VOICES IN THE MIRROR

BY GORDON PARKS

GORDON PARKS

VOICES
IN THE
MIRROR

An Autobiography

NAN A. TALESE

DOUBLEDAY

New York   London   Toronto   Sydney   Auckland

PUBLISHED BY DOUBLEDAY
a division of Bantam Doubleday Dell Publishing Group, Inc.
666 Fifth Avenue, New York, New York 10103

DOUBLEDAY and the portrayal of an anchor with a dolphin are
trademarks of Doubleday, a division of Bantam Doubleday Dell
Publishing Group, Inc.

Library of Congress Cataloging-in-Publication Data

Parks, Gordon, 1912–
Voices in the mirror: an autobiography/Gordon Parks.
p.   cm.
1. Parks, Gordon, 1912–   . 2. Afro-American photographers—
United States—Biography. 1. Title.
TR140.P35.A3   1990
770'.92.—dc20   90-34871
[B]   CIP

DuBOIS' [

For
Leslie
Sara
Dannah
Alain
Gordon III
Toni
and
David

ACKNOWLEDGMENTS

At times I find myself surprised at just still being here; somewhat astonished to have made it this far. A deep backward glance over my shoulder assures me that it was my parents' love and commonsense that thwarted fate's attempts to wipe me out on certain rageful days and nights. In their earthbound ways, Sarah and Jackson Parks blessed me with a beginning that I now understand and appreciate.

Others gave a part of themselves to keep me alive and moving —helped, in one way or another, to smooth out the wrinkles of a troubled childhood. Those who are left will remember, and I hope my words treat them gently.

I thank Deedee Moore, a good friend of many years. When this book was only a germ of an idea, she gathered mounds of research, encouraged me and worked tirelessly toward shaping its contents. Renate Haarhoff, a loving and devoted friend, spent a year's worth of reading and correcting countless misspellings. Gene Young, my former wife who urged me through a myriad of darknesses, led me to abandon my doubts about commencing a fourth autobiography. Her meaningful comments after reading the first draft were enough to whisk me on.

Finally I give high praise to Nan A. Talese, my editor, who allowed no dust to settle upon my writing hand for two years. Having taken the details of my past into her keeping, she gently, but persistently, nudged me into remembering things that my memory had denied me—significant but forgotten things that had shimmered away with time. Her wisdom roams these pages, bringing order to disorder—while rescuing me from those pernicious mistakes writers often manufacture for themselves. "Fine!" she wrote at last. And I looked into my mirror and applauded.

PROLOGUE

The sharp pain knifed up my left side, sliced across my heart and, as I screamed, my chest seemed to blow apart. I bolted up from the bed feeling that I had been shot. And there, standing in the shadows, for the third time in a week, was a black-robed figure pointing a bony finger at me. It was death. Howling with anger, I lunged at death's throat. "I've got you this time, you bastard! I've got—!" The brass lamp I was choking would not yield. Death's shoulder, which I had driven my fist into, was the corner of the chest next to my bed. Thankfully, death escaped, but the pain stayed on—in my chest, and now in a bruised fist.

That pain, always attacking during my sleep, had wracked me for six weeks. Now it was unbearable; and the dream had tested my sanity for three consecutive nights. At three in the morning I telephoned my doctor. It came as no surprise that Dr. Stanley Mirsky was at my side in less than thirty minutes. He had done as much before. He was wearing a new sportscoat and gray flannel trousers, and, no matter that I was dying, he asked my opinion of the combination. Without bothering to look, I nodded my approval, and he stuck a thermometer into my mouth.

The dream bothered him more than the pain. The latter, he knew, was the boomeranging of two foreign antibiotics—one for a bug I got in South Africa, the other for a bug I had picked up in Russia. Only time, hot milk and rest could help that. But the dreams? They were getting worse. For several months now I had suffered them, and they came with such violence that at times I dreaded going to sleep. Ignoring my groaning, Mirsky told me a joke, then took a pulse count. "It's good. You're going to be around for a while. But I'm worried about those dreams. Sure you didn't get some bad vodka in Moscow?" He was still reeling off bad jokes when dawn slipped through the window, and obviously *they* were working. Feeling considerably better, I even walked him to the door.

Hours later, still haunted by the grim illusion that had wakened me, I began searching out the disquieting foliage of dreams past. Maybe they held secrets that might shed some light on the hostility that stormed my sleep so often. Weeks crept by. Now and then some nightmare would come jostling back—frightening, disjointed and always confusing. One by one I stretched them out across the naked landscape of my memory. They told me nothing.

A few weeks later an invitation came from the city of Birmingham —the same Birmingham where, in the 1960s, racial tumult had reigned; where black protestors were chased with dogs and knocked down with water from fire hoses; where black children were bused in great numbers to prisons, and four black girls died when a bomb exploded in their church; where the imprisoned Martin Luther King wrote his impassioned letter to the conscience of the nation; and from where I once barely escaped tar, feathers and a lynch mob. But on this occasion I was being invited, along with six white photographers, to return to Birmingham to capture the "vibrancy of this thriving city—its people, buildings and environment, and help foster a deeper understanding of the city's local history." Eventually our photographs would become a part of the permanent collection of the Birmingham Museum of Art.

Birmingham, Alabama! A city blacks once called Bombingham.

The invitation, so innocent and unaware, put my thoughts to work. Surely they knew I was black, but they were saying boldly, "Come back and take a look at us now, twenty years later. Since Martin Luther challenged our way of justice we have changed. Since your escape from that murderous mob, we, like Martin, have been to the mountaintop." I couldn't bring myself to believe it, no matter how chaste the intentions. For so long I had unsuccessfully tried to scratch Birmingham's sordid past from my memory. Now it crossed my mind that the would-be assassins might even be requesting another chance at my neck. I decided to turn down their invitation. But before long the telephone rang; and the pressure was on. "Please come to Birmingham. It would mean so much to our city—and especially our black citizens." Perhaps it was the sweetness of those last words that got to me. I put Birmingham on my agenda.

Night came on. The time interval for dreams is hard to pin down, but it must have been around four in the morning when I floated into the Deep South, not into any particular city or town, but into a heavily wooded area where the air was overpoweringly sweet with the scent of magnolia. Then, one by one, large white houses began bursting up through the earth, their facades frowning, smiling, sneering, even laughing. Suddenly there was a wilderness full of them, and I felt trapped, unable to escape their presence or their glares. At first their windows appeared to be hollow, rectangular holes, but a deeper look into their recesses revealed enlarged parts of human bodies. Arms. Torsos. Feet. Hands. Some resembled sculptures; others appeared to be paintings. A toothless black head with blood dripping from the eyes sent me running from house to house, searching for a route of escape. A man and his wife, both whiter than white, sat on a porch in rocking chairs. He offered me water, but when I lifted the glass to my lips, it was empty, bone dry. I ran on, hearing their laughter swelling behind me. On another porch a family of six was roasting a goat. When all six chalk-white faces turned toward me with fanatical hostility, I started running again, but this time to a couple of friendly red-whiskered gentlemen in white suits. They, too, were in rocking chairs, but sipping mint juleps, and sensing my desperation they pointed to a shallow stream through which I could escape. They smiled broadly as I thanked them, then they were laughing so thunderously they could be heard for miles. I looked down. The sweet clear water I was wading through had turned brown, then black, and suddenly I was sinking into a swirl of red-clay slime. Sinking! Sinking! I sprang awake struggling desperately, entwined in a sweat-drenched sheet.

It was difficult, but I exiled my thoughts from the sentiments of that dream and went down to Birmingham at the appointed time to make my contribution. I spent a weekend there swimming through some emotions that had defiled the clear streams of my childhood—the emotions of black people at worship whose faith had devoured the night-fear of Klansmen in the red-clay hamlets and concrete cities of the Deep South. Born brothers and sisters through blackness, they had never stopped being a part of one another. No one can decipher the trials of oppressed people with more fire and passion than a black preacher, and I tried to touch that power with my camera.

Several months later, having returned for the exhibition of those photographs and the reception that preceded it, I found myself examining those gentle white faces that were smiling so kindly at me. How many of them had glowed beneath the light of flaming torches? How many had lifted to the voices screaming hatred toward black people? And how many of those friendly hands that shook my hand so gently had once hoisted burning crosses on some hate-studded night? To have attempted to take full measure of such things at the time could serve only to demean the honor being bestowed upon those of us who had returned for the celebration. The Southern presence was too engaging. It was difficult to look into its gathering of faces with the same feeling I once had. So I did as Martin Luther might have urged me to do. I smiled politely and shook a lot of hands that emerged from all sorts of questionable people. Before leaving the following day I was given the key to the city, and recognizing that now the mayor was black, I left Birmingham in honeyed peace. But the hostility of those terrible days and nights of the sixties still comes to visit my dreams. Perhaps the anger, held in check for so long, is still flashing out in the crepuscular zones of my subconscious.

In reflecting upon Birmingham I can't help but remember the perils of my youth. A lot of unfriendly teeth tried to devour it. Some had the roughness of nail points; others had the sweetness of poison. All of them were capable of chewing me to a pulp. Only by toughening my skin did I soften the sharpness of their bite. My youth didn't hang around very long; it departed overnight, and the teeth had kept on biting, gnawing away with a hunger that at times seemed impossible to abate. They bit chunks out of me, even attempted to swallow me whole. The problem was to keep that part of me that survived from showing the marks. Now, violent dreams sometimes unleash the anger and discontent of those earlier years, but I still prefer the ferocity of a nightmare to the blast of a gun. Yet I wonder if the violence I shunned is, at last, demanding pay. I did suppress layer upon layer of rage during my youth and adulthood—most of which was provoked by whites who held me inferior because I was black. But the energy I might have burned to sustain animosity toward my tormentors was used instead to prove them wrong. I had to get on with my life—a complex, transitory, bittersweet existence that keeps shifting with time.

ONE

I was born in the small town of Fort Scott, Kansas. Clumped in the vastness of the prairie, it was proud of its posture as part of a free state, while clinging grimly to the ways of the Deep South. Blacks and whites moved about in deceiving air, seeming to avoid any sort of relationship that might somehow damage their pride. And as they lived, so were they consumed, one race by despair, the other by intolerance. It was a place with an inner music of its own; a tormenting music that provoked our black souls. The grade school was segregated but the high school wasn't —mainly because the town fathers couldn't scrounge up enough money to build a separate one. But even inside those walls of meager learning, black students had to accommodate themselves to the taste of salt. We were not allowed to participate in sports or attend social functions. The class advisers warned us against seeking higher education, adding, "You were meant to be maids and porters." College for us, they said, would be a waste of time and money.

Both the Empress and the Liberty theaters spoke silently, with small signs for blacks pointing toward the "buzzard's roost." From there only could we watch Hoot Gibson and William S. Hart chase Indians across the silent movie screens. White eating places warned us not to poke our heads through their doors or there would be trouble, and we were not allowed to drink a soda in either of the two drugstores. Even the graveyards shunted black burials to unkempt outer fields. Law was white, and issued death to blacks with the flick of a thumb. The executioner was a tobacco-chewing sheriff named Kirby. Humiliated or enraged, most blacks had to take in whatever spirit the white town fathers gave, and that spirit usually kept them in darkness. But there were other blacks with outsized courage, who showed that death was nothing to fear. They too were gun-minded, and as mean as Kirby was, he wasn't stupid. When the opposition became too fierce his old Harley Davidson churned up dust.

In retrospect, I consider myself lucky to be alive—especially when I remember that four of my close friends died of senseless brutality before they were twenty-one. I also consider myself lucky that I didn't kill someone. There was always the opportunity to do so—out of self-defense or uncontrollable anger, and not because of any wrongdoing of my own.

Reflecting now, I realize that, even within the limits of my childhood vision, I was on a search for pride, meanwhile taking measurable glimpses of how certain blacks, who were fed up with racism, rebelled against it.

In 1921, when I was nine, the Tulsa, Oklahoma, race riot took place. Whites invaded the black neighborhood, which turned out to be an armed camp. Many white Tulsans were killed and rumors swept through our community that the fury would spread into the state of Kansas and beyond. At this time Martin, a cousin of mine, decided he would go south to work for a mill that had offered him a job. My mother, knowing his temperament, pleaded with him not to go, but he caught a freight train headed south. Months passed and we had no word of him. Then one day his name flashed across the nation as one of the most wanted men in the country. He had killed a white mill hand who had called him a "dirty nigger" and spat in his face. He had killed another while fleeing the scene.

He came one night. I remember it was raining and I lay in the darkness of my room listening to pounding on the roof. Suddenly the window next to my bed slid up and Martin, soaking wet and cautious, scrambled through the opening. I started to yell as he landed on my bed, but he quickly covered my mouth with his hand and whispered his name, frightening me into silence. He went straight to my mother's room and shook her awake. She prayed over him and then tried to persuade him to surrender. He refused. He went to our old icebox, filled a paper sack with food and went out the same way he had entered. Two weeks later, trapped by lawmen on the viaduct between Kansas City, Kansas, and Missouri, he shot one and escaped again.

None of us ever saw or heard of him after that. But I had sleepless nights wondering if he would be caught and also killed. And I said a prayer for him each night—remembering the huge slabs of peanut brittle he used to bring me, and the thrilling rides he used to give me on the back of his old motorcycle. I loved Martin like a brother. He was a gentle kind person until he was abused or wronged in some way, then he was all fury. Many years later when we were both in Kansas City, his brother Claude pointed at a beaten junkie lying on the sidewalk on Paseo Boulevard. "That's Martin," he said, shaking his head.

"Martin?" I asked in astonishment.

"Yep—my brother and your cousin, but he wouldn't know either one of us. He's in another world. I spoke to him one day, told him who I was and tried to shake his hand. 'I never laid eyes on you, man,' he said, and walked away."

Two words, "dirty nigger," and spit in the face had turned Martin Brown into a rageful murderer. To call what he did an act of rebellion is to beg the question. Those two nasty words cost three men their lives and another his soul. Unless you are black like me and millions of others who have been called "nigger" "darky" "shine" and other names that arouse anger and humiliation, I have no understanding to ask of you. When I was a child

3

the indignities came so often that I began to accept them as normal. I too fought back, but not as viciously as Martin.

I was only twelve when another cousin of mine, Princetta Maxwell, a fair girl with light red hair, came from Kansas City to spend the summer at our house. One day she and I ran, hand in hand, toward the white section of town to meet my mother, who worked there as a domestic. Suddenly three white boys blocked our path. I gripped my cousin's hand and we tried going around them, but they spread out before us.

"Where you going with that nigger, blondie?" one snarled to my cousin.

We stopped. The youngest one eased behind me and dropped to his hands and knees, and the other two shoved me backward. Pain shot through my head as it bumped against the sidewalk, and I could hear Princetta screaming as she ran back toward home for help. I caught spit in my face, and a kick in the neck. I jumped up and started swinging, only to be beaten down again. Then came a kick in the mouth. Grabbing a foot, I upended its owner, scrambled up and started swinging again. Then suddenly there was help —from another white boy. Waldo Wade was in there swinging his fists alongside mine. The three cowards, outnumbered by the lesser count of two, turned tail and ran.

Waldo's left eye began puffing up as we walked along nursing our bruises. "How'd it all start?" he finally asked.

"They thought Princetta was white."

"Idiots," he answered. "Hell, I know'd she was a nigger all the time." Waldo and I had trapped and fished together all our lives, but only through the delicacy of the situation did I resist busting him in his jaw.

Because of similar incidents Princetta had to leave before her vacation was over. She was never to come back and visit us again. As her train pulled out, I asked my mother why whites hated us so much. She was silent for a few moments, trying, I'm sure, to find an answer that would last me for a lifetime. Finally she said, "All whites don't hate you, son. And those that do are in such bad trouble with themselves they need pitying. They're not worth worrying about."

That fight was sort of a turning point. Slowly the frustration was boiling into anger, pushing me to the edge of violence, creating one emotional crisis after another. Why, I was beginning to wonder, had God made some people black and others white? One terrible night I dreamed that I was white, but my skin seemed flabby and loose, so I kept trying to pull it into shape—trying to make it fit. Finally I awoke, frantically clutching my long underwear. Shaking my head at such a crazy dream, I looked closely at my underwear. Well, the damn things *were* white. Nobody sold black underwear. At least not for boys.

Where could I begin to build pride? In church, God and the saints and angels were always white. In school the textbooks always showed my ancestors picking cotton, dancing jigs or strumming banjos. Africans were always depicted as savages. My history books never mentioned heroic blacks like Hiram Revels, Peter Salem, Benjamin Banneker or Harriet Tubman. Much later I read about Russia's great poet Alexander Pushkin and France's revered novelist Alexandre Dumas, but not until years later did anyone tell me that they were men with black blood.

So in a black and white world anything whiter than I became my enemy. At fourteen I began to strike out—suddenly, quickly and at times without reason. One day, in a fit of temper, I struck my twenty-two-year-old invalid brother (he was a couple of shades lighter than I). Immediately ashamed, I attempted to apologize. Understanding my frustration, he smiled and waved me aside, and I ran from the room humbled and with tears welling. It hurt many times worse when I was told by my sister Gladys that he was incurably ill. Just before he died the following winter he called me to his bedside. "Pedro," he said, using his nickname for me, "for the life of me I don't know why you're so mad at the world. You can't whip it the way you're going about it. It's too big. If you're going to fight it, fight with your brain. It's got a lot more power than your fists."

I remembered those words as I stood watching his coffin lowered into the grave. One day the truth of them would filter through the daily anguish of racism. But that day, still a long way off and smiling coldly, stood waiting. During those times, whites of Kansas acted as though they stood at the center of the universe; behaved as though we Negroes were just galaxies of negligible black flesh, swirling in and out of their orbit to serve them. It would have been impossible for them to understand what our lives were like; nor did they care.

5

But within our family at home life had many pleasures.

My mother, Sarah Parks, saw to it that her children ate regularly, and my father, Jackson Parks, worked the field around our small clapboard house to make that possible. He grew corn, beets, turnips, potatoes, collard greens and tomatoes. A few ducks and chickens supplied eggs, and my father always managed to have a hog to slaughter for the smokehouse, which was small and crude but served the purpose. Alongside that was a pathetic grape arbor that kept my belly feeling sweet. When my father was lucky enough to catch a big turtle, there was enough soup for a week. Mulberry, peach, persimmon and apple trees were in range for looting, and Mr. Wade's watermelon patch suffered a loss now and then. An outdoor water hydrant, which had to be thawed out during the winter, was a block away. Wooden barrels caught rainwater for washing clothes and bathing, and I remember it as being silvery and soft. I had chores befitting the youngest of the family. Those I hated most deserved my ire—getting up to fire three potbellied stoves, then emptying the slop jars in the outhouse that leaned toward the alley behind the cornfield.

There were a living room, dining room, two bedrooms and a kitchen. The beds were homemade and huge. They had to be. The girls slept in one, the boys in another—all sweet memories of small hardships to be endured by a family crammed together with love and kindness. Not once, during those years did I hear my mother or father raise a voice against one another nor, for that matter, against their children. Discipline and respect for one's elders took care of that. None of my brothers or sisters ever smoked cigarettes during their lifetimes. The boys smoked pipes after they were grown, but never in the presence of my parents. That privilege was left to my father.

Easter and Christmas provided the joyous times. I hunted for Easter eggs in the bushes and beneath the big oaks, then, scrubbed to a rawness, I dressed in my finest—which wasn't so fine—and hurried off to Sunday school. Christmas brought added beneficence. There was always the tree my father cut, to decorate; and presents to discover beneath it on Christmas morning—a small bag of marbles, perhaps a new stocking cap, rib stockings and a sack of peanut brittle. The present I treasured most was a BB gun my father and mother saved up for six months to buy. But it came with a warning: I was never to shoot at birds or animals. It was meant strictly for the red and white circular target that came with it—or perhaps, for a skunk. But my ultimate joy was banging on our battered upright Kimball piano, which I had learned to play, by ear, at the age of six.

I will always consider my parents to be my just heroes. My fourteen siblings would, I am sure, have agreed with me. They made life more tolerable for all of us with their compassion and generosity. Yet neither of them would have thought what they did to earn our infinite respect was in any way extraordinary. Sarah Parks would have defied God Himself if what He willed her to do would harm another human being. She would have exonerated her disobedience by concluding that God had, for an instant, lost sight of His own teachings. Certainly, the devil found her a terrible enemy. Neither would she allow racism to drag her reasoning into the throes of its darkness. Without considering the consequences, she once took a homeless white child into our house to feed and clothe until a distant relative came to his rescue. That our black friends and neighbors disapproved of her actions made no difference. The boy was hungry, needed clothes and a roof over his head. A good number of whites, feeling guilt for not having done something for the child, had ungrateful things to say as well, but she gave them the same short shrift she had given the blacks. The sick or disabled, no matter what their color, found her at their bedside. And although we were dismally poor, she always scraped up a basket of food to take along. She was a thrifty woman as well. One of my brothers sent me an old bank book of my mother's that he had kept for many years. Between 1912 and 1925 she had managed to save ten dollars and eighty-two cents. I looked at it in the abundant light flowing through the windows of my apartment and for several moments I stood speechless. How, I wondered, had she managed all that bountiful food for our table, those sizzling pans of baked beans, sweet potatoes, apple pies and cobblers.

Sarah Parks was forever forgiving. When a judge sentenced three older black boys to three months' imprisonment for roughing me up and throwing me off a truck, she asked the court to rescind its decision and allow her to mete out the punishment. The judge bowed to her wishes and the three were sentenced to three months' worth of Wednesday night prayer meetings. No excuse was acceptable for their absence; it was prayer meeting or jail. Years later, Elijah Wells, one of the offenders, confessed to me,

7

"Your mother knelt right there beside us every Wednesday night, and we did enough praying to last us for a lifetime. Many times I felt that I'd rather have gone to the jug instead."

In our house, dirt was as forbidden as lipstick, rouge, obscenity or jazz music. There was rainwater, scrubbing boards and plenty of blueing water for gingham dresses and overalls, and no one, including my father, would risk Sarah Parks's ire by taking to bed before sponging off in one of those tin tubs.

She laid down a standing rule about fighting blacks or whites. "Don't strike until you're struck; then it's your right to defend yourself." Never did I get any sympathy for complaining that two white boys beat me up. Instead, I was more than likely to get a switching. I was expected to hold my own against two whites, even three. I was to avoid a fight if I could; but I was never to run. That was the sin of all sins.

For years, my brother-in-law, Boissy, had provided us with dangerous moments. Twice a month, after getting his pay, he would fill his belly with whiskey, load his shotgun and set out to shoot my sister Anna and their three children, who came to hide beneath my parents' bed. Everyone—my older brothers, Andrew, Clem and Leroy, and my father—was ordered by my mother to leave the task of disarming him to her. It was always thrilling to watch her meet boozed-up Boissy midway down the path, gently take that shotgun from him and make him get to his knees and pray. It happened like that for years until the night she died. It was on that night that Boissy finally let go with a blast that blew the frame off the door and ran to hide in an adjoining cornfield. It was pouring rain at the time, and Kirby, a heartless sheriff with a posse of two, was itching to turn his guns on that cornfield. It was then that my dying mother lifted herself into heroism. With the help of two women neighbors she left her bed and went, beneath an umbrella, to the edge of the cornfield. With the same gentleness she had shown for so many years, she called for him to come out and pray. Frightened, rain-soaked Boissy came out and put his gun at her feet. Wearily she waved Kirby off and meekly her son-in-law followed her into the house—to let her pray over him for the last time. The morning my mother was to be buried, he took his shotgun and flung it into Marmaton River.

My mother spoke one language—love. In looking back, I can't find one moment when I can honestly say she was wrong. Her last words to me were about love, and making something of myself. There's no doubt that, in the fifteen years providence willed her to me, she wove the guidelines that she hoped I would follow.

My father spoke the same language, though he spoke little. He stood behind her as she laid out her dreams for her children. In all the years, my father made only one attempt to punish me, and that was for breaking a watermelon rind over my sister Peggy's head. In doing so, he wound up suffering more than I did. He aroused me from bed at 6 A.M. and instructed me to fetch three peach tree branches and braid them together. Wisely, I chose very limber ones and had the foresight to put on three pairs of overalls to cut down the sting. Being very inept at dishing out physical punishment, he stood too close to me, and the switches encircled my padded legs to lash his instead. Infuriated, he accused me of striking him.

"You're hitting yourself, Poppa," I protested, and moved even closer to him. Upon hearing the racket, my mother got up. Sensing my father's frustration, she motioned him aside and took over the job. But first she had me remove all three pairs of overalls. I knew then that things were going to be done properly. Sarah Parks could wield a switch as deftly as a conductor might wield a baton. Gracefully she waved those branches so they landed with a sharp snap. As I danced to their touch my father sighed and headed out to feed the hogs, happy, I am sure, to escape doing something he couldn't put his heart into.

My father was a compassionate man. Even today I can remember an afternoon when he halted my game of marbles and told me to let my mother know when she came home that he would be at Mercy Hospital. My mother seemed confused when I gave her his message; taking me by the hand, she hurried to the hospital. There she found him in bed. Skin had been stripped from his back, arms and legs—to graft onto a little black girl who had been horribly burned the night before. Things were pretty bad for us at the time; the crops were failing and money was short.

"But, Jackson, why didn't you ask me about doing this first?" my mother asked.

"No need for that, Sarah. You would'a said yes, anyway."

I had become a father of two myself when I finally asked him about that incident. He had all but forgotten it.

9

"It was the little Savage girl and her parents—pretty shiftless people," I reminded him.

"Aw yes, I do remember."

I then asked him something that I had wondered about down through the years. "Did Mr. or Mrs. Savage ever come to the hospital to see you, or bring you flowers?"

His reply brought me to the full measure of him. He puffed on his pipe and shook his head. "Well, no, I don't recall that they did. But I didn't do it for thanks or flowers. I was just trying to help the child—nothing else." He seemed a bit put out by my questions, and, somewhat ashamed. I said no more.

At times I suddenly remember his pausing to glance at me—wondering, perhaps, what I would eventually amount to. I feel now that in the silence of his pondering, he was probably hoping that I would carry out dreams of his own that had been swallowed up in frustration. There were moments when he seemed as secretive as stone, and it was then that I would interrupt his silence by asking a favor of him.

"Poppa, can I have a dime?"

"A dime—for what?"

"Some peanut brittle."

After a deep sigh he usually dug into his pockets and handed me six or seven cents—especially if I had done my chores well. I remember his face, mustached and as weathered as ancient wood. Rarely did it wrinkle into a smile, but when it did, it was like a mountain opening up. He walked slow in rain or snow; even a strong wind failed to make him hurry. The memory of him glows —a splendid memory, constantly spreading, leaving me searching sometimes for things he felt I had left undone.

Both he and my mother were soft-spoken, and the staunchest laws of a Methodist religion were contained in them. Those laws prevailed in every corner of our family life, in our mannerisms and attitudes toward one another and just about everyone who surrounded us. Their teachings lay buried inside us, and the words of the Lord hovered over us like swarms of bees. They bolstered the ten biblical commandments with some of their own. Frankly I had trouble with a few of them. I had a big problem with my parents' telling me to *strike only after I had been struck*. That first blow could leave you completely immobilized. The solution I found turned out to be satisfactory. I learned to duck that first blow, while allowing just enough of its touch to justify a reaction. The strike of a shirtsleeve was a strike—and that strike gave me license to start defending myself.

And there was that equally serious problem of loving thy neighbor. Some of our white neighbors absolutely loathed black people but, according to my mother, hatred was *their* problem and they would have to answer to the Lord for it. It bothered me also that the pictures of Jesus always showed him as white with blondish hair, though my Uncle Booker used to tell me that Jesus was black as coal. Never would I have plumped up the courage to question my mother about this. Even the thought of doing so seemed blasphemous. No, you learned to accept Jesus as He was, and leave Uncle Booker to his mischief. Lydia Hinkson, a white neighbor, made images of Jesus out of white flour sacks. She was just a little squirrelly, Uncle Booker thought. My buddy Elmer questioned everything and everybody. "Why," he asked our Sunday school teacher, "are all those disciples at that Last Supper white? I don't see nary a black face there."

Miss Hill's answer left us as confused as she seemed to be. "I don't rightly know, but I don't reckon there was any colored folks around then."

As a child I was taught to share, though I didn't have much to share. But there was Buster Jones, another buddy, who took advantage of that teaching. Buster would pocket your favorite marbles and give you nothing in return—beyond a black eye if you complained. "But you're to feel sorry for poor Buster," my sister Gladys would say. "Remember, he's got no mother."

Buster did have a father, but that didn't seem to count. He was a bully as well. Living by the good word kept me in line, and for a long time I went around appeasing the likes of Buster, thus losing some of my most prized possessions. Poor Buster went too far one day. He pocketed my favorite aggie, as pretty a marble as I'd ever seen. I don't remember who threw the first blow. I do remember that for the first time I kicked poor Buster's behind real good. It had never occurred to me before then that such a thing was possible.

My parents were not simply preachers of virtue. They practiced what they taught, and time has proven their worth to me. They showed their children how to live honorably, and how to die honorably. There were indeed times when their righteousness irked

11

me, but there have been more times when I longed for the wisdom to neglect certain things they found to be worthless.

For the first fifteen years of my life I was a child who said yes a lot of times when I would rather have said no. But that's expected of obedient children. Several years before I reached adulthood my mother died, and my security died with her. My family, once linked together by seven boys and eight girls, had already thinned out. Ben, Lucy, Ernest, Lewis and Mary were half brothers and sisters, and except for Mary they had all gone off before I was born. At the time of my mother's death Andrew was in Chicago; Cora, with two of her own children, was in Nebraska. Peggy lived with her husband in St. Paul, Minnesota. Clem, another brother, still lived in Fort Scott and worked as a cook to keep his family of six going. Clarabell and Leroy (who had called me Pedro) had already been taken by death. Anna, her husband and three children, had a house close by. Gladys and Lillian, my two youngest sisters, lived with my mother and father.

Shortly after my mother's funeral the plans for me were made; I, the youngest, would go live with my sister Peggy, while the two youngest sisters would stay on to keep house for my father. What little I had to take was packed in a matter of minutes, and there was still a lot of room left in my cardboard suitcase. Two hours later Dan Stover's taxi came to take Peggy and me to the station, where we would board the train for St. Paul. My father's farewell was muted and tautly drawn. He touched my shoulder and said, "Just mind your mother's teaching and you'll make it all right." He had then walked off toward the barn without looking back, sparing himself the worst. As strong as he was, it was the stronger will of my mother that kept things going.

As the taxi drove off I took a final look at what my parents had worked so hard for—the old clapboard house leaning forlornly on a dusty plot of earth. There, so much love had been, but now only silence was left. But in that silence were walls filled with memories that would take a long time dying.

A final, compelling sunset rimmed the Kansas prairie as the train started rattling north, and as it sped along, the telegraph poles blurring toward and past us, I had a feeling that I was escaping a doom that had already trapped those I was leaving behind. Just a few hours before, I had got up in the middle of the night to go stand beside my mother's coffin—hoping that being alone with her would help me cast off the fear of death. My love for her was, I knew, stronger than the fear. But that fear still roamed the quiet. Having gained the courage to lift the coffin lid, it took more courage to place my hand on her hands than her face. After I eased the lid down, a sense of relief came, but one of isolation as well. The person I loved most was gone forever. It is still difficult to explain the true depth of my feelings as I lay down beside her coffin to sleep out the night. I knew that her life had taken flight and that I felt stranded. I had brought a quilt along that she had sewn together. I covered my body and my head with it and lay on the floor trembling under its darkness. It would, for the remainder of the night, provide me with a little security. My father had found me there the next morning when he got up to feed the hogs, and perhaps he knew why I was there.

Gone now, Emphry Hawkins, shot; Johnny Young, shot; Doc Allison, shot; Captain Tuck, shot; all my friends and all dead by the gun. I had already lived so close to death and violence in my young life, having witnessed two drunken women knife each other to death in front of Joe's pool hall. So, quivering with those memories, I had lain beside the coffin, hoping that in sharing my mother's final presence, I could draw on her love and strength and somehow cut the bond between blood and fear.

By the next sunrise I would be far away from Fort Scott's Main Street, and all the indifferent white faces passing; Gunn's Park, Tower Hill and Marmaton River; the neighing of my father's horses, the grunting hogs, our strutting cock crowing above the cackling hens—all distant sounds of my childhood. But I would always remember Cheney's Mortuary, where Orlando Cheney and a caretaker shoved me, a nine-year-old, into the clammy dark where Captain Tuck's corpse lay on a slab, locked me in and left me to scream out my fright. Those first fifteen years amounted to a sprawling drama that could have warped my mind forever. To further explain the immensity of them is to take a look into even more fear and the darkness of the dreams that now take over during my sleep.

13

TWO

I entered my sister's house in Minnesota still snarled in the roots of racism, still wearing the web my mother had spun around me as protection from our baffling world. Within a few hours that web began ripping apart. I had never met my brother-in-law, but his very first handshake told me that I was to be tolerated rather than accepted. Nearly white, big and fierce-looking, he seemed formidable and unfriendly. His only words to me that first evening were about things I was not to do in his house.

It was a nice house, two-storied, spanking clean and with large comfortable rooms—and without kerosene lamps to clean, wicks to trim or wash water to have to carry in buckets through the heat and cold. Lying in bed that night I marveled at the ornamented wallpaper with deer leaping over bushes, and my thoughts leaped with them into vague imaginings of the future. Yet, there was no feeling of permanence in the softness of that big brass bed. I had a feeling that this was at best an uneasy stopover. The sharp rap of a fist sounded against the door. "Turn off the lamp! Electric lights cost a lot of money!" Without answering, I snapped off the light. The anger in his voice had turned the room to ice.

His name was David Grissam, but before long I began to think of him as Davey Grisly. He was a Pullman porter and that helped, since he was gone much of the time. But when he returned he became more and more hostile, and my sister, normally a cheerful person, seldom smiled when he was there. Having enrolled me in high school, she spent a great deal of time helping me with my homework.

The evening before Christmas a freezing north wind swooped down on the city like a hawk. By seven o'clock the temperature had dropped to ten below zero. I had been invited to a party, and I bundled up to go. Peggy, her friend Crystal Graham and my brother-in-law sat in the living room as I bade them good night and started out.

"Where do you think you're going?" His voice was menacing.

"To a party."

"No party tonight. You've been out two nights in a row."

"I'm sorry," I said, for my sister's sake. Then, for myself I added, "I'm going to the party."

Instantly furious, he rose and started toward me. When my sister rushed to my defense he slammed her against the wall, and that sent me swinging for his belly. My blows only angered him more. Pouncing on me, he flung me to the floor and began to choke me. As my sister stood screaming, Crystal came to my rescue, beating on his head with an umbrella. When his hands fell loose I scrambled from beneath him and ran out the door, with Crystal close behind. Several minutes later all my belongings, including my alarm clock and cardboard suitcase, came sailing out the window. And I charged about gathering them from the snow. Even over the howling wind I could hear my sister's sobs.

"Where will you go?" Crystal asked.

15

"I don't know."

"I've only got a room. I can't take you there."

"It's all right. I'll find some place."

"Well—well, take care of yourself."

Take care of yourself. The words hung for a few seconds in the cold air after she left. In a matter of moments David Grissam had snatched that protective web from me and booted me toward manhood. The subzero weather he had forced me into was as cold as his hate. Up until then there was only one experience I could liken it to. When I was eleven three white boys, knowing I couldn't swim, had hurled me into Marmaton River and left me to save myself. I had survived by ducking my head under the water and somehow making it to the riverbank. The river David Grissam plunged me into was far deeper and wider, and the sound of his window slamming shut was hardly different from those words shouted at me on Marmaton River, "Swim, black boy, or die!"

Alone now and with tears welling, I knew I was in for a hard time, and that I had only myself to count on for survival. There was no one I could turn to for advice or shelter. Suddenly I had to think of myself as full grown, and with a few pennies over two dollars in my pockets, frightened and uncertain, I began tromping the frozen snow. The dangerous cold made my instant adulthood imperative. I had to find shelter fast or freeze to death. I began walking and four blocks later I wandered into Jim Williams's pool hall. My face, hands and feet, numb from the cold, welcomed the stale heat that hit me. It didn't matter that the air was the color of smoke. I dropped my suitcase and went to stand over a heat vent, anticipating the warmth of school the following day, then realized it was closed for the holidays. I had been banished so quickly I could hardly grasp the truth of my predicament. Just six months before, parents, family and home had seemed like something good and secure that would last forever. Now even the memory of all that seemed half-real.

With a lump in my throat, I watched the pool players drifting around the game tables. Aiming, shooting, detached from my gloom, they seemed like ghosts. They were a tough-looking lot, and I kept my hand on the recently bought switchblade I had in my pocket. The only person who spoke to me was Tee Vernon, a big man with an engaging smile and a bulging belly, who waddled around racking the billiard balls. His conversation amounted to a friendly "Hi," but even that lifted my spirits. A few hours later, I heard someone say it was a half hour before closing time and I reached in my pocket and rubbed my money together.

I could ride out the night on trolley cars running the outer limits between St. Paul and Minneapolis, spend a couple of hours in Union Station, then head back to the pool hall. It was a dismal prospect, but there seemed no other alternative, so I set out for the trolley.

That first night's journey was one of foreboding. I slept most of the time, using my suitcase for a headrest, waking now and then to the sound of sleet pelting the trolley windows. I was aware of people getting on and off, and I envied the fact that they had somewhere to go. Once when I awoke, the car was empty and dark. The doors were open and the wind-driven sleet was sweeping into both ends of the trolley. I felt alone, confused, suspended within undecipherable space. I rubbed frost from the window and looked out. Except for the swirling sleet there was nothing—no trees, lights or landscape. Only blackness. Then came a sputtering of bluish-white light. The operator was swinging the contact pole to the power line. The car's lights flickered on and a railing came into view. We were on a bridge, high above the Mississippi River. For a few moments I felt like a dead soul.

I made this lonesome journey every night for nearly a week. On the final morning, I had only eleven cents when we arrived back in St. Paul at dawn. The trolley operator had gone for coffee. The aged conductor poked me awake, saying we were at the end of the line. He stood looking at me; in his hand was a bundle of green bills wadded together with a rubber band. At the sight of them, my hand tightened around the switchblade in my pocket. I rose slowly, looking through the window to see if anyone was around. We were alone. His back was toward me as we walked to the rear of the car. Perspiration rolled from my armpits and anxiety must have shown on my face as I pressed the button and the blade popped out.

"Conductor!"

"Yes?" He turned and looked calmly at the blade. Trembling now, I looked at him. My father's black face had replaced his white one.

"Conductor, would you like to buy this knife? I'm a little hungry."

17

He eyed me for a couple of seconds. "I don't want your knife, but come on, I'll buy you some grub."

I closed the blade. "I'm sorry, mister."

He peeled off two dollar bills. "Here, go get yourself something to eat."

I refused the money, jumped out of the trolley, more frightened and ashamed than I had ever been in my life, and stood there in the falling snow. I hurried along the icy street shivering.

When the Christmas holiday was over, and school was about to open again, I walked across town toward the warmth of it with my suitcase and three books wrapped in a leather strap. After crossing Wabasha Street I glanced up as a flock of pigeons swooped down between two buildings; they twisted, turned and as they shot upward, one struck the cornice of a building. Stunned, it fell to the snow just a few feet ahead of me. I bent to pick it up, but a growl coming from behind a truck sent shivers up my spine, and I drew back. A large dog, hunger showing at his ribs, was inching toward the bird. We eyed one another for a moment, taking the measure of each other's courage; then, suddenly, he lunged for the bird as I swung my books at him. He had managed to mouth the bird, but with the blow he yelped, dropped it and fled.

The pigeon was still, and its head fell to one side as I picked it up. The dog had broken its neck. He stood now at a safe distance, growling as I smoothed the ruffled feathers. I picked up my books, stuffed the bird into my pocket and continued across town. At a clearing near the school I pulled the bird from my pocket and looked at it closely. It was dead, freshly killed, and I was hungrier than I had ever been in my life. After gathering paper and firewood, I defeathered the bird, gutted it with my knife, roasted it over the flame and ate it.

During the third-period class I began thinking about the experience. The dog's hunger had been as great as mine. My stomach began churning, and feeling the worst coming on, I bolted past my teacher and ran into the hallway. A few seconds later I lost my breakfast. At that moment, I vowed I would never be so hungry again.

I got permission to telephone my sister from school later that morning, and I was in luck. Her husband would be gone for three days and I could spend them with her. She had saved up twenty-five dollars for me and with that I got a three-dollar-a-week room near the pool hall. It was small but the bed was comfortable, and the landlady, a Mrs. Brookins, was a kindhearted woman. Her husband found a job for me on weekends washing dishes in a beanery. Later, when the snow was gone and spring was edging in, I was glad to have stayed in school and thankful that somewhere beyond my baleful world I still had a family. During the worst moments, from somewhere or other, a sister or brother seemed to speak to me from out of the past, urging me on, telling me I could make it. I could feel their eyes, sense their touch, but then suddenly they were gone and I was alone again.

The darknesses were still plentiful—leaping in, harassing, denying me peace. Yet there was always some invisible noble-hearted something that kept beckoning me on. I can't describe it but it was relentless—although it showed up precariously late sometimes.

As a stranger to that frigid north country and its city ways, I sought out people who appeared to be knowledgeable, and began plying them with questions. There were some who just glared at me and walked away without telling me anything; others smiled and told me what little they knew, but there were others who told me lies. Never before had I met such people. If I looked hungry, they offered me a drink of bad whiskey. If I seemed lonely, some big-hearted woman might—for a few bucks—offer me her body. It was a bleak time, and I ate anguish for breakfast and supper. I finally stopped asking so many questions; I watched and listened more—especially to those who dressed as if they might have something important to say. I soon became an expert at taking the true measure of people—at least I thought so at the time. But I did watch and listen with a good deal of enthusiasm.

With the seriousness of my situation sinking in, I started taking stock of myself. I was like an uprooted tree in a strange forest. If, at that time, someone had urged me to have faith, the advice would have sounded like a joke. It never struck me that I had three valuable assets—youth, health and the inner need to some day amount to something. I was still overwhelmed by the complexity of surviving in a big city. I had grown up in a small town of dirt roads and slow-moving rivers, a prairie abundant with tall Indian grass and innocent flowers. Here, caught up in the noise and rush of things, I felt clumsy, out of place.

But I had the good fortune to be born with music in my head and fingers; and before long I landed a job in a brothel where I played the piano every night for tips. My wardrobe was pitifully meager—two pairs of bell-bottom pants, three blue shirts, a checkered red and yellow sweater, a snap-brim brown hat that had replaced the black woolen cap with earflaps I had brought from Fort Scott and a knee-length black and red mackinaw overcoat. The black rib stockings were fine for cold days, but too thick for the sharp-pointed button shoes my sister Peggy had bought for me at Bamberger's Department Store before she brought me up north. Ben Wilson, the pimp who lorded over the brothel, wanting me to dress in attire more fitting for his establishment, blessed me with my first suit. It was one of his old pinstripe numbers. To accent this sartorial splendor, I slicked down my hair with a heavy grease to get that Rudolph Valentino look, and then I was ready for the evening.

THREE

The question frequently asked of me is why I have undertaken so many professions—photography, painting, writing, musical composition and film. At first I wasn't sure that I had the talent for any of them, but I did know I had an intense fear of failure, and that fear compelled me to fight off anything that might abet it—bigotry, hatred, discrimination, poverty or hunger. I suffered those evils, but without allowing them to rob me of the freedom to expand. They came. I bottled them up inside me, closed them off and went on doing what I had to do. Why? I suppose it was good common horse sense. Perhaps it was then that those evils began churning into my subconscious, then to erupt much later through those violent dreams.

Nothing came easy. I was just born with a need to explore every tool shop of my mind, and with long searching and hard work. I became devoted to my restlessness; to chasing down poetry in the best of what I found; to opening doors that allowed me entrance into their universe, no matter how small. If I found nothing, I tried another door. Today my imagination refuses to be confined to boredom. It stays hungry and I feed it with things that surround me.

In my formative years I was ill-prepared and I tried to make up for that by exploring every possibility. If one failed me I turned to another, but I was never just a dabbler. I gave all of myself to every effort, and I still do. Calculation always figures strongly in my desire to doggedly hold on to my creative pursuits. Sometimes I play the piano with my eyes firmly shut—considering the small possibility of blindness. Under such a handicap, I would learn to photograph an object or person by the feel of the light. If I lost my legs I could still write. And if I should lose both arms I am sure I would try painting with my toes.

Despite the fears that so often invade my sleep, I sometimes awake with a poem, or perhaps a musical theme, coursing my mind. Memories too come streaming in from the past—good memories that I never want to forget, or bad memories, some of which I have learned to make peace with.

Here in the autumn of my life I still feel that there is a lot more to do, that there are other opportunities waiting to be grabbed. The signals are clear every morning when I get up; I know for sure that I will be working at something I like, and those are the kinds of mornings I've worked toward for so long.

I know too that there are a multitude of incalculable forces lying in wait to do me in; to burn me up like firewood and scatter my ashes when nothing is left. But those forces still have trouble with me. Their language is despair, and I refuse to have any truck with it. I've liked being a stranger to failure since I was a young man, and I still feel that way. I'm still occupied with survival; still very single-minded about keeping my life moving—but not for fame or fortune. I simply want to stay alive to learn more about the world we live in, a world that we, in spite of all its opportunities, are failing to live up to. I'm puzzled by all the illiteracy that surrounds us in the midst of so many schools and teachers. I'm puzzled by all the crime, poverty, hunger and bigotry. Something is wrong, awfully wrong.

There have been times when I was even puzzled about the term success. Some dubious characters have staked claims for it. To argue that Willie Sutton, the bank robber, was not successful is to lose the argument. In one haul—and there were many of them—he walked away with more money than Jessie James laid eyes on during his entire career of banditry. Other gangsters like Al Capone, John Dillinger and "Pretty Boy" Floyd graduated *summa cum laude* in their nefarious fields. I could question the morality of their accomplishments if I liked, but all of them spelled success the same way John D. Rockefeller spelled it, and all of them gained national recognition. Yet, in the end, they proved as worthless to society as skeletons of dead fish. Only another crook would choose them as role models, and unfortunately a lot of them have, and it was my good fortune not to have been one of them.

Those parental sermons had prepared me to reach for a nobler kind of success, and during those frowning, adolescent days that threatened me, it took on a strange physical bearing, and a personality as well. I imagined it tall, skinny, sly and aloof—as mercurial as quicksilver. And I envisaged it hovering secretively in dark corners and veiled in blue obscure shadows, always playing hide and seek with me.

I'm often asked if I thought of failure during those days. At that time there wasn't much to lose. I was starting in the pits, and up was the only direction available to me. What I needed most was motivation, and a need to escape my despair supplied plenty of that. There was no time for weeping, or for drumming up excuses to justify that despair. I had to do some fast growing or remain in the pits. It was a bad time, but I learned more with every setback. Luck, coupled with youth and determination, proved a worthy force against those detractors who kept the books on my strengths and weaknesses—those white teachers back in Kansas who had discouraged me, and later those Minnesota blacks who scoffed at my greenness. There were those other enemies too—cold, hunger and desolation. Had my father seen me so distressed he would probably have given his usual advice. "Think, boy. Use that good common sense the Lord gave you." For him common sense was responsible for anything that turned out to be right—a fine crop of corn, the profitable sale of a horse, or perhaps the sale of a couple of hogs. To the contrary, all failures happened because "somebody didn't use their head."

I don't pretend to be an authority on common sense. I speak from only seventy-seven years of experience—which tells you next to nothing. As a term it has been undefined fully for centuries, and will probably remain so for centuries to come. I like to think of it as wisdom, and I've learned not to confuse wisdom with intelligence. There is a difference.

No doubt it was wisdom that taught me that my most dangerous enemy could be myself. One morning, with shaving razor in hand, I had stared into the mirror and asked myself some rather bothersome questions. With hard eyes I stared back at myself and reeled off some disturbing facts, along with some advice: "You're approaching manhood and you dislike yourself. That's why you're interrogating me. *[Well, make up your mind to do something about it.]* You're so thin-skinned that the softest criticism rubs you raw. *[Accept criticism, man. It can't hurt, and it could be helpful.]* Envy of others' success hangs around your neck like a rope. *[That's stupid. Use their success to give you inspiration.]* You squander too much time on trivial things, always hurrying to nowhere, and in a rush to get there. *[Take your time, man. Think things out first, then go.]* You avoid questions about yourself that you find hard to answer. *[Figure things out. You just don't have the right answers. So admit to it.]* You talk rapid-fire just to be heard, and without having anything worthwhile to say. *[That's downright ego. Listen more. Keep your big mouth shut and keep your ears open. Your insecurity's showing.]* Well, enough for now. There's plenty left on the list for tomorrow. *[One last thing: Until you're sure of yourself, you won't be sure of anything. Think it over. See you tomorrow morning.]*"

I remember that session with the mirror so well because it forced me to take stock of myself. I was struggling for a positive image. But it was one thing to acknowledge my faults, and another thing to do something about them. I recall using four of my closest friends to learn from; to help me through the crisis. Adolph Thomas and Bud Kelly were likable, but both were gregarious and suffered from diarrhea of the mouth. George Berry and Howard Barksdale were just as likable, but they were more reserved and usually spoke when they had something worthwhile to say. The four of them were near-perfect subjects for me to observe in helping to correct my own faults, and I used them well. But the mirror went right on watching, accusing, badgering like a nagging mother. Plainly it could see that I was weary of climbing into bed every night to cover myself with agony. It had helped me declare war with myself, and all the faults that were set to foul me up. The enemy—my faults—was confronted with the truth, and truth wielded the more powerful weapon.

Little by little I grew to feel better about myself, but having knocked one fault off, I had to remember that others were waiting to take over. They seemed to live in every shadow, knowing how hard it was to live without them. It was hard, while trying to beat the cold and scrounging for food, not to feel envy for my friends with secure homes, who wore nicely cut suits and talked about plans for college. I had finally bought my first new suit after I turned seventeen. I put two dollars down on it, and Ben Myers, the man who made it for me, got another dollar or so whenever he could catch me. Even then it took me a year to satisfy that debt. As for college, poverty purged it from my thoughts.

That past comes galloping in sometimes like an enraged warrior, hawk-eyed, scowling, admonishing itself for not having cut me down somewhere along the way. Angrily, it seems to point back at the smoke-filled pool hall, to the greasy eatery in St. Paul where I washed a million dirty dishes every weekend, to a rat-infested flophouse on St. Peter Street where I mopped up the vomit of bums, to that lowly brothel where I wearily thumped out the blues on a beatup piano for two years. It seemed as though I was serving out a sentence in hell. Remembering now, I sometimes shake my head and wonder how I survived it.

In St. Paul I met a wall of indifference—raised by blacks as well as whites. I never really expected much from the whites; to them I seemed to be invisible. But I hadn't bargained for the cold shoulders of blacks. Yet, their "private" clubs appeared as bigoted as those of the whites. Their members, intoxicated with their upper lower class stations, altered my thoughts about the sense of caring blacks were supposed to have for one another. No hungry black boy would have gone unfed by other blacks in my hometown. There was always room for another plate at our supper table, regardless of how little food there was in the larder. Up there in the North, blacks mistook the hunger in my eyes for daydreaming, and their houses seemed to be doorless. They made it clear to me that people, no matter what their color, could be unfeeling.

Surprisingly, some blacks who were thought to be living close to the devil showed me the most concern. The gamblers and hustlers always had a pat on the back for me, and they found odd jobs for me that brought in a few bucks. The tarnished world they were rooted in had not discolored their regard for a youngster like me. A foggy sense of paternalism showed through their perverseness. Ben Wilson, the gun-toting gambler and pimp who had given me my finery to play the piano, ordered me out of his place when he found me at the crap table. "This joint can turn you into a bad egg overnight," he said as he showed me to the door.

My life brightened that summer when Gladys, Lillian and my father came to live in St. Paul. A brother, Andrew, had arrived from Chicago with his wife earlier in the spring, and Cora would soon move from Nebraska to St. Paul to be near them. But by now I was on my own, and despite the hardship, I wanted to stay that way. What's more, I had gone to a party in Minneapolis and instantly fallen in love. She was a beautiful peach-colored girl named Sally Alvis, but she had a father, Joe Alvis, who would have been happier if I had drowned years before in Marmaton River. Joe made my courtship miserable. He attended my weekly visits sitting in the dark at the top of the living room stairs, his eyes on the sofa, coughing or clearing his throat whenever I moved in too close to his daughter. "That Mr. High Pockets," as he referred to me, "is up to no good," he would grumble to his wife, Ida, each time I departed. And he was always up there waiting in the darkness when I brought Sally home after a party or the movies.

It didn't seem to matter to Joe that I truly loved his daughter.

In 1929 hard luck backed off for a while when I got a job at the wealthy, prestigious, white Minnesota Club as a bus boy in the day, and as a general lackey at night. There I had the opportunity to observe what success was supposed to be, and to learn the rules I needed to know if I wanted to claim success. The rarefied world inside the Minnesota Club was one of spacious rooms with high-beamed mahogany ceilings, of thick carpeting, of master and servant, of expensive clothes, wines and liquors, elegant table settings and epicurean tastes. Influential men arrived there daily and I, dressed in a uniform of blue tails, white tie and striped vest, served them brandy and coffee, and listened to their talk of stock markets, boating, traveling, golfing, financial deals and politics. I would take their coats, and the camel's hair and the velvet-collared chesterfields felt good to my calloused hands. Their suits were well cut and well pressed, their oxfords and grained brogues discreetly polished. Their faces looked scrubbed, their hair neatly trimmed and they smelled of bay rum. There was always the aroma of good food—great platters of roast pheasant, duck, guinea hen banked with wild rice; huge buttered steaks served on planks of wood, garnished with steaming vegetables; spicy rum cakes, ices and creamy desserts. I was never hungry in those days; the leftovers amounted to a feast. There was a lot an unlettered black boy could learn there, and what I learned I tucked deep inside, determined meanwhile to put each lesson into use whenever I could. I began to read more, borrowing newspapers, novels and books of poetry from the club library. And there a whole world opened up to me, one that would have been impossible to imagine on our small dirt farm back in Kansas.

Margaret Armstead, one of my grade school teachers in Kansas, had long before primed my interest in reading literary works, those beyond comic strips and fairy tales. Twice a week she would have certain of her pupils make up stories spontaneously and recite them before the rest of the class. "It's to improve your imagination," she would explain. The class itself had the privilege of selecting the storyteller they enjoyed most. My imagination must have been the wildest of the group, for it was me whom they usually raised their hands to hear. Buster Jones, my antagonist, declared that the reason for my always winning was because I was the biggest liar. If the novelists I began to read in the books I filched from the club library were also liars, then they were obviously famous and rich liars—so I thought. Nevertheless, my mind was being pushed into the foreign worlds of Thomas Mann, Sinclair Lewis and James Joyce. Justice Pierce Butler, a member at the club, had, after several brandies, engaged me in conversation. Rather blithely I told him about my interest in reading. A couple of days later he handed me an edition of Edith Wharton's *The Age of Innocence.*

During 1929 fate smiled at me more than she had for a long time. I was still in school and working evenings at the club. Then Black Thursday came—and with it panic and depression. I had no idea that my small world would be affected; surely a market crash concerned only the rich. But very quickly I, along with millions of others, was without a job. Desperately I searched for work, but I always failed to get any. On the seventh of November I went to school and cleaned out my locker. It was impossible to stay on. The blunt feel of winter returned with a snowstorm that same evening, and my hopes dwindled once more.

I still had my room at Mrs. Brookins, and what little money I had saved soon ran out, but she didn't press for her rent. Then when everything seemed blackest I got a job playing at a north side Minneapolis brothel called Mattie's. Since I was full of melancholy the music I fed them was filled with my mood, and it seemed to soothe their souls. Friends began calling me "Blue," because of the blues I played for the prostitutes and their pimps, who were ripe for big tips. "Butterfly," bemoaning the fate of a beautiful prostitute, became the big favorite, and I got one request for it after another. After a spat with Sally Alvis I composed a song called "No Love," and that had silver dollars falling like tears. The job ended with a gruesome murder one Saturday night. The dead man, with a knife still lodged deep into his chest, fell a few feet from the piano. Along with the night ladies, their customers and pimps, I fled that place and never went back. I can never forget the final moment in that room. The silence was startling.

Trouble was still coming in measured doses, and from all directions, rambling in out of order. If it didn't find me on Monday, it was bound to catch up with me on Tuesday. Had I been smart I might have saved myself some trouble by just sitting on a street corner and waiting for it to arrive. It took discipline to keep running away from it; and I ran hard if somewhat slow. Now the grass had turned to snow again, and I was still running.

FOUR

As there had been no turkey for Thanksgiving, there was no good cheer or presents for Christmas. The new year only rang in more snow and icy wind, and I was terribly desperate to get out of St. Paul. During the last week in January I decided, for some inexplicable reason, to try my luck in Chicago. I had no idea of how I would get there. That same weekend I met a trumpet player named Jess Turner. Soft-spoken, tall and consumptive-looking, he was stranded with an orchestra and wanted to get back to Chicago to his wife and children. We were standing by my favorite radiator in Jim Williams's pool hall trying to think of some way to make the trip, knowing neither of us had the necessary cash. It was Jess who finally thought of hopping a freight. "With luck we'd make it in about two days," he said.

"It would be awful cold."

"We'll wait till it warms a little."

We waited for nearly a week but the warmer weather never came. So, according to plan, Jess and I met at Dale and Rondo at six o'clock one Monday morning and took a trolley to the freight yards. The same cardboard suitcase I had brought from Kansas was filled with a few clothes, an army blanket and several bologna sandwiches my sister Cora had fixed for me; and I had two dollars. The weather was well below zero, and I pulled on three layers of long underwear, two pairs of wool socks and overshoes. Jess's landlady had held his clothing for unpaid rent, and he was poorly dressed for such weather in a chesterfield overcoat, a thin suit and patent leather shoes. He had no gloves and carried only his trumpet case. I was concerned for him and told him so, but the cold tight-fisted ways of Minnesota had numbed him into an almost suicidal indifference. He seemed to ignore the unmercifully cold wind as it pushed us along after we reached the freight yard.

"I wouldn't try it, Jess," I warned again.

"I've got to git back to my kids and wife. I ain't seen them in over three months. I'm more worried about them than this damned cold." The determination in his voice made any further warning futile. We wandered about the yard for nearly an hour, ducking railway police, searching for boxcars marked for the East. It was a hobo who finally helped us. He sensed our plight the moment he spotted us.

"Where you headin'?" he whispered as we climbed over a car coupling.

"Chi," Jess answered quickly.

"You're in the right lane. Just lay low for a spell. We'll board soon as they hook onto that line a couple of tracks over," he said.

"Why can't we get on now?" I asked.

"The yard dicks are still checkin'. Better wait a spell like I say." He motioned us down beside him in the snow beneath a flat car. "Keep low—out of sight."

We crouched and waited. Jess was already gray from the cold. But the hobo was right. In less than ten minutes a big yard cop, dressed in a red mackinaw, climbed into the car we would take and looked about. A club was in his hand. He swung down, slid the door shut and continued on his way. "They'll be hookin' on now. Then we'll run for it. Damn glad he didn't seal her up." I was beginning to respect this hobo. There was a banging in the distance. The cars on the next track lurched backward, shaking off the loose snow, then stopped.

Jess and I eyed the hobo nervously. He was getting to his feet and motioning us up with him. "Take it easy," he whispered. He stuck his head around a boxcar, observed the tracks from both directions and signaled us. "Come on. Make it snappy." We scurried across, slid the door open and scrambled up and in. Then the hobo eased the door shut.

There was very little space inside the car. Large wooden crates marked for a dye factory in Philadelphia took up most of the room. The hobo, who gave his name as Joe, pushed against them. "Better be sure none of this stuff shifts on the turns. We'd be smashed like potatoes." Jess and I put down our belongings and started pushing. The thought of being caught under such weight was frightening. "Don't worry. It's solid," Joe said. Then the three of us settled down in a space suitable for four men and sat waiting. Joe was leathered from the cold. Overalls padded with newspaper stuck from beneath his worn army coat, and his feet were wrapped in pieces of old blanket. He hadn't shaved in weeks and resembled a dirty Santa Claus with the gray-matted hair flowing down to his neck from under a red-and-black stocking cap. His breath smelled of alcohol in the closeness. But I was glad to have him with us. At last the train jerked forward and we were on our way, and I took out my blanket and offered it to Jess.

Hour by freezing hour we rattled over the countryside and only the quiet of my mind, braced against the noise and incredible cold, assured me of reality. All the problems of the world seemed to be contracted into this small and impersonal space. We were three shivering strangers, sharing our chance and hard times. Now and then the freight slowed to a stop. But before we could adjust our ears to the silence, a passenger train would roar past and the freight, having paid its respect to luxury and speed, would rattle off on another leg of our journey. When I got hungry I took out the sandwiches and we ate. Joe pulled out a bottle of cheap red wine, and we washed down the food with it.

Sometime during the first night we hit an area of paralyzing

31

cold, and although the three of us were huddled beneath the blanket, I felt a stiffness in my legs and arms. Jess, I knew, had to be freezing, but he lay there all night, his head on his trumpet case, without complaining.

The trouble came the next morning when we decided to stand for a stretch. Joe and I got to our feet but Jess could move only from his waist up. He kept pinching his legs and thighs, saying he felt like a rock. We pulled him to his feet but he began to totter. We tried to make him take a step but he couldn't move. Joe felt his lower limbs. "This ain't good," he said. "Your friend's got a bad frostbite. Better lay him back down."

After Jess was on the floor I doubled the blanket around his legs and started to rub them briskly, hoping to return the circulation. "Better not do that—his skin's likely to rub off in that condition," Joe warned. "We'll fix him up at the next stop. Better pray there's snow wherever we pull up." I prayed. And about an hour later, after we had stopped, Joe and I hopped out, filled the blanket with snow, and got back into the car.

"Pull his pants and shoes off," Joe said.

"What for?" I asked.

"Do as I say if you wanta save him." He was packing the snow into a solid form.

"Okay with you, Jess?" I asked.

"It's okay. I don't feel nothin' anyway."

I pulled off his shoes and pants, and we placed the blanket of snow beneath him up to his waist. Then, scooping up the loose snow, Joe covered the top of his legs with it, and secured the blanket. "That oughta thaw him out slow," Joe explained. "If he ain't better by afternoon you're gonna have to git him off here and to a hospital someway."

"How do you feel, Jess?" I asked.

"I don't feel," he answered bluntly.

"You will after a spell," Joe assured him. "Now I'm gonna git some more sleep."

The morning seemed endless. I thought of Sally and the uncertain hours stretching ahead. Depressed and disillusioned, I had left without seeing her. There was only a hastily scribbled note mailed saying I would be out of town for a few weeks. I could give no address but I would write, I promised. Now, lying between two men in the odor of wine and filth, I thought back to the warm breezes of summer that had played at her soft hair, the long walks by the lakes, the smell of meadow and her delicately scented skin, the promises and the tender moments of our love.

Why was I running? It was as if I were trying to escape hardship by stumbling backward into an even worse fate. Yet whatever my mother had hoped for me was still far out in the crooked distance. I wouldn't forget the afternoon when she trudged into the yard weary and sick, her gingham skirts trailing dust, the fire and spirit gone, a market basket under one arm and a blood-flecked handkerchief at her mouth. I had helped her into the house and into a chair. "What's the matter, Momma? What's the matter?" I kept demanding as tears clouded my sight. We were alone. I sat at her feet sensing that our world together was ending. I could feel it. The very nature of her silence said so.

"I'm going to ask Maggie Lee [Peggy] to take you back North with her. And I want you to mind her and go to church like you was brought up to do." The handkerchief was completely red now. "It's a better world up there in the North—color won't work so hard against you." There was a long pause. "Do right and don't get in trouble, and make a good man of yourself." I was trying to remember every word, not realizing how soon I would be needing them. "You better go to the field and look for your father. I'm awful tired."

When I returned with Poppa, she was lying on the floor unconscious. A few weeks later she came to long enough to mutter a prayer for me. Then my brother Clem told me to go to bed. Early the next morning I was awakened and told that Momma was dead. Now the fear I had shaken off such a short time before had caught up. And it lay beside me, gloating over the intensity of my shivering.

When Jess began to stir I shook Joe awake. But soon the quiet that Jess had held during the night was replaced with agonized cries that went on for several hours. "You got to git him off," Joe said at last. "It's too bad—we oughta be near Chi by now."

"I'll make it in. Don't put me off out here. Take me on to Chicago," Jess pleaded through his groans.

"But I'll get an ambulance at the next stop. They'll take you to a hospital," I said—not knowing if what I was saying was true or not.

"No. Get me home; I've gotta see my wife and kids."

I decided to let him have his way. Joe agreed and we settled in for another miserable night. We reached the Chicago freight yards early the next morning. A sparse scattering of snow whitened the area but it was nothing like Minnesota. After the train had stopped I jumped out and ran across to a signal tower for help. The man inside listened to my story rather unsympathetically, then said he had work to do and couldn't be bothered with frozen bums. But I persisted until he telephoned the yard master. In about an hour they brought an ambulance to the edge of the tracks and brought out a stretcher to take Jess away. I asked to go along in the ambulance but the driver refused me. "You'd best git the hell out of here before they take you to the lockup," he warned. They gave Jess an injection, wrapped him in dry blankets and hauled him off. I went as far as the ambulance.

"So long, Jess," I said.

"So long, kid," he said as they lifted him into the ambulance.

When I got back to the boxcar, Joe was gone and so were my blanket and bag. The morning was cold and blustery, and I walked toward the tall buildings I saw in the distance, staying close to the buildings to avoid the thrusts of cold air that swept the wide streets. I wound up on Wacker Drive and continued along the river toward Michigan Avenue. There the gales from the lake turned me about and I sought shelter in the lobby of a large building. And this was to be my tactic the rest of the morning until the chill began to leave my body. That night I found a flophouse on lower Wabash called the Hotel Southland. Rooms were advertised for twenty-five cents and up. The two dollars I had would provide eight nights of shelter. A young clerk with a badly pimpled face was on the desk. He eyed me curiously and in a very nervous voice asked me what I wanted.

"A twenty-five-cent room," I answered.

He looked at me as though I were about to draw a gun on him. "I'm not supposed to take colored in here. I'm sorry. It's the boss's rule, not mine. You understand, don't you?"

"No, I don't understand. It's damn cold out there, and I've got a quarter to pay for a bed." I glanced around the dirty, smoke-filled lobby, at the despondent and broken men sitting and lying about on the floor.

"Why don't you try the colored section out on the south side of town?"

"Because I want work downtown here and I don't have carfare back and forth."

"You're looking for work? Just a minute, maybe I can do something for you." He disappeared behind a ragged velvet drapery into an inner room. After a few minutes he reappeared with a tall fat man named John. He chewed on a cigar butt and tobacco juice coursed down his bulbous chin. "Mike tells me you're looking for a room and work. That so?" he asked, squinting down through the smoke at me.

"That's right."

"You look like a clean-cut colored boy."

"I'm a boy. I don't know what my color's got to do with it."

"Don't go gittin' your dander up. I think I got a proposition for you." I waited. "How'd you like to have a room and a job both?"

"Where?"

"Right here. I'm needin' a boy to clean this place. You'll git a room in the back and a half a buck a day."

Fifty cents a day would hardly keep me in food, and a back room in such a flophouse would be pretty bad, I thought. "Why don't you take it?" Mike urged. "At least you'll be out of the cold and have a place to sleep."

"I'd like to know why I can't just pay and sleep here?"

"Look, I ain't no expert on race problems," the fat man said impatiently. "I'm just givin' you a proposition. Whyn't you try it and see how things work out?"

"Give me twenty-five cents more a day and some food."

"Hell, fellow, you'll be makin' a buck a day with all that. That's big dough round these parts."

"Sorry," I said, turning as if I were going.

"Just a second." I had bluffed him into a decision. "Okay, I'll try it your way. Six bits a day and some grub." He threw up his hands and went back through the curtain.

"You shoulda held out for two bits more. He'd 'a paid it. This joint's dirty as hell—ain't been swept for a week," Mike whispered. He led me through the tangle of ill-smelling men and up to a tiny unheated room on the third floor. There was an army cot with a blanket on it and, like the other rooms in the place, it was separated from the hallway by meshed wire. The rooms resembled rows of chicken coops and had padlocks on their wobbly doors. They looked more like cages. As we walked along, I noticed that they were dark, the only light coming from the bare bulbs in the corridors. And they were partitioned off from one another by thin plywood. The haggard men stared out from them evilly, reminding me of trapped animals. And after Mike left I stretched out on the cot, listening to their hawking and spitting and their snarling, incoherent voices until I went to sleep.

When John awakened me at seven the next morning, an awful stench was in the place. Because of the cold I had slept in my clothes so I didn't have to dress. He led me to a hall closet, which was larger than my room; it was cluttered with rags, brooms, buckets and dustpans. There was Lysol for the toilets and a bin of sawdust for sweeping the floor. When I asked him about food he said the kitchen would be open at eight but that I should have all the corridors cleaned by then. After a breakfast of an oily, nondescript soup and stale bread, I went up to clean the rooms and toilets. And I instantly learned that poverty in the big cities festered a special kind of filth.

Some of the men were up and moving about. Others still slept. Several of them had ignored the toilets and defecated upon the floor. One drunk lay face down in his own vomit and another, claiming to have been beaten and robbed during the night, lay groaning in his bed, his blanket matted with blood. The toilets were filthy beyond use. Our hog pens in Kansas were antiseptic by comparison. Without doubt the Hotel Southland was the vilest piece of real estate in the entire city of Chicago. Cleaning the place was hard, but it was the washing of spittoons covered with slime and tobacco juice that made the work even more unpleasant. Plowing was backbreaking but it was much cleaner. The freshly turned soil had been cool and soothing to my bare feet. Keeping the plow straight in the furrows brought clean sweat. And there had been something wholesome about driving Charlie, our plow horse, the length of a field without stopping to rest.

But the Hotel Southland was a bad breath of smoke, alcohol, sour bodies and human excrement. Its pickpockets, alcoholics, bums, addicts, perverts, panhandlers and thugs were of the lowest order. They spoke with an intolerable vulgarity that was catching. Soon I was saying things of which I was ashamed. But it was the only way, I thought, to hold my own here, where profanity meant prestige and politeness invited abuse.

"Good morning," I said to a drunk on the third day.

"What's good about it, you black son-of-a-bitch?" he growled back.

I froze in anger, wanting to hit him, disgusted with myself for not having an equally ungracious reply. He stumbled on down the hall, urinating in his pants as he went, unaware of the emotions he had aroused in me.

Minutes later a scream spun me about. The same drunk, seized now with violent delirium, was trying to scale the wire partition. "Snakes!" he screamed. "They're all over the place!" He grabbed at his legs, neck and thighs as if they were biting him. "Snakes!" His screams must have only multiplied their numbers, for he gradually slipped down to the floor, shrieking and exhausted. And I imagined them curling over and under him as he lay quivering in silence. Several men came out and staggered toward his body, which twisted and contracted under the imaginary reptiles. They would help him, I thought. But instead one kicked him in the back; one searched his pockets for money; one stuck a burning cigarette to his leg—he only flinched—and another clamped a spittoon on his head. The slime and tobacco juice, mixed with the viscous sweat of his hallucination, soaked his hair, face and neck. Then the men joined hands and danced weirdly around him to a drunken chant of "He's a jolly good fellow." The man was hemorrhaging from his mouth and nose and his eyes had frozen to a stare; I was afraid he was dying. But after a while he came to and pushed off the spittoon. He tried to stand but the other men's feet pushed him back down and he lay cringing beneath their mocking dance. He looked up to me, his hand extended, pleading for help. I stood there with a broom in my hand, observing him, remembering that a few minutes before he had called me a black son-of-a-bitch. The moment was mine and all I could bring to it was revenge. I smiled at him scornfully and backed away. The others gave him a final kick and staggered off to their cages, and eventually he crawled away on his hands and knees.

This strange, indecent ritual had taught me that degradation was no respecter of color; the truth of the lesson fell trip-hammer hard. And in a wordless way I felt exalted, reassured—knowing that I would never sink to such a depth. After it was quiet again I began sweeping up the mess; and it was like clearing away the remnants of a decayed animal.

Big John was tight the first Saturday I went into his office for my pay. He was passing out cigars and corn whiskey to Mike and a policeman who had stopped in to get warm. His generosity, I learned, was seeded with the joy of his wife's pregnancy. And the nature of his talk swelled with adulterous boasting. "I'm fifty and I can still hump four chicks a day. Not one, mind you, but four—five if I'm pushed to it—'cause I take care of myself."

The cop's coat was open, and his winter underwear needed washing. He didn't seem to be listening. He chewed the cigar and sipped the whiskey without taking his eyes from the floor. Mike, on the other hand, hung on to every word his boss uttered. Maybe he was thinking about his girl. But either the whiskey or the cigar —or maybe the talk—was turning him paler by the minute.

"And I don't mean git'n on and blow'n off like a schoolboy. I mean stay'n with it for an hour or so if I'm goin' good." His red eyes turned toward me. "How much you got coming, boy?" he said frowning.

"Four-fifty. You owe me for six days." I wanted to get out for the weekend and I tried to show my impatience by pretending to ignore his boasting. Now he ignored me.

"When's the last time you got a piece, Mike?" The younger man, seeming disturbed by the question, fidgeted the cigar and gulped down the last of his whiskey.

Big John persisted. "Come on, tell us. When'd you git your last piece?" A fiendish grin played around his jowls, and Mike's bad complexion was turning to ashen purple. His thin lips were almost colorless.

"I'm sick," he gulped, and ran out the door.

Big John roared with laughter. "Sick, he says, sick. Hell, he ain't sick—he's a goddamned fruit. He likes boys—specially sailor boys—that's what he likes. He's a goddamned punk." Now he doubled in laughter and still laughing pulled open a drawer and took out a half dollar and four greasy bills and tossed them at me. The cop's expression hadn't changed. He continued chewing the cigar, sipping the whiskey and gazing at the floor. I pocketed the money and fled the derisive laughter, the smoke and the smell of dirty bodies.

So Mike was a "fruit." What a hell of a place for him to work, I thought.

It was only five o'clock, and since I hadn't been to the south side I decided to go there for the evening. As I rounded the corner toward the elevated train a Negro youth stopped me. His car, he said, had stalled and he wanted me to help him push it to an incline several feet away. "Once I get it rolling it'll start up," he said. We both pushed and near the incline he jumped in behind the wheel. The car bucked a few times, coughed and started up, and I was turning to go when a man ran from a store hollering, "Police! Police! They're stealing my car!" I wanted to run but several men grabbed me and held me until the police came. They caught the thief two blocks away, and, luckily for me, the cop who had been drinking with Big John ran up. I told him what had happened; he believed me and let me go. They took the real thief to jail and I changed my mind about the south side and went to a movie instead.

I stayed on at the Southland until the end of January, hating each day. It was a harsh and ugly time, and I earmarked every penny I saved for a coach ticket back to St. Paul, longing for the time when I could get into a tub of hot water and soak out the smell of the place.

One morning I awoke to a commotion down on the second floor. And when I moved to the staircase to look down, a man ran up and past me toward my room. Several policemen were running about brandishing their guns. They had subdued two men, who lay handcuffed on the floor, and were searching for the one who had run past me. The men, I found out later, had been involved in a holdup. Big John was with the police, helping to search the cages, and after a few seconds they stormed up toward me.

"Anybody come up this way, boy?" I pointed in the direction the man had gone, realizing that he was hiding either in the toilet or in my room. The outer door was locked and the other cages were occupied so he couldn't have escaped. They found him under my bed, pulled him out, beat him and dragged him downstairs.

Three days later I found a pistol beneath my bed. The holdup man had obviously left it there. I knew I should have turned it in immediately; my conscience and better judgment told me so. But there was something appealing about having a gun in this place; it could be a protection against the place itself. And the longer I held on to the pistol, the harder it was to part with it. Each night, after the lights were dimmed, I took it out and fondled it, admiring its shape and power.

The trouble came one Saturday when I went to collect my pay from Big John. As on every Saturday he was drunk and boasting of his sexual prowess. Mike was there and a couple of drunks were stretched out on the floor, their backs propped against the wall. Big John was puffing about, his belly shaking up and down. Deep belligerent lines coursed from his sullen mouth to his chin. I sensed trouble the moment I asked for my wages.

"Git outa here, you black bastard! Don't you see I'm busy!" he shouted, doubling his fist as if he would hit me.

Everything blurred and my body shook with rage. I looked around for something to hit him with in case I had to fight. He was too big to take on otherwise. There was nothing but his battered typewriter and frayed ledger in which he kept records. A half-filled whiskey bottle was in his left hand, and he looked as if he might hit me with it. I knew I should have backed away but my temper was out of control and I foolishly challenged him. "Give me my money, you lousy dog! I'm quitting!" He charged me like a bull, pummeled my face and body, slammed me into the wall and kneed me to the floor. Pain streaked through my groin but I managed to slide from beneath his kicking and scramble out the door.

"You black son-of-a-bitch, you won't git a cent now! Turn in your lock and git the hell out of here before I kill you!"

"Kill you kill you kill you"—the thought burned into my mind all the way up the stairs. My lip was cut, my nose bled and my groin felt as if it were on fire. I ran cold water over my wrists, arms and head; and though the bleeding stopped my anger continued to rise. I had saved sixteen dollars and that was in a money belt I had sewn together. When I lifted the mattress to retrieve it, I saw the gun. I buckled the belt around my waist and shoved the gun into my overcoat pocket. Then I walked determinedly down the stairs.

Mike was at the outer desk when I reached the office. "You'd better get out fast," he warned me; "he's half crazy. Come back tomorrow—he'll forget all about it."

I pulled out the pistol and pointed it at him from a low angle. "I won't come back tomorrow and I won't forget what he did to me in there. Now you go in there and get my money out of his drawer —and make it snappy," I ordered. My anger had carried me too far but I couldn't stop now. Mike started to raise his hands but I told him to keep them down. "This ain't a holdup. I just want what's coming to me." He turned quietly and went through the curtain, with me following close behind. Big John was seated now and he began shaking when he saw the gun pointing at his heart. I didn't know whether he shook from rage or from fear. And I didn't want to shoot, but the choice lay with him—if he charged me I would pull the trigger. I had made up my mind, knowing it would be fatal if he overpowered me again. In his mood he wouldn't have hesitated to kill me.

"Give me that gun, boy," he growled, "or I'll take it away from you."

"You try, and see what happens." The two drunks lay unmoving on the floor as if nothing unusual were happening. "Go ahead, Mike. Get my money out of that drawer." He looked appealingly to Big John, who grudgingly nodded his consent, and Mike, in his nervousness, gave me an extra dollar. I put it in my pocket and Big John sat smoldering, his hand inching toward the whiskey bottle on his desk. But I snatched it from his reach, emptied the contents into a glass and splashed it into his eyes—blinding him momentarily. He tried to rise but I knocked him sideways with the butt of the pistol. He tried to get up again but I swung viciously, catching him on the temple, and he collapsed in a heap on the floor. I ran from the building and kept running toward the Union Station, expecting any minute to hear a police siren; but none sounded. Halfway across the river bridge I slowed down and looked in all directions. No one was watching and I pitched the gun sideways into the water, then hurried on to the station. Inside I pulled the coat up around my neck to hide the bloody shirt and went to the washroom.

"Gordon?" The voice was frightening, but at the same time familiar and friendly, and I turned toward it, filled with apprehension.

"Uncle Pete," I said in a half cry.

"My God, boy, what's happened to you?" He was dressed in a Pullman porter's uniform, ready to make his run back to St. Paul and on to Seattle. "What's all that blood doing on your shirt like that?" He had recognized me and followed me to the washroom.

41

"I've got to get out of here. I'm in some serious trouble."

My uncle, suddenly involved in the peril of his sister's youngest child, reacted swiftly. "Button up and come with me. You can tell me the rest later." He took me up to his Pullman car, put me into an empty compartment and went out to receive his passengers. It was like an eternity before the conductor hollered, "All aboard." Then at last the train was rolling. And a feeling of safety grew with every click of the train's wheels as I relaxed in the comfort of the plush compartment. Momentarily my mind reached back through the trauma of Lysol, sweat, filth, cursing, drunkenness, savagery and perversion, and I welcomed the distance between me and the Hotel Southland. There was a knock at the door and, thinking it was my uncle, I opened it. It was the conductor and he was smiling. "Don't worry," he said; "everything's okay. Your uncle went to get food for you. Just take it easy—everything's okay."

"You're lucky to be alive," Uncle Pete said after I had eaten and spilled out my story. He made a bed for me and I washed, changed and crawled into the clean softness of it, thinking that I would like to lie there forever. Tonight there would be no inhuman voices coming from the corridor, and there would be no ominous morning to awaken to. In minutes I was deep in a dreamless sleep.

The next morning my uncle got me up about an hour out of St. Paul and fed me ham, eggs and fried potatoes. He admitted he was a little ashamed of not having inquired of me since Momma's death, and I had almost forgotten his being at the funeral. Even though he was my mother's brother he had always seemed apart from the family, and I sensed a distant unhappiness between him and his younger brother, Charlie. "Pete's pissed ice water since he was a kid," Charlie would say. Yet, running into my icy uncle at the train station provided me a warm thankful moment. On our arrival in St. Paul he had given me twenty-five dollars and advised me to stay out of trouble. I could never think of him as my mother's brother—and I fear he had difficulty in thinking of me as her son. Conversely, Charlie was a favorite of mine. I remember the two men getting into a heated argument over Charlie's getting drunk just before my mother's funeral. It made little difference to me that Uncle Charlie was always a bit tipsy. He kept a big smile on his face, and pulled me aside sometimes to tell risqué jokes. I saw Uncle Pete only twice after that, and he had few words for me. He died two years later, and I would find that out several years afterward. With a bottle at his side, and that smile still on his face, Uncle Charlie died in the winter of 1935.

FIVE

Just as Uncle Pete's twenty-five dollars was about to run out I got a job as *head* busboy at the St. Paul Lowry Hotel. It didn't matter that I was the *only* busboy. One day after lunch had been served and the dining room was empty I, having set the tables, decided to indulge in a little fantasy. At one end of the room was a large grand piano. Handsome and inviting, it had beckoned to me for days. I sat down and began playing, imagining that through the microphones hanging above me, my music was reaching out to the entire universe. The final chord was still echoing through the empty room when a voice came from behind.

"Nice tune you were playing. What's the name of it?"

It was Larry Funk, a white orchestra leader whose band was playing at the hotel. I was startled, and he seemed amused. "It's a song I wrote called 'No Love.'"

"You wrote that?"

"Yep, I did."

"Would you like for my orchestra to play it?"

The smile on my face was enough of an answer. He picked up the house phone and asked for Room 313; the party who answered was told to come to the dining room immediately. A few minutes later the orchestra's arranger was beside me, taking my song down note by note. Half an hour later he was jotting down the lyrics. "We'll play it on the Saturday night broadcast," Funk said as they left. And I stood there watching them go, struck dumb with a mixture of disbelief and joy. "No Love," written at the brothel just a few months before, was going to be played for a nationwide broadcast. From that moment on the hands on all clocks moved slowly. It was Tuesday. The three intervening days seemed never to end and waiting became torturous. Meanwhile I went about telling everyone I knew to listen in to the Saturday night broadcast.

Finally Saturday arrived, the dining room was filled and over the Mutual Network the entire universe (I hoped) was listening as Larry announced "No Love" and introduced me as its composer. His wand pointed at me as I stood trembling by my bus stand. It was a good but nerve-wracking moment, and I would like to say that I felt promise in it. But I didn't; inner excitement had all but paralyzed my brain.

Trouble was furthest from my mind as I left the hotel's drugstore after work later that night. Three white men passing out handbills and pamphlets approached me, but as they came nearer I sensed trouble. It came quickly.

"Here, boy," one said, shoving a pamphlet into my hand, "tell your mammy and pappy to vote like this thing says."

"Go to hell," I countered, throwing the pamphlet to the ground. A sharp kick answered against my ribs, but I was prepared. Adjusting my ring, which was set with a crystal, I doubled my fist and swung at the one nearest to me. He fell to the street, his face cut from his eye to his ear. The second one ducked my blow, but I caught the largest of the three with a hard right. He fell backward toward a plate glass window, and he grabbed me about the neck and pulled me with him. We both crashed through the window, but my neck, body and arms caught most of the glass. His friends pulled him out and they ran, forcing their way through a crowd of spectators who had gathered during the commotion. By the time I was carried into the drugstore, I was bleeding badly and the second finger on my right hand hung half severed from its joint. The drugstore employees covered my wounds with wet towels and someone called the police. As luck decreed it, three of my friends—George Berry, Leroy Lazenberry and Howard Barksdale—were walking past, and off they ran to capture my assailants. The wisest thing I did, a doctor told me later, was to tape my finger back into its joint. Eventually the police took the three white men to jail—and I was imprisoned, along with them, as a "material witness." The three of them were locked up in a cell next to mine; only bars separated us from one another. I asked for a doctor; but at two in the morning none had come. At three o'clock the lights were turned out and I curled up on my cot and tried to sleep.

Imprisoned there in the foul dark, I felt like a caged and injured animal. The other three, having slept off their drunk, had begun to mutter obscenities: "You black son-of-a-bitch—we'll kill you the next time—goddamn dirty nigger—black bastard—wait till we git you on the street again." Now one of them was urinating through the bars onto my floor. I watched from the shadows, my mind racing and searching for some way to retaliate. But there was nothing, not even a glass to throw. I could only observe their depravity with disgust. It was hard to regard them as human beings; they seemed only a shadowy white mass—one so unbearable that even to hate it seemed futile.

I closed my eyes, still hoping that sleep might separate me from the experience. And in my despair I forced my thoughts from their ugliness and into my mother's grave. Then things were easier. The mere thought of her eased the tensions and the boiling inside me.

"You 'sleep, tar baby?"

I didn't answer.

"Maybe the bastard's dead. Heh, we pissed on your floor!"

The odor bore him out, but I lay still, my mind's eye deep inside the grave. The image of my mother, slim brown hands crossed, face sharp and immobile, demanded in its repose that I remember her teachings.

46

"Wake up! Wake up, you black son-of-a-bitch!"

It was an hour later that my anger began to rise again—and suddenly out of control, I got up, lifted my cot and slammed it against the bars. The three barely stirred. Only a flat grunt came from one of them. They were asleep. Then, righting the cot, I lay back down. In my rage I had only hurt my finger and it was beginning to bleed again. Some time later the lights went on and a policeman unlocked the cell, shook the three white men awake and told them they were free. "What about me?" I asked, as he started away.

"You just take it easy, friend," he grumbled, "you've caused enough trouble for one night."

"But my finger is half off and it's bleeding again," I protested.

"Ain't no doctor around this time of morning."

"How about a hospital then?"

"You just take it easy like I told you." He flipped the light switch, went out and slammed the outer door shut. And I lay back and tried to reason things out. Why, I wondered, were the police releasing them and holding me?

There was nothing to do but wait. And in the long interim I did a lot of thinking about the white man and about his brutality—realizing that it was nudging me into a hatred of him. I lay aching until dawn, reassembling all the scalding experiences one by one. I was overwhelmed by the many injustices already fastened to my memory. I had sort of limped through the early years, accepting as normal a scar for a scar. Now I felt a permanent anger after each clash. And I was becoming more sensitive to any situation that revealed a white man's attitude toward me. I never feared him or stood in awe of his achievements. "If a white boy can do it, so can you," Momma used to say, "so don't ever give me your color as a cause for failing." She made everything seem possible, even during the bleakest years, by feeding my young mind with all the things one could do in spite of the color of one's skin.

But the injuries I received that night seemed to gather all the misfortune and futility I had known since childhood. They had, in a way, become symbolic of failure, making all the efforts of the last years meaningless. I was suffering with the others now—those imprisoned in slave ships from Africa hundreds of years before, those strung up by their necks in hatred-filled Delta bottoms, those gunned to death for "looking the wrong way" at some Southern white lady, those bent, gnarled and burned to black crispness under the white-hot sun, in the white man's field, so that the white man might live a white man's life on a white man's land.

Dawn finally broke. And when they released me several hours later, undoctored and unfed, it was raining. The same bloody towels were wrapped about my neck, arms and hands. I stood in the doorway of the jail for several moments, then I walked slowly in the downpour, letting the rain beat life back into my body. People huddling in the doorways observed me curiously, unaware of the bitterness inside me, where, only a short time before, there had been hope and joy. Ten new scars, inflicted by white men, ached beneath those towels. And my life, held now in a body of trouble and hurt, was ready to explode with hatred and revenge.

After a doctor had dressed my wounds and stitched my finger into place, I holed up again in my room. And, as the cuts gradually closed, they seemed to seal in the experience. And the bitterness, trapped inside me, began poisoning all the senses that governed my thinking.

In my distress I forgot my music; I even forgot that it had been broadcast. I slipped back into days and nights of brooding; and composing no longer enraptured me; fate was playing games again —and it was winning. My sister Peggy, concerned about my unhappiness, kept a close watch over me, inquired of my needs and tried to make things pleasant. But I didn't talk much to anyone. I was too busy encouraging the suffering and pampering the hate that had taken me over. Eventually I emerged from the memory, quietly but dangerously violent—resolved to gain vengeance upon any white person who crossed me the wrong way.

Two months later the orchestra finished its engagement, and Larry Funk casually asked me if I would like to travel with it. I was ecstatic. The events had come so close to one another, and so unexpected—a miracle, the rush of violence, then yet another miracle. The experience was akin to something beautiful blooming, then dying only to bloom again.

Larry's invitation had been shrouded in vagueness; he neither defined my duties with the orchestra, nor a salary. I didn't press for clarification. Opportunity was in the offing and there was no time for giving it a lot of thought. I quit my job, packed hurriedly and was aboard the orchestra's bus when it left for the next engagement in Cleveland, Ohio. There my duties began to take shape. Larry, liking "the husky quality of my black voice," assigned me as vocalist to several songs in the repertoire, and to the orchestra's signature theme, "Band of a Thousand Melodies." The salary however remained in the realm of obscurity—a few dollars here or there, my room and board. But these circumstances, greatly outdistancing those I had left behind, gave me small concern. The sense of something even more sublime was spreading its presence. The word was that Larry was a millionaire, and an heir to the publishing house of Funk and Wagnalls. This made my employer even more intriguing.

Next came Detroit, then on to Kansas City, where I found myself somewhat of a celebrity to black musicians, because I was the first black to be singing with a white orchestra. Even more significance was attached to all this since the Hotel Muehlebach, where we were playing, didn't allow blacks to enter its portals. Larry had had a white woolen suit tailored for me, then secured a small white grand piano and assigned me to yet another duty—that of entertaining the cabaret audiences in between sets. And a few more dollars were added to those first uncertain ones. Memories of that beat-up, tuneless brothel piano were slipping into the past. Then, quite suddenly we learned that we were being booked into New York's prestigious Hotel Park Central for a month's engagement. New York! Broadway! Harlem, just a heartbeat away! It seemed that God Himself had taken a personal interest in me.

A violent rainstorm was sweeping through New York when we arrived in the city two weeks later, and things started rocketing downhill when we reached the hotel. The doorman, with very mean eyes, informed me that I would have to go in the back way. New York? I couldn't believe it. Funk had arrived by plane the previous day and was already ensconced in his suite. Abby, the orchestra's drummer whom I had become friendly with, raised a quiet protest but I shushed him. Rather than hurt my chances for staying with the orchestra, I swallowed the insult and went in the back way. Larry, Abby assured me, would put a quick end to that situation. But, to everyone's amazement, Larry Funk skipped town that same night—owing salaries to the entire orchestra.

None of the orchestra members or I knew why he had fled the city, nor did any of us ever see him again. Downhearted, Abby went with me to a drugstore for coffee and bagels, and silently we drank black coffee. He wasn't so bad off; his family lived a short distance away in Brooklyn. But I didn't know a soul, and I only had a few dollars in my pockets. Abby didn't have much either, but he handed me five dollars as we walked toward the uptown entrance to the subway. He stood watching as I lugged my battered suitcase down the steps.

"Where do I get off?" I shouted up to him.

"Take the *A* train! Get off at 125th or 145th—any place along there!"

Harlem—that fabled distant enchanted place I had read and heard about for so many years. The sound of its name rang like a heavenly bell. Like many other blacks who had never been there, I thought of it as the Eden of pleasure; a paradise where black people walked to sweet music, and good times rolled: Sugar Hill, the Cotton Club, Smalls' Paradise—all enthroned in one big jazzy Valhalla. It had never occurred to me that I would get there so quickly. The speed of the train, rushing beneath the city's darkness, the noise ricocheting around it, left me a little dazed.

I got off at 145th Street. That was the higher number; best to think high at a time like that. It had been raining; sullen clouds hung low over the tenements, and I was apprehensive. Yet, a certain excitement accompanied my first steps into Harlem. Of the sea of black faces I looked into, most seemed troubled. Laughter cut through the heavy air now and then, but even that carried a hint of melancholy. I was black like everyone else; but I was a stranger there. This wasn't Kansas where black people always nodded to one another. It was like being cast upon an island with swarms of kinfolk who refused to acknowledge my presence.

A sign that said *ROOMS* beckoned from a gray stone tenement. I walked past a line of garbage cans, up a few steps and knocked on the door. A fat, toothless woman, chewing on her gums, opened it and asked what I wanted.

"A room, ma'am."

She grunted, said she had a room, but it would cost five dollars a week. In my best Kansas manner I told her that I would take it. She looked me up and down. "My house is a house of the Lord, and I don't like strange people coming and going, and you'll have to pay five dollars a week and a week in advance."

"Yes, ma'am." I peeled off five one-dollar bills. She took them, pocketed them, then guided me up two flights to my new quarters —a wretched room, small, dirty and smelling like a mixture of stale cabbage and iodine. There was one window with a broken pane; a rag filled the opening. Cracked linoleum covered part of the floor, and the narrow bed looked to have slept thousands of bodies. The mattress was lumpy and stained with urine; she quickly covered it with a wrinkled sheet. She pointed to a toilet at the end of the hall. Both the seat and the wooden handle on the flushing chain were cracked. "Keep it clean for the other roomers," she said. From a hall closet she yanked an old blanket and tossed it on the bed. Leaving, she reminded me once again, "This is the house of the Lord, and I aim to keep it so."

"Yes, ma'am."

It had been a battering day—dreams attained and lost in less than twenty-four hours. I lay down on the bed to rest, afraid of the oncoming night, afraid of what morning held. Darkness quivered in like an ugly beast. Was this wrecked day real, or was I suffering a nightmare? After an hour I dozed. The room was pitch black when I awoke to hear a gnawing inside the wall near my head. I put my ear close, listening—a rat was trying to eat through the plaster. I took my shoe and pounded the spot from where the sound was coming. There was quiet for a few moments, then the gnawing started again. Weary of the terrible day, I finally fell into deep sleep.

I awoke to an ominous, wet morning. Rain poured in torrents; thunder rocked Harlem. I longed for a ticket home. But where was home? Certainly it wasn't behind the filthy walls that now seemed to imprison me. I felt to be a million miles from nowhere, directionless. Larry Funk had invited me to take part in a deception, a vile false alarm. All I had to confront the day with were about ten dollars and a few glamorous memories.

I recall being overwhelmed with fear that morning, feeling that all promise had departed. Uncertainty was stalking me again, and the fear was akin to that I had when those white boys threw me into Marmaton River years before in Fort Scott. There, terror-stricken with the thought of drowning, I had kept my wits and managed to get through the murky water to safety. Now, years later in strange, faraway Harlem, it was again time for some desperate swimming. But the big-city river was a flow of mean asphalt streets and shadowed alleys, and there were no concrete banks.

Kansas had weighted me with a certain obstinacy, and for the moment I could only hope to reach out to that obstinacy to help

51

me survive. Disappointment was hounding me again, and I was suffering the leftover hurt of the journey from Minnesota—feeling like I was alone on a motionless train and waking up in misery. I had lain there for a while with memories of those recent weeks dreaming in. Intermingling with the downpour on the roof above me, they amounted to abandoned talk and music that seemed to have nothing much to do with where I had fallen. But a good family life had shaped my principles and shown me the importance of not giving up, and on that was based my determination somehow to make it.

I got up and opened my suitcase. There wasn't much of a wardrobe to pick from, surely not that tailored white suit. It now appeared to be a travesty crumpled among my soiled belongings. Perhaps I could pawn it for a few weeks' rent. I settled for a gray sweater and a pair of brown pants that went well with my tan sharp-toed shoes. At midday the rain stopped, the sky cleared and I wandered into the heart of Harlem looking for work—walking walking walking through a steady stream of slow-moving black people past bars funeral parlors African Methodist Shiloh Baptist and storefront churches past beautee shops herb stores bar-b-cue hamburger and hotdog stands past stacks of caskets and more funeral parlors past brownstones and frowning tenements past Smalls' Paradise the Apollo the Cotton Club Joe's Burgers the Harlem Lunch the Church of God in Christ the Church of Good Hope past the Master Cleaners Sam's Music Pit past hog maw, chitterling and catfish shops healing stores and more funeral homes past windows with pictures of the Black Jesus and African herbs—but not a single one with a help-wanted sign.

For the next two months I lived on a diet of hotdogs and root beer, which, at the time, cost seven cents. I was sinking deeper into fear and into debt for that wretched room at Mrs. Haskins's, and she was ready to kick me out. But being a religious woman she was merciful and grudgingly accepted my promises to pay her when I found a job.

Hunting for a job in Harlem was akin to panning for gold in an onion patch. There were none to be had. The place was a prison, owned, operated and exploited by whites who lived downtown. Its inmates were all guilty of the same crime; they were born black. And things were the same downtown—easier to walk on water than to find work there. Help-wanted ads in the newspapers were explicit in terms of who was to apply for jobs. Bus drivers, taxicab drivers, doormen, bellhops, receptionists, musicians, waiters, garbage men, street cleaners, sign painters, hospital attendants, clerks and plumbers were all needed—providing they were white. The Hotel Park Central, where I had hopes of performing with Larry Funk's orchestra, needed cooks and dishwashers, but they wanted white cooks and dishwashers. A plumber needed a helper, but a white one. A limousine service was hiring drivers—providing they were white. The ads said so. Only the rich part of town offered jobs to blacks, but those were for maids and nannies—women, not men or boys. Nevertheless, I made that long trek by foot through Central Park every morning, all the way down to Forty-second Street and beyond sometimes, only to return weary and more desperate, my face and manner showing the strain of the fruitless journey.

A tall skinny man languished on the steps when I returned one Saturday evening. He wore a zoot suit and a wide-brimmed hat. "How you doing, man?" His tone was friendly, his eyes, red and heavy-lidded, saw that I was beat. "I'm Charlie. I live on the second floor. Have a seat." I sat down on the step above him after shaking his hand, which was damp and felt like leather. "You new here?" he asked.

"Been here close to a month."

"Where you from?"

"Minnesota."

"Like it here?"

"Hardly what I expected it to be."

"What's the trouble?"

"Can't find work."

He took a single cigarette from his shirt pocket, lit it and inhaled deeply, blew out the smoke, then inhaled again, holding in the smoke for a few seconds before exhaling it again. An odor like burned cornsilk hit my nose, and I suddenly realized that Charlie was smoking a stick of marijuana. Some of the musicians in Larry's band had attempted to get me to try one, but I refused simply because I didn't smoke at the time.

"Want a drag?"

I accepted his offer as an act of friendliness more than anything else. The taste was hot and bitter, and I hurriedly blew out the smoke.

53

"Heh, man, you waste the charge like that. Hold it in. Get the full charge."

"I'm not a smoker, Charlie," I said, handing it back.

"Okay. No sense wasting a fine stick."

"See you later, Charlie." I got up and went to my room.

I had gone to bed late and I was still asleep when he rapped on my door and announced himself the following morning. I let him in. He still wore the zoot suit and big hat, looking sleepy, as if he had never gone to bed. "How'd you like to make some loot?"

"How?" I asked eagerly, knowing I had only sixty cents left.

"Nothin' to it. Come by my room after you get dressed."

After quickly pulling on my clothes I went to his room. The door was open and he lay curled up on his bed. It was too short for his long frame and he was a rather ludicrous sight, lying there, his pointed shoes hanging over the side of the bed. He still had his hat on.

"Okay, I'm ready. What am I to do?"

He observed me for a moment, then pointed to a neat pile of small, newspaper-wrapped packages on the floor. "All you gotta do is deliver some of those every day and pick up some envelopes for me. Simple as that. Okay? You get a buck for every trip you make."

"What's in them?"

"You want to do it or not?"

I didn't ask any more questions, but he was hardly the type to be sending out religious objects. When I agreed to his proposition he sat up and wrote out the names and addresses for the day's deliveries.

A few minutes later, on the third floor of a tenement house less than a block away, I knocked at door 3B.

"What you want?" a voice growled from inside.

"I'm from Charlie. Got a package for Shorty." My tone was hip, nonchalant.

The door opened to a crack and a big, dark man peered out at me.

"You Shorty?" I asked haltingly.

"That's right." He took the package, shoved a dirty sealed envelope into my hand and shut the door. Another package went to a man named Red who lived in the basement, a few yards from the 135th Street Precinct. Red seemed to be waiting for me. After taking the package he too handed me an envelope, but with an explanation. "Tell Charlie I'm a deuce short. I'll even on the next buy." Red was jet black and hairless as a billiard ball.

"You're Red?" I asked, puzzled.

He looked at me as if I were crazy. "I ain't Snow White." The door slammed in my face. What in hell is going on? I wondered. Shorty turns out to be a giant and Red is as black as the ace of spades. I finished up the day with thirteen deliveries, and thirteen dollars. Charlie wasn't happy about Red's being a deuce short. "Son-of-a-bitch is already in me for two bucks." By the week's end I had made over thirty dollars. And the feel of those dollars was precious. By now I knew I was swimming in bad blood, but since the money was doing the talking I had nothing to say.

On the first of the next month a letter came from Sally Alvis. It was a good warming letter, full of love and our hopes for the future. Too, she wanted to know all about my work with the band —that was no longer a band—and if I had been serious about asking her to marry me. I had made that proposal by mail when the band was still in Kansas City, before everything turned black. That night I wrote that everything was just fine, that the band had broken up, and that I was now thinking about forming one of my own. And of course I was serious about marrying her.

I had just sealed the letter when two cops burst into my room with drawn pistols. I jumped up only to be knocked down again. Then they were punching me in the ribs and face. "Okay, you black bastard. Where's the stuff?"

"What stuff?"

"You know what stuff, you son-of-a-bitch!" One was now bumping my head against the wall while the other ransacked my drawers and searched beneath the mattress with a flashlight.

"That ain't Charlie! That ain't Charlie! His room's down the hall!" Mrs. Haskins had come to my rescue. I was shoved to the floor and they plunged down the hall toward Charlie's room. But Charlie was long gone. Evidently somebody had tipped him off. I could hear them bulling about the room, kicking at newspapers and overturning furniture. But they found nothing. Later Mrs. Haskins went trundling down the stairs mumbling, "My Lord, my Lord." I sat nursing my wounds, knowing that I owed a lot to her Lord. The letter I had written lay crumpled on the floor. After smoothing it out I went down to post it. I hesitated for a moment then dropped it in, regretting my action before it hit the bottom of the mail box. A light rain fell over Harlem when I got up the next morning. My body was sore and my spirits were down, and my source of income had disappeared.

Despite the setback, my hopes were still alive. As they survived, I would survive. The letdown from Charlie's exit served a dual purpose—it kept me in front of the mirror, which reminded me that there were still a lot of roadblocks ahead. I was to take a deep breath, gather strength and work my way through them. I had made that circuitous journey to Harlem with a ravening hunger for honey, only to find it also flavored with salt. To most blacks who had flocked in from all over the land, the struggle to survive was savage. Poverty coiled around them and me with merciless fingers. Only for rich whites who went there to *slum* did the good times roll. At the Cotton Club where, in grand vehicles, they went most, blacks were not allowed—unless they were there to entertain. The wealthy white man's Eden was pleasured in the poor black man's Beulah Land. The hostility of the situation suggested bondage. But, strangely, it failed to provoke any substantial bitterness in the black community. And this puzzled me.

I was on the hustle again—trying for work at restaurants, grocery stores, theaters, barbershops, pool halls, garages, amusement galleries, dance halls and even churches. I asked for a porter's job at a police station near Times Square. But it was always, "Sorry." As they said in Harlem, "Nothin' was shakin'." For that matter the same went for a lot of young men across the land. Joblessness and hunger were the words.

Thankfully, President Roosevelt did something about it. In March of that year, 1933, he reached out to the country's impoverished youth through the Civilian Conservation Corps, hoping to take them off the streets and breadlines. Two hundred and fifty thousand young men between the ages of eighteen and twenty-five were to be put to work at reforestation, road construction and the prevention of soil erosion. The pay would be thirty dollars a month—approximately one dollar for a day's work. That was thirty dollars a month more than I could count on; furthermore, I was in debt to Mrs. Haskins for two months' back rent. After seeing the government notices posted at the Harlem YMCA, I pawned my white tailored suit, paid Mrs. Haskins off and, with several hundred others from Harlem, joined the CCC. Two mornings later we were transported by bus to Fort Dix, New Jersey. More precisely, we were bused into a nightmare. At least a third of our group had spent time in prisons from San Quentin to Sing Sing. Two years later, three would die under police fire and one would wind up in the electric chair for murder. I had traded purgatory for a hell where gambling, drugs and sporadic violence filled the days.

Thugs and con artists had signed on early—not for the pay but to fleece the innocents. Lumped together, their meager stipends amounted to a handsome take for this bush-league *mafia*. Loaded-dice experts and crooked card sharks transformed the tents into noisy casinos every payday, and in most pockets where checks should have been only emptiness was left. Muscled strongmen stood around, ready to take care of anybody with a serious complaint. One could distinguish himself among this lot only by flaunting a voluminous prison record. The two white army officers and a forester assigned as overseers were about as effective as dead statues. They kept records, signed papers and looked the other way. Any orders they drummed up were issued by the thug who reigned over the others. In our company, the 235th, that was a big, swaggering brute named "Michigan" Jones.

It was raining when we reached Camp Dix; acres of mud and rain-soaked tents stretched out before us. After we left the bus we were ushered into a line. Michigan then stepped forward, and with arrogant authority, scowled at us as though we were poisonous snakes. Behind him were six others struck in commanding poses, and dressed in army surplus. We stood raggedly at attention.

"I'm Michigan Jones, your section leader! Behind me is Tate, my subsection foreman. Behind him are Marcus, Fats, Studs, Rufus and Barker! They are my assistants! I give the orders and they carry them out! Understand that?" In the quiet the sound of rain striking mud grew sharper. "Okay, you dumb bastards, move your black asses over to the barracks and get outfitted."

We dumb black-assed bastards trudged off through the wetness, past the small rosy-cheeked smiling captain observing us from his tent. Dungarees, floppy work hats, army shoes, wool socks, wool underwear and raincoats. I thought back briefly to the tailored white woolen suit hanging on a rack in that pawnshop: I'd never see that again; nor the white baby grand, nor Larry Funk.

A friend I made during those first sullen days in Harlem had accompanied me into this ruthlessness. Bill Hunter was charming, bright, good-natured and an honor graduate of Columbia University—but like me he was down on his luck. He had majored in psychology, but that had very little to do with the job he was working when I met him. He was selling skinny hotdogs on Lenox Avenue. And it was doubtful that his honors would be of much use in this gloomy place where we had just arrived. En route we had made friends with a likable young man named Hubert Carter. Michigan Jones's greeting had left the three of us wanting to be someplace else.

But in a few days Bill Hunter's charm spread through the company like sunshine. His braininess and magnetism served to rally Michigan's harassed victims toward rebellion against him. Bill called everyone "brother" and always gave everyone a friendly pat on the shoulder. By the second week our tent had become the gathering place for a lot of recruits who were in dire need of some fellowship. On this, our second Saturday night in camp, there were Cat, River Frank, Spats, Hope, Shim Sham and Geechie, a bullish South Carolina field hand. Beer was being passed around; spirits were high and so was the noise. No one seemed surprised when Michigan stuck his head through the flap shouting, "Cut down on the goddamned noise!" Only Michigan showed surprise when, for the first time, nobody obeyed him.

"Did you bastards hear me? I said break off the noise!"

Geechie, his bigness and size matching that of Michigan's, jumped to his feet. "Why you call us men bawsterds all de time, mon? You go crawp in your damn boot!" The laughter became a roar. Bill's psychology major was working, posing a serious threat to Michigan's hold on the company. Sensing this, Michigan glared at Bill and me. "You two," he bellowed, "report for latrine duty tomorrow morning!"

Not to the latrine, but to the captain's tent Bill and I went after breakfast. It had been Bill's decision. "What about Michigan's orders?" I asked.

"It's enough to listen to his crap. I'm not about to carry it around in a bucket."

The captain looked up from his papers as we entered and saluted. "What can I do for you fellows?"

Bill's accented answer was straight from Oxford. "Sir, we have been maliciously assigned to a duty we feel we don't deserve."

"And which duty is that?"

"The latrine, sir."

"Yessir—the latrine," I repeated.

"Well—who ordered you, and why?"

"Mr. Jones, sir. He seemed particularly annoyed because we took it upon ourselves to entertain some recruits in our tent last evening—some who, I might add, were in very low spirits."

"And your names?"

"I'm William C. Hunter, sir, and this is Gordon Parks."

"Low in spirits. Do you find that to be the general feeling around camp?"

"Forgive my frankness, sir, but I must say yes it is."

The captain's fingers were drumming his desk. "What's your background, Hunter—your schooling, I mean?"

"Columbia, sir. Psychology major."

"I see. Good school Columbia. I'm Princeton."

"A *very* good school also I must say."

The captain lit his cigar, puffed and blew out smoke. "Forget the latrine. I will have a word with Jones."

"We are quite thankful, sir."

"Good day."

"Good day, sir." The captain had been conned. A bit of intelligence had jarred his presence, and as far as I could see, Michigan's reign was nearing its end. It came two weeks later—when Bill was promoted to section leader, and I to a subsection foreman. That meant fifteen dollars a month more to him and ten dollars more to me. It also meant that revenge would be staring at both of us every day. Without doubt, our company, the 235th, was the only one throughout the nation with two sets of leaders. That seemed to be the captain's only way out of his dilemma. But Bill Hunter was definitely in charge.

Eventually Michigan and his pack seemed to swallow their setback, while going on doing what they had come to do. They kept up the fleecings, but there was a big drop in the numbers of those who allowed themselves to be fleeced. And Bill, having the heart of a whale, furrowed on into the ranks of our enemies, cajoling them with his wiles. He even conned Michigan Jones into a dubious friendship. "Michigan," he said one morning, "I've organized a track meet this weekend, and it would sure please me if you would consent to handing out the prizes." Grudgingly, the ex-section leader gave his consent.

It was Tate, Michigan's cohort, who challenged me to a fight. He was still angered about his demotion. To prevent a free-for-all we agreed to remain in camp and fight after the company had gone to the forest. Stripped to our waists we faced one another in the deserted camp the following morning. When I raised my fists he pulled out a switchblade. I stood speechless with fright as he came toward me.

"Drop that knife or I'll brain you!" It was Bill. He had jumped from behind a tent waving an ax handle. "Drop it, brother! I mean what I say!" Tate stiffened and dropped his knife and Bill picked it up. "You're even now. Go ahead."

Tate proved a coward. The viciousness of his switchblade was replaced by timidity: he stood trembling, refusing to raise his fists. Freed of my fear and angered by his cowardice, I banged a hard right to his stomach. He doubled up, grunted, fell to the ground and stayed there. Oddly, a comment his friend Studs had made was what had sent Bill hurrying back. "Tate's a knifer," he had told Bill as they started toward the forest. He'd run from his own shadow if it turned on him." From that day on I liked Studs. Little could I suspect then that a couple of years later he would die in the electric chair for murder.

Over two million men finally joined the corps—planting trees, building fish ponds, feeding wildlife and clearing areas for beaches and campsites; in all, forty-seven lost their lives fighting forest fires. We were earning our keep, but our time would be up in October. Depression still choked the country, and employment offices, park benches and hobo villages would be filled again. There was no more to return to now than what we had left a year before. But on the eighteenth of August, Bill posted a captain's bulletin that lifted everyone's spirits. President Roosevelt had extended the CCC camps for another six months.

I was around twenty-one at the time, but having been in charge of my own survival since I was fifteen, I was much more mature than most young men my age, and I was still very much in love. Then, too, there was a sudden urge toward family life again, and that was making decisions for me, along with the weekly letters from lovely Sally Alvis back in Minneapolis, whom I wanted very much to be my bride. By now I had saved up two hundred dollars toward that end. In October I hitchhiked my way back to Minneapolis to make her my wife. But Joe Alvis refused to give up gracefully. Disgruntled to the end, he sat in the kitchen cleaning a mess of catfish and grumbling to himself as my brother Andrew, who had become a minister, married us. Joe did manage to relent long enough to give me some advice before we departed. "When you wake up tomorrow morning, offer my daughter your pants to wear. When she refuses, take them back and tell her that you'll be wearing them from then on." I took Sally back to Philadelphia by train. It was close to our new campsite at Chenango Forks. She stayed in that city with a family while I served out my last six months.

My final days in the corps were filled with uncertainty and a confusing sort of melancholy. We had entered the corps desperate and hungry. Now, with muscled bodies we resembled tough, hardened men. Hardly any of us knew what we would face in the next forty-eight hours. The same tired tenements, jobless days, jails, park benches, bloody nights, justices and injustices would be waiting. On the morning of parting we went about slapping one another's backs, but these gestures were attempts to slap out the fear in our bodies. Bill's charm was working right up to the end. It was strange to see him and Michigan Jones sitting side by side laughing.

I was happy to be leaving to live with my wife, but I would miss these men—especially Bill Hunter. Through him I had seen how courage, intelligence and compassion could overbalance evil. Not once did he do anything for himself that matched the good he did for the others. He had even talked me out of returning to Harlem. "Go back to Minnesota, brother. You've got a family coming. It's bound to be easier for you there." He came to the train in Philadelphia to see us off, ran alongside the train waving as we outdistanced him. Then he was gone.

In a few months I would be a father, and I was overjoyed, even though I wasn't yet prepared for fatherly responsibilities. I was still growing, still galloping about chasing things that were gone before I arrived.

Spring was abloom when we arrived in Minneapolis. Sally's brother and sister, David and Mary, met us at the train, and the four of us drove to Joe Alvis's house on the south side of the city. Realizing that he was about to become a grandfather, Joe had relented and he insisted that we live with him. "Plenty room for you and the young one," he said, beaming.

Common sense should have warned me against that offer, but I accepted it. A lack of funds had a great deal to do with my acceptance. To celebrate his daughter's homecoming Joe went out and caught another big mess of catfish. After supper he kept me up after midnight, asking questions about my experiences out East.

David waited on tables at the Curtis Hotel, and during that first week he helped me get a job there as a waiter. It would do for the time being but I was still restless; still longing for bigger things. The brief stint with Larry Funk's orchestra was still pushing my hopes, but there was a hospital bill in the offing and Sally had selected a baby crib beyond my means. Now she was buying blue knit suits and diapers by the dozens. We were both sure it would be a boy—although "Mom" Alvis had predicted otherwise. There was a big Steinway grand in the hotel dining room, and in between meals I used it to further my composing—listening meanwhile to recordings by Duke Ellington, Benny Goodman and other big bands.

When Dick Long's orchestra played during dinner, the old urge crept back. Rather than lugging heavy trays of food, I felt I should have been on that bandstand performing. Dick was a heavy-set, sleepy-eyed man who conducted while playing a violin, which didn't help his orchestra very much. Eventually I showed him some of my music. He was more than enthused, and two weeks later "No Love" and "Night Blossoms" were broadcast over the local network. I was on the move again.

Fall arrived orange and beautiful but touched with a little worry. Those first cold Minnesota winters were etched deep in my memory and I watched the end of the year approach with a wary eye.

The baby came on December the seventh and Sally named him for me. Joe Alvis was a little unhappy about that for he was hoping for that honor to be bestowed upon him. Perhaps that's why he gave our son the nickname of "Butch." No doubt two Gordons in his household were too much for him. Butch gulped down

Pablum like a veteran and muddied piles of diapers, and Joe loved putting the silver spoon between his grandchild's lips. Immediately he became the baby's philosopher, guardian, doctor and savior—as well as a pain in the ass to all of us. He ignored the child's feeding schedule, accused Sally of trying to starve him, and grouched if she didn't pick the baby up every time he made the slightest whimper. Joe made matters worse by firing the furnace to a blazing heat. Any complaint raised his ire. "The child's no Eskimo! You want to freeze it to death?"

By January Gordon Jr. had developed a serious asthmatic condition. Doctoring didn't seem to help, and Sally spent many nights holding up the baby's head to relieve his painful breathing. So I had not judged winter too harshly; its coming did have an ominous meaning. The stifling heat had nearly destroyed our son, and Joe was full of remorse but he was too stubborn to show it openly. When he shut himself up in his bedroom for hours, we knew he was praying for his grandchild's recovery.

With spring came relief. By midsummer, the sun and fresh air had left Butch healthy and robust again, and it came as no surprise when he won a citywide baby contest. I had strolled proudly around the huge auditorium waving his golden crown. Well, he was indeed a beautiful child, but secretly I thought he was too beautiful to be a boy. But then his mother's lovely features had a lot to do with that. The ailment had backed off, but temporarily; it would return to plague him "probably for the rest of his life," the doctor warned us.

That same summer I got an extra job playing at a roadhouse called Carver's Inn, an old converted farmhouse located outside the city. Word got around fast, and soon the hustlers, pimps and ladies were dropping in to request "No Love" and "Butterfly," and displayed their appreciation by tipping generously. By fall I had saved up enough to get an apartment. We didn't want to spend another fiery winter in Joe's flaming purgatory. He fought our taking his grandchild from him, but we compromised by moving just two blocks away. There were two rooms, a bath, and a tiny kitchen on the second floor of a small apartment building. The furniture that went with it—a dark green sofa, two overstuffed matching chairs, a small table for dining with four chairs—was all in the living room. In the other room was a small bed for our son, a chest of drawers and a larger bed for us. Braided scatter rugs graced both rooms, and a framed print of the Swiss Alps hung above the sofa. It was home, our first real home, and Sally kept it shining. We were happy enough with it but I wanted a piano to work on; Mom Alvis thought the money would be better spent on a car. "You can take the child out to the country where the air's much fresher," she advised. She had a point. I got a used Ford that called for monthly payments amounting to twenty-six dollars.

Carver's Inn would shut down during the winter months and the hotel customers didn't tip as generously as the pimps and hustlers. I applied for a better job as a waiter on the *North Coast Limited,* and got it. It was a fine transcontinental train that ran between St. Paul, Chicago and Seattle, Washington, which took about four days. It was then Mom started mouthing even more advice, too much I was beginning to think. "You're buying too many books and records and you didn't really need that victrola you just bought." "Your wife looks to be needing some new clothes, and she's working too hard to keep your place clean." "She needs a rest after taking care of the baby all day. A trip to Chicago to visit her cousin would be just the thing for her." We hadn't moved far enough away. It began to look like we should have moved across town, or maybe someplace like Canada, where Sally was born. Sally was beginning to favor her mother's counsel, but I wasn't buying it. Before long our contentment began rumbling to a halt. Eventually only Butch showed gladness when I came home after the long trips.

I tried to mend things by buying Sally a fox-trimmed velvet coat. She looked gorgeous in it. She should have; it represented all my savings. Even Joe upbraided me for spending a hundred dollars for "a rag with skunk's hair." But I was just trying to keep our marriage from falling apart. The goals we had found so meaningful were suddenly adrift. That elegant coat, I thought, might turn them homeward again.

On the *North Coast Limited* I could again see how the rich lived. It was the Minnesota Club on wheels—with all of its customs, mannerisms, expensive clothes, luggage and first-class conversations. But by far the most exciting moment on that princely train came when bandits held it up outside Butte, Montana. Having blocked the tracks so the train had to stop, they donned masks and let go with a few frightening shots, entered the club car with pis-

tols waving, and stripped the fingers and necks of all those heavily
jeweled passengers; then they jumped from the train and disappeared into the countryside. It was just like the cowboy movies I
had watched back in Fort Scott from the "buzzard's roost," only a
whole lot scarier in real life.

On quieter runs, in between meals, when the wealthy passengers were either sleeping or consuming alcohol in the lounge cars,
I read every magazine I could get my hands on. In one that had
been left behind by a passenger I found a portfolio of photographs
that I would never forget. They were of migrant workers. Dispossessed, beaten by storms, dust and floods, they roamed the high
ways in caravans of battered jalopies and wagons between Oklahoma and California, scrounging for work. Some were so poor
that they traveled on foot, pushing their young in baby buggies
and carts. They lived in shanties with siding and roofs of cardboard boxes, the inside walls dressed with newspapers. There was
a man with two children running through a dust storm to their
shanty. The names of the photographers stuck in my mind—Arthur Rothstein, Russell Lee, Carl Mydans, Walker Evans, Ben
Shahn, John Vachon, Jack Delano and Dorothea Lange. They all
worked for the Farm Security Administration, a government
agency set up by President Roosevelt to aid submarginal farmers.
These stark, tragic images of human beings caught up in the confusion of poverty saddened me. I took the magazine home and studied it for weeks. Meanwhile I read John Steinbeck's *In Dubious
Battle* and Erskine Caldwell and Margaret Bourke-White's *You
Have Seen Their Faces*. These books stayed in my mind. During
layovers in Chicago, I began visiting the Art Institute on Michigan
Avenue, spending hours in this large voiceless place, studying
paintings of Monet, Renoir and Manet.

I might have remained a waiter on the *North Coast Limited* forever, but two incidents changed my course. At a Chicago movie
house I watched a newsreel of the bombing of the United States
gunboat *Panay* by Japanese fighter planes. Courageously the cameraman had stayed at his post, shooting the final belch of steam
and smoke that rose when the boat sank in the Yangtze River.
When the newsreel ended, a voice boomed over the intercom.
"And here he is—the photographer who shot this remarkable
footage!" Norman Alley, the cameraman, had leaped on the stage
to rousing cheers. And I was carried away by his bravery and

dedication to his job. From that moment I was determined to become a photographer. Three days later I bought my first camera at a pawnshop for $7.50. It was a Voightlander Brilliant. Not much of a camera, but a great name to toss around. I had bought what was to become my weapon against poverty and racism.

The second incident, one that forever banished me from that superior train, recorded itself rather harshly several months after the pawnshop purchase. The dining car steward I worked under, a Mr. Barnes, became terribly unhappy with "black boys" who spent time between meals reading books and fancy magazines. He was considerably more at ease with those who shot craps or lolled around up in the bunk car behind the noisy locomotive. "Parks," he quipped one afternoon, "you must be studyin' up on becoming the first Nigra president of the United States." The look I gave him, when I half rose from my seat, sent him scurrying from the dining car in unusual haste. We were serving dinner, and approaching home that same night, when he provoked me with a vicious bump in the back as I was placing a bowl of hot soup before a woman passenger. The soup went in her lap as I chased Barnes to the pantry, picked up a bread knife and put it to his throat. Two waiters grabbed me from behind, urging me to give them the knife. I did. Barnes got off with a kick in the shins. It was ten below zero outside and Christmas was coming. It would be a sorrowful holiday; I knew I was through. I went to the bunk car, dressed and lay across a bunk and waited for the train's arrival in St. Paul.

Neither Sally nor Butch was home when I reached there that night. A folded note lay on the bed, and it appeared foreboding. I looked about, unnerved. The top of the clothes chest was bare, and ordinary things like Sally's house slippers and shoes were gone. I picked up the note, looked at it for a few seconds, then opened it. Just one crisp sentence: "We have gone to Chicago." I sat down on the bed and felt the world crashing around me. Suddenly anger rushed in. I grabbed the phone and asked for Colfax 6847.

"Yes?"

"Where's Sally and *my* son?"

"In Chicago, I suppose."

"Whose house is she at, *Mrs.* Alvis?"

66

"Don't ask me. I don't know."

"When is she coming back?"

"I don't know."

"You don't know much of anything."

"That's right."

"Well—when she does get back, tell her that I want a divorce!"

Both receivers slammed down together. "Hell! Godammit! Hell!" I put on my coat and went out to look for a woman, any woman.

Two days later I was called to the Northern Pacific's commissary. Thomson, the railroad superintendent, had two words for me. "You're fired." He had spoken softly, almost in a whisper. Then he turned back to his desk. Not bothering to answer, I walked out of his big mahogany-furnished office and went to pick up my final check. Wolters, the man who had hired me, handed it to me with a wish for a Merry Christmas. I wonder until this day if he was serious.

I had found a woman at a bar the night before, but she didn't have the skin color of a peach, a dimpled smile, or soft brown hair. We had a couple of drinks and I spent the rest of the time crying on her shoulder about my marital problems; then I bid her good night and went to my deserted apartment. And it was lonely there.

Two weeks later Sally came back—to pack up her belongings.

"Where's Butch?"

"At Mom's."

"Well—she must have told you that I want a divorce."

"It's all right with me."

"You get it. I'll pay for it."

"On what grounds?"

"Anything you like. Adultery. I don't care."

When the papers came the following week I stared at them in disbelief. She had followed my flippant suggestion. It was adultery. "Too bad! I should have bedded down with that woman I met in the bar that night. Too bad. Too damn bad!" Angry, I had spoken aloud and to myself, but a far deeper feeling of loss and hurt negated all that I had blurted out. I truly loved Sally, and suddenly I was wondering how I had managed to lose her. Where was she now, and whose would she become someday? Silently I damned Ida and Joe Alvis—and myself for putting my family under their roof. After reading and rereading the divorce papers I flung them on the floor, and from there they stared at me throughout the night. And I lay sleepless on our bed staring at the ceiling with the streetlight glued to it. That bed would no longer be the breath of our marriage. The universe was slowly rolling backward.

Jealousy then all but consumed me. It had been hanging around since my courting days. I had won Sally Alvis's hand in spite of the arduous pursuit of her by three other young men who longed to claim her. Chalmer Lawson had taken off after her at the tender age of sixteen. Bill Thomas and Bill Mcquerry had joined him in his quest not too long after. Each of them, however, had an advantage over me—Joe Alvis's blessing. As an alliance they had made things difficult for me, but none of them was aware of my staying power.

Begrudgingly, they had all backed off with the announcement of our engagement, but with news of the divorce they began moving in again, and with Joe Alvis's encouragement. Rumors began flowing. Mcquerry had proposed marriage; Lawson and Thomas were said to have engaged in fisticuffs over Sally's affections. But I still loved her deeply, and jealousy, the beast, was smiling again—still sharpening its horns.

Two months passed before I went to see my son. Sally's reception was very cool, so cool I decided to take him out for a walk.

"He's not leaving this house for one minute." Her defiance was resolute.

"I'm taking him for an hour," I insisted. "He is my son after all!"

I reached for him and a tug of war began with our voices rising to a heated pitch. Suddenly Joe Alvis was descending the stairs with a double-barreled shotgun. "Get out of here!" he ordered, placing the gun within a few inches of my forehead.

Foolishly I held my ground, staring angrily into the barrels, scared stiff but pretending not to be. To have backed away would have exhibited cowardice before my son. But at that precarious moment I was reliving one that my own father once experienced when Boissy, my boozed-up brother-in-law, placed a shotgun against his head in that final attempt to get at my sister hiding beneath a bed with her three children. "You'll have to kill me first," my father had said evenly. He had survived the threat when

Boissy, distracted by the entrance of my cousin, whirled and blasted the front door. Miraculously my cousin had escaped injury.

My situation was no less dangerous now. Sally tried breaking the impasse. "Pa, put that silly gun down," she said weakly. "I can handle this." The gun stayed at my forehead as she slumped into a chair. Perhaps my son saved me. He took my hand. "Please go, Dad. Please go." When I bent to kiss him, Joe dropped the gun to his side. Sally sat beautiful and withdrawn as I left, appearing to be desperately unhappy in her father's house. I was not the least bit sorry about that; it gave me a ray of hope.

McQueeny was arriving for a visit as I approached my car. He greeted me sheepishly. "How're you doing?" My answer was a withering look as I got into the car and roared off.

Throughout that day and night, my mind kept rushing back to that terrible moment. It was one I couldn't easily forget, and the folly of it quadrupled each time it came barreling back. It was the third time I had come close to death, and my anger toward Joe Alvis stayed on for hours. No amount of reasoning could lull it into cooling. I was a husband passing a lonely night without his wife; a father robbed of the presence of his son.

I tried several beers, hoping they would help exile my feelings from the memory, but they only inflamed me more. The moment stayed on, cloying at me, tightening about my throat like an uncomfortable collar. My young son had been exposed to a garish scene that he would have cause to remember.

Thinking back to his moments of fear recalled my own fright when that shotgun threatened my father's life. When called to mind, the two near-tragic episodes always leave me depressed and shaken. One was brought on by Boissy Brown's drunkenness, the other by Joe Alvis's uncontrollable temper. The deeper meaning of their violent behavior dwells in the past, unexplained to either my son or to me—terrible moments that each of us would remember with pain. Had either man pulled the trigger two fathers would have been murdered while their young sons looked on.

My life has been interrupted by disasters now and then. Arriving unexpectedly, they seem to have divided up my quietudes with things that lambaste me. I have learned to accept them without too much surprise; to know that each hour can be as changeable as the wind. The years have also taught me that understanding rhymes with forgiveness. Strangely, I remain sympathetic to the memory of both Boissy Brown and Joe Alvis. Time, and their own deaths, have rescued them from their shortcomings.

To my astonishment, the commissary called two mornings later. The superintendent, having heard the whole story, was feeling repentant. "Mr. Thomson says you can have your job back—providing you apologize to Mr. Barnes."

"No shit! You can tell Mr. Thomson, for me, that I'd eat snowballs in hell first!" And for about a month I did just that.

Starvation was suddenly warded off when a semiprofessional basketball team offered me a berth that winter. The game had owned me since I was six. My court then had been our backyard. Elmer Kinard, a friend, had helped me nail slats of wood together to construct a backboard. The hoop we attached to it was torn from a discarded pickle barrel. There, after school and on Saturdays (since Sunday play was forbidden) we spent long sweaty hours ducking and dodging while aiming an oversized rubber ball through the circle of rusted tin—dreaming of one day becoming members of the Fort Scott Whirlwinds, the black high school team. Coached by our grade school principal, it had gained fame throughout Kansas, Oklahoma and Missouri. The white high school team, on which the black athletes were denied a chance to play, was pathetically inferior. Being forced together by segregation had brought the black teammates to a higher skill of shooting and ball handling. Having played so long together they performed like a well-oiled machine. In retrospect I remember the Whirlwinds as being the only black institution to gain high respect from the town fathers. Returning as winners from state championships, they were met at the train station by whites and blacks alike to celebrate the homecoming. Eventually those backyard sessions paid off and, as a sophomore, I had the thrill of being named a Whirlwind.

Now, approximately six years later, the semiprofessional team known as the House of David was taking me on as a right forward. (Semi, I soon realized, meant half—and half the time the team was barely eating.) There were no substitutes, only five of us traveling in manager/coach's Harry Crump's battered old Ford, and he was robbing us blind. Our trickery on the floor could not compare with Crump's at the box office. The house could be packed but he always came up short with a plausible explanation. "I get a manager's share, a coach's share, and there's the wear and tear on my car." Crump charmed and frustrated us with his thievery, while managing to project that it was he who was being robbed.

Two awesome snowstorms hit the Northwest that winter, and we got stuck in both of them. One caught us between two towns in North Dakota one night and came close to taking our lives. The snow had come suddenly, blowing in hard and fast, and after a few miles we couldn't see the highway. A power line snapped, sending eerie streaks of light alongside and above us. Then came the sight of cattle standing frozen in death. It was frightening and we stopped. Wrapped in Harry's sheepskin I got out and walked ahead and he kept his lights on me. Then the old jalopy slid to a stop. The drifts had become impassable. We all got behind the damn thing and pushed. It refused to budge. With our clothes wet and the temperature dropping, we got back into the car and huddled together, hoping that our body warmth would keep us alive. When daylight finally came our bones were stiff and we were practically buried. We had all but given up when a huge plow came burrowing through the whiteness, throwing it high into the air. The big blades clanked to a stop a few inches from the car: the driver had seen us just in time. He pulled us out and got us started; and as we drove along we could see even more dead cattle.

Farm women were waiting with hot coffee and doughnuts when we reached the next town. And they were a good sight. There were some, on the road behind us, who never arrived to eat or drink again. The plow didn't reach them in time.

Harry Crump came off that disastrous tour hugging his pockets, which were so full of money. There was plenty of room in ours. They were, in fact, all but empty.

Little by little winter left. Perhaps it was just tired of hanging around. I saw Sally again when she came to a party with her new boyfriend from Chicago, and I escorted a beautiful girl to the same party. Henrietta Bonaparte had large soulful eyes, honey-colored skin and snow-white teeth. She was a poem in her crimson velvet gown. Sally took one look and lost both her earrings—and she came to ask me to help her find them. Graciously Henrietta suggested that I go. Sally was lucky. They had fallen, accidentally, into her party bag. She thanked me and we danced several times and she said that Butch missed me and I said that I missed him and that

I would come see him the following weekend and she said that would be fine and I went over and we went for a ride in the moonlight and the next week we got married—again. But we moved a long long way from Joe and Ida Alvis this time. Three months later we were expecting our second child.

SIX

Suddenly it seemed that all the confusion between Sally and me had been absurd. She was back. No more despair in my cold bed, and my son's asthma attacks appeared to have subsided. Two weeks later the problems of work had also backed off when I got a porter's job on the *400,* a fast train that ran between Minneapolis and Chicago. Hope had a way of blooming, exhausting itself, then blooming again. Hold on to the dreams. Barnes and others, in trying to rob me of them, had only hardened my determination.

The new camera had helped dispel my gloom. The first few rolls

I had taken with it were earning respect from the Eastman Kodak Company. The manager of its Minneapolis branch showed surprise when he found out they were my very first attempt, and he emphatically assured me that they were very good. Too, he promised me a showing in their window gallery if I kept progressing. Dubious, I thanked him, smiled and told him I would hold him to his promise. After that hardly a thing faced my Voightlander that I didn't attempt to glorify—sunsets, beaches, boats, skies, even an elaborate pattern of pigeon droppings on the courthouse steps. I wasn't rushing to the bank with proceeds from those first efforts but experience was mounting, giving me a sense of direction. The gentleman at Eastman lived up to his promise; six months later he had my photographs placed in the company's show windows.

The *400* allowed me layovers in Chicago. There, visual imagery multiplied tenfold, with skyscrapers, boats plying Lake Michigan, bridges and the inner-city canals. But before long I realized that such imagery, although it was fine for the family album, was hardly the kind to put steak and potatoes on my family's table. A beautiful sunset over the lake was just a beautiful sunset—no more. Natural instinct had served to aim my sights much higher, and those Farm Security photographs with all their power were still pushing my thoughts around. Before long I had deserted the waterfronts, skyscrapers and canals for Chicago's south side—the city's sprawling impoverished black belt. And there among the squalid, rickety tenements that housed the poor, a new way of seeing and feeling opened up to me. A photograph I made of an ill-dressed black child wandering in a trash-littered alley and another of two aged men warming themselves at a bonfire during a heavy snowfall pleased me more than any I had made. They convinced me that even the cheap camera I had bought was capable of making a serious comment on the human condition. Subconsciously I was moving toward the documentary field, and Chicago's south side was a remarkably pitiful place to start. The worst of it was like bruises on the face of humanity.

I increased my visits to Chicago and to its Southside Art Center, which sat formidably in the heart of the black belt. Once a stately mansion owned by the rich, it was now a haven for struggling black artists, sculptors and writers. The gallery walls were usually weighted with the work of well-known painters who used their art to encourage protest from the underprivileged and dispossessed. How effective they were remains questionable, but for me, at the time, their approach to art seemed commensurate with the people they were attempting to serve. A large impressive painting by Isaac Soyer displayed in the front window had pulled me into the art center. The painting was of a building that brought memories of Mrs. Haskins's old place back in Harlem. Before going in I had stood looking at it for several moments, wondering if Mrs. Haskins's old gray stone tenement was still standing; if the grimy stone was even grimier, and the unwashed windows still unwashed. I had entered the art center's doors glancing to see if some young man sat now on the stoop where I had sat by garbage cans, enclosed in a world I was trying to forget. Soyer's painting had been staring at me from another block of time that I was glad to have survived.

On exhibit inside were the works of Soyer, Charles White, Ben Shahn, Max Weber and Alexander Brook, along with the merciless satires of William Gropper and Jack Levine. Oppression was their subject matter. With paint, pencil and charcoal, they had put down on canvas what they had seen, and what they had felt about it. Quite forcefully they were showing me that art could be most effective in expressing discontent, while suggesting that the camera—in the right hands—could do the same. They had forsaken the lovely pink ladies of Manet and Renoir, the soft bluish-green landscapes of Monet that hung several miles north at Chicago's Art Institute. To me these classicists were painters who told far different tales, and for several weeks the difference between the two schools—one classical, the other harshly documentary—would expand the possibilities of the artistic directions I could take.

Vogue was one of the magazines left behind by passengers. Along with its fashion pages I studied the names of its famous photographers—Steichen, Blumenfeld, Horst, Beaton, Hoyningen-Huené, thinking meanwhile that my own name could look quite natural among them. Spring was in the air and I was back in St. Paul feeling aggressive. Energy pulsed through me, urged me toward the impossible as I walked the business area. Suddenly something propelled me toward Frank Murphy's fashionable store for women —rich women. I can't explain what took over when I reached the imposing entrance; but I walked in boldly and asked for Frank

Murphy. The tall, elegantly attired man I had approached observed me with smileless eyes. "I'm Frank Murphy," he said sharply. "What can I do for you?" For a disquieting moment I wondered about that myself.

"I would like to photograph some fashions for your store." I had, without forethought, voiced a fantasy—but not an outright lie —and he had all but walked me out the door when his wife turned from a customer. "What does the young man want, Frank?"

He gestured hopelessly. "To shoot fashions."

Madeline Murphy looked me over quickly. "Well, Frank, maybe he can. Have him wait. I'll talk to him." Frank Murphy looked at his wife as though she had lost her wits. The customer left and she walked over to me. "Have you samples of your work?"

"No, ma'am, I don't."

Frank cut in. "Our clothes are photographed out East." My heart sank.

"Quiet, Frank. Can you really photograph fashion?"

"Yes, ma'am," I lied.

Madeline Murphy gave me a long, hard look. "All right, you'll have the chance. How many gowns do you want?"

"Ah—ah—six."

"And how many models?"

"Three—three will be enough."

"Can you be here tomorrow after we close at six?"

"Yes, ma'am—I'll be here."

"Fine. I'll have the models and dresses ready."

I was stunned. I didn't have an appropriate camera, lights or film, but I was suddenly plumped up with courage.

I arrived at the appointed time—with the camera and lighting equipment lent to me by a noble-hearted fellow, Harvey Goldstein, who had a camera store near the Minnesota campus and let me have film on credit. He always told me I would amount to something. "And when you do," he would say, "let it be known that I was your godfather." The camera was a 4×5 Speed Graphic, and as Harvey drove me to the store, he tried to show me how to use it, but being intimidated by Frank Murphy's prestigious store, he dumped me and the equipment at the door and fled. The dresses and models were indeed beautiful and, surprisingly, I did a good job of lighting them while Frank Murphy watched with a skeptical eye.

76

The big blow fell at exactly two o'clock in the morning, when I developed the film. With the exception of one negative, I had double-exposed the entire lot. My wife got out of bed when she heard my head bumping against the wall. The whole universe had collapsed. How could I bear to face Madeline Murphy? She had been so impressed with watching the session that she had asked me to shoot sport clothes at her country club the following day.

"I'd blow up the good one and show it to her," Sally suggested as she went back to bed. I sat moaning for an hour before her remark sank in, and early the next morning I got Harvey out of bed to make that print. And it was a big one. When the Murphys arrived, there it was—elegantly framed and standing on an easel at the entrance to the club.

"My dear boy," Mrs. Murphy exclaimed. "It's exquisite. Where are the others? I can't wait to see them!"

I was tempted to concoct a lie of some sort, but she deserved the truth, so I mobilized my scruples and gave her the truth—the whole truth. Madeline Murphy didn't bat an eye. "Would they all have been that good?" she asked.

"Oh, by all means. The one there is the worst of the lot."

"Then we do it all over tomorrow evening," she said. You could have heard Frank's groan a block away.

Shortly after, my photographs filled Frank Murphy's windows. I passed those windows many times during that first week—and spent a lot of time staring at them and smiling.

Fortunes have a way of feeding on one another. My photographs in Frank Murphy's windows caught the eye of Marva Louis, the wife of Joe Louis, the heavyweight champion. Fashion coursed through her blood and she urged me to move to her city, Chicago, where she would assure me of beautiful fashions and women to photograph. That combined with an offer from the Southside Art Center to use its studio and darkroom facilities led me to pack up my family, which now included our daughter, Toni, and move to that big city in 1940. Somehow I had survived those icy Minnesota winters, but many other manipulative things lay in wait to confuse the geography of the approaching months. I didn't know what lay before me, but I was moving ahead—at least, I thought so, and that was enough. For a long time I had been inclined to believe that fate moved me with its own persuasions. Now I suspected it was backing off for a spell, and it was time to take things into my own hands. By doing so I hoped that fate was becoming more compliant with my dreams. In any case, I had decided to help shape my own destiny.

It makes me think back to a close friend, Jasper Caldwell, who after one of his numerous failures, would always say, "Look, man, everything turned out as it was meant to be. Nothing I could do about it." Jasper departed this planet without trying to do much about anything. His philosophy became his excuse. In looking back at those days that died before he did, he failed to realize that they expired without help from him; that his neglect of them had a lot to do with what he failed to accomplish. I sensed the danger in misleading myself into thinking I did my best by those efforts that came to nothing. One's memory can be deceptive. To placate you it often refuses to remember things as they really were, preferring to see them as *you* want them to be. That is always a good time to listen to the mirror.

Chicago welcomed me cautiously, offering me a few society matrons to photograph along with its devastated black area on the south side with its storefront Bethels, God in Christs, African Methodists and Pilgrim Baptists—all kept going with the pennies, nickels and dimes of poor black people. Chicago offered me many things that first year, but not many of the golden arms Marva Louis had promised. During that first year there my family learned to spell *suffer.* But just when food and money hit the zero mark, fate resurrected my hopes. A collection of photographs I had taken in the impoverished area of the black belt came to the attention of the Julius Rosenwald Fund, a cultural foundation established by its namesake to aid promising blacks and Southern whites. Writers, painters, sculptors and scholars had been recipients of fellowships —but never a photographer. I was considered to be promising, so my work was sent to be judged by a jury of Chicago's most esteemed white photographers and, to a man, they turned thumbs down. To allow my application yet another chance, my work was then sent to a jury composed of painters and sculptors. While I awaited their decision, time crawled ever so slowly. Worry set in. The postman arrived with nothing but bills. After three weeks the jury was still out, still feeding my anxiety and sleepless nights. The fourth week an envelope, with the fund's masthead, appeared in the small pack of mail. I was fearful of opening it; it seemed to be shaped with rejection. I handed it to Sally so that she might read the bad news. She tore the envelope open, read its contents and smiled weakly. "You *are* a Julius Rosenwald Fellow."

It was the first time I ever saw my wife weep. Perhaps I too would have wept, but I was too numb with happiness. Now we could look forward to the sum of two hundred dollars each month. To celebrate our good fortune, we planned a party on Gordon Jr.'s birthday: December 7, 1941—fourteen years after I departed my father's house back in Kansas.

Then suddenly bombs were dropping on Pearl Harbor. The news was astonishing. For me other staggering news was to come shortly after. Through the prodding of the fund, I was to serve out my fellowship with the Farm Security Administration; with those same photographers whose work had beckoned to me when I was a waiter on the *North Coast Limited.* It was an extravagant moment as we began packing, and for the next two years Washington, D.C., would be our home.

SEVEN

I have one formidable, overwhelming and justifiable hatred, and that is for racists. Thorn-wielding is their occupation and I can attest to their proficiency. Throughout my childhood they kept their eyes glued to my tenderest parts, striking me, impaling me, leaving me bloodied and confused—without my knowing what had provoked their hostility. I came at last to think of them as beasts with cold hearts; of lost souls impassioned with hatred, slithering about in misery, their feelings severed of all humaneness and spreading over the universe like prickly cloth. Rancor seems to have been their master, and any good that befalls the targets of

Sarah Parks, author's mother. *Dabbs, Fort Scott, Kansas.*

Andrew Jackson Parks, author's
father. (One of the first
photographs the author took.)
Gordon Parks.

Congregation portrait of the African Methodist Episcopal Church. (Author is second from the right in first row.) *Courtesy of Gordon Parks.*

Author surrounded by wealthy supporters at the Southside Community Art Center in Chicago. *Courtesy of Gordon Parks.*

Author with his second
camera. (A self-portrait.)
Gordon Parks.

Author leaving New York's
Harlem YMCA in 1942.
Cecil Layne.

Author and youngest son David during the winter of 1945. *Arnold Eagle.*

Author's first wife, Sally, with daughter Toni. Des Plaines, Illinois, 1941. *Gordon Parks.*

The Parkses leaving for Paris on the *Queen Mary,* 1950. (Standing, left to right) Gordon Jr., Sally, the author, and Toni. David is seated in front. *Cecil Layne.*

Author and Madeline Murphy at the Minnesota Club, where she held a luncheon for him in 1970. *St. Paul Pioneer Press.*

Author with *Life* reporter Patricia Blake on airstrip near Puerto Rico in 1955. *Courtesy of Gordon Parks.*

Author with son Gordon Jr. at home in White Plains, New York. *Robert Lucas.*

New York marquee advertising *The Learning Tree*. *Cecil Layne*.

Author at the recording session of his first piano concerto in New York. Joe Eger is the conductor. Vivian Rifkin is at the piano. *Courtesy of Gordon Parks*.

their grudges sets them to brooding. And though the wind sings with change they remain deaf to it; change to them is the unbearable music of imaginary monsters, which they resist. Their actions and attitudes easily identify them. Their smiles have a curl. Their voices, no matter how gentle, are bedded in loathing. At times I can only look at them in a curious silence, wondering about their feelings, and the climates that bred them. I recall having a sort of innocence about the source of their bigotry, but naïveté was no antidote for the bleeding. Washington, D.C., in 1942, bulged with racism.

I arrived there in January of that year with scant knowledge of the place, knowing only that beneath the gleaming monuments and gravestones lay men who had distinguished themselves. What I had learned along the way had little to do with this sprawling city where Washington and Lincoln had been empowered. Sensing this, Roy Stryker, the photographic mentor at FSA, sent me out to get acquainted with the rituals of the nation's capital. I went in a hurry and with enthusiasm. The big blue sky was without clouds and everything seemed so pure, clean and unruffled. It appeared that the entire universe was pleasured in peace.

My contentment was short-lived. Within the hour the day began opening up like a bad dream; even here in this radiant, high-hearted place racism was busy with its dirty work. Eating houses shooed me to the back door; theaters refused me a seat, and the scissoring voices of white clerks at Julius Garfinckel's prestigious department store riled me with curtness. Some clothing I had hoped to buy there went unbought. They just didn't have my size —no matter what I wanted.

In a very short time Washington was showing me its real character. It was a hate-drenched city, honoring my ignorance and smugly creating bad memories for me. During that afternoon my entire childhood rushed back to greet me, to remind me that the racism it poured on me had not called it quits.

Not only was I humiliated, I was also deeply hurt and angered to a boiling point. It suddenly seemed that all of America was finding grim pleasure in expressing its intolerance to me personally. Washington had turned ugly, and my angry past came back to speak with me as I walked along, assuring me that, even here in the nation's capital, the walls of bigotry and discrimination stood high and formidable. In all innocence, I had gone to a restaurant

81

to eat, to a store to buy clothing and a movie theater for enjoy-
ment. And Washington was telling me, in no uncertain terms, that
I shouldn't have done it. Now I was hurrying back to Roy
Stryker's office like an angry wind.

When I reached there he looked at me for a few moments without speaking. He didn't have to. The gloom shadowing my face
told him everything. "Well," he finally asked, "tell me—how did
it go?"

I answered him with a question. "What's to be done about this
horrible place? I've never been so humiliated in my life. Mississippi couldn't be much worse."

"It's bad—very bad. That's why I was hesitant about taking you
on here. The laboratory technicians here are all from the Deep
South. You're not going to have an easy time. Their attitude about
photographers is not the best. To them they are a glorified lot who
roam the world while they slave away in the back rooms doing the
dirty work. And slaving for a black photographer isn't going to
improve that attitude. You're on your own here, and you'll have
to prove yourself to them—with superior work." He rubbed his
chin, thinking. "As for that city out there, well—it's been here for
a long time, full of bigotry and hatred for black people. You
brought a camera to town with you. If you use it intelligently, you
might help turn things around. It's a powerful instrument in the
right hands." He paused, thinking things through for me. "Obviously you ran into some bigots out there this afternoon. Well, it's
not enough to photograph one of them and label his photograph
bigot. Bigots have a way of looking like everyone else. You have to
get at the source of their bigotry. And that's not easy. That's what
you'll have to work at, and that's why I took you on. Read. Read a
lot. Talk to other black people who have spent their lives here.
They might help to give you some direction. Go through these
picture files. They have a lot to say about what's happening here
and other places throughout this country. They are an education in
themselves. The photographers who produced those files learned
through understanding what our country's problems are. Now
they are out there trying to do something about those problems.
That's what you must do eventually."

Eventually. All well and good—but I was still burning with a
need to hit back at the agony of the afternoon. I sat for an hour
mulling over his advice and the humiliation I had suffered. It had

grown late; the office had emptied and Stryker had left for the day. Only a black charwoman remained but she was mopping the floor in an adjoining office. "Talk to other black people who have spent their lives here," he had said. She was black, and I eased into conversation with her. Hardly an hour had gone by when we finished, but she had taken me through a lifetime of drudgery and despair in that hour. She was turning back to her mopping when I asked, "Would you allow me to photograph you?"

"I don't mind."

There was a huge American flag hanging from a standard near the wall. I asked her to stand before it, then placed the mop in one hand and the broom in the other. "Now think of what you just told me and look straight into this camera." Eagerly I began clicking the shutter. It was done and I went home to supper. Washington could now have a conversation with her portrait.

Stryker appeared astonished when I laid the enlarged photograph on his desk the following afternoon. "My God," he said. "You're going to get us all fired." I smiled, but to myself, knowing I had found a little justice in that sea of bigotry.

Stryker's advice was sound but not easy to follow. While some black people talked freely about racial problems in Washington, some, especially older ones, viewed my curiosity with suspicion. Feeling hopelessly ensnared in the city's bigoted ways, they looked upon change as an impossibility. Yielding to racism, they had given up. White, to them, spelled power and no amount of complaining was going to alter the spelling. Indeed, to one beaten soul, I was what his oppressors would have taken me to be—a young troublemaker.

This aged government messenger, fearing retaliation after I insisted upon eating in the *white* section of our cafeteria, took me aside on the third day. "Young man," he said pleadingly, "don't keep bulling your way into that white area. You're just making it bad for all the rest of us. We colored have been eating in the back of this place for years, and it ain't hurt none of us. Do you think you're too good to eat with us?"

I looked at his wrinkled face, his gray hair, feeling sorrow for him and the others bowing to jim crowism inside this government enclosure. "I've nothing against eating with you, sir, but I'm not to be forced to eat in the back just because I'm black—no matter how mad it makes that cafeteria manager. I'm sorry." He shook his head sadly and walked away, never to speak to me again. Several months later he was missing, and I was told that he suddenly died. I was sorry for him, very sorry. I was sure he had died resentful.

Photographing bigotry was, as Stryker had warned, very difficult. It didn't have a repulsive body with a head of horns. Yet it was there like a stone wall, revealing itself in a voice, a mannerism or some empirical way. The evil of its effect however, was discernible in the black faces of the oppressed and their blighted neighborhood lying within the shadows of the Capitol. It was in those shadows that the charwoman lived, and I followed her through them—to her dark house, her storefront church; to her small happinesses and daily frustrations.

Roy Stryker had also been born in Kansas, but most of his childhood was spent on a ranch in the wilds of Colorado. His family life had been far different from mine. Even in the raw, primitive surroundings he had good books to read, and his father indulged him in political and economic theories. Later Roy punched cattle and worked the gold mines. No doubt this experience contributed to his sense of self-reliance.

After serving in the infantry during the first World War, he had studied economics at Columbia University. There his professor was Rexford Guy Tugwell, who later became a member of President Roosevelt's brain trust. During that period the revealing photographs of New York's slums taken by Lewis Hine and Jacob Riis had made Roy conscious of the power of photography. After graduating he taught economics at Columbia for ten years, then Tugwell, now the Assistant Secretary of Agriculture, had called him to Washington to help prepare a pictorial documentation of rural America and its problems.

Stryker arrived in Washington realizing there would have to be a picture file, but without any idea of who would produce it. He was no photographer. He did have a Leica camera, but at a family reunion his aunt's ten-dollar Brownie had managed to get everything, while his fancy Leica drew blanks. After that he seldom picked it up.

Roy had no plans, but he did have a mandate from Tugwell. Get moving. He pitched in, and by the end of 1936 the first photographers of the FSA staff were beginning to come together—Arthur

Rothstein, Carl Mydans, Walker Evans, Ben Shahn and Dorothea Lange. Marion Post Wolcott, John Vachon and John Collier would come later. It had been these same photographers and their photographs that opened my eyes to the potency of the camera while I was still working on the *North Coast Limited* four years before.

Now, through his sense of economics, and his deep concern for the underdog, Roy Stryker—having directed the taking of 270,000 pictures that crammed the FSA files—was one of the most important documentary figures in the photographic world.

The Administration's New Deal policies gave hope but little more. Racism seemed to multiply through the days and nights, distinguishing itself in this city where hatred had become normal —despite its claims toward democracy, and statues of heroes. I read and reread Richard Wright's *Twelve Million Black Voices*. FSA photographs accompanied his text, which explored so forcefully the black man's struggle against oppression throughout America. It became my bible, a big part of my learning, and the inspiration needed to keep my camera moving where it might do the most good.

While, to most whites, Washington was a beautiful city, with its wide tree-lined avenues, dazzling statues, malls and historic buildings lying adjacent to the peaceful flow of the Potomac, to the black citizens it was an ugly place made so by the bigots who occupied it. But I was learning to point my camera toward the well-springs of their evil, and in time they attempted to have that image of the charwoman removed from Stryker's files. They failed. She remains forever to stare at them and all who come after them—in front of the American flag with her mop and broom.

It was not only black people who suffered the catastrophic time of poverty brought about during the administration of President Herbert Hoover. Those FSA files showed hungry migrants, the crumbling South, shameful city ghettos, eroding farmlands, gaunt faces of men, women and children caught up in the tragedy that had overtaken the land. These injustices could be laid only to greedy men who gutted the earth for cotton, overworked the farms and exploited the tenant farmers and sharecroppers. These same men owned the ghettos and the ravaged people who inhabited them. The FSA photographers, scornful of self-glory, used their cameras to speak for these people who couldn't speak for themselves. They were good men and women who also helped me survive the indignities Washington flung at me. Through their friendship, encouragement and understanding I was able to gather in the strength to shore up my doubts and weaknesses. So, in those checkered days I tasted both poison and honey.

Closely attuned to the liberal mind-set of President Roosevelt, the FSA was from its inception a venture that had proved questionable. The government, after all, had its share of blame to shoulder for the mess the country was in. By creating those picture files, it appeared to be sharpening the blade to cut its own throat. Powerful conservatives, constantly frowning at New Deal policies, worked relentlessly to gut the operation. At the close of the year Stryker, sensing the futility of the struggle, warned us that the end might be near. He was right. Shortly afterward, the FSA was abolished and absorbed into the Office of War Information (OWI), with Stryker's staff cut in half. The ax fell on Friday the thirteenth. Miraculously, I was still there on the following Monday, but now the photographers would be shuttled off into different directions. Perhaps it was miraculous too, that the Southern laboratory technicians singled me out for a going-away party. Pleased at the gesture, Stryker explained it. "They're hard-rock Southerners, but they have respect for superior work." And all along I thought they were waiting to do me in.

Despite the racial pressures, what I had learned within the year outdistanced the bigotry I encountered, and the experience had proved to be so important to my training as a documentary journalist—far more important than those technical aspects involving the use of a camera. I had been forced to take a hard look backward at black history; to realize the burdens of those who had lived through it. Now, I was much better prepared to face up to that history yet to be made. Another significant realization had taken hold—a good documentary photographer's work has as much to do with his heart as it does with his eye. The smoke from those bonfires in Washington gave off some more signals about using the camera to serve a humane purpose. I had learned that it *can* lie; that not only was it capable of being untruthful, but also that it could be Machiavellian. It all depended how its users chose to see things. They could wait for a pleasant smile or a frown to cover their subject's face before tripping the shutter. With deliberate intent, an extremely low angle could change a comely face into one of ugliness, and the most righteous human being could be made to look evil. What individuals actually stand for, good or bad, now urges me to try to catch the truth of them. I learned to use the camera as a means of persuasion as long as that persuasiveness is conducted with a sense of fair play. Yet, I remained aware of the possibility that what may appear as truth to me may not be acceptable as truth to others. That's the way things are.

My new boss at the Office of War Information was Elmer Davis. I never met him, as the first assignment I received from him was given to me through Roy Stryker's office. It was to cover the black pilots of the newly formed 332nd Fighter Group—the first of its kind to be initiated after the creation of the black 99th Pursuit Squadron. I was to remain with the pilots throughout their training, stay with them during their first overseas missions, then, from inside England's RAF bombers, show them on escort duty over enemy targets. In less than two weeks I was outfitted in the regalia of a war correspondent and sent to Selfridge Field in Michigan, an air base near Detroit.

Toni, our daughter, had been born three years before. Sally was now pregnant with our third child, David, and none too happy about my going off to cover a war. But I was determined not to miss the opportunity, so it was decided that, during my absence, she would stay with her mother back in Minnesota.

I approached Selfridge Field in an army command car the following week, burning with anticipation. It would be a thrill to be among so many black fighter pilots. I had already donned my foreign correspondent's uniform, and the American eagle shone brightly on my officer's cap. Suddenly there came a thunderous roar. I stuck my head out the window and looked up. Flying wingtip to wingtip, two squadrons of P-40s rocketed over the car. It was a moment to be remembered. I smiled, recalling Richard Wright's words from his novel *Native Son:* "Look at those white boys fly." Now black boys were up there manning the controls!

The 332nd Fighter Group had already been forced into inglorious battle here at home—against an enraged force of Southern senators and congressmen who fought these men's right to become pilots in the United States Air Force. Those same politicians, once apprised of my assignment, began harassing the OWI officials who were responsible for my being there. A new battle line was forming, to prevent the group from being "glorified" by the press.

. . .

Unaware of the problems they were cooking up, I went ahead with my duties—delving into the more personal lives of those young men, recording their activities and flying with them daily on simulated strafing missions. They were fine young men being trained for war and death, but they went about their exciting business with dedication and enthusiasm. Death's hand reached a number of them before they expected it. Twice in one month I saw harrowing mid-air crashes of two fighter ships in training. A month later I listened to the intercom as another ship plummeted and exploded into the earth. Those were days of excitement interwoven with tragedy.

And there were indignities to confront even as those men trained to defend people who spattered them with intolerance. The body of one pilot, Judy Edwards, who spun out up near Oscoda, Michigan, had to be shipped by truck to Detroit for embalming—because the white undertaker in that area refused to prepare it for burial. In general, the treatment given those airmen by whites surrounding the base was, by far, worse than what they would have received in the countries of America's enemies. Nevertheless, those pilots went on preparing to defend the lives of the very same zealots.

The congressional enemy was still at its dirty work as well. Two days before we broke camp to move to our port of embarkation, Colonel Davis, the group commander, informed me that my traveling papers were "out of order." Unless they were corrected, my mission would be terminated. Astounded and confused, I hitched a bomber ride to Washington. From there I would go to the Pentagon in Virginia to have my papers put in order.

At the bus stop for Virginia the following day I met Captain Lee Rayford and Lieutenant Walter Lawson, two pilots from the 99th Pursuit Fighter Squadron. Both had returned to the States after completing their required number of missions. Captain Rayford was the holder of the Purple Heart, the Distinguished Flying Cross, the Croix de Guerre, the Air Medal and the Yugoslav Red Star. He had been shot down over Austria by a Messerschmitt. Both pilots were now eligible to remain Stateside and teach, but both had elected to go back to the war zone. They, too, were en route to the Pentagon.

We took seats behind the driver. Flushed with anger, he got up, demanding that we go to the back of the bus. We looked at him in disbelief. "I mean it!" he bellowed. "This bus ain't moving till you go back where you belong! If you don't, I'm calling the MP's and having you put off!"

"You'd better start calling," Rayford replied. "We're staying where we are."

Two white Air Force captains and a major sitting opposite us stirred uncomfortably. An aged black woman seated in the back got to her feet, trembling with rage. "Don't you move!" she shouted. The other white passengers were dead quiet as the driver stood glowering at us. One of the white officers spoke. "Fellows, we know how you feel, but the major has an appointment at the Pentagon in half an hour. He wonders if you would mind moving back so we can get on our way?"

My two friends were outranked. But there were no bars on my shoulders. The American eagle on my officer's cap was equal to the major's. "Major, I'm from the Office of War Information." I said "Would you like to order these two highly decorated officers to the rear? Otherwise, we have no intention of moving."

He thought for a long moment, then glanced at the driver. "Pull out, man. Can't you tell when you're licked?" Exasperated, the driver threw himself into his seat, slammed the bus into gear and we were off to Virginia. "Hallelujah!" the old black woman shouted. We parted smiling when we reached the Pentagon, but our anger seethed inside us.

Savagely, the curse of bigotry had come rushing in upon us like a storm, wrecking the two airmen's purpose for journeying to the Pentagon in the first place—that of returning to defend a country which, at that precise moment, was harshly offending them. Having courageously flown in forward seats of their aircraft against Hitler's vaunted *Luftwaffe,* it was highly unlikely that they would, at the order of a vindictive little bus driver, take a back seat on a Washington bus.

Horrible though the incident had been, it had called upon the three of us to override ignorance with determination. We were not strangers to the agonies and complexities black people face everyday in this country. You learn to grapple with them or go under. My intentions by now were to somehow rise above them by harnessing the frustration and anger and using them to my advantage.

The officer in charge of overseas transportation scanned the papers I handed him. "Nothing wrong as far as I can see."

"Then why was I sent back here?"

"Beats me. Everybody short of the President signed them. Far as this office is concerned they are in order."

"Fine. Now where can I make contact with the 332nd Fighter Group?"

"I can only give you directions to Newport News, Virginia. You'll have to play it by ear from there. Their exact location is classified."

After a hairy ride through an electric storm and a night of sleuthing, I was picked up by two WAC's and taken to the port where the 332nd Fighter Group waited to embark. As we entered the security gate my mind was still on the bus incident, and on one Rayford had related to me as we rode toward the Pentagon. It concerned his squadron's first escort duty with American bombers over enemy targets. "We'd just swept down to cover them when the intercom crackled with a voice as Southern as corn bread—'Heh, look! They sent a bunch of coons to bring us home!' Man, I wanted to turn my guns on our own bombers!" The memory of that was still snapping through my thoughts like rifle fire. The car lurched to a stop. I had finally made it to Camp Patrick Henry.

The pilots stopped their gambling, drinking and letter writing to give me a rousing welcome, and I showed my appreciation with two bottles of scotch and several cartons of cigarettes I had wrapped in my battle gear. Besides women, they were the things they would crave most. Money was useless now and they gambled it away with abandon. If my luck held, I would be at sea within four days.

The 332nd had already experienced trouble during their short stay. A black ground crewman had been beaten by white paratroopers, and the camp's movie house had tried to keep them out. And there had been some gunfire. Things had become so bad that new traveling orders had arrived. The 332nd Fighter Group would sail two days earlier than scheduled. This pleased me. Then, a few hours before we were to embark, Colonel Davis sent his orderly for me. He looked up at me with ice in his eyes when I entered his quarters. "Parks, I'm sorry. Your papers are *not* in order. A message just arrived from the Pentagon."

I protested. Oh, how I protested. But to no avail. The colonel was a West Pointer. For him an order was an order. Anesthetized to the colonel, and all that was around him, I turned and started out. "There must be strict secrecy about what you have learned here," he said. "You must realize the dangers of any word about our movements."

"I understand, Colonel."

"You could be detained under such conditions, but I'm sure that won't be necessary." I felt betrayed. "There's a chopper flying into Washington in about an hour. You can hitch a ride on that if you like."

"Thanks, Colonel."

"My pleasure."

"No need to worry, Colonel." I went back to the barracks, packed hastily and slipped out to await the helicopter the colonel had ordered. I couldn't bring myself to say another good-bye to the pilots. I had lost.

The helicopter to Washington began circling the city at dusk. Far below I could see the Capitol standing quiet and strong at one end of the mall, the Lincoln Memorial at the other. It was a beautiful sight, but one coupled with human ugliness. As we dropped lower I could see the tops of stores, theaters and restaurants whose doors were still closed to black people. I thought back to the fighter pilots. They would soon be out to sea sailing toward war and death, ignoring temporarily their differences with the country they were leaving to defend. This was the price for questionable equality.

From Washington I called Sally in Minnesota—she was awaiting David's birth and my return from abroad. At least I could report that I was safe. An hour later, I took another plane to New York. As my taxi reached the high point of the Triborough Bridge, a stretch of dreary Harlem rooftops widened on the horizon—waiting. More poverty. More bigotry. But now I was better prepared to confront them. Living in Washington had been like living in white-hot shade but it had been just another obstacle to push aside. Life, having carried me along smoothly for a year or so, was dumping me into a well again. And again I would have to rescue myself. That was how life went about getting me ready—for the next well, blind alley or stone wall. The problems awaiting me were accountable to those wells, alleys and walls.

EIGHT

I was back in New York and woeful about facing that jungle of uncertainty again. It would have been easier to approach the time ahead knowing that the obstacles wouldn't be loaded with the extra problems of being black. But such expectations were already lodged in my thoughts. The past attempted to remind me that the future was never sure, and that I shouldn't cower to former disappointment; nevertheless I was fearful and disheartened. Another winter was edging into Harlem, and I was foreseeing a repetition of a past I hoped was gone forever. "New York's just another town. You can make it," I began telling myself.

Perhaps I halfway believed this, since after little deliberation I had set my sights on New York's loftiest portals of fashion journalism. In retrospect it seems like a dubious choice after the experience in Washington. Then maybe it was my blundering luck in Frank Murphy's fashionable store in St. Paul that encouraged me. Furthermore if it was time to reach for something, then why not the sky?

I had taken a cheap room at Harlem's YMCA. I can't recall where or how I met an admirable woman by the name of Sarah Little. I do remember showing her a set of my photographs, and it was she who took them one morning to Alexey Brodovitch, the art director at *Harper's Bazaar*. I met Mr. Brodovitch later in the afternoon, and the expression on his face remains with me; it was half frown, half smile. "So—you're Gordon Parks," he said nervously.

"Yes, I am."

"And these are your photographs."

"Yes, they are mine."

He rose from his desk, then circled it. "They are marvelous photographs."

"Thank you, sir."

He sat down at his desk again. "I'm sorry to be so frank with you but—but there is a very inflexible rule here in the Hearst organization that forbids our hiring Negroes. I'm sorry—terribly sorry. I love your work but—"

"It's quite all right, Mr. Brodovitch. I understand."

"I'm—I'm terribly sorry. I—"

Faking a smile, I picked up my photographs. "Thank you so much, Mr. Brodovitch. And thanks for your time." I left him sitting there, troubled.

On the way out I ran into Sarah Little. She was smiling hopefully. "Well, tell me, how did it go?"

I remained silent for a long moment, then with telltale averted eyes I let it out. "He said he loved my work, but he also said I couldn't work here because I was a Negro." I touched her shoulder. "Thanks so much for what you did."

Sarah Little's face became purple with rage and, without answering, she headed for Brodovitch's office, went in and slammed the door shut. I've always regretted not hearing their conversation.

Edward Steichen, the renowned photographer, was wolfing

down a huge corned beef sandwich in his Fifth Avenue office when I told him what had happened. Roy Stryker had suggested that I go see him. He stopped eating long enough to write down a name and address, mumbling, "Brodovitch the son-of-a-bitch." He thrust the piece of paper into my hand. "Go see this man. See what he has to say."

I thanked him and headed for *Vogue* magazine to see Alexander Liberman. I felt somewhat wilted; Mr. Brodovitch had left me wary. Liberman shook my hand and offered me a chair. As he carefully examined each photograph I sat waiting for another letdown. Finally he laid the photographs on his desk, saying simply, "I don't know what will happen but we must give you a chance." He rose from his desk. "Come along. I want you to meet Tina Fredericks, the editor of *Glamour,* our other fashion magazine."

Liberman chose my first assignments carefully; and just as carefully, he took stock of my performances, giving me advice along the way. He didn't rush me into *Vogue*'s high-fashion pages, instead I was given casual wear to photograph for *Glamour,* and Tina Fredericks watched over me like a mother hen. Like Liberman, she too was anxious for my success; gently, cautiously, they launched me into a fashion career within Condé Nast's prestigious publications. And before long I realized that it was a launching with demands stretching beyond my ability to make presentable photographs of comely women wearing beautiful clothes. Too, I was remembering those revered photographers' names I had seen on *Vogue*'s pages when I was a waiter on the *North Coast Limited.* Steichen, Blumenfeld, Horst, Beaton, Hoyningen-Huené—I had stumbled into their domain, and into the possibility of seeing my credits alongside theirs. But there were trials to overcome, and new rules to work by.

Foremost was consideration for what the designers were attempting to express with their creations, and the settings I selected had to be complementary to their efforts. Equally important was the need for good taste in blending the clothes and the backgrounds into graceful compositions. Renoir, Matisse, Reubens and others I had studied at Chicago's Art Institute between layovers were recalled from that time, and they came to my aid. Then, through necessity, I had to give paramount concern to those models who were used to braid those rules of fashion photography together.

These women, chosen for their beauty and ability, were meant to wear clothes in a way that showed the designers at their very best—but not to overpower their creations. Very few models thoroughly understood this; most were more concerned with the art of showing themselves off. Beautiful, easily recognizable faces raked in big money, and flirtation with the camera's lens became an obsession at times. The sensual wink of an eye or a mischievous smile could reduce the gown they wore to insignificance. That the wink or the smile failed to contribute to the mood I was creating seldom crossed their mind. It then became my responsibility to lull them into expressions more fitting to the clothes they were wearing. This consumed time—expensive time.

Yet, some models were instantly inspiring. Moving like ballerinas, and with poetry in their manners, they were a pleasure to work with. Others were granite-faced, colorless as winter leaves, and motionless as tree trunks. A large part of a photographic session was often spent trying to loosen up their mummied expressions. At times I longed for a course in psychology; it would have proven so helpful. But during those sweet, laborious hours I learned to make the best of what was present. I was also becoming aware of the vast difference between documentary work and fashion photography. In one lay the responsibility to capture a prevailing mood, while in the other was the obligation to create a mood.

Six months passed before Alexander Liberman gave me my first *Vogue* assignment. For me it was an important one—to photograph the outstanding evening gowns of that winter's collection. Quietly I rejoiced. It was to be a task both arduous and demanding, although Liberman didn't seem the least bit apprehensive about entrusting me with it. Sensing my worry, he probably felt that I was doing enough worrying for the two of us.

The eight pages of color that appeared two months later were, to me, the apogee of the chance he had given me. That chance had helped set me on my way to those hallowed pages in *Vogue,* and for the next five years my fashion work would continue to appear in them.

Madeline Murphy. Alexander Liberman. Roy Stryker. The memory of them prevents my looking at all white faces with the

95

same set of eyes. During those early years when I was inclined to loathe all whites, one would invariably emerge to prove me wrong.

Roy Stryker had moved on to Standard Oil Company (N.J.), with offices in New York's Rockefeller Center. Now he was building an impressive file on rural America, and he had begun urging me back into his world while I was free-lancing at *Vogue*. He had become my major influence and I was glad to be working with him again. His philosophy about documentary photography was simple and straightforward. To him the camera was a serious tool of communication, his FSA photographers serious journalists, not news hounds who went to dog fights to make *noun* and *verb* pictures. "My kind of pictures give you *adjectives* and *adverbs*. News pictures are all dramatics, subject and action, while the FSA photographs reveal what is behind the action. They present a much broader statement—frequently a mood, an accent, but more frequently a sketch, and not infrequently a story."

I never quite understood the real purpose of that Standard Oil file. I can only assume that it was meant to improve the company's image, which was suffering at the time. But since my bank account was also suffering it made no difference. The pay was good, and for photographers America's photogenic rural areas were rich with people, farmlands and small towns. Just two weeks before I left on assignment, my camera had been trained on thinnish, delicate women swathed in satin and silk. The following week found me on a Connecticut tobacco farm photographing a farmer's wife carrying a stack of tobacco leaves under her arm. The blue jeans she wore were not from some fashionable boutique, but most likely from Sears Roebuck, and a multitude of those Voguish ladies would have envied her wholesome smile.

A few brows had puckered when Stryker hired me. The only blacks on the premises were porters and messengers. But if they wanted Stryker they had to accept whomever he brought along. Consequently the photographic staff was a mixture of Jews, Catholics and me. For a few months the thirtieth floor where we worked from was avoided by some of the employees. They seemed to regard it as one of the company's dirtier filling stations with a smear of black across the front. But there was a sense of warmth and friendliness on that floor, and in time it became an oasis for those who sought warmth in that icy citadel.

For a while I allowed myself to hope that here, within this awesome skyscraper named for the Rockefellers, bigotry was slowly giving in to intelligence. Clean-cut young men in Brooks Brothers suits and Ivy League ties walked the corridors with official-looking papers in their hands, and courtly gray-maned executives conducted business from big plush suites: 30 Rockefeller Plaza reeked with respectability.

I didn't think there was anything exceptional when Stryker assigned me to take portraits of the top Standard Oil officials for a forthcoming exhibition. There should be no problems; they were, after all, gentlemen of high intelligence. It wasn't an assignment to hail with joy, but it was rather obvious to me that Stryker was counting on my training at *Vogue* to lend the project a style that befitted the stature of my subjects.

With special portrait equipment, I started working the executive floors; and as I worked I took heart. No eyes lifted with surprise upon my arrivals, and congeniality prevailed with every sitting—until I reached a certain vice president's suite. (For simplicity I will refer to him as Mr. Esso.) His secretary eyed me nervously, then entered his office and closed the door. Quickly she came back to tell me that Mr. Esso wasn't in. Actually he was already on the phone with Stryker—informing him that he wouldn't be photographed by "a nigger."

"Fine. I'll send someone else."

Stryker, flushed with anger, did send someone else, but not from his staff. He sent a news photographer who took a couple of flash shots and left.

Excrement hit the fan when the photographs were assembled in a large exhibition room. The festivities would open with a cocktail party and buffet. Mr. Esso was on the telephone to Stryker again, complaining bitterly that his portrait was "grossly inferior" to the rest. "Who took the others?" he asked angrily.

Coolly, Stryker had answered, "That nigger you turned away."

"Well—well, you'd better send him back. This affair's only two days off!" he snapped, and banged down the phone.

• • •

Both of these conversations had taken place between Stryker and Mr. Esso without my knowledge, otherwise I would never have gone back. The vice president didn't greet me as the others had. He didn't greet me at all. He just sat silently sorting out papers until I had arranged the lights and the chair he was to sit in. "I'm ready, Mr. Esso."

"What am I expected to do?"

"Sit in that chair, sir." He sat in the chair, and glared at the camera, his face a block of stone. Again I wished for that course in psychology. "It's a lovely day."

"I haven't noticed."

"Would you shift your shoulders a little to your left?"

He shifted slowly, and I released the shutter. "Are you a New Yorker, Mr. Esso?"

"Georgia—Atlanta, Georgia."

"Never been to Georgia."

Silence.

"If you crossed your legs you might appear more relaxed."

He stayed as he was. "I am relaxed."

"Could you lean forward, just a little?"

He leaned forward. I released the shutter. He glanced at his wristwatch. "How long is this going to take?"

"Not long, sir, but I would like a few more minutes."

"Go ahead."

"Would you mind placing your right elbow on the arm of the chair and place your thumb and forefinger on your cheek?"

"The right?"

"The right, sir."

Mr. Esso was finding it hard to follow my request. All directions went to the left. I released the shutter anyway. "Those are a couple of fine-looking children on your desk, Mr. Esso."

He allowed me a hint of a smile. "My son and daughter. They *are* fine-looking, I'd say." I clicked the shutter.

"Your son's the spitting image of you."

The smile widened. "So they say." I snapped the shutter.

"His hair's a bit darker than yours."

The smile widened even more. I clicked the shutter.

Mr. Esso shook his head sadly. "I take horrible pictures."

"I don't know why. You're a rather handsome man, I'd say."

"I always wind up looking like a baked potato."

"That beats a cucumber."

He chuckled, and smiled again. The hardness in his eyes had softened. The shutter clicked. "Maybe you don't give the photographer enough time."

"I don't have a lot of free time."

"I'm finished. Thank you very much, sir."

"You're sure?"

"I'm sure." I started packing up. He went back to his desk and lifted another picture.

"My wife."

"Very attractive, sir."

"I think so. You sure you have enough?"

"I'm sure. Thank you." As I left he was glancing at his watch.

A week later the same vice president requested me for his family's portrait. That session went well; but not until his bountiful check arrived did I finally hear the full story. Stryker had shrewdly triumphed over deep-seeded prejudice. And though I realized that his motives had been upright, I felt that somehow I had been used; and I doubted that the result would dispense an endless flow of justness in Mr. Esso's heart.

Roy Stryker was a man who provoked opinion. Certain photographers, feeling he was too concerned with their personal lives, spoke of him with disfavor at times. John Vachon, while conceding truth to Roy's importance in the documentary field, snarled at his "righteousness." Walker Evans, I was told, had left FSA disgruntled with Roy after their long association. Through cause and effect, Roy had a good amount of criticism and praise. The irony of these contentions was that, with all his kindness, he could be as scheming as the devil himself, but he never made any alliances with him. His deviousness invariably had a noble purpose—to keep us straight and on our toes.

I myself fell prey to these multiplex traits of his when my third child, David, was born in Minneapolis. "Get out there right away and bring your family back here to live," was his immediate and fatherly advice.

"But I don't have enough money to do that at the moment."

"Then I will get the company to advance you enough."

I did as he advised, but the two older children, after living two months in Harlem, rebelled against the city life. They began pleading for a house somewhere in the country away from the heat and noise.

"They are right. Find a nice little place and get them out of there," Roy further advised.

With another advance he arranged for me from the company, I found a beautiful little bungalow in White Plains, New York, and bought it. Three months later Stryker laid me off—and for no reason he attempted to explain. *He was keeping me on my toes.*

For the first time in our relationship I wanted to curse Roy Stryker. But I didn't complain; instead I hightailed it back to *Vogue* and, at the suggestion of Franklin Watts, a publisher, I put together an instruction book on using flashbulbs in photography, and another book titled *Camera Portraits.*

Amid the pleasant confusion of working at fashion for *Vogue* and the publishing of the two books, Roy had the effrontery to call me back to work with him again. Inwardly I was happy about being called back, but with disguised pleasure I said, "It will take me another three months to fulfill my present commitments. Sorry, Roy." My words must have sounded like an impetuous pile of crap to him, and I longed to see his face at the other end of the line.

There was a long moment of silence. Then he answered, "Fine, I'll be waiting."

The Second World War had ended with victory bells tolling throughout America. But black people were still suffering poverty and discrimination. Young black men, having served overseas, were now returning to fight the kind of tyranny they had helped put an end to in Europe. All across the country blacks were gathering, their voices kindling that awful fire that threatened to flame across the land. A few liberal voices were promising new laws in our behalf, but the Civil War and two world wars had taught us that bigotry could not be legislated from a man's heart. It was up to black people to take things into their own hands, and they were on the move. And I was ready to move with them. Just about every landscape I had traveled had prepared me. But I was unsure from where I could fight most effectively. Certainly not through the chic pages of *Vogue* magazine, nor in the ultraconservative offices of Standard Oil Company. I decided to put in two more years of work paying off my debt to the company and then move on. Stryker's contract there was coming to an end. During our final meeting he seemed to have grown tired, very tired. "Well, what's next, Roy?" I had asked.

A weak smile wrinkled into his face. "In a few months I'm heading back to Colorado—to stay, to breathe in some fresh air, and pray for some sanity to come to this country." Winter was deep in his face and hair. He resembled a man who, after killing a lot of fires, was pulling in the hose and going for some rest. I thought back to my first day in Washington, when bigotry had me aflame. Always I would be mindful of his helping me to survive.

NINE

Most blacks were weighted with the denial of opportunity but I had been fortunate to be able to shove aside those restrictive boundaries. Now what I wanted was what so many photographers, black and white, found almost impossible to get; a staff job at *Life* magazine. That publication wasn't exactly trumpeting the black man's cause, but it would be a prestigious base for me to work from since it was so well known and reached millions of readers throughout the world. So one morning I took my portfolio to Wilson Hicks, the magazine's picture editor, and asked for a job. Miraculously he decided to give me a try.

Wilson Hicks later explained his decision to me: "There was a scarcity of documentary photographers on the staff, and none with fashion experience, and we sorely needed someone to cover the Paris collections. It was that simple."

But even later I learned it *wasn't* that simple. Hicks had to be cajoled into my acceptance by two senior editors, John Dille and Sally Kirkland, who ran the fashion department. I could serve both their needs. He wanted a powerful documentary story for an upcoming issue, and she was frantically preparing for the French collections.

Eyeing me with skepticism, Hicks had thrown out a question that caught me off guard: "Have you something in mind that you'd like to do?"

"Yes I do," I lied, never expecting things would get so far so quickly. "A gang war is taking place up in Harlem, and I'd like to cover it." Then hurriedly I concocted a deeper reason. "Such a story might help black kids realize the folly in murdering one another."

Hicks wasn't impressed. It would be easier to freeze snowballs in hell, he replied dryly. But after a terribly long moment he caved in. "Okay, I'll go along with that idea, but I can only offer you five hundred dollars."

"So little?" I was astounded.

Dille cut in quickly. "Take it—just take it. Everything will work out." Reluctantly I agreed to the price. It was an opening. Once outside Hicks's office Dille assured me that I would work with an unlimited expense account. This made *very* good sense. It had been a tense session, but both Sally and John were contented, and I was secretly ecstatic—yet apprehensive as well. It was indeed a tough assignment, and I was now struck with the impossibility of pulling it off.

The next morning I drove up to Harlem in the Buick Roadmaster I had bought—against Stryker's advice—in search of a gang leader. It was like searching for a bubble in the sea. For a week I drove around up there, with Hicks's doubts overlapping my own. Why would any sensible gang leader, having just blown away somebody, want his face spread over the pages of *Life* magazine? And why should he take me, a stranger, into his confidence? Doggedly I kept on with the search.

I was at the 125th Street police precinct one morning talking with a detective friend, Jimmie Morrow, when luck arrived in the person of a sixteen-year-old, freckle-faced boy with a prizefighter's build and demeanor. The obscenities he was hurling at the desk sergeant were strong enough to get his head cracked, but the sergeant sat quietly, red-faced.

Amazed, I turned and looked at Jimmie questioningly. He smiled. "That's your man if you can talk him into it."

Red Jackson was *the* Harlem gang leader. Now the crown prince of the Midtowners, he was cursing out the desk sergeant for failing to give his gang the protection it had been promised—not from the police, but from a rival gang that had killed a Midtowner the day before. The police, recognizing him as the most powerful leader in the slaughter that was taking place, had asked him to pull back and help cool things off. Now, having lost one of his gang, he was giving vent to his anger.

I followed him into the street. "Hi, Red."

He turned on me with a look of hostility. "Who are you, man, a cop or a stoolie?"

"Neither. I'm just a friend of Jimmie Morrow's."

"He's a cop."

"Yeh, I know. He told me who you are."

"So?"

"I've got a problem I'd like to talk with you about."

He looked at me from head to foot. "What's your problem?"

"I'm a photographer with *Life* magazine and I would like to hang out with you and your gang."

"You ain't got a problem, man. You've got a death wish."

His answer was chilling, but it had merit. "I'm willing to take the chance. How about it?"

"You must take me for a real patsy. Why would I do something stupid as that?"

"Jimmie Morrow was telling me about your problems with the desk sergeant. Maybe I could be some help to you in some way."

His eyes narrowed. "The only help you can give me is by kicking that fucking sergeant in the balls for lying to me. Later, man." He started walking off.

"Can I give you a lift somewhere?"

"I've got carfare."

I opened the door of the Roadmaster. "Come on, I'll take you where you're going."

"That your rod?" Evidently he liked what he saw.

"Yeh, it's mine."

"Okay. I'll let you drop me at 116th Street." He got in, and as I drove along slowly he patted the upholstery admiringly. "Man, this rod must have cost you some big bread. How long you had it?"

"About four months. Do you like it?"

He rubbed the dashboard. "It's a fucking gas. How fast will it go?"

"Over a hundred on a straightaway."

"You ever let it out all the way?"

"Never had any cause to."

We stopped at a red light. "What's this shit about *Life* magazine?"

I thought deeply and then took a chance on the validity of those thoughts. "I'm going to come clean with you, Red. This story I want to do is a big one and an important one."

"What makes it so important?"

"You—and a lot of other black kids are knocking one another off for some stupid reasons. Think of yourself as brothers, then you'll see that it doesn't make any sense."

The light changed and we drove off. "That sounds like some of that sergeant's bull we fell for. Tells me to lay back. Said he'd take care of things. Then wham, a Midtowner's pulled out of the river with four slugs in his head. I know who did it and their asses belong to the Midtowners, man."

"So you go on killing one another?"

"You have to kill to live in this fucking place, man. Don't you understand?"

"I'd hate to find out tomorrow that you'd got it."

"I would, too, but you have to expect to take the lumps."

We were approaching 116th Street and time was running out. "I want to help you get rid of those lumps."

"How? How're you going to do that?"

"With your help. Look, Red, you can't like facing death every day. Nobody does, not even your enemies. If I get a good story that appeals to all of the gangs, then things might really cool off."

He laughed derisively. "Hell, man, those cats won't even see your magazine, let alone read it. They don't even read anything. I don't."

"They'll read it if they see your picture."

"My picture?"

"Yeh, and the rest of the Midtowners."

We turned into 116th Street. It was teeming with black people, and it was a hot day. Fire hydrants, turned on by the Midtowners, were flooding the streets and cooling off the neighborhood kids. He pointed at a squalid tenement. "This is where I get off." He got out and slammed the door shut. "Thanks for the lift."

I made one more try. "How about it, Red?"

His eyes had shifted to a second-story window where a scantily clad girl leaned on the sill. "I'll talk to my war lords about it. Pick me up here about this time tomorrow. I'll let you know what they say. Later," he said as he headed for the second floor. I didn't feel as though I had made any sort of an impression, but I expected that my new Roadmaster had, and I drove back downtown with my hopes pinned upon it.

Red wasn't easy to find the next day. No one, it appeared, had even heard of Red Jackson. Obviously I was being taken for a detective, and I felt deceived. After hanging around outside his building on 116th Street for two hours I was driving off when a younger replica of Red came up to the car. "You the cat who brought my brother home yesterday?"

"That's me." I felt relieved.

He turned, cupped his hands around his mouth and hollered, "Red!" After a few seconds the window on the second floor went up and Red stuck his head out. His torso was bare. "Yeh!"

"Your man's down here!"

The girl came to his side and he put his arms around her naked shoulders. "I'll be down in a few minutes. Tell him to cool it!"

The few minutes lasted for another hour. By the time he arrived my car was surrounded by Midtowners. The four war lords had bunched themselves together in the back seat. The front seat was left for Red. Obviously he had spread the word, and it looked as though the Midtowners had agreed to take on a chauffeur with a big new Roadmaster. No other gang in Harlem could make such an extravagant boast. Red got in and nodded toward his henchmen in the back of the car. "They're Herbie, Joey, Butch and Jimmy. Fellows, this is Mr. Parks."

"Hi—fellows. Good to meet you." Silence. "Well, Red, where to?"

"Just cruise around. Want'a look the turf over."

The turf, spreading between the Harlem and the Hudson Rivers, and that space between 116th Street and 135th Street, was inhabited by more people than a lot of small American towns with a mayor. And it was a long, nervous cruise that lasted until four in the morning—interlaced with hotdogs and soft drinks I gladly supplied.

A week had passed before Red asked me when I was going to start using my camera. It was a small one and in my jacket pocket. I smiled and patted it. "Whenever something happens." With his Humphrey Bogart look, Red lit a cigarette, took a long drag and blew out the smoke. "You know, Mr. Parks, we like you—but we don't like double-crossers."

"I dig you, Red," I replied coolly but uncomfortably, with the thought that there might be a very thin line between betrayal and honest reporting. It was not the time to discuss the delicacy of that difference. "Always remember this, Red—you can trust me, and I hope to trust you."

"You're on," he replied, and we slapped hands.

That trust was cemented by two incidents that took place shortly after that. I had casually mentioned that my exposure meter was suddenly missing.

"That little black thing with a needle and numbers?"

"Yeh. The guys were playing around with it the other day."

The following morning Herbie handed me the meter—with a great big apology. Then one afternoon the police burst into the basement of the Midtowners' headquarters. Someone had reported a rumble in progress. When I pulled out my *Life* magazine credentials and convinced them that I was doing a "social study" on Harlem youth, they left immediately. Red was flabbergasted. "Goddamned flatfoots would'a cracked our heads if you hadn't been here, man."

In the weeks to follow I found how indifferent death could be in this warring place, where honor meant spilling blood over the most trivial thing—an accidental bump on the shoulder; a dispute over a stolen bicycle; an invasion of the wrong territory; a girl's innocent wink; or a game of stickball. Teenagers, talking death, took blood oaths to die together. Mothers feared a knock at the door; afraid it was the police to say that a son was dead. All the Midtowners had knife or bullet wounds, and they wore them with bravura. They were like badges of courage. Such passionate allegiance, Red explained, had good reason.

"It's for protection. You wise up fast here in Harlem. You join up with somebody or keep getting your ass kicked. They say, 'You belong to a gang, cat?' 'No.' 'You got some loot?' 'No, I ain't got none.' Then—bop! Bop! Bop! 'Next time you better have some!' If you've got some the next time they take it and you get bopped anyway. If you're a Midtowner, they think twice before starting any shit, 'cause they know they'll have to rumble."

As the Midtowners moved toward the first rumble I experienced with them, it was drizzling. Dusk had fallen and there was an ominous feel in the air. As we rode along Red calmly told me how he became boss of the Midtowners.

"Cappy was our leader then, and I was right beside him. The Harlem Dukes had us outnumbered, and they was coming at us hot and heavy. Pow! Pow! Pow! Cappy went down and blood was popping out of his head and I knew he was gone. I grabbed his .38 and started shooting with two guns, shooting and running. Pow! Pow! And two of their cats fell. Then the bastards turned tail while I kept banging away at their asses. Next day I was made the head man."

Now the Midtowners were about to settle matters with the same Harlem Dukes. One had called Red's sister a bitch and spit on her shoe. She didn't know his name; no matter, that was reason enough for a rumble. The point of encounter was on Eighth Avenue near 135th Street, less than two blocks from the 135th police precinct. We left the car at 125th Street, met twelve other Midtowners and started walking. Red, wearing dark glasses and an old trench coat I had given him, looked every bit the leader. The others, packing revolvers, zip guns and chains, moved along stealthily. Red had given orders two hours before, and they were ready. A police car passed, slowed, then went on.

I was carrying a small camera the *Life* technicians had rigged up. The infrared flash, they told me, would hardly be discernible—just a small flicker of light in the darkness. My feelings were split.

Those of the reporter pulsed for action. Yet, in human terms I worried about the possible consequences. Swiftly and silently the Midtowners walked into rival territory. Then Red's hand shot up, signaling us to stop. He gave a quick nod of his head, and three of the most powerful of them slammed their weight against a basement door. My nerves were scrambling as we broke into the Dukes' den, taking them by surprise.

Tiger Johnson, the rival leader, leaped to his feet, but before he could grab a lead pipe, Red knocked him to the floor with a brutal right. The Midtowners aimed their weapons, and seven of the Dukes stood motionless as Red put a switchblade to Tiger's throat. "Which one of you bastards spit on my sister? Tiger's eyes snapped toward a boy crouching beside him. "I'm sorry, man," the boy mumbled.

"Get to your feet, punk!" Red ordered. The boy rose slowly with fear in his eyes, and fear was bolting through me as well. "Open your shirt, punk!" The boy opened the buttons at his chest. When Red placed the point of the blade just above his heart I snapped the shutter and froze. "Say it again, punk, and make it loud."

"I'm sorry, man!" Sweat was rolling down his face and chest. Red flicked the blade upward for about a quarter of an inch. The boy moaned as a thin trickle of blood came, and I felt like turning away. "You're lucky I don't cut out your fucking heart and make you eat it!" Inwardly I sighed a sigh of relief. He spat on the boy's chest and dropped him with a terrible right. "Frisk these other punks!" That was done quickly with expertise, then we backed out of the place—with the Midtowners' arsenal swelled by four pistols, five knives and six zip guns. Then we were out of the block as swiftly and silently as we had come.

Three weeks later Joey, a Midtowners war lord, was knifed to death by the Sabers, another gang. On the third day Red and Herbie, his chief war counselor, went to the funeral home where Joey's body lay. "You had better travel light," Red had warned me. "We may have to do some running." I went as lightly burdened as possible, wearing a pair of sneakers. Only Red and Herbie went in to see the body. The others waited outside to stand guard in case the Sabers showed up.

The funeral home attendant came to stand beside us as we viewed Joey's body. "Would you mind leaving us alone with our friend, man?'' Red's request was more like an order, and the attendant obeyed it. I cringed as Red lifted his war lord's head and examined the cuts on the neck and skull, then placed it back in position. ''The fucking bastards did a good job on him,'' he mumbled. ''They gonna get the same treatment. Let's go.''

A few minutes later we *were* running from an attempted Saber ambush, and people were hurrying for shelter as we fled to an empty second-story hideout to escape the Sabers. Once there, Red knocked out a window, reached for his .38 and prepared to start firing. From a dark corner I photographed him. It was that photograph that made him known throughout the world. Further violence was avoided when two police cars from the 135th Street precinct careened into the block.

Twelve days later a Saber was killed, but a Midtowner's stomach was badly slashed during that rumble. Since the police would be searching the hospitals, two of the Midtowners stitched the gaping wound together with needle and thread. I had seen enough bloodshed to last me for a lifetime, and I believed I had the story I had come for. Two weeks later the Red Jackson story was on the stands.

There had been some contention between the editors and myself during the layout of the story. They had wanted to show Red on the cover with a smoking gun in his hand. I fought against it, even destroyed the negative to be sure it wasn't used for such a purpose. After the story was published I brought the Midtowners to my house in White Plains to spend a day with my two sons, hoping that among the trees, fields and horses, they would lean toward a better kind of existence. They were, for that Saturday, just kids eating hotdogs and swilling down soft drinks and riding my sons' horses. It was a good day for them, for my family, and for me. I remember sitting by Red as he tossed pebbles into a stream. ''Why'd you bring us up here, Mr. Parks?'' (It was never Gordon as I had once suggested.) ''My family wanted you to come. Wouldn't you like to get out of Harlem someday, away from all the violence?'' I asked.

He had smiled sadly. ''Oh, I'd like to, but not a chance—not a chance.'' Then he asked a favor of me. ''Why don't you let your son Gordon spend a weekend in Harlem with us? You won't have to worry. We'll take good care of him.''

''I'm sure you will, but you'll have to promise—no rumbles.''

"No rumbles," he promised, and we slapped hands. Gordon did go to spend a weekend with Red. And a promise made was a promise kept. "Dad, I had a hell of a good time," my son reported when he returned.

The most disturbing thing about that assignment was the double edge it presented; if a war did break out boys would die; without the uncommon violence they indulged in, the story itself would have died.

As things went, another Midtowner died when gunfire cut through the noise of Harlem two months later. While reading about it I seemed to be there, but observing safely from behind a steel curtain, devastated, knowing there was nothing I might have done to prevent the tragedy. I had tried to lay the horror of gang war before the nation, hoping that somehow a way could be found to end it. Perhaps someone paid attention; the following year passed with just a few Harlem gang murders. For the time being it seemed that youth's killing of youth was slowly coming to a halt.

Now, forty years later, hard drugs have become the rainbow, and again youthful gangs roam city streets killing one another—protecting their little kingdoms of heroin and crack. Gunfire erupts nightly, and unfortunately black teenagers are caught dead-center of the catastrophe. Despair settles in and they try burning it out with alcohol and hard drugs. In a short time they fade into mere shadows of themselves; into nothingness, then early death. Spun from the loom of such disaster is a remarkably cold statistic. The average black male in Harlem is fortunate to live past the age of forty. Pausing now to look back, I see myself in the distance—leaving there with a sigh of thankfulness.

Red Jackson's fate was less final than it had seemed when I found him leading the Midtowners in Harlem back in 1948. After almost forty years a letter came assuring me that, for him, time had beneficently wielded its power. With learned humility he wrote:

"Dear Gordon, I saw my picture in *Life* again the other day, and it brought back some bad memories. That story was a big ego trip for me. At fifty-six, I've been through the mill, and along the way I've met dozens of ghetto kids that wound up the same way I did. Now, with your help, I would like to reach some of them and tell them how quickly glory faded from me, and that there's a much better way to go. I might wind up saving some of them. Even one would be worth it. I would like to help a few Harlem kids to get an education. That's the key: Education! Would you believe that at my age I'm preparing to take the test for my High School Equivalency Diploma? I love it! And I'd love to hear from you again. Yours truly, Red Jackson."

A door from Red's sordid past had finally opened up, and he had chosen to walk through it to a better kind of life. Time had deceived both of us. Now I could firmly believe he would make it —something that I had for so long doubted. The letter had been dated January 5, 1987. He had taken a long step from his old unhappiness.

TEN

Response to the Harlem essay brought me some recognition. Sympathetic letters, along with a few vitriolic ones, poured in from *Life*'s readers. Others arrived from company officials. Henry Luce, *Life*'s founder, also penned a congratulatory note, and I was pleased to have done something that neither Wilson Hicks, nor I, thought possible to do. Hicks called early one morning with some good words, then casually he added thirteen more. "We have decided to send you to Paris to cover the French collections."

I sat silent for several moments—stunned.

"Are you there?"

"I'm here. Just a little dazed."

"Well, pull yourself together and start packing. You sail for Paris a week from today."

Paris. The enchanted place I had never expected to see. Sally, my wife, was clipping roses in the backyard, and I went to the window and hollered the good news to her. *"Life's* sending me to Paris!"

Her reaction was strangely calm. She looked at me as if I had informed her that I was going to the grocery. "And what are they sending you for?"

"To shoot the French collections."

"Ah, terrific," she said icily, and went back to clipping roses.

Her reaction was one to which I should have attached a deeper meaning, but I didn't. I crossed to the center of the bedroom and stood there with Hicks's words still sounding in my ears. An entire universe seemed to waltz around me.

Paris. As I showered, my mind drifted back to a winged, childhood fantasy. My brother, Clem, had planted it into my subconscious when he came home from Paris after serving in the First World War. He had been struggling behind a horse-drawn plow, getting the field ready for spring planting, and I was at his side. "What was Paris like?" I kept asking him.

"I'll tell you about it later, Pedro. Can't you see I'm busy?"

I had persisted. "But why can't you tell me right now?"

He had reined the horse to a stop, wiped away sweat and looked at me with a tired, big brother's impatience. Then, with a mischievous smile, he said, "Pedro, it's a great big beautiful place with lots of beautiful girls and famous artists. Now, let me get on with this plowing."

"Is it big like a mountain?"

"Yep, Pedro, big like a mountain." Then he had snapped the reins across the horse's rump and gone on with his plowing—leaving that image to linger in my imagination for most of my childhood. It was my capacity for daydreaming that bestowed the long flaxen hair on the beautiful girls, and bright red berets on the famous artists, but how the caves I envisioned got into the sides of that big Paris mountain is still a mystery. I had secretly resisted being awakened from that charming illusion for several years. Now, that childish mirage was about to be shattered forever.

• • •

Sally Kirkland and I sailed for Paris a week later aboard the *Queen Mary,* and Joe Thorndike, the managing editor, came to the pier to see us off. It was a very high moment: managing editors didn't usually take time off for such things. After champagne in the lounge he left, but he stood there waving from the pier as the huge ocean liner backed away.

I had asked my wife to see us off, but she refused, saying that she always found farewells disturbing.

"I'm sorry you won't be there," I said as I was leaving the house.

"I know. Well, have a nice trip," she had answered, and quickly shut the door.

It would take five days to cross the Atlantic, ample time to rid myself of the anxiety I felt. High winds, storm clouds and monstrous waves defiled that first day at sea. Both Sally and I, along with a lot of others, kept to our rooms and ate very little. The mere thought of food made my insides feel green. The second day was bathed with sun; the sea was calm as a mirror and that night the dining room was filled. The required dress was evening gown and black tie, and I felt a bit awkward in my very first tuxedo. Then, too, my left patent-leather slipper was just a bit tight, and I was wishing that I had taken the salesman's advice and got a larger pair. But such minor suffering failed to turn the course of the evening. There were bars and music, fore and aft, and a concert hall nestled in the center of the ship where a pianist played Mozart concertos with a string quartet. The luxurious *Queen Mary,* with its gymnasiums, swimming pools and sweeping decks, was a far cry from the leaky little fishing skiff I paddled about on Marmaton River back in Fort Scott. Surrounded by infinite, black horizons, the ship seemed to be inching its way to France. Only when one looked at the prow knifing the water into frothy dark pools could one sense its power and swiftness.

I telephoned my wife on the third day, feeling she would be pleased about our voices meeting so far out over the Atlantic. The call went through at noon, New York time, and the connection was remarkably clear.

"I'm over halfway there. Just wanted to say hello to you and the kids. Wish you were here. How are things back there?"

"The same as they were when you left. This town's hot as an oven, and I'm frying potatoes for *your* children."

Her voice, curled with cynicism, had stripped away any desire for further conversation. "Well—give them my love, and take care of yourself."

"Right now I had better take care of the potatoes before they burn up."

"This is a great ship."

"I hope you enjoy it."

The only thing left to say was good-bye. I said that and hung up —sensing that I shouldn't have made that call. It had only served to chafe the ears of a very chilled spouse.

A cablegram arrived from Wilson Hicks the following morning. He was offering me a job on the staff—and at a salary that sent my thoughts skyward. Sally, a smart business woman, smiled. "Tell him you'll think it over, but that you want at least a third more than he is offering."

Having followed her advice, I began sweating it out—through Cherbourg, on the boat train to Paris and in the car whisking us to our hotel. Another cable awaited me at the Hotel Crillon. "Okay —you're on the staff with a third more than previous offer. Congratulations."

I cabled back: "I'm happy and honored."

World War II had bent Paris to its knees, but it didn't appear to have been permanently befouled by Adolf Hitler's brutal occupation. He was dead now, his name suspended in hatred. Recalling his back turned upon Jesse Owens's Olympic triumphs years before gave me reason to speculate. Oh, how it would have galled him to know that another "inferior" black was occupying the same suite he and his mistress, Eva Braun, once lived in. Machine-gun and mortar-shell holes, exploded into the hotel's facade by French Freedom Fighters, were still there, reminding Parisians of those battering days when storm troopers patrolled the boulevards.

Now the city was glittering again; gaiety was creeping back; the River Seine had never stopped its peaceful flowing, and sidewalk cafés were blooming like roses. Nevertheless the Nazis had left Paris in want. Cigarette butts were still being lifted from gutters, and even cheap wine demanded a heavy price. But the great fashion houses had maintained the elegance of prewar days. Their

116

plush, coffin-gray salons stayed packed with rich clients from all over the world, and the pungent aroma of costly *parfums* filled the air. I can't forget the smartly clad lady furtively plucking a cigarette butt from a Dior ashtray—nor will I forget her scornful glance when she realized I was watching.

So much had happened so suddenly, I hardly had time to consider my good fortune. Melodious names of the great fashion houses were bouncing against my ears—Chanel, Dior, Molyneux, Schiaparelli, Fath, Balenciaga and others that I found difficult to pronounce. But soon I was referring to them so casually one would have thought I was brought up in their showrooms.

Patiently, Sally Kirkland apprised me of the characteristics that set the houses apart: "Chanel's clothes are comfortable and easy to move in, and her suits are classics. Molyneux designs for elegance and grace, and his things are very fluid. Schiaparelli is famous for crazy buttons and shocking pinks, and loves to play around with different colors. Dior's gowns are very feminine and he's well known for creating the New Look. Balenciaga works for perfection, whether it's an evening dress, suit or coat. He hates the press and pretty mannequins. Jacques Fath is all discretion, but his things can be very witty and sexy. His evening dresses are extremely flirtatious." So went my daily designer education.

For me it was a golden time, crowned with dazzling gowns and beauteous mannequins—Dorian Leigh, Bettina, Janine Klein, Jackie Stoloff, Suzy Parker, Carmen, Dovima and others whose faces graced the pages and covers of prestigious fashion magazines. Sally had found a studio for me, but it was rarely used. Paris's outer face was too compelling. No enclosure, no matter how dramatic, could have transcended the blue-haze mornings when blood-red sun filtered through the fog and mist. My backdrops became the marbled bridges spanning the Seine, ancient buildings, embowered streets and inflowing boulevards. My memory was once more reaching back to the paintings of Degas, Matisse and Renoir I had seen in the Chicago Art Institute back in the late 1930s, allowing them to influence my selection of color and composition. The same allurements that had once kindled their imagination were now kindling my own. But within this visual splendor there hung the unfading memory of my father's cornfield, and my brother's stopping the horse to plant that whimsical imagery of Paris into my head. Surely the artists and the beautiful girls were still there—but no caves. Their invention remained a mystery.

During those first nights in Paris I lay cuddled in my own warmth, smiling whimsically, recalling the storminess of my earlier years. Moments of failure and heartbreak strolled through my thoughts in a strange silence—Jim's pool hall, the homelessness and hunger, the brothels, the bone-chilling freight car ride to Chicago, the flophouse and its miserable inhabitants came fluttering in like dusty dreams. Ugly and unforgettable, they had split me apart and overlaid me with fear. Now, lying in the splendor of the Hotel Crillon, it was hard to unscramble those harsh memories, and to determine what they meant to where I had landed.

When, after two weeks, the assignment ended, I felt as though I had been whirling about in an awakening storm that had suddenly died. It was over. The rich ladies had chosen their new wardrobes and gone home. Now all those fashion palaces with the melodious names would begin threading needles for the next season's collections.

Sally Kirkland flew off to London. I stayed on for another week, absorbing the city's treasures—its historical landmarks, museums, concert halls and its Left Bank bistros and cafés. Inwardly I dared to hope for a chance to live and work here someday, but such a sweet possibility seemed, for the moment, out of the question. Only a day before I was to sail home, yet another cable arrived: "Beautiful story. You get cover and twelve pages." That welcome news flowed into even better news: "Proceed to Rome Bureau then Stromboli for the Bergman-Rossellini affair. Maria Sermolino goes with you. Luck, Wilson." Ingrid Bergman and Roberto Rossellini, also impressed with the Harlem essay, had both agreed to my coming.

Daphnis and Chloé. Romeo and Juliet. Now—Roberto and Ingrid. For all six, love was the terrible creature. I took the morning plane to Rome.

Roberto, the Italian director, and Ingrid, the great actress, were on Stromboli, a volcanic island in the Tyrrhenian Sea, attempting to make a picture while suffering out their extraordinary love affair—one most of the world thought of as scandalous. She had deserted her husband, and child, and she was having an affair with Roberto. This was unthinkable to millions who idolized her. She had forsaken the most sacred principles of their proper postwar society.

Stromboli swarmed with reporters and photographers—all sent to capture a single, impassioned embrace. Any publication with the good fortune to publish such a picture full page, would have sold out moments after it hit the stands. Exasperated, Rossellini had ordered all newsmen off the island. They were exiting as Sermolino and I came ashore. Rossellini was standing knee-deep in the water, screaming at the last boatload of reporters departing his sanctuary. "Go! If you try to return I will choke you with my own hands!"

"*Addio,* tyrant! *Addio,* wife stealer!" one reporter shouted back. Enraged, Rossellini splashed deeper into the sea, but the boat was well out of his reach. Sermolino and I introduced ourselves. Bergman greeted us with a warm smile despite the confusion. "We've been expecting you." Rossellini, still ruffled, bowed stiffly, frowned, then pointed to an old house perched on a cliff high above the sea. "That's yours," he said, and strode off. Uncertainty lay ahead. The irate director was bristling with anger toward the newsmen he'd disposed of—because they were trying to accomplish what I had been sent to accomplish.

Rossellini moved through the next day hardly speaking, and I was careful not to point the camera in his direction. I simply went about photographing the island. It was a strangely beautiful place, formed from the volcano rising out of the sea. The beach sand was jet-black—proof of eruptions over the years. After three days Rossellini sullenly invited me to visit the set. He seemed to have a complete change of mood. Later he asked me and Sermolino to dinner. That night at Bergman's quarters, the four of us ate lobster by candlelight and listened to the recorded music of Vivaldi. It wasn't exactly a relaxing evening. One could sense the anxiety coiling inside both of them, see the uncertainty on their faces. There was good reason. Dr. Lindstrom, the jilted husband, was sailing toward Stromboli to have a showdown.

Meanwhile disapproval of Bergman stormed in from everywhere, and in every conceivable language. Her idolators raged that she had showed herself to be imperfect. They felt Rossellini undeserving of her. They felt scorned. It wasn't so much "Ingrid, what are you doing to yourself?" but "What are you doing to us?

You are murdering *our* image of *you.*" They felt deceived by the angelic smile.

Robert Graves implied that boys and old women are foolish for falling in love, and he obviously felt the same about girls and old men. Bergman and Rossellini were neither of these. They were dead center of an age that yields to passion. Now, like Romeo and Juliet, they were clinging to one another while the storm howled around them. It was as though the Tyrrhenian waves buffeting the island had become their enemy. The disgruntled newsmen had regrouped, returned in an armada of boats of all sizes and shapes, their long lenses trained on Stromboli. Rossellini had no control over the sea. Bergman seemed to be content with her decision. Rossellini—a bit rotund but rakishly handsome, stayed at her side, feeding her love and encouragement, spitting at the world, declaring, "I love her! I adore her! Nobody will take her from me!"

I began to like Rossellini. During his better hours he was charming and beguiling. And I grew to respect Bergman highly; in spite of her trials, she was easeful, never allowing her friendliness to waver, and she had a gift for making you feel comfortable in her presence. My good feeling for her was beginning to threaten the magazine's intention for sending me to Stromboli. *Life* wanted what every other publication around the world wanted—that unguarded moment of passion. She knew it and he knew it, yet they accepted me with trust. My loyalty was split, and the rules existing somewhere between their trust and my obligation to the magazine left me unhinged. If the moment arrived either *Life* or the melancholy lovers would suffer. In either case I would be at odds with my conscience.

The moment flashed in when I least expected it.

A week of filming had ended. Everyone had left the set except Ingrid and Roberto. I stepped from a closet where I had been unloading film from my camera. They stood in the center of a large room, weary, drained from their ordeal, holding one another close—a comforting rather than a lustful embrace. Instinctively I raised my camera; then just as quickly, I dropped it to my side. The moment that slipped away was undeserving of betrayal. I slipped out, hoping that I had gone unnoticed.

On Sunday morning Bergman knocked at my door. She and Roberto were going for a walk along the shore. "Would you like to go along?" she asked. I answered that I would.

"Then hurry along—and bring your camera. Roberto and I would like some pictures together." She *had* seen me two evenings before, and now she was, in her own way, showing gratitude. I spent the morning with them, walking apart, photographing, trying not to impose upon those few peaceful hours they were sharing.

The picture was going badly, and the crew was becoming agitated and restless. Rossellini was becoming tyrannical; the distractions were taking their toll. As I was leaving the set one evening Ingrid stopped me, then took me aside. "Would you like to stay on and assist Roberto with the filming?"

I was moved beyond delight. "But, Ingrid, he would never agree to that."

"I think he might. Let me try." She tried, but without success. We never found reason to discuss the possibility again, but a desire had been awakened in me. I went to bed preoccupied with thoughts of someday being able to direct a motion picture. They were towering thoughts with frail possibilities, but they didn't go away.

A couple of weeks later Sermolino and I left Stromboli. It was, I remember, just after dawn and the sea was angry. The newsmen in their boats were still out there, roughing it on the great waves. I remained on deck, my camera focused on wisps of black smoke curling from the volcano's mouth; hoping that it wasn't about to erupt. Ingrid and Roberto were still asleep in their inland refuge, and I hoped too that they would soon be left alone. Sermolino eventually came to stand beside me, and together we watched as Stromboli disappeared slowly beneath the sea.

I never knew how long their passion flamed, or when their love grew thin. But certainly they loved while suffering the agonies of it. Later three children were born to them, and in time both Ingrid and Roberto took the final trip west.

My memory of them has never diffused, I recall so distinctly their walking the shore of Stromboli that Sunday morning, harrowed, moving uncertainly through a seascape of blue sky and black sand. During those moments they appeared to be more in mourning than in love. Gulls played above them. Waves rippled in over their bare feet, and an old fisherman touched the bill of his cap as they passed. Surely her mind was on those who had judged

121

her so harshly but he, blind to the entire universe, seemed content to let people think what they chose to think. They had stopped for a moment and he took her hand in his. Only love was left. As they moved on silently I had wondered if love was enough.

My wife was still in a snit when I arrived home, and it didn't improve her disposition to find that I was to hurry off on yet another assignment. I decided to face up to her disgruntlement before leaving. The conversation lasted far into the morning, only to end up with bitterness, but she made me understand that being the wife of a *Life* photographer had some serious drawbacks,

"You're out enjoying the world, and I'm stuck here with *your* children. Do you think that's fun for me?"

No, I hadn't thought of that; I had been too busy just trying to get there. "I've worked damned hard toward this all my life." I posed a difficult question. "Would you have me give it all up now?"

"That's for you to figure out."

As I packed I was afraid I had already figured it out. It was clear; I was growing, and she seemed reluctant to grow with me. On the plane west I gave serious thought to those earliest years of her own life. Until she was adopted by Joe and Ida Alvis she, along with her brother and sister, lived in orphanages. Deserted by their parents, they had gone from place to place, at times without one another. Now, with Joe and Ida nearing their end, perhaps that sense of youthful insecurity was creeping back, and since I had become her sole security maybe the worldliness that was suddenly engaging me was becoming threatening for her. This possibility deserved deeper thought, and I spent the rest of the flight in self-recrimination.

En route to Los Alamos, New Mexico, I would be snapped into the awareness that I was back in America, and the moment arrived unexpectedly, filled with the smell of violence and possibly death. It came in a small Texas town at a bus station where I awaited an army car to carry me to my destination. Having recognized me, a white female journalist ran over, planted a kiss on my cheek, then hurried off to catch her bus. It was noon and terribly hot, and I was drinking from a water fountain when the Texas drawl curled over me.

"We don't like niggers kiss'n white ladies down this way, do we, Bart?"

Still bent over the fountain, I glanced up, then took two more gulps. Bart was curling the cord of a venetian blind into a lynch knot. "Nope, Hoagy, and this is what we do to smart-ass darkies who do crazy things like that. But we beat the shit out of them first. Hangin' ain't a'nough."

By now I was much too angry to be afraid. When I stood up to face them I saw the word *Gunsmith* on a small building opposite the station, and brushing past them, I headed for it.

I'd never had any desire to seriously shoot a gun. There was that BB gun my parents had given me many Christmases before, and I had shot targets with a .22 rifle that belonged to my friend, Emphry Hawkins. My father also had a dislike for guns, but having handled them back in Oklahoma where he was born, he possessed a knowledge of them. More than once I had heard him tell my cousin Martin, "Boy, you don't pull out a gun unless you've got the guts to use it." He also talked about firing logs—a thick section of a tree's trunk that caught bullets when testing a gun. "A bullet just disappears into one," he would say.

All these memories were racing through my thoughts as I crossed the dusty road. I entered the shop and asked the gunsmith for a .45 automatic—and in a manner that said I knew how to use it. Three ruffians had followed me, but they stood outside peering in. The gunsmith glanced at them, then back at me.

"A .45 automatic?" He was stalling.

"That's what I asked for." He took one from a shelf and handed it to me. I handed it back. "Load it." He loaded it and handed it back. "Have you got a firing log?"

"Right there in the corner."

I turned. There it was, just as my father had described it. I aimed, pressed the trigger. Nothing happened. "It won't fire. Give me one that will."

He took another glance outside. "Did you release the safety?"

"I sure did."

He handed me another .45. "Try this one."

"It's loaded?"

"Sure is."

I released the safety, aimed and fired three quick bursts. The bullets disappeared into the log—just like my father had said. I paid for it, and with my hand still on the trigger, I walked out, with every intention of using it. The three backed away as I came out, but they began following me, cursing now, getting closer. "You black bastard. You son-of-a-bitch!"

Back in Kansas that last insult would have called for action. I turned and raised the gun, just as the army car pulled up. My driver, a military policeman with a gun strapped to his hip, stepped out, glancing at the big red and white *LIFE* logo on my camera bag. "What in hell's going on here?" he asked.

"That local welcoming committee has been giving me a few problems," I answered. The three stood quiet as I got into the car. Surely killing was on their minds too. We were a good way out of that town before I stuck the .45 into my camera bag.

As we sped along I told the driver what had happened. He didn't express any shock, as I had somehow expected him to do. With his eyes intensely glued to the highway, he appeared unusually calm. The terror of the moment was over, and only now, riding along, did I feel a little fright.

Los Alamos, with its uniform houses, shopping mall and supermarket, resembled a multitude of other American communities throughout America. Mothers pushed baby carriages down the clean sidewalks; children rode bicycles, skipped rope and played on grassy lawns. It was a peaceful-looking place, full of fresh air and glistening sunlight. But clusters of factory-like buildings occupying a secluded area of the small town presented a far less nonchalant presence.

A Mr. White was the official assigned to show me around these buildings. He was a rather cheerful fat man with a quick, unnerving laugh who puffed a lot as we walked. The following morning we donned hard hats, inserted earplugs and put on glasses with black lenses before entering the restricted area of one building. "Few people are allowed in here," he said, "but your magazine seems to have a lot of pull with the right people."

I agreed. As we passed through an extremely thick door a roaring noise assaulted my ears, and despite the plugs, it was nearly unbearable. Soon I was walking a short distance from awesome machines bolted into thick slabs of concrete, belching fire and flames. There was a constant, thunderous booming that was at times a little frightening. And building after building seemed to shudder with this same incessant booming. In their soundproof privacy they seemed miles from the peacefulness that reigned just a short distance away. Next came huge rooms with men working at planning boards, and the quiet was a tremendous relief. Then came the smaller private rooms where men of science sat, thinking and studying blueprints. Most men were strangers to their special intelligence; they would have been lost for a way to talk comprehensively to those scientists.

Later at lunch I casually asked Mr. White about the purpose of all those awesome machines and blueprints. He smiled, laughed one of his quick laughs. "Technological advancement." And that was all he said about them. Then he asked a question that rang a little offbeat. "What did you think of the outcome of the presidential elections?"

"Truman gave Dewey quite a rump-kicking, and I expect he deserved it."

White's brow wrinkled but he managed a smile. "Don't tell me I'm eating with a Democrat?"

I smiled. "I'm afraid you are."

His eyes twinkled behind the bifocals. "Your magazine gave Dewey a lot of help." He wagged a finger above his ham sandwich. "Dewey's a good man. He would have made a great president."

"Perhaps, but we'll never know."

Mr. White fell quiet.

"I hope I didn't spoil your lunch. Perhaps Truman will prove to be better than you expect."

"I doubt it." He paused. "He's got guts. I'll say that for him. He proved that to the Japs." Then he added quickly, "Guts is what this country needs most right now." A definite ferocity had entered his voice.

I was not totally unaware of the real purpose of all I had seen that morning. I could only stare at those fire-belching machines incredulously as I photographed them. Los Alamos was planning death for the future. Only a handful of scientists and politicians knew the full meaning of the place back in 1942—dark, terrible meanings that later made the entire universe shudder. Behind these same thick, soundproof walls, where the bombs for Hiroshima and Nagasaki were secretly in the making, death was being prepared for 100,000 Japanese.

I stayed there for nearly a month chronicling men at the machines, at blueprints, wives tending to their homes while watching their children at play through bay windows. Only when I was leaving did I look back and realize that those mothers and children didn't really know what their husbands and fathers were actually doing there.

The same military policeman drove me back to that small Texas town where I had the trouble. The three toughs were nowhere in sight. Only the small gunsmith shop sat there as a reminder.

After reaching home I thought back to that trip, and stared at myself in the mirror as one stares at something saved in a storm. The incident in Texas had been so poisonous. My wife shuddered when she saw the gun as I unpacked. "My God, what are you doing with that?"

I told her as I kept unpacking, becoming more and more agitated as I talked.

After a long silence she said, "Well, that's America for you."

Later, I called the police chief in White Plains. I wanted to turn the gun over to him. After hearing how I came about buying it, he said, "Bury it. Throw it in the river." Instead I wrapped it in newspaper and stuffed it in the uppermost part of a hall closet. Two months later I came close to using it again. Over the radio came the report of a convict's escape from a prison for the insane near Valhalla, a few miles away. The entire neighborhood was on edge, and I slept lightly that night. At three in the morning I heard someone walking down our graveled drive. I listened until the noise subsided, but shortly afterward there was a sound of glass crashing in the living room. Hurriedly I put a call through to the police, then went for the gun. The escaped man had broken out a glass panel in the door of the living room. He had stuck his arm through the opening and was attempting to open the door through the shattered panel. I switched on the porch light above him and I could see that he was bleeding profusely. He stared at me blankly, with his hand still inside the door.

"Get out of here or you're a dead man." I spoke as quietly as possible, hoping not to awaken my wife and children.

126

He withdrew his arm slowly, raised his other hand and I mistook the wrench he held for a gun. I was close to firing when two police cars with lights flashing sped into the block. He ran off through the darkness but they caught him a few minutes later. Sleep was impossible the rest of the morning, and as I lay awake I made a resolve to rid myself of that gun. For the second time I had come very close to using it.

ELEVEN

Poverty, crime, fashion, broadway shows, sports and politics were among the fifty-two stories I was assigned to during my first eighteen months at *Life.* But those special problems spawned by poverty and crime touched me more, and I dug into them with more enthusiasm. Working at them again revealed the superiority of the camera to explore the dilemmas they posed. Not that I dismissed the other assignments lightly, I just could not attach an equal amount of importance to them.

• • •

Then someone of high influence at *Life* magazine decided that I had distinguished myself, and used persuasiveness to give me the "plum" most *Life* correspondents long for—a two-year assignment to the Paris bureau.

The Paris assignment was one of my most yearned-for goals. What little time I had spent there seemed frivolous when compared with the two years ahead. Since my family would go with me, Paris, I sincerely hoped, would lift my wife from her sense of unimportance.

Happiness was the children's immediate reaction. In each one there was a joyful surge to learn French with the help of Berlitz recordings, and I felt joy in analyzing the effect the new language was having on them. Somehow they were gradually becoming more polite, and even our boisterous six-year-old son, David, was taking on charm. A suitable amount of sorrow arrived however, when it was made clear that Gypsy, Champ and Charlie, the horses, had to be sold. For Gordon Jr. especially, it was a grievous shock; he loved those horses. Now he would miss riding, feeding and caring for them.

"You'll get more horses when we come back," I said, in an attempt to console him.

"Not like them, Dad. They are special." He was right.

"Aw, let's take 'em with us," David said with his usual cockiness.

"That's stupid," his sister Toni had replied. "Don't you know they can't learn to speak French?"

"What about the car, Dad?"

"We *are* taking that for sure."

After two bustling months we had selected a good home for Bangor, the cocker spaniel, sold the horses, rented the house and bought up a lot of bathroom supplies unlikely to be found in Paris. Soft toilet tissue headed the list. Then, with half the neighborhood at the pier to see us off, we sailed. I had chosen the *Queen Mary* for a couple of reasons—it added a postscript to my first trip, then too, my wife could now see how I had really been enjoying myself while she was back home frying those potatoes.

To the family the five-day crossing was much the way I had described it to them. Only David ran into trouble on the first day out. He ate more for breakfast and lunch than the entire family consumed. It was our waiter who, during dinner, pulled David's chair back when his face took on an agonized look.

"Right this way, Master David," he said politely.

David rose unsteadily and started running. The garbage pail in the ship's galley became his destination. The next morning his appetite was as hearty as ever, and from then on there wasn't a deck on that massive ship that failed to share his presence. One day he emerged from the unknown, smeared with dirt and grease. He had taken lunch down in engine room—an exciting, throbbing world where few passengers had the audacity, or permission, to enter. And with a breeziness, he told us about the "big monster" machines that were powering the *Queen Mary* across the ocean. Despite my admonishments for taking such liberties, I secretly wished I had been with him. Departing the ship at Cherbourg, we were ushered into an area set aside for diplomats—elevated to this status through rumors I was sure David had spread. I now discovered that throughout the crossing I had been looked upon as an African prince en route to Arabia.

The gun I bought in Texas had also taken the trip, but I deposited it with customs, with the understanding that it could be reclaimed when we left the country. I had no intention of doing that.

Because of David's pleading, the car's top was down as we drove toward Paris. A disagreeable easterly wind had swept the decks as we made port, but now, two hours later, warm sun streamed through the poplars along the road, making them strangely distinct. Standing like sentinels, they seemed to be guarding the countryside. For an absurd moment my memory flashed back to a road outside Mankato, Minnesota—this brought on by the timelessness of roads throughout the universe.

We came to a large sign that confused my sense of direction, and I hailed a boy on a bicycle. *"Garçon, s'il vous plaît, la direction à Paris?"*

"À droite ici."

"Merci," I said, and turned left.

"Dad, he said *à droite!"* Toni informed me.

"I heard him. Why do you think I turned left?"

"But, Dad, *à droite* means right."

"Aha, I was just testing you, girl," I said, turning the car back in the other direction. I could feel my wife smiling.

A few miles down the road a motorcycle policeman pulled up alongside the car and motioned me to a stop; he pulled out a ticket and explained that I was speeding.

"But I don't understand French, monsieur. What did you say?"

As he stood puzzled, scratching his chin, Toni chirped up—in good French, "I'll explain to my father, monsieur." She did. The policeman patted her shoulder and handed her the ticket after writing it out. As he sped off I gave my daughter a look she would always remember.

Further on, a cloud of smoke fanned out from beneath the hood. We limped into a gas station. The mechanic immediately knew the problem; it was a very common one, I was told later. The workmen aboard the tenders often put kerosene in transmissions instead of oil—a little trick they played on tourists with fancy foreign cars.

The lights of Paris were snapping on as we reached there. Everything was smiling. We drove along the Seine, passing ornate bridges, stone walls and ancient buildings. We drove on over cobbled streets, coming at last to Avenue de la Grande Armée, proceeded for several blocks, then turned into a street in Neuilly, and there it was—7 Rue Ybry. The house, a four-story English Tudor, was easily recognizable. In my pocket was the picture of it sent to me in America. The Paris bureau had arranged for everything—even a maid and butler. The rooms were large and there were spacious hallways with venetian-marble floors and curving mahogany banisters on the stairways. The kitchen was large enough to service a small restaurant. It was a good house. Dinner had been prepared; Marie and Claude served it, and the children had their first glasses of watered-down wine. For all of us it was an auspicious beginning.

"*C'est un bateau!*"

"It's a boat!"

"*Bateau! Bateau!*"

"You're crazy! It's a boat!"

I was in the bathroom shaving when I heard the two young voices rising to a pitch. Looking from the second-story window to the sidewalk, I saw David and a boy about his age. They were having trouble trying to communicate. It was time to intervene; I

131

called them upstairs to the bathroom, and in my best French I explained to Jean Luc Brouillaud that, in English, the toy he held was called a boat. To David I explained that, in French, it was called a *bateau*. Grinning, they began an English-French game of identifying objects in the room—the floor, ceiling, even the bidet. It seemed to be in the cards; David would learn the language much quicker than any of us.

Toni and David were enrolled in a school with all French-speaking children. It was an arbitrary decision that left me somewhat concerned; even the instructors couldn't speak English. Part of me felt it might be an intolerable situation I was putting them in; the other part advised that they would certainly learn much quicker. Their minds were young and agile. There was hardly a choice for Gordon Jr. Approaching sixteen, his mind-set was already too firmly bedded in his mother tongue. To have been instantly plunged into French translations of algebra, science, mathematics or other demanding subjects would have proven disastrous for him. So he was sent to the American School, where French was also taught.

The Paris bureau, overlooking the sprawling Place de la Concorde, served as the principal headquarters for *Life*'s foreign correspondents. From different parts of the world they flew in, snatched a few hours of Paris and flew off again. David Douglas Duncan, Bob Capa, Chim and others I didn't know, roamed the office, talked out their experiences, picked up money or supplies and took off. It was an unpretentious, sparsely furnished place with a relatively small staff. John Boyle, an affable Irishman, headed the *Time* bureau. John Jenkinson was the *Life* chief. The reporters were Lee Eitingon, Dita Camacho, Dodie Hamblin and Natalie Kotchoubey, a descendant of Napoleon Bonaparte. Dmitri Kessel and Nat Farbman were the other photographers. It was an uncommonly resilient staff, held in high regard for its coverage throughout Europe. For me, it was a rather secure sanctuary for learning; everyone extended help and friendship. Yet, caught up in family responsibilities, the others mostly kept to their separate worlds, and I admit to eventually doing the same.

I needed Paris. It was a feast, a grand carnival of imagery, and immediately everything good there seemed to offer sublimation to those inner desires that had for so long been hampered by racism back in America. For the first time in my life I was relaxing from tension and pressure. My thoughts, continually rampaging against racial conditions, were suddenly becoming as peaceful as snow-flakes. Slowly a curtain was dropping between me and those soiled years.

Paris became my beautiful mistress, seducing me with Bach, Mozart and Brahms, Proust, Sartre, Camus and others I hadn't bothered to stop and listen to. Usually, with Gordon Jr. or Toni, I attended concerts or visited museums on weekends—pointing out Degas, Braque, Bonnard, Picasso, Van Gogh, Chagall and other masterful painters. It was gratifying to see my children gaze with childlike absorption into every painting. Perhaps I was reacting against the intellectual voids of my own childhood, but I wanted them to know that they now stood in the presence of a grand past —one that had survived the Huns, the Hundred Years War, the English, the Black Death, the Prussians, countless revolutions and two world wars—and that the space between it and Fort Scott, Kansas, was very wide.

I sat at tables in Café des Deux Magots on the Left Bank, where Balzac or Baudelaire might have sat. I haunted the tree-lined quais along the Seine, the marbled bridges and open-air book stalls. I walked the Rue de la Paix, Place Vendôme and Montmartre, high above the city in the shadows of Sacré-Coeur, to look down upon the classical age of Molière, seeing Notre-Dame where Napoleon I was crowned emperor. I was moving through centuries of history, and not unaware of the possibility of its help in shaping my future. Being a part of it was like feeling at once young and old.

I confess to have not always taken a camera along on these sublime excursions. But my mind was following another seductress—poetry. Twice on one afternoon it told me, quietly and enticingly, that when I was seriously indulging myself in it, there was no need for a camera. Walking along rue Boissy d'Anglas in a drizzle, I watched two young lovers rush toward one another. Falling into a passionate embrace they stood kissing, and remained so for several minutes while, just a few feet away a news vendor shouted, *"Le gouvernement fout le camp encore!"* Then ignoring the drizzle, and their government's fate, they passed the vendor and moved off toward the Seine—still kissing, still stopping every few feet to embrace.

The afternoon was turning to dusk. At a corner a few blocks away stood an older man and woman. Seeming directionless, they gazed blankly into a puddle of water at their feet. Her face bore a troubled look, with the lips twisted upward at one side. She wore a baggy black coat. The fur on its collar was worn and, like her gray hair, slick from the drizzle.

The man, grimy, thin and sunken into himself, rocked from side to side. His khaki leftover from some past war had obviously been issued to someone much larger, and his shoes looked to have taken shape from another pair of feet. He stood with his ankles close together, rocking as though his heels were weighted with lead. I hesitated, observing them too closely and too long; and their eyes lifted to stare at me. Then strangely they turned and, for a few seconds, stared at one another. Hurrying on, I had a dim feeling that their snickering was meant solely for me. Two small moments with such disparate meanings; yet both with the makings of poetry. No camera could have captured the romantic or satirical implications of either one. From then on if I was without a camera, I was sure to be carrying a diary. Two weeks later I rented a piano and bought a typewriter; two natural instincts bottled up inside me, verse and musical composition, were asking for freedom. Somehow I would have to accommodate the urging although I had been sent to Paris for far different reasons.

"Paris est toujours une ville en grève!" our butcher complained one morning. He was right; it was a city of strikes. It seemed there was one every day. That afternoon the Communists disrupted the city with a massive shutdown of the transportation system. Strikers filled the avenues and boulevards and the dreaded *Compagnie Républicaine Sécurité* was called out to assist the police. Photographers gave those particular *gendarmes* distance and respect, and instead of going in close we used our long lenses when the head-beating was given with truncheons and capes, which were lined with lead. Many members of the *Sécurité* were also members of the party, and didn't like being photographed roughing up fellow members. Jacques Leland, a young Belgian photographer, was showing his bravery during the height of the violence that ensued. He kept going in too close despite our warnings, and the third

time a cape caught his ankle and tripped him up. He scrambled back to safety, but the fourth time a truncheon smashed in his face and he went down screaming. He was a bloody mess when we dragged him back into our ranks. It was too late. His right eye hung on a string of skin dangling over the crushed cheekbone. Crying and cursing, he did something I will never forget. He tore the eye loose and flung it toward the *gendarmes.*

Having been sent hurriedly into Europe I knew little of what history had left behind there. What I did know had been gleaned from newsprint and hearsay. But before long I realized it suffered social, economic and political problems akin to those in America. Lingering also in its present and past were heroes, royal families, traitors and certain dictators who had got on with their dirty work. Some, having indulged heavily in brutality, arrogance and greed, had fled pageantry and pomp to hole up in exile. Taking substantial amounts of their country's wealth, a few were still living out their enforced leisure in loneliness and disgrace. Others, whom luck deserted, languished in prisons. My assignments took me into the presence of several of them. The first was handed to me three days after the collapse of the violent strike in Paris.

Natalie Kotchoubey and I flew to Estoril, Portugal, a tropical resort-like place alongside the sea. Natalie, the daughter of a baron and a princess in her own right, and I were being sent to find and photograph a gathering of deposed monarchs and would-be rulers who had fled their countries to live in luxurious exile. They were a wealthy, spiritless group—King Carol of Romania and his mistress, Madame Magda Lupescu; King Humbert of Italy; the Hungarian admiral and statesman Nicholas de Nagybanya Horthy; Don Juan de Bourbon, pretender to the Spanish throne and several others of less importance.

Finding them wasn't as difficult as we had imagined. Carol spent most of his time at a private shooting range slaughtering doves while Lupescu sat on their spacious veranda knitting, eating bonbons and arranging elegant parties. Humbert II was usually at his beautifully appointed mansion on a rocky knoll above the sea working on his memoirs. Don Juan, an excellent golfer, could be found most of the day on Estoril's private course. Horthy spent long hours in his Rube Goldberg-like laboratory doodling at outrageous inventions that neither he, nor anyone else, would find use for. If we were unable to find some notable at home, Natalie discreetly left her *petit* calling card, and the next morning the door magically opened.

Such high living was in bitter contrast to that of the impoverished Portuguese people who surrounded them. For a small pittance some royal households employed up to ten servants whose pay hardly proved substantial for even one. Beggars were plentiful and homeless children roamed the streets and beaches. Even the landed gentry were finding it hard to make ends meet. Rich with inherited land, they could find nothing to work to their advantage. Crops and industries were failing and dwindling herds of cattle roamed the spacious ranches in hunger. Only glorious memories of the past inhabited their days. Antonio de Oliveira Salazar, a ruthless dictator himself, had taken in the royal exiles while leaving his own countrymen in dire straits. He spent most of his time and energy, along with government funds, putting down rebellions in Portugal's African colonies, where the native population had suffered for many years under that government's rule.

Salazar's inscribed portrait was prominently displayed in the splendor of King Carol's living room, and in those of the other exiles as well—except for that of Don Juan. The relationship between him and the dictator was obviously wobbly. Carol and Lupescu, always elegantly attired, appeared to be a pleasant enough couple, and they always showed up at the fox hunts, at which foxes were glaringly absent. All the others would be there as well, appropriately outfitted, mounted on sleek horses—living out the fanciful illusion of the hunt. Carol also seemed gracious and gentle. It was difficult to associate him with the infamous assassinations and massacres that took place during his dictatorship and the fascist Iron Guard that eventually opposed him. His other side emerged now only when he was joyfully murdering doves. After bringing down one he would smile contentedly and hand his gun to an aid for reloading. Watching the birds burst apart and flutter to earth always upset me. To me it was useless slaughter and it had seemed so throughout my childhood. Then, the only bird I would aim my BB gun at were the huge hawks that swooped down to steal our chickens. It might seem a bit ridiculous but even now I will let a fly or bug escape into the open—with the thought that it might have a family waiting somewhere.

Unlike Carol, Humbert II was extremely uncommunicative. Answering questions dryly, he never elaborated or explained. He appeared morose, somber and secretive, and obviously he was longing for his throne, which he had occupied for just a short time after his father, Victor Emmanuel, abdicated. He yearned in vain; Italy was through with kings. But I came to admire Don Juan and his family for their openness and warmth. He seemed to be the only exile working at something other than gaining another kingdom. A younger daughter who was blind studied the piano, and at times we played for each other. She had a capacity for seeing beyond her blindness, speaking at times about the sound of birds, or the beauty of her surroundings, as though she actually saw them. During such moments my thoughts flew back to my uncle Jim, who was blind too but always seemed to see the beauty of things despite his sightlessness. As I led him about, with my hand in his, he taught me things about nature that eluded my own eyes. One June day as we walked across a field he astounded me by saying, "The cornflowers must be beautiful in all the green around here." They were, I remember, very beautiful. Somehow I felt that Don Juan's blind, sensitive daughter had found happiness where fate had sent her father, and that he would defend that happiness by remaining where she seemed so content.

Peace and contentment had deserted the aging Admiral Horthy forever and his mind was rambling toward insanity. One afternoon, standing amid an awesome array of glass tubing, bottles, chemicals and beakers, he abruptly stopped his tinkering and began mumbling his thoughts about the First World War and the time he commanded the Austro-Hungarian fleet. Repeatedly pounding his fists against the wall, he damned Béla Kun. "The scoundrel! The scoundrel! He's the one who stole my power in Hungary! What an outright bastard he was!" Stopping for a moment, he went to gaze blankly out the window. Then he went back to his bottles, vigorously shaking the contents of one to a meaningless foam, mumbling again. "But the scoundrel got what was coming to him. Deserved every bit of it." Then he was up from his workbench suddenly, strutting about with his fat hands on his bulging hips. "But it was me, mind you, me, who kept that foul Emperor Charles from regaining his throne. And the whole empire was thankful to me for that." He stood shaking his head as if reliving his trials. "Ah, but how soon people forget. How soon they forget." He returned once more to his workbench. "With him gone I put myself in a terrible fix. With him gone I was a regent of a confounded country without a king." He paused for several moments. "You're an American no doubt."

"I am," I answered.

"Americans. Ah yes, Americans." He smiled rougishly. "It was the Americans who saved me from the damned Nazis." He got up slowly and went to lie down on a couch. Then he was asleep, snoring loudly as we departed.

With our assignment finished Natalie and I took the morning plane back to Paris. From the air I looked down at Estoril, falling rapidly behind. In the sunny solitude of white houses were the splendid homes of the exiles. I could think of the place only as a royal morgue nestled into a sweep of white sand beside the sea. For the once-crowned heads, Estoril, with its genteel boredom, plush balls, lavish parties and make-believe fox hunts, appeared to be their last fling at a good life. They were still bluebloods after all —but turning gray and wrinkled while swapping memories and hanging on to meaningless titles.

On July 16, 1951, King Leopold III of Belgium yielded his throne after prolonged pressure from leftist and liberal parties, and I was sent to cover the occasion. That morning, along the broad avenue facing the palace, crowds of Belgians, some crying, others rejoicing, jostled one another as they awaited the appearance of the fallen monarch and his son, Baudouin, who would ascend the throne. When they strode out together a great cheer went up. Leopold smiled weakly, waving. Baudouin, sensing that he was losing the freedom of his youth, stood unsmiling but with the erectness born to kings. And Leopold was probably wondering how he had failed Belgium during its occupation by the Nazis.

He had led his troops bravely. It was only after defense became impossible that he—over the opposition of his cabinet—surrendered unconditionally and thus provoked an accusation of treason. With my camera trained on his profile I saw the strain; the lines that had set in while he was a prisoner. Surely the smile frozen on his face belied the bitterness that was in his heart. He was no longer Lord of the Royal House, or master of the Lowlands, or the Belgian Congo. Yet there must have been some virtue in the relief. From then on it would be his son's business to worry about the rising tide of African nationalism. I wondered if he, like his father, would continue the exploitation and abuse; if he even knew or cared about it. It was hard to tell as he stood there in the depth of such fervent ceremony. At times he looked to have just awakened to a dream, not knowing where he was. It was understandable; so few young men faced such responsibility.

A week later I watched as Marshal Henri Philippe Pétain was buried on the bleak isle of Yeu. He had been jailed there since 1945 after being sentenced to death for collaborating with the Nazis. De Gaulle had later commuted the sentence to life imprisonment. His wife, heavily veiled and broken with grief, the local mayor, a long procession of curious townspeople and a few stray dogs followed the coffin up a winding road to the edge of the village. It was an unheroic farewell to the once lavishly decorated hero who had stopped the Germans at Verdun in 1916, and had once served France as her Premier. There were no praiseful words; no French flag to drape his coffin; no sounding of bugles or rifle fire as he was lowered beside other unhonored dead—only a few consoling words from an aged priest who could do nothing more than advise the widow to keep her own life moving.

I remained at the burial site until everyone was gone except two gravediggers. They finished their lunch and then as if to show contempt for the traitor—tossed scraps and an empty wine bottle in beside the coffin. Now the discarded hero would be left to rot.

Time buys experience, and I wasn't yet finished with the complexities of royalty. Several weeks later Natalie Kotchoubey and I were traveling again—this time by car with three mannequins to the resort town of Biarritz near the Spanish border. There, for their more prestigious clients, the *haute couture* were giving the Napoleon III ball. I was to cover that, then get on with a fashion assignment with the mannequins. The Duke and Duchess of Windsor headed the list of guests; King Farouk of Egypt with his infamous entourage of women and henchmen would also attend—thus creating a social problem for the Duke and Duchess, who loathed him. Several miles outside of Biarritz there came a sudden blast of automobile horns. Then, from our rear, ten limousines roared down upon us, forcing our car off the road. King Farouk was on his way. Farther ahead an injured horse lay beside the cart it had been pulling, and an old man, a hit-and-run victim, stood waving a stick at the vanishing fleet.

We had just settled into our suite when the concierge came to inform us that we would have to move to another floor. The king wanted only his party on the floor we had been assigned. Remembering the ditching Farouk had given us, I refused despite the concierge's pleading, and Natalie, the mannequins and myself went to refresh ourselves at the lounge. When we returned an hour later our rooms were in great disarray. Clothes were on the floor and every drawer had been emptied.

Furious, I went to complain to the manager. He listened with little patience and made a telephone call. Soon I was confronted by an Irishman and two squat Egyptian strongmen. The Irishman extended his hand, palm up. It held the cartridges from the gun I had bought en route to Los Alamos. I had failed to leave them, along with the gun, behind in Cherbourg. Unpacked, they had been found in one of my bags.

"These yours?" he asked coldly.

"You should know since you ransacked our rooms—and I'm damned mad about it."

He ignored my anger. "What part of Egypt are you from?"

"What makes you think I'm from Egypt?"

"What part?" His anger was rising.

A clerk came, handed him my hotel registration card; he read it and observed me skeptically. "You're with *Life* magazine?"

"That's what it says."

"What's your boss's name?"

"Which one. I've got several."

"The top one."

"Henry Luce. Happen to know him?"

"I was brought up in New York. Where's the gun?"

"That's my business."

"Right now it's *my* business."

"Then take care of it the best way you can."

He nodded to the strongmen. I stood rigid as they patted me down. They nodded back negatively and the three of them started off. "How about my cartridges?"

"Since you don't have a gun you won't be needing them. You'll get them back after we've left. My apologies for your rooms. We must be careful." Knowing the widespread dislike for his boss, I understood his concern. Our party remained on the floor, but an armed guard was posted down the hall from our quarters.

· · ·

140

At the banquet that night Farouk indulged in some of the antics that had brought disfavor upon him. He kept pelting the bare back of an Englishwoman with small chunks of bread. Angered, her husband finally got up and charged the King's table—only to be manhandled back to his seat. When I tried to record the incident with a wide-angle lens, two strongmen placed themselves in front of my camera.

The Duke and Duchess dined elsewhere. At the ball they kept to a small anteroom until Farouk's party left.

The months sped by. In between assignments I worked on poetry and getting the feel of the piano I had rented. There was also a piano in our house in the south of France, and I spent two glowing summers there with my family. The children especially loved nearby St. Tropez with its *petit* carnivals and colorful waterfront, and we had picnics in the wooded area above the town during weekends, and took motor trips along the beach at Cannes. Then up the winding road toward home, inhaling the aroma of bread baking and *parfum* wafting from the hillside factories. For me there were tennis courts in the rear of Cannes's renowned Hotel Carlton—a holstery for royalty and movieland's celebrities.

It was there, on these courts, where I had a more personal encounter with Farouk. He had been watching from his hotel window as I played with the tennis coach. A telephone ring interrupted us, and he came back with a message that both amused and intrigued me. His Majesty was requesting a set with me. I agreed. Ten minutes later he came—with two bodyguards, a half-dozen embossed towels, four rackets, and a large carafe of white wine packed in ice.

His Majesty weighed close to three hundred pounds and his expensive white flannel shorts seemed to have been tailored by a tent-maker. As he chose a racket a bodyguard mumbled to me, "His Majesty dislikes running too hard. Try to keep the balls in the center of the court."

"Oh?" I said, remembering his treatment of me at the hotel in Biarritz.

Farouk nodded at me. I nodded back, thinking that this was his way of acknowledging my presence. When he nodded again I realized he was ordering me to the far side of the court. He didn't want the sun in his eyes.

Either I wasn't good enough to keep the balls in the center of the court, or maybe I kept thinking back to Biarritz. After puffing for a few sharp crosscourt shots, he stopped abruptly, downed some wine and headed for his suite without as much as another nod. The following day, Dino, the coach, presented me with a racket. The note attached read simply: "From His Royal Highness, King Farouk of Egypt." A rather puzzling postscript read, "Learn to control your *balls.*" The present still languishes in my hall closet.

Paris was in December's embrace when I arrived back there from Cannes. And another strike was in full force; this time the heat was off. The bureau had obtained permission for me to photograph the Duchess of Windsor selecting her spring wardrobe at Elsa Schiaparelli's salon, but even the Duchess was suffering from the cold when I arrived. As she reclined on a satin chaise longue, her legs were being warmed by a great mink lap robe. Schiaparelli fawned over her as the mannequins pranced back and forth showing the fashions. The shoes were shown by a mannequin who was making her first appearance. Motioning at her Schiaparelli said, "She's ugly as sin, but have you ever seen such gorgeous legs and feet?"

"Beautiful," replied the Duchess.

The mannequin, who couldn't understand English, smiled graciously, most happy that Her Highness seemed pleased.

Later that afternoon I nearly cost Comtesse Maxine de la Falaise her lovely Right Bank apartment. I was photographing her in an adjoining apartment that belonged to the building's owner. There were candles in the wall chandeliers, and to enhance the mood I lit them. We were nearly finished when the owner arrived and found her candles burning. Running to extinguish them, she burst into a tirade, threatning to sue *Life*—and eject the startled Comtesse from her suite. It took a carton of new candles and a couple of days of cajoling to smooth matters out. It seemed there was still a shortage of candles in Paris.

TWELVE

My grateful feeling at the absence of racial bigotry in Paris soon received a jolt. A black friend due to arrive from the States had asked me to find him an apartment, preferably near our place in Neuilly. An advertisement in *Paris Presse* seemed to fit his needs and I telephoned the number listed for inquiries.

"*Oui,* monsieur. The apartment is vacant and you will find it very nice."

"Fine, I'll be there in a few minutes."

"*Oui.* I'll be expecting you. My name is Madame Defoe."

Madame Defoe blanched when she opened the door to me.
"Oui, can I help you?"

"I'm the gentleman who called about the apartment."

"But—but, monsieur, it—it is already taken."

"Taken? And in less than twenty minutes, madame? Obviously you are mistaken or lying."

She was quiet for several moments, seeming anguished. "Monsieur, I'll have to admit to that, but do come in. I want to explain myself." She took me through the house to stop at a window overlooking a garden. There, playing in a sandbox, was a dark-skinned child. With tears welling in her eyes, she pointed at him. "He is my daughter's son who I keep through the day, and I love him dearly. But white Americans who live here are from the American embassy—and they pay me a good sum, but they warn me that if I let black people move in they will move out. Monsieur, I'm a widow, and I just can't afford that."

"All from the embassy?"

"Most of them."

I faced once more the bitterness of American bigotry and I left as she poured out her apologies. I didn't relish calling about another apartment that was also advertised. But when I reached it the man awaiting me had a welcoming smile. I inspected the place, gave him an advance and, with that grateful feeling intact again, I left.

Toni came home from school one Wednesday in a snit saying she wasn't going back because of a book that a teacher assigned her class to read. When I read the passage that offended her I agreed. Published in England, it referred to American blacks as "darkies" and "pickaninnies." I confronted the headmaster and explained why neither David nor Toni was at school. He expressed shock and immediately banned the book from class. It had never occurred to me that Toni could express such rage; and I was proud of her reaction when bigotry touched her small universe.

Gordon Jr. didn't fare as well when he bolted class at the American School and came home to complain that his French teacher was working him too hard. "What's more," he bragged, "I told her where to get off." I marched him back to school and instructed the teacher to double his load and find punishment suitable to his behavior. Being a rather sensible young man, he avoided any further discussion about being overworked.

Being black in Europe had remarkably little to do with how I was accepted, but one evening a few moments of confusion did come about because of my black ancestry. Todd Webb, a white American friend, and I were drinking wine at a bar in a Left Bank bistro. A bearded man—having lifted one too many—barged into our conversation. Introducing himself as Boris, he spoke to Todd in a thick Russian accent. "Why do you drink with this black man here in France and not in America?"

We eyed him skeptically as Todd answered him. "Not only have my friend and I eaten together in America, we have slept at one another's homes. Perhaps that should tell you something."

Boris wasn't buying that. Turning on me, he asked if I had experienced the same intolerance in Europe that existed against me in the United States. I said with honesty that I hadn't. My answer revved up his attack on Todd. "Ah, did you hear that?"

"But I agree with him completely," Todd answered.

"Then you admit that white Americans hate blacks?"

Suddenly I had found myself defending and damning America at the same time. Boris was becoming a bore. "Listen. You have good people here and you have bad people here. It's the same in my country. My friend here happens to be one of the good people. Now if you don't mind—"

"My friend, if you choose to defend the murderers of your people, then you can do so. *Bon soir!*" he bellowed, and stalked off. Todd and I remained silent for a few moments, then ordered two more brandies.

Richard Wright, the distinguished black writer, had been invited by the French Government to move his family to Paris. Exasperated by rocks shattering his windows when he and his white wife bought into a white neighborhood, he had accepted. I couldn't help but wonder if it wasn't his being immersed in the Southern fear that had driven him to become such a powerful writer. Would Europe soften him; douse the fire that had for so long compelled him? A fixed protagonist against bigotry, his text for the book *Twelve Million Black Voices* spoke with such power and eloquence about this country's mistreatment of blacks few whites who read it could escape their conscience. In Washington during 1942 that book had become my catechism, telling me that I was at the cross-roads; that voices were rising and black men were moving forward —and that I should be moving with them.

Psychologically, Wright was obsessed with fear, fascinated with it. It had been the thread weaving through his most forceful works. It seemed to have led him to an understanding of the forces that create hatred and strife. And there had been plenty of both in Natchez and the smaller towns alongside the Mississippi River where he had spent most of his childhood.

I telephoned him one morning to ask him out to lunch.

"That would be fine."

"Where would you like to go?"

After giving several moments of thought to that he chuckled and replied, "To Maxim's."

Sure that he was joking, I chuckled as well, but he was quite serious, and I admit to being mildly shocked, having pictured myself with him at some Left Bank bistro that I thought would be more to his liking.

Before hanging up he said, "Forgive me my choice, but just for once, and no more, I want to see what that fancy joint is really like." I called and made reservations. The prices there didn't fit my pocketbook but this lunch would, for me, be very special. It would be shared with an individual whom I sincerely admired.

Maxim's was filled with the rich and famous. Next to our table sat Rita Hayworth and Aly Khan, the wealthy prince. Having met Hayworth, I introduced Richard to her, and she spoke with high praise of his most famous novel, *Native Son*. An extremely modest man, he seemed surprised to know that she had even heard of him. As we ate he watched everyone in his sight; listened to the chattering with an intense curiosity. When I picked up the check he insisted upon seeing it. Then, shaking his head, he said, "Good Lord, I could feed my family for a month for that." He had seen enough. "Come, my friend. There's a good little bistro on the Left Bank I frequent—and it's got some very good cheap wine."

There, I spent the first half hour with him talking about those ordinary things two black Americans talk about in a foreign land— the differences in people, food and economics, family and work. By now the wine had warmed us, loosened us up. "Richard," I said, "the very first thing I read of yours was *Uncle Tom's Children*, and I enjoyed it."

146

"So much rubbish," he answered gloomily. "It was naive, a mistake, a terrible mistake. A white slave owner's daughter could have read it, wept with guilt and felt her soul was thoroughly cleansed. But I learned after that. One has to write cold and hard about black life in America and not allow whites to face the words with the consolation of a few tears."

"You couldn't have found a better teacher than Mississippi."

He emptied his glass. I emptied mine and we ordered more wine. "Mississippi, my friend, was a brute. It killed and still kills blacks by the thousands. Killing blacks is a part of its grandeur and cotton is still God down there. All I had to fall back on, to save me, was constant fear, and that left so many black people helpless. Yes, sir, I learned how to live Jim Crow down there, to fear whites and, most importantly, keep away from them. As a kid I watched my father sharecropping his life away—and on some of the richest land in America. We lived under white hatred and I was educated by it. That's why I wanted so desperately to write about it. I didn't want to just write ordinary books, but something akin to bombs." For a moment there was a strained silence. "Have you read *Native Son?*"

"Several times, and I have never quite understood the character Bigger Thomas. He puzzles me."

He put his wine down, turned and gazed out at the Seine, far beyond it probably and into the past. "I could not have written *Native Son* without Bigger. When I was a kid I knew several Biggers, and none of them seemed to have any fear inside them. The white bosses always called them 'bad niggers,' because they wouldn't kowtow to them. 'I'll kill that goddam nigger one of these days,' they would say. And more often than not they did. I was scared of one of those Biggers myself. He was big, tough and a little crazy, and kept his foot in my behind—always damning me for not standing up to the whites. 'You're already dead, boy, so what you so a'feared of? That white man's gonna have to kill me all over again. I'm not takin' his shit.' Richard smiled, remembering that particular Bigger. "You know I secretly admired that guy. He was crazy but, man, he had guts."

Curiously interested in my reaction to Europe, he wanted to know if I, like he, had considered staying on, giving up on America altogether. My thoughts about that stood clarified. "No, never. I've too much at stake back there. You've done your bit, now I

147

have to go back and do mine." Then, looking into my wine, I added, "Black people are on the move back there, and I want to be moving with them." He smiled, knowing I was quoting Richard Wright from *Twelve Million Black Voices*. I hoped I had pleased him.

We left the bistro and walked across the Pont Neuf, and as we walked he said rather fleetingly, "You know, Gordon, the substantial differences between black and white folk are not so much blood and color. I truly feel that it is what they both hope for that will bring a stronger kinship than any words or lawful legislation." I had no immediate answer to that. I could only hope he was right.

When we reached the Right Bank he hailed a taxi, and I was never to see him again. He died a year later. The little time I did have with him seems suspended, and I remember it over and over again—along with the power of his words when, during my first days in Washington, they had nudged me toward a more diligent use of my camera. I have had cause, too, to be mindful of the inscription he penned in my daughter Toni's copy of his *Black Boy*. Bearing a lifetime of his experience, it says simply, "Freedom belongs to the strong."

After years of gazing into the past, I realize that I did very little during those first months in Europe to persuade my wife that Paris wasn't her natural enemy. It is rather late to realize that, in certain ways, she felt even more insecure. She was living far away from close friends in, what was to her, a strange land with a strange language. Moreover, my assignments kept me away for long intervals, leaving her to cope with three children with problems far more intricate than those they faced back in White Plains. And their problems became her problems. Instructing a child how to, in English, explain something to a teacher who only spoke French wasn't easy. Planning menus with Marie, the maid, who didn't speak a word of English must have been just as difficult. Then there was the ever-puzzling value of the franc, which was as changeable as the weather. No doubt at times she felt defenseless against such odds. Coming home to listen to her frettings led me to think that perhaps she was simply inventing problems for herself, or maybe I just preferred to think so. In any case it was my choice to try to understand her or not. In hindsight it appears that I chose the latter, and for her the most trivial things continued to translate themselves into major annoyances. Our butcher didn't improve matters by lifting his hat and bidding her good morning from a *pissoir.* Sally just couldn't bear the idea of Frenchmen relieving themselves in public. The maid was adding to the problems. She was suspected of pocketing francs given to her for shopping.

"A normal custom with French maids," I reminded her. "Furthermore she gets much better bargains at the market than you could. Forget it. She's a fine cook and an excellent housekeeper."

One evening Sally talked seriously about her wish to design hats. Such a desire could not be taken lightly, and the next morning found me at Dior consulting with Suzanne Luling, a woman with many contacts in the fashion industry. Within a few days Sally was hired as an apprentice to a good hatmaker just off Rue St. Honoré. Within the first month Suzanne called me to say that Sally's talent for designing was being recognized.

Such praise from Monsieur Debouchet, the chief designer at the establishment, was somewhat astounding. I hoped my wife was making a niche for herself in the fashion world, yet I dared not say much about it because our marriage had become a rather baleful situation. Nevertheless I did encourage her, and she continued to work there and to flourish until the house closed down for summer vacation. Only then did I move her and the children to the vacation house near Cannes. With them settled in I returned to Paris. I felt content with them there on a hillside flowering with fruit orchards, smothered in pink bougainvillea, and overlooking the Mediterranean. The house came with an Italian housekeeper who was also a fine cook. Taken along were sufficient supplies to enrich Sally's ideas for new designs. All this, I was now certain, would coax the still hovering insecurity out of her.

I did little more than stare at the handsome new piano I had rented, but my thoughts were still on some piano concertos by two Russian composers who had recently seized my imagination. I had not met either of them, but like Prokofiev, I had a mother who, like Maria Grigoryevna, devoted her energies to her son. I had once seen Rachmaninoff in the late 1940s when during a snowstorm he walked against a red light on Fifth Avenue. I had rammed my car into the curb to keep from striking him. He had walked on into the traffic seeming not to sense the danger he was in.

• • •

But doubt reminded me that without formal training I should perhaps leave piano concertos alone. But the long presence of my mother's past advice came snapping in. "There's hardly anything you can't do if you're willing to try hard enough." Remembering such reassuring advice helped me put optimism to work. After several weeks I had devised an intricate mathematical system for using numbers that corresponded to notes—allowing me to establish themes and harmonic structures. Rachmaninoff and Prokofiev would have probably frowned with disdain, but circumstance had willed me a different set of rules. A tape recording of my first efforts convinced me that those rules were working, and I began composing with confidence.

The first real encouragement of my ability to compose came from a man who was well respected in the world of classical music. Dean Dixon, a fine conductor—but black and therefore unacceptable to America's large symphony orchestras—had given up on America and come to Europe to work. Here his performances were receiving outstanding notices and attention. Upon hearing my tapes, he promised to perform my "concerto" whenever I finished it. I was startled. Vivian, his wife, and a fine pianist, shared his enthusiasm. She anguished at my fingering, wondered how I did everything so awkwardly and made it sound right.

"It's far too late for you to start studying formally," Dean advised me. "You are already doing what you would only be taught to do—harmony, form, counterpoint, melody and cohesiveness. It's all there. And someone can be found to assist you with the final construction." Dean and Vivian were leaving Paris for a concert tour—and leaving me with newly found inspiration. And alone now with that shot in the arm, I was ready to seriously do something about it.

A week later there came a letter from Vienna where Dean was conducting: "Besides continuing your composing, I think you should start out on a planned listening program. Choosing a very few excellent works but listening to them dozens of times. I know that it sounds like a quite impossible thing but it really can be done and done very simply. For example, you get the work on a tape or record. After taking it home your very first listening to it is with you sitting together with it in a room, just the two of you, and your giving it a *very* hard listening-to, trying to learn as much about it as you possibly can, and trying to understand as much of it as possible. Then I would immediately take a second listening, but during this one I would start doing something else: make a telephone call, talk to Sally or one of the kids, sort pictures, read a book or magazine, have a meal, etc. Do anything you want to as long as you are within hearing distance of the music. And for the next 10 or 20 times, listen to it in this fashion. Painting would be an excellent 'other-thing-to-do' in this way. For your 21st listening, you go into the room *alone* with the music again and try listening again as hard as possible. Then, for the 22nd to the 40th, listening while doing other things, then coming back around the 41st time to the concentrated listening again.

"You see, Gordon, what we are trying to do here is to get you as conversant with the masters of our craft as you are with the popular boys. . . . The main thing you want from the big boys is *form.* We shall see where it goes from there. Thus, I would suggest as a starter something like Haydn's Clock Symphony, or the Beethoven 3rd, or the Ravel Daphnis and Chloé Suite No. 2, or the Mozart Symphony No. 40—any of these will be good.

"Oh, yes, I forgot to mention to you where I come in on this 'listening' picture with you. I am the guy who sneaks in on the 13th or 25th or 61st listening and asks you questions.

"It is really too bad that you are in Paris while I am in Vienna. Best regards to all, and keep looking like you did the other night; man, you really looked fine, as the boys would say. Dean."

It was a letter so inspiring that I could only stare at it, read it over and stare at it again. All my life I had been waiting for such a letter. It excused all my excuses; it was time to go shopping for records.

There was another letter that day—a very short one from E. Simms Campbell, the noted illustrator for *Esquire* magazine. He was bitterly concerned about a wrathful term that was growing rapidly in America—"McCarthyism." He had good cause. Joseph McCarthy, a senator from Wisconsin, was on a relentless hunt for Communists, who, he declared, were infiltrating the country. Even the State Department had been accused of harboring some. McCarthy's charges against the State Department were dismissed by a senate subcommittee, but he was still going about repeating his claims in radio and television appearances. Challenged to produce evidence, he refused and made new accusations. Simply, he was exploiting the public's fear of of the Soviets. At widely publicized hearings, he was bringing in unidentified informers who, through reckless accusations and flimsy evidence, were ruining distinguished careers.

The letter also included clippings of the Julius Rosenberg espionage case. After a trial that lasted twenty-three days, he and his wife, Ethel, had been found guilty of giving classified military information to the Soviet Union. Now they were to die in the electric chair during April of 1951. Their conviction had seemed to fit neatly into Joe McCarthy's scheming.

E. Simms was highly amused by the UFO scare that was sweeping the country. Many Americans were seriously considering the possibility of an invasion from some distant planet. There was also a snapshot of his daughter, Elizabeth Ann, who was about Toni's age. Elizabeth was already showing signs of becoming a great beauty. The photograph, and the letter, were placed beside Dean Dixon's letter.

Sally and the children were still in the south of France, and I had been sleeping late when Marie knocked at my door. "A man called for Madame, but I couldn't understand his name. I told him you were sleeping and he left a number for you to call."

Monsieur Debouchet's name sprang to my mind. I got up, showered, dressed leisurely and put in a call to him. He had called to say he wished to give Sally a chance to design the spring collections. Excited, I hurriedly telephoned her to pass on the good news. There was a peculiar silence on the other end.

"Are you there, Sally?"

"Yes—I'm here. I'm just thinking it over."

I answered with restrained patience. "Thinking it over? With such news you should already be packing."

"I'm very satisfied down here. The kids are enjoying themselves, and I think it's best that we stay here for the rest of the summer."

"Do you realize what this could mean to you?"

"Perhaps you don't realize how much being here means to me."

Then for several moments I was silent. "Okay, Sally, I'll call Debouchet and give him your answer. Say hello to the kids. Talk to you later." Baffled, I hung up. Then came the urge to fly down there and force her back, but that urge dissolved into a shrug. I called Debouchet, and with her "profoundest regrets," thanked him.

Sally and I never spoke about designing hats again. Providence seemed to be playing a game of cat and mouse with us, giving a pound of one thing while taking away a pound of another. It was all being weighed up and charged to our life accounts, and at times trying to keep the books straight was confusing.

In between assignments I lost myself in composing. By mid-September I had recorded the main themes of a four-movement concerto on the piano and sent my efforts on to Henry Brant, a composer living in New York. At Dean's suggestion I had prevailed upon him to help me with the overall construction. Our plan was to complete the orchestration when I returned to America.

THIRTEEN

The winter of 1950 had arrived amid news of General Dwight Eisenhower's takeover as supreme commander of the Allied forces in Europe. When he set up headquarters in Paris, Dodie Hamblin, a reporter in our bureau, and I were assigned there. Having been selected to take his official portrait, I hurriedly gathered the proper equipment.

"You have exactly ten minutes," a young major curtly informed me when I arrived.

"That's hardly enough time to set up the lights."

He was firm. "That's it. Just five minutes more would wreck his schedule for the entire day."

To my dismay, Eisenhower spent the first seven minutes asking about the equipment and inspecting the camera.

Just as I was about to begin, the door opened. The major stood there, his eyes informing me that my time was up."

"It looks like I'm being kicked out, General."

Eisenhower's eyes shifted from the camera he was holding to the major. Then he waved him away as though he was a worrisome fly. "You're from the States?" he asked.

"Yes, sir. Born not too far from Abilene, where you spent your childhood."

"Where's that?"

"Fort Scott, Kansas."

He chuckled. "Golly. I used to get goose pimples over a pretty girl who lived there." He devoted another precious minute of my time to the beauty of the prairie, the june bugs, cornfields and mulberries. If five extra minutes would have truly wrecked his day, the hour he granted me must have completely destroyed it. As I passed the major on the way out he stiffened and frowned. I allowed myself a polite smile, hoping I hadn't set myself up for some future hostility. From then on if the general spotted me, and he had a moment, talk about cameras became the priority. He was an incurable camera buff.

Dodie Hamblin and I were then assigned to cover him on his travels, but keeping up with his plane as he shuttled in and out of the NATO countries for two weeks was hard on the body—and sometimes the soul. Mine, for one, suffered serious introspection on an unforgettable flight.

Along with a planeload of foreign correspondents, Dodi and I were following the general's Constellation toward Hamburg, Germany, when his pilot radioed back to warn us of dense fog, heavy snow, sleet and very high wind. The general was advising us not to follow him. His plane, unlike ours, was equipped with highly sophisticated landing gear. Ours was a chartered DC-7, and the pilot, a Texan who had never flown in Europe before, had only a map, guts, and a dangerous ego. "If Ike's pilot can make it so can I."

"But suppose *he* can't make it?"

"Then I will. Hell, man, bad weather was born in Texas." He flew on toward Hamburg.

Soon we were in the thick gray of nowhere, bouncing all over the sky, unable to see the wingtips. Walls of snow and sleet slammed against the windows. The wings iced over, forcing us to a lower altitude. And we worried journalists sat silent and pale in the buffeting, exiled to our private thoughts—waiting for fate to take over. By now half of us had lost our lunch in paper bags. Dodie pressed close and I took her hand in mine, feeling for sure that we were about to die. It was then that I politely asked God to land us safely.

He didn't respond immediately; evidently He felt I should pray some more. Then WHAM! We had hit an air pocket, plummeted down a hundred feet, and the plane shuddered from the impact. Death flashed through my thoughts and I had braced for it when there came a startling CLANK!

"Good Lord, we hit something," Dodie said shakily.

"Just the landing gear locking into position." I tightened my grip on her hand. We dropped fast, lower and lower until a blurred redness flashed beneath the port wing. Then, more flashes on both sides. The Texan had made it, and after a few moments of silence a cheer went up for him. He stepped out of the cockpit, extremely calm, refusing even to acknowledge our cheers. Putting on his cowboy hat, he managed a smile and said, "Welcome to Hamburg, folks."

Waiting for something of great consequence to happen at Eisenhower's headquarters proved to be dull business. Aside from the coming and going of a few diplomats and scurrying military personnel, nothing much happened to engage my camera. The headquarters were housed in a four-storied princely old building with an aura of furtiveness around it. It was staffed by other generals, colonels, majors, captains and a goodly number of lieutenants to do paperwork. For those of lesser rank there was only the futility of a banal existence.

The one photograph I made on the premises worth mentioning —beside the Eisenhower portrait—was a group of dour-faced cameramen huddled outside in the rain. It had been rumored that British field marshal Bernard Montgomery was arriving. He never showed up. I did a lot of waiting as well, but between the waiting there were alternatives—demonstrations, strikes, fashions, theater, fashionable balls and more demonstrations, most of which were much more challenging to cover than the military headquarters, where nothing much of anything happened. The strikes and demonstrations kept the eye alert and constantly roving. Trying to capture a moment that every other photographer in the area wasn't also recording was the problem. Many years before Roy Stryker had given me sage advice. "Avoid the pack. They all come away with the same picture." Remembering this, I searched for a position or angle the others overlooked—providing it wasn't too close to the dreaded *Compagnie Républicaine Sécurité* with their lead capes. Occasionally a celebrity capable of whipping up unusual enthusiasm arrived. Such was the black welterweight, and later middleweight, boxing champion, Sugar Ray Robinson.

The return of Napoleon Bonaparte on his white steed couldn't have charged Paris with much more excitement than did the coming of Sugar Ray in his pink Cadillac. *"Le Sucre* Robin-son! *Le Sucre* Robin-son!"* became the chant as he drove down the Champs-Élysées. Paris, the irresistible seductress, had opened herself to him; and gratefully he was partaking of her wiles before later going on to London in 1951 to defend his crown against Randy Turpin. Handsome, heralded and self-confident, he would party, hit golf balls, take Turpin apart and return home to even more hero-worship.

The world was still at his feet when he departed for London. To cover his workouts and the highly publicized encounter, I went to London with him. *There were no workouts.* Sugar Ray played at golf through the days, and at card tables late into the nights. Turpin, a dockside-type brawler, trained like a man possessed. Pound for pound the man he hoped to wrest the crown from was the greatest fighter of all time. The public, sportswriters, and probably Turpin himself, knew his chances were terribly slim. He trained on. Sugar Ray played on.

When the two men faced each other in the ring, there wasn't a sportswriter of consequence who expected Turpin to answer the sixth bell. Not only did he answer it; he took the round. No cause to worry, I thought, Ray's just stalling, giving the audience its money's worth. But by the tenth round I wasn't so sure. Ray was fighting as if in a trance, appearing sluggish, tired and at times pitifully inept. During the fourteenth round I glanced at his wife

157

Edna Mae, remembering that three days before she had come to me in tears.

"Why is Ray doing this, not training, playing gin rummy all night?"

I didn't have the answer, nor had I felt she expected one. "Have you talked to him about it?"

"Until I'm blue in the face," she had answered, "but he's not listening." Now, in this next-to-the-last round, her hands covered her eyes.

Ray had to win by a knockout in the final round or, I was sure, he'd lose his crown. There was no knockout and at the end Turpin's hand was raised in victory. A mighty roar rocked the stadium—Great Britain had a new hero.

Sugar Ray didn't return to his hotel that night; he didn't want to see the reporters, the crowds, Edna Mae or anyone else. The two of us slipped out a side door and I found a cheap obscure hotel near the stadium. Early the next morning the two of us took the boat train to Paris. The pink Cadillac, Sugar Ray's wife and fifteen-man entourage, would come later. Thankfully no one on the train recognized him in the dark glasses and slouched hat lowered over his forehead.

"I'll kill him the next time. So help me I'll kill him." He said little more than this during the entire trip back to Paris—that seductress who had lulled him into a weariness that stripped him of his title. Now she would greet him with a frown. Ray wasn't so bad off. He would have another chance at Turpin.

More and more during the last months of 1951, John Jenkinson, Paris bureau chief of *Life,* greeted me with troubled looks. He had shown no special friendship for my wife, so when he asked her out for lunch the invitation had puzzled both of us. Nevertheless, she accepted and the conversation, she said, never got much beyond the food and the weather.

Two weeks later a confidential letter arrived from Wilson Hicks. It was friendly and warm enough but the last paragraph eased into the message he had been so gently leading toward: "You've had a very successful run there, but your wife's *tremendous unhappiness* with Paris influences our decision to bring you back before your time expires. The magazine doesn't like being held responsible for family discord—especially where children are involved. And the understanding here is that a divorce is imminent if you stay in Paris much longer."

In short, I was being reassigned to New York—and conversation about Jenkinson's invitation for lunch hung in the silence. The damage was done. A cable of strange consequence fell accidentally into the hands of Natalie Kotchoubey. For Jenkinson, it read: "I'm waiting and I'm ready." It was from Tom McAvoy, a photographer in the Washington bureau—and godfather to Jenkinson's daughter. I felt quite strongly that I was the victim of a conspiracy between Jenkinson and McAvoy. I began packing for home with remorse, while sharing remarkably little conversation with Jenkinson. There was however a strong sense of knowingness floating between us.

We returned on the *Queen Mary* two days after the Christmas of 1952. I had remembered the gun at Cherbourg, but I had forgotten it just as quickly. It was, I hoped, off my hands forever.

By now mid-Atlantic cables had become almost as common as doorbells ringing. Another came on the second day at sea: "Winston Churchill and Anthony Eden are aboard. Try for interview and pictures. Wilson." Now I understood why the two men keeping vigil outside the cabin a few doors away observed everyone with steely eyes. The Prime Minister's secret crossing, if it was meant to be a secret, wasn't one anymore. I tried several times but he wasn't seeing anyone or talking to anyone.

It was the final morning and New York would appear on the horizon soon. I was up early for the first glimpse. At the far end of the promenade deck three figures were approaching. As they came nearer I realized that it was Churchill and Eden. Then the stunner —the small girl skipping between them was Toni. And me without a camera. "This is my daddy," she said as we met.

"You have a delightful child," Churchill said.

"Thank you, sir, and she's had better luck tracking you down than I have. *Life* magazine's been cabling for an interview and pictures."

He grunted. "I'm talked out, and I'm getting too homely for photographs. Settle for a brandy and a good cigar?"

"I would, sir."

"Then come into my cabin for a few minutes."

The telephone rang after my second sip of brandy. Eden answered it and his expression told me that privacy was needed, that someone of high importance was calling. My few minutes were up before they hardly started. As I got up to leave, Churchill handed me a big cigar. "Thank you, sir," I said, and left.

His reply was directed into the telephone—and not to me. "Good morning to you, Mr. President. I've been awaiting your call."

I kept that cigar for years until it flaked into nothing, and then I smoked it in my pipe.

After leaving Churchill's cabin I had gone back on deck to watch New York appear on the skyline. The Time-Life skyscraper would be there spiraling above Rockefeller Center, and in a few hours it would be filled with scores of workers—all white except for a handful of black messengers and porters.

New York was an island and now I had become somewhat of an island. In escaping Harlem I lost black friends along the way. I was black and I felt black, but my aspirations had propelled me toward things most blacks were denied. Soon I would be in that same skyscraper full of offices wherein my face would be the only black one. Having already lived out that dubious experience at *Vogue* and Standard Oil Co., I felt the sadness of knowing so many others like me were being held back. For me it seemed at times like I had won a rather pyrrhic victory.

Almost two years in Europe had brought my past and future together. There I had been accepted without judgments based on color; there I walked the boulevards, silently proclaiming myself free, whole and respected. I had found it without racism and more in accord with those democratic principals my own country pro-pounded but failed to live up to. Yet I was not unaware that America, with all its shortcomings, still had more to offer black people than any country in the world. The sad thing was that America made it so hard for black people to realize this.

Five days aboard the *Queen Mary* had given me time to think back. Approximately forty years' worth of dreaming formed the geography of my memories; memories strewn through Kansas prairies, Minnesota snowbanks, big-city ghettos and now Europe.

Flushed with confidence, I reached the bureau the following morning—feeling perhaps a bit too cocky. With Europe still soaring inside, I was eager to descend upon America and let it know how much I had learned. It was foolheaded to be so pompous. To America I was less than a pebble of sand, but it didn't hurt to bathe for a while in innocence; to raise a glass to my delusions. Having completed over fifty assignments in Europe, I felt more experienced than those fledglings moving in from places like Yale, Harvard and Princeton. No Ivy-League professor could possibly have lectured upon those avenues of my own learning.

The Paris bureau had been rather tranquil and serene. It would be exhilarating to be a part of the fierce energy of the New York bureau, the nerve center that fed vitality to all the domestic and foreign bureaus. There, as in Europe, photographers and reporters were constantly on the go. A mother gave birth to quintuplets in Canada. Indians rioted in Calcutta; civil strife flared in Spain. A plane went down over Iceland—within a short time a *Life* team was on its way. The magazine was a leviathan basking in journalistic glory.

But before I threw myself back into this world completely, I had another love to attend to. Nearly two years had passed since I started on my piano concerto back in Paris. It felt more like aeons, and Dean Dixon's promise to give it a performance was now beginning to seem like so much water in the air. Henry Brant and I had finished work on the score soon after I returned and for months it lay in the silence of my hall closet. Then a cable from Dean arrived: "Your work is programmed for Venice concert on the 10th of July. Send score quickest. We expect you to follow it. Dean."

The score went in June. I arrived a day before the concert. The large posters smiling from the walls of the city stopped me, smiled at me, and I smiled back. The composers: Elgar; Piston; Britten; Ireland; Gershwin and Parks. Joy did the talking; nothing was left for me to say. Minutes before it happened I felt weightless, remembering back to the listening listening listening—to Haydn, Beethoven, Mozart, Prokofiev and Rachmaninoff; listening alone late into the night; listening beyond the voices of my children, beyond abandoned conversations. At the time I had felt gifted from so much listening, but now I was too terrorized to be enraptured with the moment. At last, in the splendid courtyard of the Doges' Palace, it was about to happen, and I sat like a zombie pierced by some ephemeral ray.

Vivian, Dean's wife, sat at the piano, and one hundred musicians, all looking toward Dean, awaited the rise of his baton. The evening, the entire scene, seemed to be adrift in space, and as the baton rose a vapory nervousness streaked through me. The first chord struck the evening. Pigeons fluttered up from the surrounding buildings. What happened after that is to me a blur. The music streamed through my ears like broken stars. I tried drinking it in, but heard only pointless sound. The four movements seemed to have loped into the air and disappeared in a flash. It was over. A hand touched my shoulder and I rose shakily to acknowledge the applause—feeling a joy so strange it was hard to express.

When I called Sally the following morning she said, rather coolly, "I knew it would be a success. You always have success. Maybe that's your problem." As I hung up I felt a deep sadness for her.

Spring brought final truth to our relationship. We no longer understood one another, nor did we try; the sharing of twenty years was dead, and I had gone in search of new companionship. I found it in M, a lovely woman from South Africa. While Sally had discouraged my attending the concert because of "financial reasons," M had insisted upon my going. "Nothing should stop you. You will hear your music performed by a big symphony for the first time. It should be a grand moment, and you can't miss it." When I grew doubtful she bought the ticket, thrust it in my hand and drove me to the airport. Waiting in the hotel room she had reserved for me in Venice were two dozen roses and a bottle of champagne.

Happiness was in her voice when I telephoned her after the concert, and she was full of "good news," but that, she said, would have to wait. I pressed, but to no avail. Yet somehow I knew. M was expecting our child.

I took her into my arms when she met me at the airport. "You, my dear, are pregnant."

"You, my dear, are right." We embraced and tried to smile away the seriousness of the problem. But in the clarity of the next morning we realized the dream had to be cast aside until later.

A doctor was consulted and a private nurse was engaged. On the appointed morning fate would send me off to Chicago on a brief assignment, but I was to return by early evening. Strangely, she voiced no objection to my going. It was, after all, a matter of being away for just a few hours. But when I returned that same evening M had shut her door to me—and forever. The telephone fell silent to my voice, and a month's worth of letters went unanswered.

Six years had gone by when, on one summer's day, we met accidentally on Fifth Avenue. We managed a quick hello, then passed on like two strangers. A once-deepening love wrenched away perhaps by my insensitivity.

FOURTEEN

There was no special black corner established for me at *Life*. I was assigned to any and everything, but if I could bring significance to a story because I was black, it was given to me. I went also as a reporter—not *Life*'s black reporter. Into the hell that I was about to be sent, this distinction made little difference. It would have been imprudent to announce that a reporter of any color was arriving to spread his presence. The subject was *Segregation in the South,* that bastion of lynch knots, Klansmen and hatred of black skin.

As I packed to go I thought of the terror we blacks had suffered there at the hands of white Southerners—the shootings and lynchings which went unreported at the order of Klansmen, who hid their consciences behind hoods, who heated up the hot Southland nights even more with torches and flaming crosses. So many black people had been murdered, butchered and hung from trees beneath those garish flames.

Determinedly I packed. In need of an assistant, I spelled out his specifications to the editors: he would have to be black, young, intelligent and fearless, with a vast knowledge of the South. Two days later I put my will in order. The next afternoon, I took a plane for Birmingham, Alabama.

The city was dozing a lazy Sunday afternoon away when I reached it, but racial tension was so thick in the air I seemed to smell it. This was the Deep South, the hostile territory, a place where a black man eyed a white face fleetingly. To look too deeply into one sometimes invited trouble. The black cabbie drove me toward the "colored" side of town, past racist symbols that stuck out like prickly thorns—drinking fountains, *White* and *Colored*. Real estate signs, *White Only*. Parks, eating places, playgrounds, schools and churches—*White Only*. With a small camera tucked in my pocket, I was where, for so long, I had intended to use it—Alabama, the motherland of racism.

The cabbie dropped me off on a street corner where the directions I had been given told me to wait. It was a lonely corner packed hard with centuries of red clay. Farther down the road were rows of lean-to houses, weathered and worn by the years. Two black boys, bare-shouldered under their bib overalls, passed on the dusty road. They were barefoot. Both carried fishing poles and a string of catfish—a bittersweet memory of my own childhood. Older blacks, born to this downside of life, moved sluggishly through the heat like leftovers from another time. A car stopped. The young black man stepped out to greet me. It was Sam Yette, who had been sent by *Life* to guide me through the perils of his birthplace. Soft-spoken, intelligent and possessing a sense of humor, he seemed likely to meet all the requirements.

There are rare instances when truth is best served by silence. So it must be with the name of the man who was to accompany us. I will refer to him as Freddie. He was one of *Life*'s Southern bureau chiefs, a white sent to act as a sort of liaison, to help fend off any possible danger that might await us. Long after dusk he finally showed up, and the place of his arrival was obscured by darkness. After a weak handshake, he hushedly informed me that my assignment was ill-founded; that there was insufficient segregation in Birmingham to warrant it.

Unbelievable!

After expressing such doubts to the editors in New York, he should have been eliminated from the story immediately. For some reason, he wasn't. But, as a rule, *Life* staffers had a fierce loyalty toward one another. He went off to arrange our "protective source," which I was to find out from the local NAACP office, was the White Citizens' Council—a group as distinguished for hatred of blacks as the Ku Klux Klan. For protection, Freddie had called in redneck killers. After putting a call through to New York, Sam and I went into hiding. Kenneth McLeish, a senior *Life* editor, arrived the next morning and, after a discussion with Freddie, assured me all would be fine.

Somehow Freddie never got around to traveling with us. For the first two days after our arrival only blindness would have prevented our knowing that we were being followed constantly by three men. To take out a camera would have been to put our lives in jeopardy. On the third night, in the wet darkness, we slipped out of Birmingham and drove toward the small hamlet of Anniston. Willie Causey, a black sharecropper, lived there, and by photographing his miserable existence I hoped to strike at the roots of Southern bigotry. Freddie, I decided, was not to know about my plans until I was finished. His responsibility then would be to help protect the Causeys from any harassment after the story was published.

We drove into Anniston at dawn. It was all red clay, shacks and tall pines with crows cawing from the branches. The air boiled and the roads were eroded by water and time. Willie was a poor man with a wife and five children. Mostly he cut pines for a living. Home was a two-room shack with a tin roof, a tiny kitchen and a porch slanted toward the earth. It sat near the road's edge on a gutted half acre of red clay that turned to slime during the rains. A huge iron cauldron sat in the center of the backyard for washing clothes. A secondhand refrigerator, Mrs. Causey's proudest possession, took up most of the kitchen—and it had taken Willie five years of hard work to pay for it. Mrs. Causey taught black children in a nearby one-room shack that was their school. A potbellied stove sat dead center of the ancient desks. After giving the white man his share of monthly pine cuttings, Willie had around twenty-five dollars left for beans, greens and hog fat. He and his wife slept in one room; the five children slept in the other, and they seemed to sleep throughout the day, moving slowly, quietly. It was as though old age were already closing in on them. They seemed not to be aware of any other kind of life. There wasn't even a radio to put them in touch with the big city lying just a few miles away.

They were trapped in a wilderness where Klansmen burned crosses, where fear and hunger were the way of life. Others like them shared their fate—to the north, east, south and west. But, in the near distance, angry black voices were beginning to cry out against segregation, against bigotry and poverty. At last the easy white days of mint juleps and magnolia blossoms were under threat—and by hands that for centuries had picked the cotton.

Hidden beyond the pines, I worked for a week, recording the plight of the Causeys. On the seventh day we left for Birmingham by a back road. Lucky for us that we did, because, unknown to us, the townspeople had become aware of our presence—and they were on the way with rope, tar and feathers. Meanwhile, back in the city, I melted into the workday motion of the people, shooting casually at those water fountains, playgrounds and other chaffing monuments set up to keep "colored people" in their place. All of these would have to fall if democracy was to have its say.

I had left Willie Causey's family feeling concerned about how they would fare after their story was published. "You're not to worry," Freddie assured me, "I'll be in constant touch with them." I found myself searching for a single reason to believe him. We bid him good-bye and headed toward the railway station. The train to Nashville was due in an hour. In that city, I was to photograph a black college professor boarding a bus in the segregated area. Freddie preferred driving by himself to Nashville. He would meet us at the bus station at two o'clock the following afternoon.

At the Birmingham railway station, the signs read, Interstate White/Intrastate Black. "We're traveling interstate, boss," Sam quipped as I hurriedly photographed the "separate but equal" facilities.

"And we're traveling into trouble," I said as we took seats on the white side. Then, brashly, Sam broke a most sacred Southern law: he walked over and drank from the white water fountain. A woman gasped, and consternation rumbled throughout the room. It was too late even to think about the sin Sam had committed. The indiscretion echoed through the entire place, and a few minutes later a scruffy bunch of workmen entered by the back entrance. Menacingly they stood staring at us, mumbling about things that happened to uppity niggers who intruded upon their sanctuary, who had the audacity to drink from their white fountains. Both Sam and I were scared, but we sat there with a coolness that evidently surprised them. When our train pulled in, they followed us to our Pullman, still mumbling obscenities. Nervously, we boarded our car, expecting blows that never fell.

We had escaped harm too easily and I still sensed danger. Sam had a lower berth, so I advised him to share my compartment where the door could be locked. He refused, and I took the exposed film to bed with me. About a half hour out of Birmingham I heard scuffling. Sam was being attacked. I reached his side wielding an oversized flashgun, hitting one of the assailants across his neck with a vicious blow. Their planning was well timed. The train had stopped, and they ran for the exit. Obviously, they had been after my film. For the rest of the trip, Sam felt it best to share my compartment.

We set our trap. Instead of photographing the professor in the afternoon—as Freddie had proposed—we did it at ten in the morning. A black university student had offered to arrive at the bus station in my place at two o'clock. He was grabbed by the local police and only after proving that he wasn't a *Life* photographer was he released. By that time, Sam and I were on a plane to New York. We had come to the end; it was as though I were waking from a nightmare, feeling dirty and betrayed.

The townspeople of Anniston came down on Willie Causey with true Southern wrath. They took all of his belongings and put his family on the highway and warned them never to return. Upon reaching Birmingham on foot, Willie telephoned me collect in New York and explained what had happened.

"Did you notify Freddie?"

"I sure did. He promised to help, but I never heard from him again."

Freddie, the bureau found out, had taken his family and gone on a month's vacation. When two of *Life*'s editors went to Anniston and attempted to get the Causeys' belongings returned to them, they were met in the mayor's yard by several men armed with rifles and shotguns. The mayor was a lady who spoke with crushing authority. "If Willie cares about his life, he'll stay out'a here. And if we'da caught that nigger who took them pictures, we'da tarred and feathered him and set him to fire."

You might say that things ended reasonably well for Willie Causey. *Life* relocated his family and gave them twenty five thousand dollars—more than a sharecropper could ever have dreamed of. It is interesting to note that Willie took half, and his wife got the other half. Then they did something they had wanted to do for a long time. They told each other good-bye. As for Freddie, he was called back to New York and given a little inconsequential desk outside some inconsequential office.

My world has been abundant with the likes of Freddie. They are forever gathering around, speaking a strange language of their own. They appear harmless, and in brotherly manner they walk beside me—hiding a dagger in their hand. No matter that I tire of them; they keep sprouting here and there, refusing to die off. After inviting themselves into my life, they try settling into it. Then comes a storm and they are gone, leaving me to the troubles.

FIFTEEN

Perhaps, like me, you sometimes wonder about providence—that divine intervention that is said to govern our existence. It would seem that it has the power to put our bodies together, wrap them in different colored skin, take the measure of them, and then, at its own discretion, send us off in many directions. Is it reasonable that in the same hospital a child is born blind with two limbs missing, while another is born bright-eyed and healthy? And if a man is born to evil, why then should he be expected eventually to overcome that evil? Should society expect the same of a black youth appointed to the ravages of Harlem since birth as it would of a white youth assigned to the wealth of Park Avenue? It would be easy, perhaps, to conclude that such questions are predetermined by one's lot. But neither that blind child nor a young black behind bars would find such a response comforting. However, I must believe that there is some indefinable power that created us; that monitors our actions and that, to a great extent, we are accountable to. There is an old German proverb that I find hard to dispute: *Der Mensch denkt, Gott lenkt . . .* Man thinks; God leads.

"But who's God, man, and if He's around, tell me who made Him up?" Ed Martin, the young inmate at Elmira, was seething with anger after I asked him if he believed in God. "If you know Him, tell Him I didn't ask Him to send me here through the belly of a whore who left me on a doorstep because she didn't want me. Look, man, with all the shit I've been through since then, I'd just as soon not have been born." His answer wiped me out and burdened me with his confusion. He seemed to have turned his wrath against anybody committed to God. For the rape and murder of a nun he would remain in prison for the rest of his life. At thirty-five he had already spent fifteen years behind bars. If his birth could be ascribed to divine intervention, then there were even more vexing problems to ponder.

Martin was one of several inmates I had spent a week talking to about the misfortune of having to spend their lives behind bars. How much of it did they bring upon themselves? To what extent did they feel that fate was responsible? Only a few admitted to willful wrongdoing for the sake of it. Most of them, including Martin, blamed fate for their problems. "So I was born in trouble's lap, man. Wasn't nothing I could do about it—even if I'd wanted to." Fate, being in a highly ethereal state, was unable to speak up for itself; unable to defend its position with the likes of a James Baldwin, a Richard Wright or a good number of others who had escaped its grasp.

Life's editors had just assigned me to photograph these men in a story called "Crime Across America." Chicago, a mecca of criminal transgression since Al Capone's reign of gangland terror, would provide the prelude for the journey. San Francisco, no less a haven for malefaction, would serve as the epilogue. Murder, drugs, racketeering and prostitution—all bunched into a world of their own—were the obvious subjects of such an odyssey.

"There's a thin line between a cop and a crook. I know; I've been both." This pronouncement was made by Chip, a member of the Chicago homicide squad. To be, or not to be—a crook. Chip was pointing a finger at fate again. In the weeks to come, I sometimes wondered if he had made a choice. He confiscated drugs, sold drugs and used drugs. He ambushed crooks, pistol-whipped them, then, if they could pay off, he let them go free. Otherwise, he slammed them into jail and added them to his dubious list of arrests. Chip was part madman. Just before kicking in an addict's door one night, he winked, then whispered to me, "Get your camera ready. I'll plug him so you'll get a good shot."

I shook my head. "Not for me."

"Just in the arm—or the leg?"

"Nope, not for me."

Both Chip and his partner, Jimmy, were masters of disguise and subterfuge. It depended upon the district. Laundrymen in a laundry truck with peepholes; deliverymen in bakery trucks; street cleaners sweeping the gutters—and always they had a "pigeon" stashed nearby. On one particular night we were parked near a stakeout in a milk truck. The "pigeon" was sweating; the barrel of Chip's revolver was pressed against his cheek. "Okay, fucker—you git in there and try to make a buy. If you come out smoking a joint, you can keep walking. If nothin's there, you git your black ass back to this truck. Try running and I'll blow your ass apart. Git going."

The pigeon went in, came out smoking and sauntered off into the darkness. Nervously I followed Chip and Jimmy into a dark alleyway. With their guns drawn, and a crowbar, they climbed up two sets of fire escapes, then stopped before a shaded window. "You ready?"

"I'm ready."

The crowbar smashed out the window's pane and we scrambled through—to find only three small black children huddled in fear, screaming. Then their mother burst through a curtained door. "What's this? What are you doing here?"

"Shut up! Where's your old man? Where's the stuff? I know you've got it stashed somewhere! Where is it?" Chip pointed the gun toward her heart as Jimmy burst into the outer room. A tall black man stood against the wall with his hands raised as I entered. "There's nothing here, man—nothing," he swore to Jimmy.

They searched for an hour. Having found nothing, we had started down the stairwell when Jimmy noticed a padlock on a door beneath the steps. He stood back and sent the crowbar smashing against the lock. It popped open. Chip howled with joy. There it was—enough heroin and cocaine to supply Chicago's south side. As they pushed the handcuffed dealer down the stairs I heard the wailing children. Their voices grew fainter as we went. Happily, Chip stumbled down the stairs with a big box full of cellophane bags.

Homicide. Death in the day; death in the night. A prostitute, throat slit, lying in her own blood; in the half light of a dingy room—the foul, sweetish odor of drugs, incense and death hanging in the stale air.

Three hours later at the county morgue, a heavy-set woman dressed in black entered the door Chip held open for her. A bare lightbulb popped on above the corpse and she was asked to step in closer and look at it. She took her time before stepping closer, then she looked at the dead man coldly, at the five bullet holes in his face and neck. Then she glanced up at Chip. "Well—what do you want from me?"

"I want to know who he is. Do you know him—his name?"

She stood silent for a moment, looking disdainfully at the corpse. "He's Carmine Loretta. I should know the bastard. He shot my father and sister. Finally he got what was coming to him." Before the morgue attendant could cover Loretta, she spat on him, hatred etched deeply in her face, then turned and left the room.

Later that week, on a burning hot afternoon, Jimmy and Chip were leading a narcotics squad, and with drawn guns they edged into a field. Weeds, nearly six feet high, concealed our approach toward the objective. I hadn't been told what it was, but I was to stay close to Jimmy. We stopped for several moments—waiting. Then Jimmy's revolver was waving above the weeds, signaling for the attack. Cautiously we burst into a small clearing in the center of the field. And there, reclining on a velvet couch alongside his tin shack, was a black man smoking marijuana. I will never forget his coolness. Smiling, he blew smoke at Chip's gun barrel. "Well, sweetheart," he said. "You've just fucked up ten years of happiness." He got up slowly, broke off the top of a weed and stuffed it in his pocket. "Okay, gents, I'm ready to go." He took a final look at the bountiful crop before we pulled away, and shook his head.

"What a fuckin' waste." For ten years he had nursed that field of marijuana. Now they were pouring kerosene all over it—preparing to burn it all down.

Late evening brought a murder that left me distrustful of my senses. While on a weekend furlough, a mental patient slit the stomach of his pregnant wife. Remorsefully he sat on the bed bemoaning her death. "I was only trying to get the child out early —to keep my wife from so much pain."

The weeks had gone slowly, and I wasn't even halfway across America. Chip was dutifully concerned about my getting whatever I needed. "Did you get a picture of a junkie taking the needle?" he asked.

"That would be impossible."

"Nothing's impossible; come on." In a matter of minutes he had supplied the dope, the needle and the junkie—even a dark room in the back of the precinct. The grizzled man took his belt off, tightened it around his arm until his vein swelled, then sent the needle home. Ecstasy seemed to have overtaken him. Chip patted his shoulder. "Don't forget, Joe. For that you owe me one." If Joe heard him, he didn't let on.

Leaving Chicago didn't change the picture. From within the shadows of prisons across the country, I heard about the storms that had shattered so many young lives. It was disturbing that so many of those I saw behind the walls were black, or members of some other racial minority.

At Minnesota's Stillwater Prison, "Baby" Eubanks and six of his fellow inmates had been charged with murdering one of their fellow men. "We need your help," Eubanks said to me. "The guards did it—they beat us to it. The dude deserved to die for taking advantage of young guys for sex."

"What are you in for, Baby?"

"Murder—but I've served enough time for parole. Would you be one of my sponsors?"

"I'll look into it. If I can, I will."

I never found out who killed that inmate, but after a lengthy conversation with the warden, he promised me a "thorough look" into the case. Not long after, the charge was lifted. Eventually, I sponsored Eubanks for parole—with the condition that if he made it out, he would not visit his old haunts again and get into more trouble. He promised to honor that request, and he made it out.

But, his sense of honor was long gone. He went back to Minneapolis's north side, got into a fight and was stabbed to death. The irony of it—if Eubanks had remained at Stillwater, he would probably be alive today.

Then, there was José Santos—in a Missouri prison for peddling drugs. He had been incarcerated about a year before he was to get a bachelor's degree. He was a bright, handsome man with a deep scar on the left cheek. He stared at me for several moments when I asked him how he got it. Then, very dryly, he said, "I caught a piece of shrapnel overseas."

"And why the drugs?"

"It's hard to say. After I got back, everything went zap. I was off my rocker most of the time—didn't know night from day."

"Did you try to get help?"

He chuckled. "Hell, man, I used every inch of space between God and the devil looking for help. People don't care about helping you anymore. They're all off doing their own thing. I stopped begging for help, took things in my own hands and landed up here in good old Missouri State."

Having at last reached San Francisco, I entered Joe Hudson's cell on San Quentin's death row. He looked up, offered me a smoke and his wooden stool. He had one more day to live. I didn't ask him why he was there; I knew. He had knifed to death a young boy who was using the urinal next to him.

"Had you ever seen the kid before?"

"Never."

"Were you angry about anything?"

"A little. The undertaker I'd apprenticed for never got around to letting me work on a corpse."

"That's all?"

"That's all."

"How do you feel about it now?"

"I'm sorry for the kid—and I hate myself."

"Are you ready to die?"

"I've no right to live after doing such a thing."

"I'm sorry for both you and the kid, Joe."

"You coming to watch me go?"

"Would you like for me to be there?"

"It might help a little."

"Okay—I'll be there."

"Say a little prayer for me, will you?"

"I'll do that."

I was about four feet from the chair when they strapped him into it at six o'clock the next morning. (A cocky little guard had placed me there at the last minute, and certainly not out of the generosity of his heart. Terror was on his mind, and that terror was intended for me. For him there would be entertainment in observing my reaction to a death so close.) The condemned man's face had gone ashen, and a solitary tear rolled down his cheek when he glanced at me. He seemed to be questioning my standing so close. Another guard brought a stethoscope and adjusted it over his heart. There had to be a precise moment of death to enter into the record. The other guard patted his shoulder, probably advising him to inhale "it" quickly, to get it over with fast. At the last moment Hudson asked for a Bible. One was thrust into the cubicle and placed firmly into his hands. At last he sat alone, head down, thumbing the Bible—waiting. A minister's voice came from behind me: *"The Lord is my shepherd; I shall not want. He maketh me to lie down in green pastures: he leadeth me beside the still waters."* The condemned man thumbs on—Samuel, Kings, Chronicles, Ezra, Esther, Job, Psalms—*"He restorth my soul; he leadeth me in the paths of righteousness for his name's sake."* Through the green glass I perceived my own image emerging from within his. Proverbs, Isaiah, Jeremiah (the warden's arm was raising), Lamentations—*"Yea, though I walk through the valley of the shadow of death, I will fear no evil: for thou art with me; thy rod and thy staff they comfort me."* The warden's arm dropped. The pellet dropped. The gas was rising. Joe's head snapped backward and his thumb dug into Lamentations. The Bible fell free and snapped shut. His image parted from mine, and there was intense quivering from the top of his head to his neck. His nervous system was being eaten away. *"Thou preparest a table before me in the presence of mine enemies: thou anointest my head with oil; mine cup runneth over."* The quivering reached his belly, his hips, his legs; and there was a final protest as it reached his toes. Then he was still. *"And I will dwell in the house of the Lord for ever."*

It was over. Without reason he had murdered dispassionately; his judgment was served dispassionately. As I looked at him

Ella Watson, American Gothic, Washington, D.C., 1942. *Gordon Parks*.

Pool hall in Fort Scott, Kansas, 1949. *Gordon Parks/Life Magazine © Time Warner.*

Mrs. Lucy Jefferson of Fort Scott, Kansas, 1949. *Gordon Parks/Life Magazine © Time Warner.*

Red Jackson, Harlem gang leader, New York, 1948. *Gordon Parks.*

Roy Stryker, 1946. *Gordon Parks.*

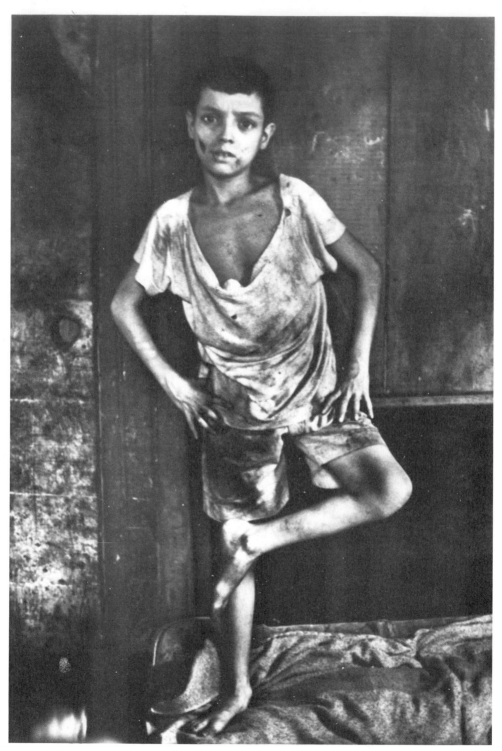

Flavio, 1961. *Gordon Parks*.

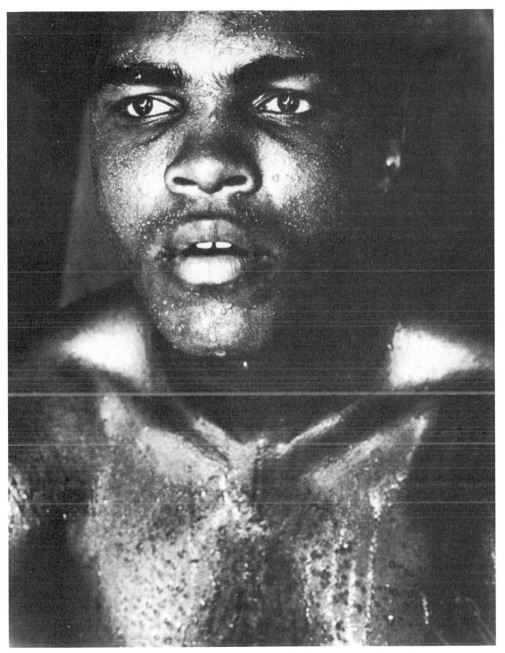

Muhammad Ali, after Cooper fight in London. *Gordon Parks*.

Bessie Fontenelle at the welfare office, New York, 1968, surrounded by her children. (Left to right) Kenneth, who died in the fire; Richard; Norman Jr.; and Ellen, who was on the cover of *Life*. *Gordon Parks*.

Bessie Fontenelle and little Richard the morning after she scalded her husband with boiling water. *Gordon Parks*.

Ingrid Bergman, Stromboli, Italy, 1949. *Gordon Parks/Life Magazine* © *Time Warner.*

Author aboard ship approaching Stromboli, Italy, 1949. *Maria Sermolina*.

slumped in death I failed to distinguish the profanity of one act from the profanity of the other. One evil, cloaked in cold judicial morality, had just fed upon another. As we filed out the young guard asked me if I enjoyed the show. I could only look at him with despair. He followed me. "Too bad you wasn't around a few weeks ago. Two colored boys went at the same time. One cut his jugular with a razor before we could strap him down and blood was all over the guards, windows and chairs and he was hollering, 'Don't kill me, don't kill me,' and the other one was laughing like a hyena and hollering, 'Come on, man. Don't let whitey think you're scared' and the bastard kept laughing right to the end." My despair deepened and I hurried on.

As I left the prison compound that small blotched part of my own past leaped out before me. Life, so priceless, seemed for the moment, so unreasonably cheap.

I came to the tranquility of home with the scent of prison life in my mind and clothes; the heavy clinging odor of heroin and cocaine in my film. Even now, years later, it seems to linger in the transparencies that recorded those dark days and nights. At times, doubting myself, I have asked others to either confirm or reject my contentions. Strangely, most have nodded their heads in agreement. I don't like reliving those terrible hours, but they stay on, burning in deeper.

With the publication of that essay came invitations to speak before groups concerned with the problems of crime and ways to fight them. Against a mature judgment I accepted a few. But I had no reassuring answers; I too was begging the questions, eating the same despair. I could at best conclude with things they already knew—crime was as inevitable as the sunrise, and spreading like a fearful stain. Some people were doomed to walk the wrong side of the road.

How could I explain the awesome, unreasoned murder committed by Joe Hudson—or his judicial murder? His crime was like a drop in a deluge when compared with so many others taking place around the clock. It would take the faith and visions of saints to hope that other such crimes wouldn't happen again, but no prayers of ministers, acolytes or priests could prevent them. The prisons were bulging even more, and the lists of inmates were growing. Steadily the cry for *capital punishment* was building.

"A death for a death!" one man had shouted. "That's the only way to deal with the likes of a Joe Hudson!" I looked at him with his fist spiking the air, wondering about what he might have said had his own son been meted out the same judgment. I was inclined to believe he might have said, "No, no—never."

He went on. "You seem to have a soft spot for this Hudson fellow. Why? He deserved just what he got."

"I have sorrow for him and his victim. Both were caught up in the agonies of fate."

"What would you have suggested they do with him?"

I thought for a moment. "Lock him up and throw away the key."

"That's not good enough for me."

"Obviously not, but for me it's the only answer I have until society finds a better one."

"Joe Hudson was a blight on our society. We are a nation of civilized people!"

With Birmingham coming to mind, I paused for a few seconds. "Well, at least we presume to be civilized. But I find it hard to understand civilized people killing other human beings, no matter what law they are governed by."

Perhaps the only slightly redeemable thing about my assignment through the world of crime was the realization that I had managed to escape it. So many young lives behind prison walls have been stopped forever. It is one thing to place the fault, another thing to point at where the fault lies. The truth of it is slippery. Without my upbringing I might have been behind those prison walls. Now I want to give my children what their grandparents gave me. Love is the significant charge. Culture and education can be rubbed into them with time.

SIXTEEN

For generations the problems of poverty have grown steadily worse. Now, the entire universe seems paralyzed by its dimensions. Starvation and homeless people have created a cycle of despair so big, so urgent and complex, no single government body can handle it alone. Big business, unions, church groups and finally we private citizens must join the fight against human misery, or in the end all of us must bear the cost.

I have, for a long time, worked under the premise that everyone is worth something; that every life is valuable to our own existence. Consequently, I've felt it was my camera's responsibility to shed light on any condition that hinders human growth or warps the spirit of those trapped in the ruinous evils of poverty. It is not easy to do away with, whether its victims are black or white.

I couldn't go on forgiving myself for my apathy toward those who were unable to do for themselves. I looked closely at those asleep on the sidewalks. I looked closely at those searching the rubbish cans for supper. To me, they were ghosts of my own past, and I couldn't help but feel trapped inside their misery. They seemed to swarm all around me, tormenting my mind. I began to think of them as people who slept out their nights on pillows of stone; who staggered to their feet every morning lost in nothingness.

I've never lost my fierce grudge against poverty. It is the most savage of all human afflictions, claiming victims who can't mobilize their efforts against it, who often lack strength to digest what little food they scrounge up to survive. It keeps growing, multiplying, spreading like a cancer. In my wanderings I attack it wherever I can—in barrios, slums and favelas.

Catacumba was the name of the favela where I found Flavio da Silva. It was wickedly hot. The noon sun baked the mud-rot of the wet mountainside. Garbage and human excrement clogged the open sewers snaking down the slopes. José Gallo, a *Life* reporter, and I rested in the shade of a jacaranda tree halfway up Rio de Janeiro's most infamous deathtrap. Below and above us were a maze of shacks, but in the distance alongside the beach stood the gleaming white homes of the rich.

Breathing hard, balancing a tin of water on his head, a small boy climbed toward us. He was miserably thin, naked but for filthy denim shorts. His legs resembled sticks covered with skin and screwed into his feet. Death was all over him, in his sunken eyes, cheeks and jaundiced coloring. He stopped for breath, coughing, his chest heaving as water slopped over his bony shoulders. Then jerking sideways like a mechanical toy, he smiled a smile I will never forget. Turning, he went on up the mountainside.

The detailed *Life* assignment in my back pocket was to find an impoverished father with a family, to examine his earnings, political leanings, religion, friends, dreams and frustrations. I had been sent to do an essay on poverty. This frail boy bent under his load said more to me about poverty than a dozen poor fathers. I touched Gallo, and we got up and followed the boy to where he entered a shack near the top of the mountainside. It was a leaning crumpled place of old plankings with a rusted tin roof. From inside we heard the babblings of several children. José knocked. The door opened and the boy stood smiling with a bawling naked baby in his arms.

Still smiling, he whacked the baby's rump, invited us in and offered us a box to sit on. The only other recognizable furniture was a sagging bed and a broken baby's crib. Flavio was twelve, and with Gallo acting as interpreter, he introduced his younger brothers and sisters: "Mario, the bad one; Baptista, the good one; Albia, Isabel and the baby Zacarias." Two other girls burst into the shack, screaming and pounding on one another. Flavio jumped in and parted them. "Shut up, you two." He pointed at the older girl. "That's Maria, the nasty one." She spit in his face. He smacked her and pointed to the smaller sister. "That's Luzia. She thinks she's pretty."

Having finished the introductions, he went to build a fire under the stove—a rusted, bent top of an old gas range resting on several bricks. Beneath it was a piece of tin that caught the hot coals. The shack was about six by ten feet. Its grimy walls were a patchwork of misshapen boards with large gaps between them, revealing other shacks below stilted against the slopes. The floor, rotting under layers of grease and dirt, caught shafts of light slanting down through spaces in the roof. A large hole in the far corner served as a toilet. Beneath that hole was the sloping mountainside. Pockets of poverty in New York's Harlem, on Chicago's south side, in Puerto Rico's infamous El Fungito seemed pale by comparison. None of them had prepared me for this one in the favela of Catacumba.

Flavio washed rice in a large dishpan, then washed Zacarias's feet in the same water. But even that dirty water wasn't to be wasted. He tossed in a chunk of lye soap and ordered each child to wash up. When they were finished he splashed the water over the dirty floor, and, dropping to his knees, he scrubbed the planks until the black suds sank in. Just before sundown he put beans on the stove to warm, then left, saying he would be back shortly. "Don't let them burn," he cautioned Maria. "If they do and Poppa beats me, you'll get it later." Maria, happy to get at the licking spoon, switched over and began to stir the beans. Then slyly she dipped out a spoonful and swallowed them. Luzia eyed her. "I see you. I'm going to tell on you for stealing our supper."

Maria's eyes flashed anger. "You do and I'll beat you, you little bitch." Luzia threw a stick at Maria and fled out the door. Zacarias dropped off to sleep. Mario, the bad one, slouched in a corner and sucked his thumb. Isabel and Albia sat on the floor clinging to each other with a strange tenderness. Isabel held onto Albia's hair and Albia clutched at Isabel's neck. They appeared frozen in an act of quiet violence.

Flavio returned with wood, dumped it beside the stove and sat down to rest for a few minutes, then went down the mountain for more water. It was dark when he finally came back, his body sagging from exhaustion. No longer smiling, he suddenly had the look of an old man and by now we could see that he kept the family going. In the closed torment of that pitiful shack, he was waging a hopeless battle against starvation. The Da Silva children were living in a coffin.

When at last the parents came in, Gallo and I seemed to be part of the family. Flavio had already told them we were there. "Gordunn Americano!" Luzia said, pointing at me. José, the father, viewed us with skepticism. Nair, his pregnant wife, seemed tired beyond speaking. Hardly acknowledging our presence, she picked up Zacarias, placed him on her shoulder and gently patted his behind. Flavio scurried about like a frightened rat, his silence plainly expressing the fear he held of his father. Impatiently, José da Silva waited for Flavio to serve dinner. He sat in the center of the bed with his legs crossed beneath him, frowning, waiting. There were only three tin plates. Flavio filled them with black beans and rice, then placed them before his father. José da Silva tasted them, chewed for several moments, then nodded his approval for the others to start. Only he and Nair had spoons; the children ate with their fingers. Flavio ate off the top of a coffee can. Afraid to offer us food, he edged his rice and beans toward us, gesturing for us to take some. We refused. He smiled, knowing we understood.

Later, when we got down to the difficult business of obtaining permission from José da Silva to photograph his family, he hemmed and hawed, wallowing in the pleasant authority of the decision maker. He finally gave in, but his manner told us that he expected something in return. As we were saying good night

Flavio began to cough violently. For a few moments his lungs seemed to be tearing apart. I wanted to get away as quickly as possible. It was cowardly of me, but the bluish cast of his skin beneath the sweat, the choking and spitting were suddenly unbearable.

Gallo and I moved cautiously down through the darkness trying not to appear as strangers. The Catacumba was no place for strangers after sundown. Desperate criminals hid out there. To hunt them out, the police came in packs, but only in daylight. Gallo cautioned me. "If you get caught up here after dark it's best to stay at the Da Silvas' until morning." As we drove toward the city the large white buildings of the rich loomed up. The world behind us seemed like a bad dream. I had already decided to get the boy Flavio to a doctor, and as quickly as possible.

The plush lobby of my hotel on the Copacabana waterfront was crammed with people in formal attire. With the stink of the favela in my clothes, I hurried to the elevator hoping no passengers would be aboard. But as the door was closing a beautiful girl in a white lace gown stepped in. I moved as far away as possible. Her escort entered behind her, swept her into his arms and they indulged in a kiss that lasted until they exited on the next floor. Neither of them seemed to realize that I was there. The room I returned to seemed to be oversized; the Da Silva shack would have fitted into one corner of it. The steak dinner I had would have fed the Da Silvas for three days.

Billowing clouds blanketed Mount Corcovado as we approached the favela the following morning. Suddenly the sun burst through, silhouetting Cristo Redentor, the towering sculpture of Christ with arms extended, its back turned against the slopes of Catacumba. The square at the entrance to the favela bustled with hundreds of favelados. Long lines waited at the sole water spigot. Others waited at the only toilet on the entire mountainside. Women, unable to pay for soap, beat dirt from their wash at laundry tubs. Men, burdened with lumber, picks and shovels and tools important to their existence threaded their way through the noisy throngs. Dogs snarled, barked and fought. Woodsmoke mixed with the stench of rotting things. In the mist curling over the higher paths, columns of favelados climbed like ants with wood and water cans on their heads.

We came upon Nair bent over her tub of wash. She wiped away sweat with her apron and managed a smile. We asked for her husband and she pointed to a tiny shack off to her right. This was José's store, where he sold kerosene and bleach. He was sitting on a box, dozing. Sensing our presence, he awoke and commenced complaining about his back. "It kills me. The doctors don't help because I have no money. Always talk and a little pink pill that does no good. Ah, what is to become of me?" A woman came to buy bleach. He filled her bottle. She dropped a few coins and as she walked away his eyes stayed on her backside until she was out of sight. Then he was complaining about his back again.

"How much do you earn a day?" Gallo asked.

"Seventy-five cents. On a good day maybe a dollar."

"Why aren't the kids in school?"

"I don't have money for the clothes they need to go to school."

"Has Flavio seen a doctor?"

He pointed to a one-story wooden building. "That's the clinic right there. They're mad because I built my store in front of their place. I won't tear it down so they won't help my kids. Talk, talk, talk and pink pills." We bid him good-bye and started climbing, following mud trails, jutting rock, slime-filled holes and shack after shack propped against the slopes on shaky pilings. We sidestepped a dead cat covered with maggots. I held my breath for an instant, only to inhale the stench of human excrement and garbage. Bare feet and legs with open sores climbed above us—evils of the terrible soil they trod every day, and there were seven hundred thousand or more afflicted people in favelas around Rio alone. Touching me, Gallo pointed to Flavio climbing ahead of us carrying firewood. He stopped to glance at a man descending with a small coffin on his shoulder. A woman and a small child followed him. When I lifted my camera, grumbling erupted from a group of men sharing beer beneath a tree.

"They're threatening," Gallo said. "Keep moving. They fear cameras. Think they're evil eyes bringing bad luck." Turning to watch the funeral procession, Flavio caught sight of us and waited. When we took the wood from him he protested, saying he was used to carrying it. He gave in when I hung my camera around his neck. Then, beaming, he climbed on ahead of us.

The fog had lifted and in the crisp morning light the shack looked more squalid. Inside the kids seemed even noisier. Flavio smiled and spoke above their racket. "Someday I want to live in a real house on a real street with good pots and pans and a bed with sheets." He lit the fire to warm leftovers from the night before. Stale rice and beans—for breakfast and supper. No lunch; midday eating was out of the question. Smoke rose and curled up through the ceiling's cracks. An air current forced it back, filling the place and Flavio's lungs with fumes. A coughing spasm doubled him up, turned his skin blue under viscous sweat. I handed him a cup of water, but he waved it away. His stomach tightened as he dropped to his knees. His veins throbbed as if they would burst. Frustrated, we could only watch; there was nothing we could do to help. Strangely, none of his brothers or sisters appeared to notice. None of them stopped doing whatever they were doing. Perhaps they had seen it too often. After five interminable minutes it was over, and he got to his feet, smiling as though it had all been a joke. "Maria, it's time for Zacarias to be washed!"

"But there's rice in the pan!"

"Dump it in another pan—and don't spill water!"

Maria picked up Zacarias, who screamed, not wanting to be washed. Irritated, Maria gave him a solid smack on his bare bottom. Flavio stepped over and gave her the same, then a free-for-all started with Flavio, Maria and Mario slinging fists at one another. Mario got one in the eye and fled the shack calling Flavio a dirty son-of-a-bitch. Zacarias wound up on the floor sucking his thumb and escaping his washing. The black bean and rice breakfast helped to get things back to normal. Now it was time to get Flavio to the doctor.

The clinic was crowded with patients—mothers and children covered with open sores, a paralytic teenager, a man with an ear in a state of decay, an aged blind couple holding hands in doubled darkness. Throughout the place came wailings of hunger and hurt. Flavio sat nervously between Gallo and me. "What will the doctor do to me?" he kept asking.

"We'll see. We'll wait and see."

In all, there were over fifty people. Finally, after two hours, it was Flavio's turn and he broke out in a sweat, though he smiled at the nurse as he passed through the door to the doctor's office. The nurse ignored it; in this place of misery, smiles were unexpected.

The doctor, a large, beady-eyed man with a crew cut, had an air of impatience. Hardly acknowledging our presence, he began to

examine the frightened Flavio. "Open your mouth. Say 'Ah.'
Jump up and down. Breathe out. Take off those pants. Bend over.
Stand up. Cough. Cough louder. Louder." He did it all with such
cold efficiency. Then he spoke to us in English so Flavio wouldn't
understand. "This little chap has just about had it." My heart sank.
Flavio was smiling, happy to be over with the examination. He
was handed a bottle of cough medicine and a small box of pink
pills, then asked to step outside and wait.

"This the Da Silva kid?"

"Yes."

"What's your interest in him?"

"We want to help in some way."

"I'm afraid you're too late. He's wasted with bronchial asthma,
malnutrition and, I suspect, tuberculosis. His heart, lungs and
teeth are all bad." He paused and wearily rubbed his forehead.
"All that at the ripe old age of twelve. And these hills are packed
with other kids just as bad off. Last year ten thousand died from
dysentery alone. But what can we do? You saw what's waiting
outside. It's like this every day. There's hardly enough money to
buy aspirin. A few wealthy people who care help keep us going."
He was quiet for a moment. "Maybe the right climate, the right
diet, and constant medical care might . . ." He stopped and
shook his head. "Naw. That poor lad's finished. He might last
another year—maybe not." We thanked him and left.

"What did he say?" Flavio asked as we scaled the hill.

"Everything's going to be all right, Flav. There's nothing to
worry about."

It had clouded over again by the time we reached the top. The
rain swept in, clearing the mountain of Corcovado. The huge
Christ figure loomed up again with clouds swirling around it. And
to it I said a quick prayer for the boy walking beside us. He smiled
as if he had read my thoughts. "Papa says 'El Cristo' has turned his
back on the favela."

"You're going to be all right, Flavio."

"I'm not scared of death. It's my brothers and sisters I worry
about. What would they do?"

"You'll be all right, Flavio."

The following morning I filed a cable to *Life*'s New York bureau,
the longest cable I have ever filed in my life, all about Flavio da

Silva's life in the favela of Catacumba. Forty-eight hours passed before I got a reply:

CATURANI FOR PARKS FROM TIM FOOTE—LOOKS LIKE YOU'RE
ON TOP OF A GREAT STORY—FLAVIO SOUNDS TRAGIC BUT HE
SOUNDS WONDERFUL—INSPIRING—STICK WITH HIM AND
KEEP US INFORMED—KEEP A DIARY—REPEAT KEEP A DIARY
BEST TIM FOOTE

MARCH 22, 1961

Reached shack at 7:30. Zacarias was crawling around naked in the filth outside. Albia and Isabel were swinging in a greasy hammock hung across the room. Flavio was cooking. I stepped backward to photograph the two in the hammock and upset a pot of beans. The girls laughed and laughed. Flavio started laughing but it brought on convulsive coughing. He became so weak I had to hold him. Later he scraped up the beans and dumped them back into the pot. I can almost see him dying now. I've started buying food for the family. Can't resist it. José da Silva is ecstatic. His back improves with each sackful I bring in.

MARCH 23, 1961

The kids are unpredictable. Albia and Isabel wiggle beneath my arms and grip my fingers. I'm not surprised to feel the prick of a pin or a nail. They seem to be testing my response to their need of attention. Nair hardly has time to give them any love, and José seems incapable of doing so. To ignore them for long is to abuse them. Their reaction is sullenness or violence. Maria is always plastering her hair with grease. When I found it was hog fat I brought her a bottle of perfumed oil. She grinned, sniffed and combed it in. She reached for Luzia's broken mirror to observe herself. Luzia snatched it away from her, spit at her, then me. Then she stomped my toe and ran. Maria put on a wrinkled dress, kissed my cheek and went out to let her friends smell her hair.

. . .

187

The favelado's fight against hunger and disease had spawned a hatred in them for those outside their world. That hatred was turned against a local television cameraman who had been sent to show me at work. He was blond, broad-shouldered and about six feet four. To protect the Da Silvas, I moved to another section of Catacumba. As I photographed the shacks, the cameraman followed closely, filming me. Suddenly a bunch of young toughs were gathering, coming toward us.

"Keep working and walking," the cameraman advised. He sensed trouble, and it came almost instantly. They began shoving him about, spitting on his face, on his arms and in his hair. I turned, cursing them. "Keep moving! Keep moving!" he shouted. "Don't mind me!" It took ages to reach the bottom of that hill, and I felt ashamed that my dark skin had spared me. As we crossed into the traffic two young favelados ran past us. Then came the screeching of brakes and a scream. The smaller one was caught under the speeding car. His crumpled body rolled to a stop about fifty yards away. The car slowed for a moment, then sped off with scores of favelados screaming behind it. The angry mob encircled the dead child. Some cried. Some cursed and others lit vigil candles and crossed themselves. Eventually someone brought a sheet that was embossed with fancy initials. It was probably a part of some rich family's laundry. Blood was seeping through as the cameraman and I moved off.

"The bastard never even stopped," I said.

"And it's good he didn't. They would have killed him on the spot. He'll report to the police in a few hours. That's all that is required here in Rio."

MARCH 27, 1961

It was unbearably hot today. José da Silva, looking more dead than alive, lay shivering and feverish beneath a crusty blanket. "God, what's to become of me? What's to become of me?" A huge black spider crawled over his leg and little Isabel smashed it with her fist. José shrieked and his hand shot up and struck her face. She stood crying until Flavio dunked some bread in coffee and pushed it into her mouth. She quieted for a moment, then for no reason she turned and kicked Zacarias in the head. Luzia shoved her to the floor. Mario smacked Luzia. Flavio went after Mario, and trying to get away he plunged headlong into Nair, who was entering the door. She cuffed him and he fell to the ground screaming, "What'n hell you hit me for?" Isabel, her sullen tearful gaze on Luzia, sat in the corner, muttering, "Bitch! Bitch! Bitch!" After cleaning her feet with stale coffee, Luzia went outside, doubled herself up on the ground and began sucking her thumb. Nair picked up Zacarias and tossed him onto the bed; then she sat on a box and buried her head in her arms.

It was Saturday night. I sat at my hotel's sidewalk café nursing a drink. A slender girl with sad eyes came to my table. "Would you like fun, señor?"

"No, thanks."

"It is very cheap."

"No, thanks."

"I need money for my sisters and brothers. They . . ."

"Here," I said, handing her about two dollars' worth of cruzeiros. Then I went up to my room, changed into my work clothes and, ignoring José Gallo's advice, took a taxi back to Catacumba. By then it was past midnight. The driver let me out at the foot of the mountain, and sensing that I was a foreigner, he asked, "You know where you are going?"

"It's okay," I answered. He drove away and for a moment I stood gazing up into the darkness, wondering, a little frightened. There was danger up there but there was also truth. To grasp the reality of the Da Silvas' plight, I would have to live as much of it as possible; feel the misery of the nights along with that of the days.

A third of the way up the darkness became menacing. Gallo was right. This was no place for a stranger to be after sundown. The fork turning off to the Da Silva shack had been easy to find in the daylight, but in the blackness I suddenly feared I had passed it, and standing there in the still point of that blackness, I lost all sense of direction. I climbed higher. A small animal scurried across my feet, a dog lunging after it. Then came the fierce screeching of a cat, the brief sound of struggle, then quiet. I made out the limp form of the cat hanging by its broken neck from the mongrel's mouth as it trotted away.

Farther up a man sat in his doorway rocking a child in his arms. A woman lay asleep behind him, and vigil candles burned at the head of a makeshift bier. The child's face was set in death under the flickering light.

"*Boa noite,* señor."

"*Boa noite.*"

"I'm looking for José da Silva's place."

"A few steps to the left, then soon you see the house."

All fear passed away; I was on the right path. When the path narrowed between two huge boulders I knew I was there.

Flavio was having a bad night. His hacking cut through the darkness as I approached the shack. When I knocked and called out my name, Nair opened the door and motioned me in. A strong scent of eucalyptus filled the place. Flavio sat on a box in the weak light of a kerosene lamp inhaling steam from a pan of hot water. Zacarias was sleeping soundly in his broken crib; the others were sprawled together on the one bed.

Surprised to see me at such an hour, Flavio smiled weakly and waved his hand. Speaking was obviously too difficult. The asthma attacks grew worse during the night, and his breathing was pained and labored. Yet, he kept smiling, seeming to know by instinct why I had come. Hoping to turn the course of his suffering, I smiled back, but my eyes, like his, struggled to show any joy. In the yellowish gloom there was only wretchedness; above Flavio's wheezing came the uneasy snoring of seven children and their father. Eventually Nair and Flavio would join them. Then there would be nine. Before lying down, Nair forced a spoonful of liquid between Flavio's lips. It was a mix of cold coffee and kerosene. Grimacing, he swallowed it. When he finally fell asleep I lifted him into bed beside the others.

It was three o'clock when I blew out the lamp. I sat on the floor with my back to the wall. My ankles ached. Climbing Catacumba every day had swollen them to twice their normal size. The family's snoring rose and fell in uneven rhythms, punctuated by Flavio's coughing. The blue-black sky looked unreal through the huge spaces in the ceiling. I sat in a strange darkness watching embers cool and flake into the ashes.

The sleep I fell into slipped into a nightmare. Cristo Redentor cracked into a million pieces and tumbled backward onto the slopes of Catacumba. There was a river of floating coffins filled with garbage and human limbs. Mario, not Flavio, lay dead upon a makeshift bier. I awoke in a sweat. I went back to sleep, but when I awoke again it was dawn. Flavio was up by seven, tiptoeing about, trying not to awaken the others. When the family began to stir he soaked hard chunks of bread in cold coffee and placed them in a pan beside the bed. It was Sunday morning; that called for a special breakfast.

APRIL 7, 1961

As I had promised, I took Flavio and Mario to the Copacabana beach today. When I arrived at seven they were already waiting at the entrance to the favela. They were unwashed, dressed in their tattered shorts and without shirts. Gallo was a bit put out with them for not cleaning themselves, but he realized that their eagerness had got the better of them. When they scrambled into the back seat he threw up his hands in disgust, then drove off. As we rolled through the valley of gleaming white buildings Mario's hand closed tightly about Flavio's.

Then, suddenly, the vast, curving waterfront with the thronged beach came into view. It was already hot and hundreds of multi-colored umbrellas cast pools of shade over the white sand. Boys their age flew kites and ran about the beach. "Flav, is this here all the time?" Mario asked. "Yes, yes of course, stupid."

We stopped at the far end of the curving stretch of sand and they got out. Copacabana Beach, with all its finery, was only a short distance from their deathful world, but they had never been there before. At first they were afraid to move about on the wide expanse of sand. Obviously it seemed unreal to them. They had drummed up enough courage when a large jet roared over from behind the buildings. They ducked and cringed. When the noise died, they joined hands and warily approached the water's edge. A wave broke against their legs and they screamed and ran, but after an hour they were running unafraid along the foaming surf. Gallo went off and came back with beef sandwiches, cookies and sodas, but for once their souls were hungrier than their stomachs. When it was time to go Mario begged for one last ride along the serpentine beach. We turned and made the trip again as the brothers sat holding hands, perhaps for the first time in their entire lives, taking in the vision of white sand and sea.

I tried pushing myself to believe that Flavio and Mario's trip to Copacabana might give the incentive for them eventually to escape Catacumba. But I knew differently. I had only exposed them to a doubtful dream. Flavio met me on an upper path near the shack the following morning. His eyes twinkled when he saw two sacks of groceries in my arms. He offered to carry one and I gave him one. He sniffed at the top. "Ah, meat and oranges. Thanks. Thanks." The roar of a big jet shot his head upward. He loved watching them, watching their vapor fleecing the cold air. I'm sure he never thought of the possibility of ever flying in one of those "silver birds," as he called them.

"I go back to America tomorrow, Flav."

"You go to stay?"

"Yes, to stay," I answered, thinking for an instant of his being up there flying beside me, then rejecting the thought as quickly as it had come.

"I go with you to America."

"Maybe someday, maybe someday. Zoooom! Up and away we'll fly!" We both laughed at such an impossibility, then fell silent as we climbed to the shack. All the kids gathered around as we started pulling out the groceries, pushing and shoving, trying to see what we had brought. They gazed at the meat, vegetables and fruit with a sort of sad gaiety. When Flavio took out the candy sticks bedlam broke loose. For a few moments happiness took over the Da Silva shack.

That afternoon Gallo and I went to see the clinic doctor, hoping to arrange for more medical care and substantial medicine. He wasn't the least bit encouraging, and repeated only what he had said before. We passed Da Silva's store, where he lay asleep on a bundle of rags. Nair was washing at the tubs. We exchanged smiles as she continued to rub. Then silently José and I drove toward my hotel, suffering a double sadness. Flavio's story was finished, and if the doctor was right, death would soon be knocking at his door. A dream had cracked apart. "Poor Flav," José finally said. A sense of the boy's absence was already in his voice.

APRIL 9, 1961

With José Gallo, I said good-bye to Flavio and his family.

"Gorduun, when do you come back?" he asked.

"Oh, someday soon," I lied.

"You come back to favela to see Flavio, yes?"

"Someday soon, someday soon."

He walked with me to the car, rubbing my hand as we went. There was a scream and I looked back to see Maria chasing Mario with a stick. Flavio stood grinning as we pulled away. "Come back! Come back!" He turned and hobbled back toward the hill; back into the jungle that was Catacumba.

The plane to New York took off at midnight. As we gained altitude, Rio, far below, sparkled like a jewel. Cristo Redentor, brilliantly bathed in floodlights, stood with its great concrete arms stretching into the night. Behind it, somewhere down in the big darkness, were Flavio and his family. We banked steeply out over the ocean, then there was only the glow of moonlight on the wings.

En route to New York from Kennedy Airport the following morning, a depressing thought struck: my essay on poverty might not be published. A ridiculous thought, but it kept bouncing back. That rejection bin on *Life*'s thirtieth floor was overflowing with good stories that failed to make it into print. An extraordinary event, an earthquake, a declaration of war, could send your story to that bin—never to be revived. It all had to do with the capricious nature of news.

Actually I had cause for concern. Poverty had been intended as only one part of a five-part series titled "Crisis in Latin America." *Life*'s top editorial board had approved the series on the condition that a single photograph would represent each of seven Latin American countries. If this decision held, all the effort I had put into Flavio and Catacumba would come down to one photograph. That just couldn't happen, no matter what that board had intended. But it did. In the layout approved by the managing editor, one photograph of Flavio da Silva, lying ill, was juxtaposed against a lady of extreme wealth from Rio de Janeiro. Despair struck when I saw it; and despair stayed as I went back to my office to pack my belongings. My mind was set. My days at *Life* magazine were over. I put forward the resignation to the managing editor:

Dear Ed:

The layout shocks me. I gave so much to that story, perhaps too much. I can think of it now only as an exercise in frustration. To use one photograph of that dying boy juxtaposed against one of some socialite is, to my thinking, a journalistic travesty. You will, perhaps, think I am out of my senses. At this point I probably am. Nevertheless, I feel that I can no longer work here. With regret, I offer my resignation.

A copy went to Tim Foote, the editor who had encouraged me throughout the ordeal at Catacumba. "Wait," he advised. "Give it some time." It was Friday. I decided to wait out the weekend.

It seems reasonable that miracles happen on the sabbath. The one that descended upon the sabbath of that particular weekend gave Foote and me cause to rejoice. In a *New York Times* article, Dean Rusk, the Secretary of State, warned that "if our government didn't give immediate and sizable aid to the poor of Latin America, Communism would surely spread rapidly throughout the hemisphere." We were in. On Monday, Flavio's story was rescheduled and laid out for eight pages. It was published in the issue of June 16, 1961, titled "Freedom's Fearful Foe: Poverty."

No one at the publication was prepared for what happened next. Thousands of letters poured in, some even offering to adopt Flavio. Money rolled in from every quarter of the nation—over thirty thousand dollars before the month was out. A note came from the publisher's office:

We have never seen any reaction from readers quite as spontaneous as this one. Queries are coming in from bureaus asking where people may direct money, food and clothing.

Then, from Denver, came an offer that electrified us. It was from the Children's Asthma Research Institute: "Without charge we will definitely save him. All you have to do is deliver him to our door." Overnight, preparations were in motion that would send me to bring Flavio to America. Then came the disturbing wire from the Rio bureau:

FLAVIO HAS TAKEN TURN FOR THE WORSE. DOCTOR RIBEIRO THINKS FLAVIO A TUBERCULAR VICTIM. UNCERTAIN WHETHER ASTHMA'S ORIGIN IS ALLERGY OR CONGENITAL. IT'S AN APPALLING, CRIPPLING STRAIN. HIS NORMALLY

SALLOW SKIN TURNS BLUE AND HIS THROAT SWELLS IN
EFFORT TO BREATHE. HE HAS SUFFERED THREE BAD SPELLS,
BUT KILLING HIMSELF TO KEEP FAMILY GOING. PRIME NEED
IS TO HOSPITALIZE HIM AS SOON AS POSSIBLE TO PREVENT
EARLY DEATH. LIFE'S READERS' CONTRIBUTIONS CAN
PROBABLY SAVE HIS LIFE. WE HAVE TO HURRY.

Most disturbing was the possibility that Flavio might be tubercu-
lar. This could prevent his entering this country. I suggested that
President Kennedy be asked to help. The President's message:
"Bring him on." Two days later I was speeding toward Rio.

SEVENTEEN

When my plane touched down in Rio at midnight, Gallo was there—waiting with hopeful news. Flavio's condition had improved, and a comfortable house had been found for the Da Silvas in the Guadalupe district several miles outside the city. *Life* would advance money for the purchase and a van to transport them. En route to my hotel Gallo described their new home and the neighborhood where it was located. Compared with the favela, it sounded like heaven. There were lovely trees and that *real* street that Flavio longed for. In the backyard was a small cottage surrounded with flowers and rosebushes, and there

196

was a good school nearby. For the ravaged family of Flavio da Silva, clear weather seemed to be ahead.

Gallo flushed with excitement when I informed him that arrangements had been made for him to return with us to Denver. He too would be going to the United States for the first time. I had grown to admire the sleepy-eyed, quiet-spoken Gallo. Tragedy had struck his own life when his eight-year-old son, Carlos, suffered brain damage and was left unable to speak. Despite this, his concern for Flavio never lagged. Pain was etched in his face for both of them. Since he was to take Carlos to a doctor the next morning, we arranged to meet later at the Da Silvas.

I arose early, took a taxi and got out across the street from the entrance to the favela. I stood for a moment looking up at the mountainside, finding it hard to realize I was back. But it was still there, throbbing with misery. As I started to move off, little Baptista's voice rang out, "Gorduun! Gorduun!" He was darting across the traffic to meet me.

"Wait! Wait, Baptista!" It was too late. A screeching of brakes, a thud. The car had knocked him down, passed over him, stopped, then started off again. But almost instantly a dozen or more favelados surrounded the car, screaming threats at the driver. Baptista was prostrate and unconscious when I lifted him from the pavement. The crowd thickened; growing more violent, they began rocking the car, trying to turn it over. The frightened driver sat helpless with the doors locked. Then Nair's hysterical voice pierced the noise. "My God! My God! They've killed my child!" she screamed, pushing her way through the crowd.

With Baptista in my arms, I beat on the car door. "Hospital! Hospital!" I shouted. It must have seemed like the only way out for the driver. He unlocked the rear door and I motioned for Nair to enter. She got in and I placed Baptista in her arms and we sped away. The happy reunion I had hoped for had evaporated in disaster.

As Baptista was attended to behind closed doors, Nair stood wringing her hands, weeping and mumbling prayers for her son. Gallo and José da Silva arrived after an hour. The father was barefoot with his pants rolled above his knees. "How's the boy, Nair?" he asked gruffly.

"He's in God's hands."

José got on his knees and prayed. Baptista was his favorite child.

All four of us were praying when we heard Baptista crying. At least he was alive. Another hour passed before the doctor came out. "Your boy has a fractured collarbone," he said to Nair. "There seem to be no serious head or internal injuries. He's lucky, very lucky. Don't worry. He should be all right." Then the doctor disappeared. I had last seen the driver at the end of the corridor. He too had disappeared. We returned to the favela with Baptista, whose shoulder was in a cast, the right arm in a sling. The gleaming white bandages seemed out of place in the dirty shack. For a brief period, Baptista appeared to be somewhat of a hero to his brothers and sisters. They looked at his bandages with a kind of awe. Gallo, after a respectable wait, gave them the good news. Flavio would be going to an American hospital and they were to have a new home far from the favela. "There will be new furniture, good food and new clothes for all of you. Your father is to have a truck." Happiness filled the Da Silva shack. As his brothers and sisters danced about wildly, Flavio sat on the floor with a broad smile on his face, obviously overcome with the good news. Nair slumped to the bed with Zacarias in her arms. José da Silva, finding all this hard to believe, eyed Gallo with disbelief—thinking perhaps that we were involving him in some sort of trickery. Flavio reached up and took my hand. "I'm glad you came back. I didn't think I'd ever see you again." His voice had a warmth and calmness that held me speechless. I could think only of his wish for "a real house with pots and pans and a bed with sheets."

Gallo and I stayed on for the remainder of the afternoon, filling the parents in on the wonderful reactions of the Americans who were responsible for their good fortune. Nair expressed concern about the need for Flavio to be away for two years, but she realized that it was necessary. For some reason we couldn't quite figure out, José showed concern about being so far away from the favela. Gallo reassured him. "You're going to have a better life where you are going, and a chance to earn a decent living." Still, the suspicious man sat scratching his head in puzzlement. Gallo and I left the area before sundown. The day, begun so disastrously, was ending much better than we had expected.

It was natural that the Da Silva children would spread the news that they were asked to keep secret. They shouted it to the hills. In doing so, they incurred the wrath of their fellow favelados, and Nair was forced to carry a broomstick to ward off attacks on her children. Hostility erupted among those who were forever doomed to the evils of Catacumba. "Why them and not us?" The question they shouted was a good one, but one without an answer. It became clear that the Da Silvas would have to be moved out as quickly as possible.

When Gallo and I arrived with the van early the following Monday, the entire family was washing up with their last bucket of water. Flavio hobbled about, wrapping their few belongings into bundles. Friendlier neighbors who had shared the hill with the Da Silvas for over twelve years stood outside the shack looking on with mixed feelings. Some hated to see them go; others were happy for them. "Maybe Flavio will live now," one woman said.

After an hour we started down the mountainside. Everything they owned was carried in a few makeshift knapsacks. Tearfully, Nair stood for a few moments taking a final look at the terrible dun-colored enclosure that had been home to them for so long. It had, after all, been home—regardless of the dirt, stink and rot. Several neighbors followed us to the bottom where a hundred or more favelados had gathered. The mood was tense and solemn. A few good-byes came from the crowd. One woman came forward and kissed Zacarias, then Nair. Another woman grabbed my shoulder. She held a small sickly child in her arms. "What about us? All the rest of us stay here to die?" I looked at her, answerless, then moved away. As the van pulled out Flavio strained for a last look at Catacumba, for their shack near the top. "Look! Look! There it is!" he said, pointing at the deserted hovel.

"Good-bye, favela," Mario said. He was smiling. I glanced back. The surly crowd was still there, watching from a lengthening distance. They would go on starving, diminishing with the onslaught at Catacumba.

We stopped at Sears, Roebuck to buy the entire family three sets of new clothes. Entering the store, the children were startled by popping flashbulbs: a score of newsmen went after them like hawks after chickens. Bedlam followed us as the newsmen posed them with toys they had never dreamed of owning. Zacarias was photographed with a teddy bear three times his size. Mario was asked to slop about in men's cowboy boots. Albia was hoisted onto a motorbike where she hung on in fright. Luzia was squeezed into an oversized dollhouse. Sanity returned only after Gallo corraled the family into a corner and barred the press.

José chose three blue suits. Nair selected six gingham smocks, and something new for the child in her stomach. The girls got cotton dresses, underwear, shoes and stockings. The boys were given shirts, pants, sweaters, pajamas, socks and shoes. Then came the toys—dolls, water pistols, cars, trains, footballs, baseballs, bats and cowboy outfits. All the children insisted on changing their clothes openly and in the aisles. At the last minute, it was discovered that Zacarias's shoes were two sizes too large. They were quickly changed, and the Da Silvas marched from the store transformed.

The half hour trip to the Guadalupe district became tumultuous, with the children grabbing at each other's possessions. José da Silva, unnerved by the noise, hollered for quiet. Quiet lasted for only a few moments, but a startling hush fell over the family as they pulled into their new neighborhood. A good part of that neighborhood had turned out to greet them—along with another barrage of newsmen.

With their arms loaded with clothes and toys, the family entered a gate to the yard almost timidly. José bowed nervously to the neighbors who, one by one, returned his greetings. Once inside, the entire family fell completely silent. "My God," Nair said as she looked about. "Is this all for us?"

"All for you," Gallo murmured softly.

Flavio ventured out in front of the group and looked things over. Then in a half whisper he asked, "Will my family really live here when I am gone?"

"It's their home forever," Gallo answered.

Suddenly, like a dam bursting, the children were all over the house, pulling out drawers, bouncing on beds, flushing the toilet again and again. Having moved cautiously into the kitchen, Nair rubbed her hand against the new refrigerator, then the stove. The neighborhood women had washed every plate, knife, fork and spoon. There were two large bowls of potato salad. *Feijoada,"* a rich dish of rice mixed with beans, meat and vegetables simmered in a large pot on the stove. Nair cried openly. José went to the kitchen door and surveyed the backyard, the little cottage surrounded with flowers. "I can't believe this," he murmured to himself.

By eight o'clock the neighborhood women had personally served the Da Silvas supper, cleaned up the kitchen, made up the beds and departed. For the children the magical day was coming to an end. Mario and Baptista giggled at one another as they buttoned up their first pajamas. Luzia was drying her doll's face after washing it in the bidet. Albia and Isabel had fallen asleep on the bedroom floor, entwined in an embrace. Flavio, helpful to the last, undressed them and lifted them into their bunk beds. This would be his last look at them for two years. Our plane was scheduled to take off at midnight. Maria was the last to get into her new nightgown. She stood silently watching Flavio pack the clothes I had bought for him the day before, including a pair of saddle shoes he valued most. At the last moment he pulled them out of his suitcase. "I'll wear these," he said proudly. Maria and Flavio didn't say good-bye. They faced each other, smiling awkwardly. He giggled and pushed her. She giggled and pushed back, then ran into the darkness of her room.

Nair had avoided Flavio most of the day. Not once had she spoken to him or touched him. Her withdrawal seemed more pronounced as she sat alone in the kitchen, wiping aimlessly at her kitchenware. By ten o'clock her manner had become one of stoical indifference. When it was time to depart Flavio went to her and touched her arm. "I've come to say good-bye, Momma." Nair remained quiet. Puzzled, Flavio looked toward me. I motioned for him to try again. He put his arm around her. "I have to go now, Momma." Suddenly, in a spasm of grief, she enclosed him in her arms, sobbing hoarsely, "God protect you, son. God protect you." Confused, Flavio took some coins from his pocket and pressed them into his mother's hand. Then hurriedly he picked up his suitcase, took my hand and pulled me out the door.

José had decided to see his son off. Undoubtedly he was by now the most celebrated son in the Western Hemisphere. A battery of cameramen, floodlights and television cameras met us at the terminal, and hundreds of people closed in to get a look at Flavio. Strained to the breaking point, he ducked under my arm and broke into tears. I hurried him through the crowd, and the airline officials rushed us straight to the plane. At the bottom of the ramp I asked José how he felt about someone adopting Flavio.

Scratching his head, he answered, "I don't care how long you keep him. Just bring him back well." He touched Flavio's shoulder. "Be a good boy." Then he moved off to the edge of the airstrip. He stood there watching as the big jet moved toward the runway. Gallo leaned across the aisle and pointed to him standing in the half-darkness. "That poor guy is still wondering about what happened to him."

At last Flavio was about to fly in the "big silver bird." He tensed and grabbed my arm as we began streaking down the runway. As we shot up into the darkness I could feel his fingernails digging in. "Next stop, New York," Gallo said. Flavio relaxed into a smile. After a good dinner and a trip to the cockpit (where he saw "men in police uniforms driving the plane"), he fell asleep.

A huge limousine met us at the New York airport—with two white-clad nurses. *Life* magazine was taking no chances. Flavio da Silva was a precious property. After a day in New York we flew on to Denver. There, an ambulance, a good-sized crowd and more newsmen awaited. The bulbs started popping and flashing, and once again Flavio ducked beneath my arm. He stayed there until we were whisked off to the Asthma Institute. In less than an hour he was undergoing an examination by three doctors. Despite their gentle manner he appeared bewildered, refusing to remove his clothes. Someone suggested that he might cooperate if I removed mine. This worked—until we got to the shoes. But then this had been the case since we had departed Rio. He had slept in them at the hotel in New York. They were, after all, his first pair of shoes. It came down to force. Gallo and I held him down and a doctor pulled off one shoe. When Flavio shrieked with pain the doctor examined his foot. It was covered with sores and blisters. We decided to cut the other shoe off. When we did, Flavio burst into tears. Promises to get him another pair failed to calm him. After he had cried himself out the doctors went on with their work. A couple of hours later, in a new pair of sneakers, Flavio was pumping wildly on a playground swing, surrounded by admiring boys and girls. It was evident he wouldn't lack for friends. There were a hundred and fifty children to make sure of that. He would no longer have to survive on stale coffee, hard rice and black beans. His meals would be prepared under the supervision of trained dieticians and allergists who were dedicated to saving his life. Nonetheless, he was in a strange place with only a few words of English to express his needs and feelings. Surely he would feel isolated and fearful for a while, and it was disturbing to think of all the adjustments he would have to make. In the months ahead the doctors would have to try to undo what twelve years of poverty and hardship had done. There had been times in the favela when I felt he was getting ready to die, that his overtaxed, ravaged body had decided it could not go on. Now I could only hope that there was enough time left for them to save him.

Before leaving, I had tea and sandwiches with Gallo and Flavio, and I again promised him another pair of saddle shoes. Gallo would stay on for a couple of weeks to interpret and quell the uneasiness. We embraced and said good-bye. As my plane climbed into the clouds I saw, far below, the plane's shadow, the "pilot's cross." To the fighter group I had once flown with as a correspondent, this was a sign of good luck. From my jacket pocket I took a note handed to me by a Dr. Falliers. It read: "Flavio's enlarged chest cavity confirms suspicion that he has one of the severest types of asthma. And X-ray indicates that at twelve he has the bone structure of a boy about nine. His weight and height are those of a six-year-old." I sighed and looked down for the pilot's cross. It was gone.

But Flavio survived and healed and emerged from the experience with an enviable command of English. I flew back from Europe the day he arrived in New York en route back to Brazil. We spent the day taking in the sights and stuffing ourselves with hotdogs, popcorn and cold drinks. We even took a boat ride around Manhattan. The following morning, after two years away, Flavio was flying homeward, well, happy and a few inches taller.

EIGHTEEN

In May of 1957 Gordon Jr. had been called up by the army. It was the morning of his departure and both Sally and I were in fear of losing him. The night before had been a troublesome one for us, and the disagreement we had was still gnawing at us. As Gordon packed, Sally strode uncertainly about the living room, obviously nervous and upset. I wanted to go to her; to calm her, to urge her not to worry about him. The words were in my heart but stuck there, boxed in. And as she walked, her frustration grew, until she could no longer bear it. As I knelt to fasten Gordon's suitcase she snatched a pitcher of water from a table and dumped it over my head. Wiping my face, I stared at her. "Why did you do that?"

"The next time it will be boiling water," she replied.

It was a bad moment for the three of us, and I truly believe she was instantly sorry for it. She had yielded to frustration, and lost complete control for a moment. Her anger had flashed like lightning, then it was over. She put her arms around Gordon and walked him to the door.

En route to the station he and I discussed the washout of my marriage, both of us realizing that the whys and hows of it were far too many to alter. Just before boarding the train he said something that was hard for him to say. "Dad, it's all over between you and Mom. Toni, David and I have known it for a long time. We also know you're holding on because of us. She meant what she said about the boiling water next time. We will understand if you decide on divorce."

I managed a smile. "You are not to worry. Your mother and I will straighten things out." Inwardly I doubted that, and he did as well.

Gordon's absence during the following months left a hole in our family life. It was like awakening mornings to find a favorite flower missing. At noon on August 31, I had been eating in a restaurant when a premonition of fear struck, not for myself, but rather for someone close. I experienced a chill for a moment, then it was gone.

Two weeks later a letter came from Gordon. He had been on war maneuvers in Desert Rock, Nevada, that same afternoon. The convoy truck, carrying him and three other soldiers, had broken down as they were escaping the radiation belt of an atomic test. They had sought safety beneath piles of heavy canvas until they were rescued by an emergency squad. Perhaps the two incidents had nothing to do with one another but they were cause for serious thought. For the next six months he underwent close observation by the medical corps, then strangely he was sent home—permanently released from all army duties. We were grateful for his early return, but with it came an inextinguishable fear that he might suffer serious complications in the future.

I have doubts about just how good a father I have been to my children. I do know I have loved, fed and clothed them well, and sent them to good schools. The house by now had been enlarged to twice its original size, and there was a spacious garden hemmed in by flowers, as well as a glistening swimming pool. There were more horses, a private tennis court nearby where David, Gordon and I spent long hours, and reasonably gentle slopes for skiing during the winter months. Good books and good musical recordings filled the shelves. Toni, studying the piano with Vivian, Dean Dixon's wife, worked at a large concert grand. Naturally, thoughts of Toni's performing the works of her father someday lingered in my mind. When the strains of my favorite Chopin prelude came from downstairs, I knew Toni was attempting to play a frown off my brow, or perhaps, about to barter for a new dress. If the house drowned in Rachmaninoff concertos, the boys, sensing my serious mood, took off for the tennis court or the stables. In other words, they had it made.

I suspect they felt nothing special about those glorious times, and perhaps for good reason. In an interview I had made it clear that no child of mine would suffer as I once suffered. Dad was simply living up to his word.

Yet, despite all the good things, they were living under a strain. Their parents' marriage was moving more and more into bitter weather. The pain of it was on Sally's face as well as mine. And as the days wore on the pain refused to wear off. A multitude of large and small agonies had delivered themselves one after another, then the worst—she began questioning the children's love for her. This left them, and me, baffled. Eventually the entire household took on a brooding atmosphere.

Then one night, with my mood extremely vulnerable to the situation, I experienced a terrible nightmare. A reptile slithered about in my right arm, trying to find a hole through which it could escape. In desperation I dug my fingernails into my arm, grabbed its head, jerked it out and began flailing Sally with it. In terror she fled our bed.

Regaining my composure, I felt my arm. There was no reptile, but blood spotted the sheet. I had torn a small hole in my skin. The uneasiness of that moment stayed on, driving me at last to a psychiatrist friend. "It's time," he advised, "for you and Sally to get a divorce."

The end came quietly one Sunday afternoon. "Would you like to keep the house?" I asked.

"No. It's too large, and full of bad memories."

"What about the children?"

"I can't understand them. They don't really love me. It would be better if they stayed with you. I've leased an apartment in New York."

The flame had burned out completely. Nothing left then but the ash of a twenty-odd-year companionship. And suddenly it was, in the sorrowful quiet, like a downdraft from a mountain. Nervously the children filed in to bid her good-bye. She kissed their cheeks and left. I watched from the window as she went to her car. Sadness was all over her—in her face, her shoulders and walk. I felt a deep sadness for her, wondering what wrong I had wrought upon this lonely woman who had suffered my three children into the world; children she could not bring herself to understand. In the beginning my love for her had been measureless; she had meant everything. I loved so much the feel of her; her dimpled smile and soft brown hair; her innocent silence on nights when she wanted love. When she drove off I turned from the window feeling alone, knowing that what we had shared wouldn't be forgotten. The decision she had made was, she honestly felt, the best for all of us. Despite what others thought, I felt it was an unselfish decision. After all, it was she now without family or home.

The overnight transition of becoming a father with three children and no wife did not totally confound me. The immediate and sensible answer to that particular problem was a good housekeeper. I was, however, mystified by the sense of independence my children began to exhibit. In considerably little time Toni developed into a good cook, and both David and Gordon assumed manly duties they had avoided in the past. Even more surprising was the attention they gave to me. They became good, warm companions. Toni was attending the Boston Conservatory; David liked the idea of going off to a prep school, and Gordon expressed an eagerness to find work and an apartment in New York. Things were working out, and the days ahead looked hopeful.

For me there were still untried paths, and Carl Mydans, a fellow *Life* photographer, urged me onto one in the last week of 1962. During intervals between assignments, we spent time reminiscing about our pasts. He had become especially interested in knowing about my childhood in Kansas, and I talked freely of those days.

"I'm amazed that you haven't written about it," he said one afternoon.

I laughed. "It's not so amazing to me. I can't write."

"Did you ever try?"

"A bit of poetry and a diary. That's it."

"I think you have a novel inside you."

"Now I am amazed. I've had no training whatsoever. You can't be suggesting that I write a novel."

"Why not try? Paper's cheap. You had no musical training either, but you had a piano concerto performed. Doesn't that make sense?"

Indeed it did. Partially to appease him, partially to affirm my own doubt, I went home that weekend and tried. In retrospect, it wasn't much of a try. What took shape were seven triple-spaced pages having to do with a Kansas tornado that stormed across my memory. With misgivings I thrust the pages into his cubbyhole the following Monday, then avoided him for the remainder of the day.

"Mind if I show these pages to someone?" he asked as we left the building.

"If you like. I don't mind." I couldn't muster up the courage to ask him for an opinion. Two days had passed when a call came from a gentleman who gave his name as Evan Thomas. He was inviting me for lunch the next afternoon. "What's it all about, Mr. Thomas?"

"I'm a close friend of Carl Mydans."

That was enough. "I would be happy to lunch with you, sir." I rushed to Carl. "Who is Evan Thomas?"

"He called?"

"Yes, to invite me for lunch."

Mydans smiled broadly. "Evan Thomas is a vice president at Harper and Row. If you don't mind, I'm going with you."

Most certainly I didn't mind.

Evan's first sentence stunned us. "Look, I want your novel," he said as we headed toward our table. "It's your first novel and we can only offer you five thousand dollars."

"But, Mr. Thomas, I . . ."

"Perhaps we can go to ten, but no more."

We were seated now and I swallowed hard. "What I was trying

to say, Mr. Thomas, was that I probably can't write a novel—but since you offered me all this money, I'm damn sure going to try."

As we left Evan warned me that news traveled fast; that other publishers would be after me. "Some can outbid us, but we will give you fine editing, and that's so important to a first novel." He was right; a few days later Ken McCormick, an affable man at Doubleday, offered twice as much, and introduced me to his staff, who, he promised, would lend me every assistance.

Perhaps Evan was unaware of how he got me to ignore that much higher bid, but surely I knew. At our next meeting he brought along a young lady whom he introduced as "your editor." Gene Young was a tall attractive Chinese woman, and from the moment I saw her I decided I was going to be an author for Harper and Row. After a cocktail Evan had left us at the bar to get acquainted. Later, as I walked her to the train station, she seemed merely to tolerate my presence. With a slightly heavy heart I accepted the news that she was married. Perhaps it was for that reason that I saw as little of her as possible. From then on we talked mostly by telephone, but the memory of her grew, and the few times I did see her left me with the kind of longing that was impossible to push aside.

I began writing on the first day of the New Year. In Kansas a meal of black-eyed peas and pig's feet brought good luck on that day. The peas were soaking.

Memories started gathering, rolling in from the bittersweet arena of cornfields, dusty roads and muddy riverbanks that formed the geography of my youth. I reached back for witnesses of that time. Marcus, my bullying nemesis of those turbulent days, appeared with a scowl to claim his role as chief antagonist. My parents were secure in their roles. Then, along with myself, all the sub-major characters took positions, leaving space for all the minor ones to squeeze into place. A murder helped the plot, and I spent several days melting back into the memory of it.

Facing that blank first sheet of paper was like staring into trackless space. Without realizing it, I was three hundred and three pages from the end, notwithstanding the destruction of hundreds of attempts, but the first seven pages I showed Carl would survive. Now, my thoughts were taking me back through the green fields and winter landscapes; the tornadoes, Sunday schools, prayer meetings, puppy loves, passions, killings, funerals—and towering walls of bigotry. Remembering was suddenly a tempestuous voyage backward, and I was trying to resurrect an often angry childhood.

Everything seemed pale and fogged, but reality remained in my father, mother, sisters and brothers—along with our clapboard house, with its ornamented wallpaper, potbellied stoves and creaky flooring. All the friends and enemies of my childhood stared at me, some dead, some alive, waiting to be included on those forthcoming pages. My memory went on, pointing at things that meant something, or nothing. Ideas came, caught fire and then sputtered away. A month crept past. Two months. Then some words my mother once spoke to me came back, bringing meaning with them.

Confused by intolerance, I had asked her if we had to stay in Fort Scott forever. "I don't really know, son," she had answered, "but you're to let this place be your learning tree. Trees bear good fruit and bad fruit. And that's the way it is here. Remember that."

Some of these words became the title, and all of them would be my inspiration throughout the book. My past began forcing me back, and then turmoil would gallop through me. Gene, my editor, sensing this turmoil, began nursing me through it—advising, constructing, helping me to make peace with it. "Plot, character building, style and the kind of stimulation that will keep the pages turning." She drilled these essentials into me during our long sessions. I found that writing a novel required considerably more than stacks of paper and a typewriter. Impatience became my worst enemy. Tearing up mediocre pages was no less than excruciating. But Gene, observing such pages without sympathy, persisted. And lovely though she was, at times I couldn't help but think of her as a tyrant. Wearied, perhaps, of trying to push me toward perfection, she relented near the end and began readying the manuscript for publication.

I finished *The Learning Tree* exactly one year from the day of starting, and six months later the novel was published. The dedication read simply: To Momma and Poppa. In a golden circle at the upper right side of the cover were three words, "A Harper Find." The inside jacket explained, "From time to time there appears on the Harper list a book by a newcomer outstanding for its qualities

210

of freshness and popular appeal. It is designated a "Find" by Harper salesmen in all parts of America, on the basis of their own enthusiasm, and the cooperation of booksellers is enlisted to see that the book gets the attention it merits."

Elizabeth Ann Campbell, the daughter of my friend, E. Simms Campbell—and my daughter's dear friend—had arrived from Switzerland when I was midway through the book. I hadn't seen her since she was about thirteen years old. Now, at twenty-one, she had returned full-blown and beautiful. After a visit to the house she invited me for lunch one afternoon, then a dinner, and then a party. It seemed as though we had suddenly discovered each other, and before long we were exploring the legends of love. Finally, on one fine summer's day, she arrived to spend the "weekend" with Toni. I remember that my heart quivered a bit as she alighted from the car and came down the driveway radiant in soft, beige linen. With some foresight and maneuvering, that weekend lengthened into still another; then bits of her wardrobe began arriving from New York. I pretended not to notice, but space was made in the clothes closet and more hangers were bought. It was the hospitable thing to do. Then suddenly it came to me; Elizabeth and I were living together.

Elmer Campbell, the renowned illustrator, was equally renowned for the rack of rifles and shotguns mounted on the wall of his den. After dreaming of them one night I shivered awake and elbowed Elizabeth into consciousness. She sat up on her elbows. "What's wrong, lamb?"

"Neither of us have thought about what Elmer Campbell might do when he finds out you're sharing my bed."

Gently she patted my brow. "Don't worry, lamb. The old boy's in far-off Switzerland. He'll just cuss, storm about and threaten to blow your rump off, but don't worry, lamb, all his guns are in a New York storage house." She lay back down and instantly went to sleep; but I slept fitfully. Throughout the night Elmer was on the chase, banging away at me with his prize shotgun.

A week later, at three o'clock in the morning, the telephone rang. Sleepily I picked up the receiver. "Hello, and who's calling?"

"You goddamned black bastard, you know damn well who's calling!"

Knowing for sure who it was, I asked again, "Who's this?"

"It's Santa Claus, you bastard!"

Liz had jumped out of bed and hurried to the downstairs phone. Vivian, her mother, had done the same thing back in Zurich. "Mother—"

"Liz, this is Viv. What are you up to?"

"Gordon and I are in love, Mother."

"Do you really love Liz, Gordon?"

"Why—why of course I do, Viv. We—"

"You're a goddamn lying bastard!"

"Mother! Will you shush Dad up. Gordon and I intend to get married." (The first I'd heard of that.)

"Married my ass! He's a liar, a son-of-a—"

"Daddy!"

"Don't Daddy me! I want you out of that house tonight! Do you hear? Tonight!"

It went on like that around three every morning, and for hours at a time. By the end of the first month Elmer had run up a twenty-five-hundred-dollar telephone bill. Things cooled somewhat when he got it, but then another call came at four one morning. The conversation was brief this time—very brief.

"You know, old boy, she's twenty-one and you, you bastard, are a hundred and twenty-one. Ha! Ha! Ha!" The telephone clicked off before I could confirm his remark.

It was a little too late. Elizabeth had already found a marrying preacher with a nice little church. "Come on, lamb, why not try it for a year? If it doesn't work out, well *tant pis.*" She got my best dark suit pressed and coaxed me away from the *Learning Tree* long enough for a blood test. When that test expired she hauled me down for another one. Finally, on one beautiful fall day, we took our vows. During the reception a case of champagne arrived. The note read: "With our deep love. Happiness. Viv and Elmer." I had inherited another father-in-law with a loathing for me, and a love for shotguns.

When copies of the *Learning Tree* arrived, I had stuffed my pipe with tobacco, lit it, made a cup of tea, stirred delight into it, and sunk into the pages. It was like dipping a cup into a well of memories. As Carl Mydans had predicted, there had been a novel in that well. Gene Young and Evan Thomas made it possible for me to plumb the depths. One opportunity fed upon another; Evan immediately pushed me into a sequel.

Vivian, Elizabeth's mother, had offered her some rather questionable advice. "If you want to keep Gordon, get him a small apartment in New York where he can write in peace. Now don't flip out—and you might consider getting him a mistress to go along with it. I've known him for a long time. He's a true Sagittarian. Put chains on him and you've lost him." Elizabeth cut the advice in half; she got the apartment, on New York's Beekman Place. I can't say whether or not this arrangement contributed to the marital bliss that carried us beyond those first doubtful years, but happiness reigned. Our few differences were handled in a strictly Elizabethan fashion. All threatening arguments were abruptly shut off with the placing of a flower on my desk, along with a peck on my brow. More of Vivian's sage advice.

NINETEEN

We preach freedom around the world, and we mean it. . . . Now the time has come for this nation to fill its promise. . . . We face . . . a moral crisis as a country and a people. . . . A great change is at hand and our obligation, our task, is to make that revolution, that change, peaceful and constructive for all." President John F. Kennedy, on the night of June 11, 1963, was fervently delivering his message to the American people. Shortly after midnight in Jackson, Mississippi, a white Southerner aimed his gun at the back of Medgar Evers, a black civil rights leader, and hit his mark. During the funeral white

Southern police waited with clubs, guns, water hoses and dogs to wreak havoc upon the mourners.

"And I shall oppose the black man's civil rights with every means and resource at my command!" Senator Richard Russell of Georgia was shouting his answer to the President's plea. Confronted by two U.S. marshals, Alabama's governor, George Wallace, stood pale and trembling in the doorway of the state's university, blocking the entrance of two black students, Vivian Malone and Jimmy Hood. The Klan was shooting blacks, burning and bombing their churches. In Birmingham "Bull" Connor's men were clubbing black men, women and children. Two thousand five hundred filled the jails.

Black people, especially in the Deep South, were besieged by racial calamity. The first year without a single reported lynching in America had been back in 1952. Angry black voices were trumpeting from every corner of the nation. Tired of being driven, lynched and exploited they had begun asking themselves, "What are we waiting for?" It wasn't the Supreme Court. What little help it had offered had been choked off by Klan terrorism. While the court had finally declared school segregation unjust in 1954, it had taken federal troops to get the students to their desks. Even as they sat down, "Lynch 'em! Lynch 'em," echoed through the corridors.

A few years before, Medgar Evers's murder might have gone almost unnoticed. So many blacks had been killed in the South that keeping an accurate count was all but impossible. Over seven years had passed since Rosa Parks refused to budge when a white man demanded her seat on a Montgomery, Alabama, bus. Two years later terrified black children braved white mobs to enter the Arkansas schools. Then, in 1960, came the sit-ins; disciplined with passive resistance, those who joined them had endured cursings and beatings. While one group wiped away blood and spit, another group walked in to take their place. A year later freedom riders rode with terror through Louisiana and South Carolina. In Anniston, Alabama, where I had escaped the lynch mob, one bus was firebombed, its windows smashed, its tires slashed, and the young riders beaten.

In August of 1963, hardly two months after the Medgar Evers murder, Martin Luther King hurled in the emotional wrench at the Washington Mall. His "dream" pushed blacks to harder resis-

215

tance, but shortly after, a bomb thundered inside a Birmingham church and four black children died.

With Martin Luther King, blacks began to march into the "freedom summers"; against dogs, tear gas and mass jailings; against the 1964 killings of James Chaney and two white sympathizers, Andrew Goodman and Michael Schwerner. Stacked together like cordwood, the blacks marched on, singing their battle cry, "We Shall Overcome." They were beginning to know who they were, what they meant to America, and what America meant to them. The 1960s were to be a decade of demonstrations, riots, more bombings and death, but it was clearly a revolt that had to be employed to alter the country's conduct toward black people. The symbols and images that for so long disfigured black minds had to be jettisoned. Blacks had combined to mutiny against a common fate. The forces had grown month by month, all armed with the same powerful weapon—blackness.

It was as if a cannon had sounded to summon black people toward oneness—the NAACP, the Urban League, CORE, the Black Muslims, SNCC, the Black Panthers, and Martin Luther King's Southern Christian Leadership Conference. From within the ranks sprang fiery young insurgents referred to as "Prophets of Rage": among them, the Muslims' Malcolm X, SNCC's Stokely Carmichael, the Black Panthers' Huey Newton, Eldridge Cleaver and Bobby Seale. Uncommonly militant, they were lions with a roar, and they wanted their roars to be heard around the world.

Life magazine was eager to penetrate their ranks for stories, but the black movement thought of *Life* as just another white establishment out of tune with its cause. As the magazine's only black photographer, I was in a peculiar position. As such the black militants regarded me with dubious eyes. And no doubt my editors pondered whether or not they could rely upon my reporting objectively—because I, too, was black. Eventually both my editors and the militants came to terms with their doubts—and I was thrust into those aggressive black strongholds where, for a while, I had to shake off the strangeness of being considered a friendly enemy. I sensed the delicacy of my situation. I was about to set a precedent for other blacks who might want to report for the magazine in the future, and I was also keenly aware that my sympathy lay with the black movement. Clearly that meant that I would become an objective reporter, but one with a subjective heart.

216

Somehow it will all work out, I told myself, and I stopped worrying about it.

Both the younger activists and the older moderates were plunging toward the fulfillment of King's dream, but one engaged in the rough and tumble tactics of the streets, while the other attempted to subdue white tyranny through reasoning. Consumed with bitterness, the younger men stared at the problem with hard eyes and scorned parlor diplomacy. I found myself envying their courage and willingness to die for what they believed. Openly defiant, they were boldly confronting the same police who longed to do away with them. Their brashness alienated some of the elders, but young blacks across the nation gulped in their words and proudly became their followers.

But gaining acceptance into the redoubts of such tough-minded insurgents was all uphill. It took weeks to make telephone contact with the Panther leaders. Their forays into the shadowy ghettos were understandably secretive since their every move was watched by lawmen. Stokely Carmichael, living out of a suitcase and moving cautiously through the South, was gone before he arrived sometimes. Malcolm X, obedient to the will of the Muslim leader Elijah Muhammad, stormed his contempt for white America inside the black ghettos of big cities. Stuck within those perimeters, he was easier to find—and I found him one afternoon in 1963 at 125th Street and Seventh Avenue in Harlem.

With controlled rage he was letting five hundred or more blacks know what he thought about a cordon of white policemen who stood to the rear of them. The wooden platform creaked as he walked about shaking his fist at the lawmen. "Take a good look at those white devils behind you! They know where the dope is! They know who the pushers are! They know all the whores and pimps! They are a part of them! They take payoffs from them! Those are the same rotten white devils, standing around with pistols on their hips, who help the pushers, whores and pimps stay in business!" He pointed at the police captain in charge of the cordon. "We Muslims defy you pale-face devils! Touch a Muslim and may God have mercy on your souls!" The crowd roared. The police stood silent, refusing even to look at their tormentor. Malcolm was all but sticking his face into the barrels of their guns.

He had cooled when I approached him in the Muslim restaurant on Lenox Avenue about an hour later. I introduced myself, then asked him about my chances to report from inside the black Muslim world. His smile betrayed his skepticism. "I know your work, *sir,* and I think you could do a good honest job. But it's not my decision to make. Only the Honorable Elijah Muhammad can do that."

"Would you take me to him?"

"He's in Arizona at the moment. That climate is better for his asthma."

"I'd be happy to fly out there with you."

He thought for a moment. "Well—let me call him to see how he feels about your coming."

The consent came the following day, and about twelve hours later we flew out to see Elijah Muhammad, who was known to his followers as the Messenger. The plane had just lifted off the runway when I turned to Malcolm. "What do you think my chances are?"

"Sir, it might be fatal to try and second-guess the Messenger. We'll just have to wait and see."

Frankly, I had reservations about the philosophical doctrines that counseled the Black Muslims. To me their cry for separatism gave credence to the same Supreme Court "separate but equal facility" ruling that had weighed heavily on black self-respect for over fifty years. America had built its wealth on the bodies of the black man, and his blood had also been spilled in America's wars. Now he should share in its prosperity. But to have hated all whites—as the Muslims seemed to do—was to diminish the sacrifices to be made later by Andrew Goodman, Michael Schwerner and others who would give their lives for the movement. The list would grow between 1964 and 1966. The Reverend Bruce Klunder, Reverend James Reeb, Viola Liuzzo, Jonathan Daniels and Vernon Dahmer—all white, and all to be slaughtered for their dedication to the black struggle.

Nonetheless, the Muslims had an admirable sense of caring for the poor; of reaching out to black inmates incarcerated in prisons across the nation. They were like a large family waiting to help the ex-inmates when they left prison; to persuade them against the use of drugs and further wrongdoing. Invited into Muslim homes and mosques, former convicts were eventually indoctrinated into the strict discipline inside the world of Islam—no pork, no drugs or alcohol, no smoking, and absolutely no unlawful acts of fornication. "Wake up, clean up, stand up," was the message for them. Softly, but forcefully, Malcolm explained the aims of the Muslims as we flew across the country. And I listened, inwardly accepting or rejecting what he had to say. I knew, however, that the skin the Muslims wore was the same color as mine. Somehow I would have to survive the struggle as their brother—but on my own terms.

Secretly, the question of *Life*'s editors clawed at me. Could they be trusted to print things as I reported them? Or would they try to reshape the meaning of my words to their own thinking, leaving me to the shrieks of betrayal by black militants? It was already clear to me that my neck was on the line; that somehow I would have to control the text. That meant writing it myself, and that's what I was determined to do. Even if Elijah Muhammad accepted me, I would be walking a tightrope—on one side the raging fire, on the other a conservative white publication. The afternoon was rife with imponderables when Malcolm and I entered the Messenger's door. His decision would influence the Black Panthers and all the other militants in their acceptance or rejection of me. If the answer was no, they, more than likely, would shut their doors to me as well.

Seated, Malcolm and I awaited the Messenger in a spotlessly clean living room, comfortably middle class and air-conditioned against the Arizona heat. On a coffee table was the Muslim newspaper *Muhammad Speaks,* and sternly staring at us from the front page was a photograph of Elijah Muhammad. The room's walls were bare, except for a much larger photograph of him with the same penetrating stare. On his head was a brocaded toque with the crest of Islam woven into it. He wore a dark suit, a white shirt and a small black bow tie. The same image prevailed as he came into the room coughing. Hurriedly we rose to our feet, and Malcolm bowed and introduced me. Muhammad was slightly built, frail and obviously having trouble breathing. After easing into a large armchair he motioned for us to be seated, glanced at me and smiled. "I'm not at my best today, and I have very little time to spare." He coughed and after a pause he made his mission and prophecy clear: as spiritual head of the Muslims in the Western world, he would lead the black man out of his hell on earth. Both his manner and speech were subdued but his condemnation of the "enemy" was ardent and incessant.

"The white devil's day is over. There is none a black man can trust. He was given six thousand years to rule. His time was up in 1914. These are his years of grace—seventy of them. He's already used up most of those years trapping and murdering the black nations by the hundreds of thousands. Now he's worried, worried about the black man getting his revenge."

I was beginning to feel a bit uncomfortable, like a black man in white man's clothing, sent by the very "devils" he was so heatedly criticizing, but he made no attempts to convert me. Once he warned, "Don't forget, young man. You've been living in the white Christian's world for a long time. Don't let them blind you. You don't need them."

He seemed to regard me with neither favor nor scorn. He said neither yes nor no to my request for permission to do a report on the internal workings of his sect. Extremely tired, he said, "Give me time to think it over, then come back to see me." He smiled weakly, got up, bid us good-bye, then left us in silence. In less than fifteen minutes we were headed back to the airport. Muhammad had seen me and exposed me to his doctrine; then, in a matter-of-fact way, he had let me know exactly where he stood.

"*Sir,* I think he likes you," Malcolm said as we drove along. He said little more. I didn't answer; I was thinking and feeling a little scorched from the heat of Elijah Muhammad's words.

The pilot announced our position over Chicago and I looked down, thinking of the months I had lived there in the black belt of that city; remembering the filth, fear and poverty, the bloodshed; the police brutality, storefront churches—voices singing, praying, shouting for mercy. I remembered the cold nights of winter when the hawk of misery spread its wings over the black ghetto—and then the robberies and murders that followed. And I remembered the hopelessness that seeped into so many black souls. Now, from this height, Chicago shone clean in the late afternoon sunlight. But I knew that, within the brightness below, torment and suffering were still there. With oddly mixed emotions I pondered what Elijah Muhammad's words meant to those blacks still suffering.

His soft-spoken anger kept flowing back. And I began to wonder whether or not my achievements in the world he called white had cost me a certain objectivity. True, I had stepped a great distance from the mainstream of black life, not by intention but by circumstance. In fulfilling my artistic and professional ambitions in the "white man's" world, I had had to become completely involved in it. In a way I missed the easy laughter of Harlem and the security of black friends about me. Although en route to my home in Westchester I occasionally drove through Harlem, there was hardly ever enough time to become a physical part of it again. And at times I found myself not really knowing where I belonged—a social oddity in one world, while emerging a stranger to another. At times I wondered if what I had achieved was worth the isolation. But if I had to bridge two worlds to escape the misery of one, that was the price to pay, and it seemed the price was small. I felt then, as I feel now; there is nothing ignoble about a black man climbing from the darkness on a white man's ladder, providing he doesn't forsake the others who, subsequently, must escape that same darkness.

I waited two weeks, called Malcolm, and the two of us flew back to Phoenix. Elijah Muhammad was in better health, but even more vindictive toward the "enemy." I listened patiently, feeling all was lost. Nothing I could say, or think of saying, seemed convincing enough to allow me into his confidence. Covered with defeat, I got up, preparing to go. Then, with sudden enthusiasm, he made an offer. "The Nation of Islam will pay you half a million dollars to do a film on its members. Would you like to do that?"

I had a hurried talk with my conscience. "I'm very pleased, sir, but I'm afraid you would want to control such a film."

"Of that you can be sure, young man."

"Then I have to refuse the offer. I'm a journalist, and I suppose I'm stuck with that. I would have to do things in my own way. But thanks anyway."

He stared at me, through me. "You know, in spite of your place in the white man's world I've come to like and respect your principles."

"Thank you, sir." My hopes soared.

"I'm going to allow brother Malcolm to escort you through the Nation of Islam. If we like what you do, I'll send you a box of cigars." He paused and smiled. "If we don't—we'll be out to visit you. Good luck. Now I must go to my bed."

Malcolm smiled. I had endured the storm. As we left I realized I had the assignment, and the responsibility of pulling it off. Suddenly I found the task ahead somewhat unnerving. The possibility of the Messenger's visit wasn't the most welcome thought. The problems of covering this intricate Western black arm of the Islamic faith would be difficult. Even before we reached the airport I was reaching out to my past, looking into the rocky holes of my youth. But nothing relevant was there to help explain the prophetic utterances of Elijah Muhammad. The Muslims had created a spiritualism of their own—uplifting, cleansing, demanding, but at the same time passionately violent. With a dedicated membership stretching out across the country from the East to the West Coast, the Muslims didn't appear to be seeking power; they seemed already to have it. And Malcolm X obviously felt a certain pleasure in moving about in the glare of that power, spreading the words of the Messenger. Before boarding the plane I called the New York bureau, saying that I had the assignment and would return there the following Monday. The enthusiastic response assured me that *Life*'s editors would be circling my desk all day—asking questions and offering advice.

Malcolm was far too complex to become more than superficially acquainted with over a weekend. During a Saturday rally in Chicago at the corner of Forty-seventh Street and South Parkway the following afternoon, he pounded home Elijah's anger and rage, firing up a huge crowd of listeners. "Death's no stranger to us Muslims, so the white devil's foolish for trying to threaten us with it. A true Muslim faces death head-on; and I'm a true Muslim. Elijah Muhammad's mission is to bring the white devil to his knees —and he will!" Scores of black fists shot into the air. And you knew those who shot them there were true believers. "The thinking American Negro realizes that Elijah Muhammad offers him a solid, united front. He is tired of the unfilled promises of the lethargic, so-called Negroes who have been thoroughly brainwashed by the American whites. 'Have patience,' Roy Wilkins and Whitney Young say. 'Everything's going to be all right.'

"Patience? The black man in this country has been sitting on the hot stove for nearly four hundred years. And no matter how fast the brainwashers and the brainwashed think they are helping him advance, it's still too slow for the man whose behind is burning on that hot stove!"

Again the fists shot into the air. "Tell 'em like it is, brother Malcolm! Tell 'em like it is!"

"The black man has died under the flag. His women have been raped under the flag. He has been oppressed, starved and beaten under it—and still after what happens down in Mississippi, Georgia and Alabama they ask him to fight their enemies under it. I'll do my fighting right here at home, where the enemy looks me in the eye every day of my life. I'm not talking against the flag. I'm talking *about* it!"

His humor was as dry as it was caustic, and he used it like a weapon to end his tirade. "I watch some of these big-time *Nee*-groes who get a little money in their pockets heading back South to show off, riding along all puffed up like turkeys. They ain't going no place, brother. It's the train that's moving—and they're just standing still."

His fiery words were still ringing in my ears as we boarded the plane for New York later that evening. I had felt the excitement of them and felt stirred by them as well, but I could no more dismiss the events that had molded me than I could cast off the cloak of my skin—no matter how appealing Malcolm was as an individual. Yet I concluded that the Muslims were striking a responsive chord in many blacks, even those moving in sophisticated circles who once had held themselves aloof from the day-to-day aspects of "the problem." It had come as a shock, one afternoon at a chic garden party, to hear two well-to-do black women extolling black nationalism. One was even considering joining the Muslim's New York mosque. At the same gathering I heard another black woman berate a blond matron for the white's treatment of "her people."

"You mean *our* people," retorted the fair-skinned matron. "I happen to be black too." I was afraid she would not have admitted that ten years before.

The Muslims, with their sharp and unrelenting attacks, their aggressive pride, were awakening blacks long insulated by their middle-class possessions and aspirations. Behind their Islamic chanting and semimilitary rituals that I would later witness, there lay a cause—one which called to black slum dwellers and suburbanites alike.

Tired from his day of work, Malcolm slept most of the way to New York with his chin resting on his hand, mumbling incoherently now and then—and with anger on his face. He seemed to be a prisoner of his own strength, declaring war on the enemy even as he slept.

That Sunday, away momentarily from the wilderness of confrontation, and in the sanctity of his home, he was a far different man; gentle and soft-spoken to his wife, Betty, and their daughters. Here, all was peace, free of the anger that kept him going. Munching an apple, he moved lazily about their small house, smiling easily, looking to be a young man whose heart was all future. His family was happy to have him home. Betty appeared to be a strong woman, still she must have been concerned about the danger that stalked him every day; about those vicious railings within a gunshot of the police he constantly harassed.

He went to touch her shoulder and she patted his stomach. "You're getting skinny," she said. "When's the last time you ate a good meal?"

"No time to eat."

"You'd better learn to take time. You're thin as a rail."

He grinned. "That's from worrying about you."

At seven o'clock he switched on the television for the evening news. A commercial showed a blond model spraying perfume over her neck. "That white lady's sure trying to smell good," he quipped. Two murder stories followed, then one about racial unrest in Birmingham. Suddenly his own voice was booming from the television set, and all of us turned to watch as he fired up the crowd back in Chicago the day before. "Elijah Muhammad's mission is to bring the white man to his knees—and he will!"

Betty stood for several moments observing the telecast, then slowly she turned away. "Tell 'em like it is, brother Malcolm," she said, then went off to prepare supper. For her it was another few moments of his inviting danger upon himself, and no doubt it bothered her. As he watched himself the scowl had returned to his face for a few seconds, and I had wondered if he was unhappy with his performance, but I was careful to keep my silence. Even on this peaceful evening with his family his thoughts were still in the world of confrontation.

• • •

Malcolm had made me somewhat aware of the rigorously enforced discipline Elijah Muhammad imposed upon his followers, and very little I was to see contradicted what I had heard or what he had told me. The laws were explicit—in Muslim homes, schools, stores, restaurants and mosques, there was to be no dirt, smoking, pork, liquor or boisterousness. Women wore white, hooded gowns. Men wore dark suits and white shirts, their hair closely cropped and their black shoes discreetly polished. Neatly dressed children attended schools of Islamic teachings, and the boys patiently waited for the girls to enter the doors first. A warm bond existed between the parents and their children. It was warming to see young brothers with heads bowed, facing the east, praying to Allah—in a Harlem ghetto.

Of their father I asked, "What would you do if they renounced your faith?"

Unhesitatingly, he answered, "Turn them from my door and never allow them to enter it again."

In the mosques lessons of a more sinister nature were being taught—ways to disarm a policeman; ways to kill an attack dog with bare hands. Elijah was building his nation on the everyday needs of underprivileged black people whom society had long since rejected. His converts—dope addicts, thieves, murderers, prostitutes, pimps and hustlers—had emerged from prison to be trained to be respectable human beings.

Could this be why his voice, barely audible in person, was drowning out those conservative voices of the NAACP, the Urban League and CORE? Malcolm X claimed the only answer as we were having tea in the Muslim restaurant on Lenox Avenue. "Elijah Muhammad truly cares about black people. He teaches them that, at a time like this, they can't afford the luxury of economic or religious differences. We must work together if we are to attain freedom. The Messenger wants to unite all black men, whether they're Muslims, Methodists or Catholics. Trying to go it alone means failure. If I have a bowl of soup, then you have a bowl of soup. If you die for what is right, then I must die beside you. You are a black man and I'm your brother."

"Martin Luther King wants the same thing."

"King's passive resistance tactics are for the birds. There's no philosophy more befitting the white man's way of keeping his foot on the black man's neck. King's following Gandhi's tactics. But

225

Gandhi was a big dark elephant sitting on a little white mouse. King is a little black mouse sitting on top of a big white elephant.

"But he stirred the black rebellion to life, and swept us all into common protest—the NAACP, the Urban League, the sit-downers, freedom riders and all the rest.

"Martin's way won't work. He and all the other so-called black leaders have lost control—if they ever had any."

Malcolm was as inflexible as iron. As we parted after finishing our tea, he said, "Going to Los Angeles day after tomorrow." He smiled. "Things are getting hot out there." He wrote out his West Coast telephone contact and handed it to me.

"I'll arrive within a couple of days."

"Then I'll see you there, *sir.*" Sir—there was nothing to do about the icy term but accept it.

Harlem's air was fetid and hot when, a few moments later, I walked into an angry mass of black people at 125th Street and Seventh Avenue. Violence was close to erupting, spurred on by a fiery little woman atop a box screaming: "We're on the move! We're crossing the line—even if it means death! We'll keep coming till they're ground to dust under our feet!"

Hovering on nearby rooftops and poised in doorways, disgruntled white policemen stood watching with nightsticks in hand.

"Give 'em hell, baby!"

"Preach on! Preach on!" The crowd was roaring approval.

Los Angeles' police proved to be much less intolerant—and more aggressive. Three days later when I got to the mosque where Malcolm was to speak it was surrounded by police cars, ambulances and angry Muslins. "The pigs," I was told, "busted into the mosque and shot up the place." Now they were bringing out the wounded on stretchers. I counted up to six. "Was brother Malcolm inside?"

"No—he hadn't come yet."

I felt relieved. "Anyone dead?"

"Brother Ronald Stokes. They shot him in cold blood." Fourteen Muslims were charged with "assault and interfering with an officer."

Three months later during the trial I sat in the front row with Malcolm. On his lap was the newspaper *Muhammad Speaks.* The

226

red headline blared, SEVEN UNARMED NEGROES SHOT IN COLD BLOOD BY LOS ANGELES POLICE! Directly in front of him sat the all-white jury. On the stand was Officer Donald Weese, the killer of Stokes. Malcolm stared at him with sphinxlike eyes from the moment he took the stand until he got off. During the preliminary hearings it had been established that Weese, though he knew the Muslims were unarmed, shot at least four others besides Stokes and beat another one down with the butt of his gun. The following questions by Attorney Earl Broady and answers from Officer Weese are from the court records of the trial.

QUESTION: Mr. Weese, when you fired at Stokes, did you intend to hit him?

ANSWER: Yes, I did.

QUESTION: Did you intend to hit him and kill him?

ANSWER: Yes. The fact that I shot to stop and the fact that I shot to kill is one and the same, sir. I am not Hopalong Cassidy. I cannot distinguish between hitting an arm and so forth, sir. I aimed dead center and hoped I hit.

QUESTION: You are saying, sir, to shoot to stop and to shoot to kill is one and the same thing in your mind?

ANSWER: That is correct.

QUESTION. Did you feel that to protect yourself and your partner it was necessary to kill these men?

ANSWER: That is correct, sir.

Leaving the courthouse that evening I recognized a white reporter who was covering the trial for a Los Angeles daily. "The Muslims are going to be convicted," he said. I asked him if he thought they were guilty as charged.

"The state has no case whatsoever, but they can't afford to lose this one. They have to get those cops off or the Muslims can sue them for millions," he replied.

Later, when I relayed his words to Malcolm X, he said, "Oh, he told the truth, *sir*. He was an honest devil, because that's what will happen—but things won't end there. Believe me."

En route to New York, Malcolm and I stopped at Phoenix to discuss the trial with Elijah Muhammad. He spoke with more emotional intensity than I had seen him show before. "Every one of the Muslims," he said, "should have died before they allowed the aggressor to come into their mosque. That's the last retreat they have. They were fearless, but they didn't trust Allah completely. If they had, it would have been a different story. A true Muslim must trust completely in Allah."

Mr. Muhammad was weak from a periodic fast, but he went on although fatigue slowed his voice. "There is one thing good about what is happening down in Birmingham. The black man can at last see what the white devil is really like, what he really feels about him. Birmingham bears witness to the fact that he is a devil and can't do right, what with water hoses stripping dresses from our women and our youth being chased and bitten by vicious dogs. By now the black man should realize that he must fight for his rights if he is to attain them. The white man is more vicious than the dogs he sets upon us. He's never satisfied with the black man no matter what his position. You can lie down and let your back be his doormat, but soon he'll get tired of that and start kicking you. "Turn over, nigger! You're layin' on the same side too long," he'll say.

Before leaving the Messenger, I asked two questions I had been saving for him. "Just what is salvation for the black man?"

Without hesitation he crisply replied, "We must accept Islam. We are the initial people."

"Why?"

"Because it is something universal, wherein man submits himself completely to God—a black God."

"What is your overall purpose—your goal?"

"Universal peace and brotherly love—two things the white man will never be able to accept."

It was nearing plane time. A white-suited chauffeur ushered us out toward Muhammad's limousine. I got in, and through the rear window I could see him and Malcolm embracing, their cheeks touching as they bade farewell.

Just before the story closed, *Life*'s editors decided we needed a photograph of all the Muslim leaders together. I suggested to Malcolm that we fly to Phoenix on the same plane. He, in turn suggested that I call Elijah's eldest son, Herbert, about that. I did—and his reply mystified me. "It won't be necessary for brother Malcolm to come."

"But we want all the leaders."

With clarity he answered, "Then it *isn't* necessary for brother

Malcolm to be there." It had never crossed my mind that Malcolm X was not to be a leader in the black Nation of Islam. I didn't bother to call Malcolm back. The editors were as mystified as I was, but the decision had been made, and I felt it wise to let the matter sleep. The photograph that ran was of Elijah Muhammad, Clara, his wife; his sons, Elijah Jr. and Herbert; Raymond Sharrieff; and Elijah's grandson, Hasan Sharrieff.

To assess the findings of the Los Angeles jury, I had studied the transcript of the trial. It was exhaustive, but it shed the truth: there was no effectual evidence against the defendants. A *Life* editor frowned when he came to the passage where I took issue with the verdict.

"A jury's word is final. I find it dangerous for the magazine to oppose its decision."

"I'm opposing it, not the magazine. The essay is written under my byline.

"Well—the company lawyers will have to decide."

"Then let them read this." I handed him the transcript. Two days later the lawyers passed judgment, and the passage would remain as I had written it. The magazine might have hinted at a disclaimer, but it didn't.

In sticking to my guns, I had the advantage of having seen the bullet-pocked corpse of Ronald Stokes—and I had seen the cold hatred in the eyes of his murderer. Too, I had sensed the danger of bending facts that would have soiled my credibility. The young editor questioning my conclusion was at a disadvantage. Muslim mosques, so glaring with black idolatry, were worlds into which he would never be allowed to enter, much less understand.

During those months of my coverage Malcolm and I had seen a lot of each other—tested, measured and felt one another out. After the story was published we met on the street, and casually he addressed me as "brother."

"Thank you for that, Malcolm. It's the first time you called me brother."

He smiled. "You earned it. You traveled the fire with me." Later he honored me by naming me as his daughter's godfather.

Not all of Elijah Muhammad's aims and motives were ever clear to me. I found much of his religious philosophy rather naive and confusing. It was obvious from which stratum of black society he hoped to draw support for his program: the indigent, unprivileged blacks who were seeking a messiah to lead them to a land promising freedom, justice and equality. And he insisted that only within a black state could that ultimate goal be achieved. That was far from my belief.

But somewhere, between his extremism and Martin Luther King's passiveness, the black rebellion had come alive. Fire hoses, police dogs, mobs or guns couldn't put it down. The Muslims, the NAACP, the Urban League, the sit-inners, sit-downers, freedom riders and black nationalist groups had all been swept into a vortex of common protest. If the leaders had lost control they were nevertheless still moving forward, and black people were being pulled along after them like leaves caught up in the wake of a speeding car. Even Martin Luther King was seeing his nonviolent movement swept into a long-fomenting universal revolt. And as the blacks pushed on, resistance in the Deep South stiffened. "Even here in the North the 'enemy' is plentiful!" screamed Malcolm.

He was right. Because for all the civil rights laws and the absence of Jim Crow signs in the North, the black man was still living the last-hired, first-fired, ghetto existence of a second-class citizen. His children were idling into delinquency and crime; in too many places they attended schools as inferior and as neatly segregated as any in the Deep South. A revolt in Englewood, New Jersey, against segregated schools there was just as important as the revolt in Birmingham or Nashville. There had been no time like this in the United States since the Civil War.

The times cried out for bold, principled leadership of a kind that had never really been attempted in the country before. Attorney General Robert Kennedy, after running head-on into the fanatical resistance of Alabama's Governor George Wallace on the segregation issue, had been quoted as saying, "It's like a foreign country. There's no communication. What do we do?"

Through my essay in *Life* I had answered, "You keep trying, Mr. Kennedy. You keep going back for more, again and again, until you begin to realize what it is like for a black man to 'go slow,' to 'take it easy' while under the boot of a racist like 'Bull' Connor. Go down there sometime when the fire hoses are on full blast, when the dogs are snarling and tearing black flesh, when women, children and men are on their knees singing, crying and praying for deliverance from the agony of this beautiful land.

Then go back and tell the President that if it's greatness he seeks, this is indeed his chance for it." After seeing a telecast of black protestors' heads being doused at a sit-in with ketchup, salt and pepper, those words had poured from my insides like scalding water.

I would not have followed Elijah Muhammad into a black state —even if he had achieved such a complete separation. I had worked too hard for a place in the society where I existed. Nevertheless, to the Muslims I acknowledged that the circumstance of common struggle had willed us brothers. I knew that if civil racial violence did erupt, this same circumstance would place me beside them. Although I would not have allowed them to be my keeper, I was, inherently, their brother.

Late one evening Malcolm and I were driving into New York City from Brooklyn. We were talked out, and I drowsed as he fought the headlight glare of oncoming traffic. Unexpectedly he had said, "We sent a little white college girl out of the restaurant in tears today." I had sat up, awaiting another diatribe against a presumptuous, if well-meaning "devil."

But Malcolm, speaking with a gentleness he never exhibited when discussing whites, assured me that it was nothing that had been said against her. "She had come to see if there wasn't something she and her college friends could do to help blacks and whites get together," he explained.

"What happened?" I asked.

I am positive he was unaware of the trace of melancholy in his voice as he answered, "I told her that there was no chance—not the ghost of a chance. She started crying, then turned and went out."

On the evening of November 22, 1963, I was in Paris when I heard on the radio that President Kennedy had been assassinated. For several minutes I stood in disbelief. The violence that Americans were feeding on was now feeding on them. Black America's most shining white advocate against racial injustice had been murdered. The entire world, hardened to millions of extraordinary murders, found it impossible to pardon this one. The universe was saddened, stunned by the news. I spoke a prayer for him and our country.

Paris seemed shocked to silence when I reached the lobby of my hotel the following morning. The concierge spoke softly. "It's terrible for America, monsieur—and for us here."

"Yes, it is terrible," I agreed.

Then he brought me up short. "Tell me, what is Mr. Johnson, your new President, like?"

"I don't know. I don't really know." That was all I could bring myself to say. The gloomy reality that had struck millions of other black people had suddenly struck me. A Southerner was now President of the United States. It was an unpalatable certainty that had to be admitted. If the concierge wished to know more he would have to wait—as we blacks would have to wait.

Working on the new book brought Gene and me closer when I returned to New York. We lunched frequently and our friendship took on an added warmth, and no longer did I mind her pushing me harder toward becoming a better writer. Then, at dinner one night, I allowed caution to wear off—looking up from a big steak as I abandoned it. "Gene, forgive me, but I think I've fallen in love with my editor."

"It's the wine," she answered evenly. "Authors do silly things like that from time to time." After that it was never quite the same. We grew even closer, and in my confusion I welcomed that closeness. A few weeks later, in Evan Thomas's apartment, the three of us lifted our glasses to the success we hoped for for *A Choice of Weapons*, the title which had come to me the night of President Kennedy's assassination. As we drank, Gene's eyes met mine and lingered much too long. And at that moment we both realized we were looking love straight in the face.

Tortuously slow, the black revolution trudged on. Its young insurgents were still fortifying themselves with more effective ways to address their problems; some, like the Black Panthers, were acquiring an arsenal of firearms to protect themselves against white police who, they claimed, had increased their harassment of them. They had viewed my reportage on the Muslims with questionable favor, but as yet they had not blessed me fully with their confidence. They would wait. *Life* magazine would wait and I, while working at other assignments of a less serious nature, would wait. All of us, it seemed, were in a holding pattern.

Because of this I was able to spend more time with my children during the next two years. And it was valuable time. Growing rapidly toward adulthood, they often needed fatherly guidance to wrap around their own aspirations. They had not allowed themselves to idle in boredom. Gordon's dream was to own a stable one day, and his love for horses had pushed him into a job at a Westchester polo club. David, a good athlete, wanted to become an instructor of tennis and skiing, and worked hard at both sports. Meanwhile Toni, to my mild discontent, had married Jean Luc Brouillaud, a young Frenchman, and they had presented me with my first grandson, Alain. Jean Luc was the same kid David had argued with about that *bateau* on the family's first morning in Paris.

It was a winter evening to enjoy. The children were entertaining a living room full of their friends. The sky was beginning to fill with stars and a rosy twilight glowed against the woods surrounding our house. I sat with Elizabeth in the dining room bouncing Alain on my knee as a car came down the driveway. To my surprise, it was Malcolm X, and hurriedly I went out to greet him. He looked somewhat handsome in his new goatee and Astrakhan fur hat. "I was out this way and decided to drop in on you. Hope you don't mind."

"I'm delighted. Been thinking about you." I had also been reading about him, about his recent expulsion from the Nation of Islam. But not until he broached the subject did we talk about it.

"I guess you know. Elijah Muhammad's out to get me."

"I knew there was a problem."

"A big problem. My house was firebombed a couple of weeks ago."

"I heard about that too. What about your family? Are they all right?"

"Danger is danger. They are also vulnerable."

"What about police protection?"

"Nobody can protect you from a Muslim but another Muslim. I know. I invented many of their tactics."

It all puzzled me. He had been Elijah's most devoted disciple. I thanked him for the cards he had sent from abroad in the past year; they had come from Saudi Arabia, Kuwait, Kenya, Ethiopa, Nigeria, Ghana and Tanganyika.

"I visited Mecca to get closer to the orthodox religion of Islam —and Africa to learn from its leaders. Their problems are insepa-

233

rable from ours, but Nasser, Ben Bella, and Nkrumah awakened me to the dangers of racism. It's not just a black and white problem. The cords of bigotry have to be cut with the same blade."

"Those were interesting times we shared."

"Those were mad days back there. Sick days. I'm glad to be free of them. We need martyrs now—that's the only way to save this country. I learned it the hard way, and it took about thirteen years. But I'm on my own now, and I've got some good, sensible people with me. I did many things as a Muslim that I regret now. I was just a zombie—like all the rest of them. I was hypnotized, pointed in a certain direction and told to march."

Elizabeth brought in tea, and we lifted our cups to his future. He drained his cup and got up to leave. "Well, I suppose a man's entitled to make a fool of himself if he's ready to pay the cost." He pulled on his coat. "I'm speaking at the Audubon Ballroom up in Harlem Sunday afternoon. If you're in the vicinity drop in. There won't be a lot of bodyguards searching people. My followers are trying to create a new image that makes people feel at home."

"I'll try to drop in if I can get away."

"Fine. *As salaam' alaikum,* brother."

"Peace be with you, brother Malcolm."

Two days later he lay dying on the stage of the Audubon Ballroom, his life oozing out through gunshot wounds in his chest. The most strident voice in the black revolt had been stilled—and by members of his own race. His power and prominence had made him a marked man. His downfall had started even before his notorious comment on President Kennedy's assassination ("Chickens coming home to roost never made me sad"). With that statement he unwittingly made himself vulnerable. With Elijah aging and ailing, he was the obvious successor to a power he didn't really want. Now he was out of the way.

That night I sat with Betty, his wife, his four children, and a group of his stunned followers, watching television reviews of his stormy life. Unable to watch anymore, Betty went to the kitchen where she stood staring at the wall. Six-year-old Attallah took her mother's hand. "Is Daddy coming back after his speech, Momma?"

Betty put her arms around the child and leaned her head against the refrigerator, saying nothing. Only Qubilah, the four-year-old, seemed to understand. She tugged at her mother's skirt. "Please don't go out, Momma." During the evening Betty showed me the bloodstained list of likely *hit* men that had been in Malcolm's pocket when he died. I copied them for future reference, knowing *Life* would expect me to write the story. As I was leaving, two powerfully built men who had caught and broken the leg of one of the assassins pulled me aside.

"Harlem's too hot for us tonight. How about taking us to your place?"

I was then living in an apartment on Beekman Place. "Fine, but I'm driving a sports car with only two seats. One of you will have to lie in the back."

Prosperous, lily-whites on Beekman Place would have slept uneasily that night had they known whom I had brought into the building. That evening the phone rang, as expected. The editor from *Life* was calling. "Are you on the story?"

"More than you are apt to realize. Two of the principals are taking over my bed tonight."

"Do you need anything?"

"Yes. Money. They want to skip town for a while, but they're giving me plenty of information before taking off. Send five hundred if you can—and cash."

"You'll have it before midnight."

It was a nervous night. Every time a tugboat whistle sounded from the East River guns were drawn. "Put the guns away, brothers. Beekman Place is the last place in this town for anyone to be looking for you." My door buzzer went off at five minutes to midnight. The guns were out again. "It's just a friend with sandwiches and money, brothers. Take it easy. You're making me nervous too."

They left just before daybreak, and I went to the typewriter. I had three days to write the essay before it ran. After three bomb threats, *Life* published "The Death of Malcolm X" in March 1965. One day after the magazine appeared on the stands the FBI informed Henry Luce's office that my life was in danger. Four men had been assigned to my death. Pictures of them had been sent, and I recognized two of my would-be assassins. *Life* quickly surrounded me with five detectives, and within twenty-four hours my entire family and I were aboard a jet bound for a foreign destination.

It was a luxurious tropical hideaway on the sea, and my grandson, so unaware of the situation, ran about enjoying himself on the golden beach. If an attempt was to be made on my life, I didn't want it to happen around him. After two weeks I told Elizabeth I would have to return to New York to have a tooth pulled.

"But why not have it done here?"

"I don't trust the dentists here."

When I returned *Life* insisted upon my taking a suite at the Plaza Hotel. The five-man squad took up their duties in two rooms adjoining mine, and everywhere I went, they went. Where I ate they ate. Philip Kunhardt, a *Life* editor, and his wife, Katherine, came to have dinner with me in the Oak Room one evening. The squad ate at two different tables near us. Then suddenly they were up, four of them rushing toward the lobby, while one remained close by.

The two bewildered young black men, finding themselves looking into the barrels of four revolvers, explained their presence. "We're just dishwashers from the kitchen who wanted to see what the place looked like. So we just dressed up and came to take a look."

It was a strange time. My family eventually came back, but two months had passed. And everywhere I went at least four men were beside me with guns beneath their coats. Everything that approached me seemed to have the threat of death. Never before had I been so aware of the value of life. Weary of the situation, I decided to end it one way or the other. If it was the Muslims, as the FBI said, then I would give them their chance. After giving my protectors the slip, I drove up to Harlem, strode into the Muslim restaurant and asked for brother Joseph X. He was the commander of the Fruit of Islam, the Muslims' tough force of bodyguards. We had tea and talked mostly about the weather—and parted with a handshake. *"As salaam' alaikum,* brother."

"As salaam' alaikum, brother." That was the end of it. I went back downtown and asked *Life* to call off the bodyguards.

By November 1965 the bitter ordeal of Vietnam had escalated into a large-scale undeclared war, and as we plunged deeper into the futility of it, David was drafted. Several of his friends gathered at our house to discuss their draft situations—Morton and Arnold, two Jewish brothers; Joe and Harold, two blacks; Johnny, an Irishman; Jimi, a West Indian; and Bruce, a young Swede from Pennsylvania. Measuring the passion in their voices, it was hard to decide who would go and who would not. The Jewish brothers seemed hopelessly split on the issue, as were the two blacks. The Irishman and the West Indian were reluctant, but they vacillated as the argument took its course. David seldom ventured an opinion, which was so unlike him, but Bruce was gung ho. "Those Commie bastards need their asses kicked real good, and I'm one for helping do it!"

David had never talked to me about it; he had simply shown me his papers and shrugged. I wasn't going to try and influence him one way or the other. It was his life; his decision to make. But I was prepared to back up whatever he decided.

He didn't pack any clothes the day before he was scheduled to go, and I slept very little that night. But at dawn I heard him stumbling about, and I got up and peered into the hallway, seeing only a pair of ski boots, poles and two tennis rackets. Was he going to ski, to play tennis, or to the army?

"What's up, David?" I hollered up the stairs.

"My number!" he hollered back. "I'm getting ready to meet the man!"

I was relieved but unhappy. Before he left that morning I gave him a 35-mm camera and a large supply of film. "Take some pictures in your spare time, keep a diary and get it off to me whenever you have a chance. Good luck and remember, I'm not anxious to have any heroes in the family." Elizabeth and I embraced him for a long moment, then he was gone. We were worried and painfully aware of the odds against his coming back. Considering the mood of the country he was off to help defend, I could only hope that he wouldn't have to return to yet another battleground.

Outwardly, the black revolution seemed to be charging straight ahead, but inwardly its forces, all battling on the road toward liberation, were not joined without defect. Splintered, armed with desperate solutions, they had grudgingly made their own camps. Roy Wilkins of the NAACP, and Whitney Young of the Urban League, both moderates, fought the war over white corporate tables. Young turks, rallying to the Black Power cry of Stokely Carmichael, rejected the moderates and branded the Black Muslims as isolationists. Packing M-1 rifles and draped in bandoliers, the Black Panthers rejected all the others and gathered for a showdown with the police. The Black Muslims, thirsty for the white lawmen's blood, had spilled some of their own. It was no way to run a revolution. Effective leadership was crumbling to ruin.

Suddenly the possibility of assassination was weighing heavily on the minds of those who had been gaveled into the ordeal of command. By contrast, the younger militants seemed to be obsessed with a hunger for danger.

Stokely Carmichael screamed "Black Power" until he was hoarse. Eldridge Cleaver, an outspoken Black Panther, told the meanest cops on the beat that they were only fat, gristle and blood. From behind prison walls, Bobby Seale, a Black Panther co-founder, clamored for all-out revolution. Their leader, Huey Newton, the baddest of them all, lifted his M-1 rifle when seven white cops approached him outside the Panther headquarters. One asked him what he intended to do with the gun. With his finger resting firmly on the trigger, he answered, "I'm gonna unload it on all of you if you try to take it." The cops backed down. That same afternoon a dozen young blacks joined up with the Panthers. The brothers on the block had got Huey's message—and so had the cops.

What followed seems to have taken place on some distant, belligerent landscape. But it was here in America where, with its warped sense of democracy, this nation played out a frightful drama. Lawless men advocated law to justify their lawlessness; and an oppressed minority embraced the bloodiest kind of violence to espouse their rights. Young blacks from all walks of life—from the ghettos, cottonfields, barrios, universities and colleges—bowed to their consciences, banded together and prepared for the bloodletting. Seething with anger, they suppressed all fear and made themselves ready to do battle with the iron-sided forces. Throughout the remainder of the 1960s they would flirt with death day and night.

Stokely Carmichael had been propelled to the center of the black revolution by racism. An early admirer of Martin Luther King and nonviolence, he had finally turned, his patience with white society exhausted. It was his strident call for Black Power that set off a chain of reaction hardly to be equaled in our time. At twenty-five, he was now being lionized, damned and discussed more than any other leader in the civil rights movement. Conservative blacks were especially disturbed by him. They found him irresponsible and divisive. But he went on screaming "Black Power" until, for many blacks, it was *the* promise in the air.

He was breathing fury into a gathering of students at Berkeley, California, when I caught up with him. "The white man says, 'Work hard, nigger, and you will overcome.' If that were true, the black man would be the richest man in the world! My dad believed in that hard work and overcome stuff! He worked like a dog, day and night! But only death came to that poor black man! —and in his early forties! My grandfather had to run, run, run. I ain't running no more! And hell no! We ain't going to Vietnam! Ain't no Vietcong ever called me nigger! If I'm to do any fighting it's going to be right here at home! I will not fight in Vietnam and run in Georgia!" The audience sent up a dazzling roar. "Black Power! Black Power! Black Power!"

To Roy Wilkins the term meant anti-white. "Going it alone offers a disadvantaged minority little except the chance to shrivel and die." Said Whitney Young: "There's no dignity in withdrawal from society. It gives too many Negroes a chance to escape responsibility. It's better for a black man to find a dollar in his pocket instead of a hole." But CORE's Floyd McKissick quipped, "Black Power's got to be good if the white man's against it." Martin Luther King found the term confusing but he never denounced it, and he joined Stokely in linking the Vietnam protest to the civil rights issue.

Smiling sardonically, Stokely met Wilkins's charge of inciting violence with a shrug. "I'm just telling the white man he's beat my head enough. I won't take anymore. White power makes the laws, and white power, in the form of white cops with guns, enforces those laws. As for separatism, what are Wilkins and Young talking about? The whites separated us a long time ago. And they intend to keep it that way."

The three months I traveled with him were filled with tension, anxiety and justifiable paranoia. Pieced together, the threats in the South alone would have stretched a respectable distance. He was absolutely sure some "redneck" would put a bullet through his brain before the summer was over. Normally tranquil and unflappable, he seemed like a young man cocky enough to stroll into the Mississippi legislature and demand to have his dirty underwear washed there. And he had a sense of humor that sustained him during those disgruntled days and nights. Once describing an experience that was by no means funny, he managed to make it funny: "We're on a march in my favorite state, Mississippi. [The white folks love me down there.] Hell was breaking loose. John Lewis, SNCC's chairman, was showing guts—too much guts. You could hear the billy clubs cracking against his head a mile off. He goes down time and time again, moaning, 'I love you. I love you.' And they pick him up again. Bam! Smack! Bam! 'You black son-of-a-bitch!' Bam! And John, a true believer in nonviolence, sinks half conscious to the pavement. Now we're retreating, and they're coming after us with cattle prods and dogs. I holler, 'They've come far enough, baby! Open up!' Crack! Bam! Pow! The crackers begin to scatter, running, shooting out streetlights. Bang! Bang! A big army captain's telling them to put on the spotlight. 'Shut that damn light off!' A brother zings a burst past the captain's ankles. The captain hollers, 'Orders changed! *Ree*-treet! *Ree*treet! These niggers have gone loco! Retreet!' " It was impossible not to laugh as Stokely rocked back and forth screaming "*Ree*treet! *Ree*treet!"

He had tried nonviolence, but a very violent afternoon in Birmingham had shorn him of it. Seeing a pregnant black woman knocked head over heels by the jet from a fire hose; seeing people trampled by horses, lying with bleeding legs and arms, was too much. "Things blurred, and they carried me screaming all the way to the airport. From that day on I knew if I was hit, I would hit back." Somewhere beyond Martin Luther King's pacificist teachings, he turned his back on white society. Suddenly, bigotry and death in Mississippi were no different from bigotry and death in Vietnam. At the midpoint of one anguished day he said, "I'd rather die fighting in Mississippi tomorrow than live twenty years fighting in Saigon."

One night, weary, angry and confused, and aware that his role was growing beyond his youthful experience, he confided, "I don't really know where I'm headed. I'd like to go somewhere and think things over for a while. Perhaps I've gone as far as I can go at this point. I finished *A Choice of Weapons* this morning. Hell, I don't know. Maybe your way is the way to go." I felt he was groping for advice, but when I offered none he said, "Whatever happens, we've stirred the conscience of black people. We've got the community on the path to complete liberation. I suppose it's pride, more than color, that binds me to my race. Blackness is necessary, but the concern has to go further than that to reach anyone who needs it. Mississippi taught me that one's life isn't too much to give to help rid a nation of fascists. Albert Camus says, 'In a revolutionary period it is always the best who die. The law of sacrifice leaves the last word to the cowards and the timorous, since the others have lost it by giving the best of themselves.' I dig Camus."

"To die in Alabama rather than Saigon." Stokely's words had brought my thoughts back to the ravaged city from where David had written his last letter to me: "I just got out of surgery a few days ago, and my buddy Jeff Greenfield is headed back to the states in a coffin. We were on a search and destroy mission. He was to the left of me behind the track driver. Sniper fire opened up and I heard a cracking sound. I whirled around to see blood gushing from his helmet. I felt his pulse; he was gone. We hit the water firing, flushed out sixteen Charlies and shot them up like fish in a barrel. I got three kills.

"On the way back to base our track hit a mine. I caught shrapnel in the forehead and just above my left eye. No sweat, Dad, I'll be fine; just got something I'd rather have done without—a Purple Heart. Love ya, David."

He had written about taking three lives—and in a manner that was cold and swaggering. And this from a son who had once told me he would never be able to kill. But now he had done it, and with a feeling of triumph.

Stokely. David. Two young men caught up in wars being fought thousands of miles apart. Sudden death was possible for either of them, but facing it, Stokely would have more reason to know why he was about to die. Yet, that mattered little. Both had been placed in death's easy reach by stupidity and human failings. And both would go on fighting in confusion.

241

TWENTY

Another young black militant, Muhammad Ali, had entered the squared circle to give vent to his anger. With an awesome display of talent, and a tongue rough as flint, he had pounded his way into the heavyweight championship of the world in just a few years. But despite his reign over this barbaric empire, in his chest lay a heart heavy as stone. White America seemed to loathe him—and inwardly this bothered him, angered him even more. In London, during the late spring of 1966, I was packing my bags to depart for New York when he bounded into my hotel room—*"Whoomp whoomp whoomp"*—throwing lefts and rights close to my head. His young face was free of the fury it held a few hours before when he was beating Henry Cooper. Most of London was still sleeping off the defeat of its champion. And considering the physical demands of the fight, and the yelling, shoving mobs that had clawed at him later, I thought Muhammad would be sleeping too. But here he was, the improbable Louisville Kid, come to say a quick good-bye.

"Go—o-ord-on Parks." He strung out my name for several seconds, flopped across both twin beds and took a piece of paper from his pocket. "Here's the poem I've been promising you. Want to hear it?" Before I could answer he was reading.

> Since I don't let the critics seal my fate
> They keep hollering I'm full of hate.
> But they don't really hurt me none
> 'Cause I'm doing good and having fun.
> And fun to me is something bigger
> Than what those critics fail to figure.
> Fun to me is lots of things
> And along with it some good I bring.
> Yet while I'm busy helping my people
> These critics keep writing I'm deceitful.
> But I can take it on the chin
> And that's the honest truth, my friend.
> Now from Muhammad you just heard
> The latest and the truest word.
> So when they ask you what's the latest
> Just say "Ask Ali. He's still the greatest."

"Well, how'd you like it?" he asked proudly.

"Just fine." I edged toward the subject that was really on my mind. "And you were good with the press after the fight."

"Yeh? Guess I said all the right things. Well, the loud talk and everything is over now. Just being myself from now on—a good-acting champ."

Right. Just right. Exactly what I wanted to hear him say. The question was how deep it all went. The situation reminded me of the final moments I had spent with my son David, before he went off to the army. (Muhammad and David resembled one another, not only physically but in the way they walked and gestured.) Only this time I didn't offer any advice. I wanted to. I wanted to say: "Just remember—*don't let reporters rile you. Don't always ham it up for the cameras. Listen to your trainers. Be careful about your draft situation.*" But I had learned that this boy, unlike my son, was not receptive to outright advice; even when you gave it gently you got silence—no response at all.

Now he jumped up suddenly, handed me the poem and gave me a bear hug. "Well, so long, champ," he said. Then, throwing punches again, he danced out the door.

I had met Muhammad Ali in Miami a month earlier, when he started training for Cooper, the first of his summer series of overseas fights. His public image was then in tatters. He stood accused in the press of sins ranging from talking too much to outright anti-white bigotry. There had been rumblings of dislike for him ever since he became a Muslim after the first Clay-Liston fight in February 1964. Then, late that winter, when he declared, "I don't have no quarrel with those Vietcongs!" he became, in the public eye, not just a loud-mouthed kid but a "shameless traitor," as one paper put it.

At that point I began to feel a certain sympathy for him. I was not proud of him, as I had been proud of Joe Louis. Muhammad was a gifted black champion and I *wanted* him to be a hero, but he wasn't making it. I felt, however, that he could not possibly be quite as bad as he was made out to be in the press.

He lay on his bed, in the small bungalow he always rented in Miami, half-covered by a sheet, only his chest and his powerful bare shoulders exposed. He had smiled broadly as I came in.

"Sit down," he said in a surprisingly soft voice. "They tell me you're the greatest."

There were no chairs, so I sat down on the bed beside him. He had a magazine in his hand and he pointed to a word in an article about him: "What's that mean?"

I studied the word for a second. "He's saying you're 'paradoxical,' that you aren't what you appear to be—sometimes."

"Uh-huh. And just what does he mean by calling me a bigot?"

I thought of the word "racist," but I said, "He's accusing you of being just as intolerant against whites as they are to us." He went on like this for a while, asking questions but never commenting on the answers I gave.

At first I was puzzled. The conversation, if it could be called that, didn't seem to be getting anywhere. But after a time I realized that we were, in fact, *talking*—person to person, without any put-on at all—and that this was his way of saying that he trusted me. I felt free to tell him whether he was really as obnoxious as people were making him out to be.

"No need to beat around the bush, brother," he said quickly. "I know why you came." His head slid off the pillow close to the wall. "People," he went on more softly, "have wrote a lot of bad things about me. But nothin' they write is goin' to turn *everybody* against me. Every fight, the gates just get bigger and the White Hopes get fewer."

Then, in a great swoosh, he sprang out of bed. "Come on, man, let's go see a movie!"

We were in my rented car, and he reached over my driver and flicked on the radio. The voice of the late Sam Cooke was blasting out "Shake."

Muhammad began singing along with him. An announcer's voice cut in: "Cassius Clay returned to Miami today to start training for his forthcoming fight with Henry Cooper in London. Cassius . . ."

The announcer went on, but the champion had stopped listening: "Cassius Clay! I'm on everybody's lips. But still they won't call me by my right name."

Now he was directing the driver: *"Turn right, brother.* A white man is something. Yes, really something. *Left here, brother.* There's pressures and strains when you're successful and controversial like me. Gotta always be so careful about how you act, what you say. Everybody's waitin' to burn you."

"Then why get burned so often?"

"Maybe, sometimes, I just like to see how people take it."

I wondered whether it was also to see if people really cared about him.

Muhammad's brow knit when we hit the cinema district: "What's all those signs say?"

"There's *Cast a Giant Shadow.* Looks good," I said. "Or Paul Newman in *Harper.*"

"Naw, naw. Something rough—with ghosts, no love and sex and stuff. What's that? *Goliath and the Vampires.* That's for me, brother! Find out when it starts."

"It's half over," I protested feebly.

"Come on. Let's go anyhow. The last half's always the best."
We went—and it was awful.

Later Muhammad chose to stroll through Miami's Negro section. The rented limousine crept along the street behind us while greetings came from all the doorways and windows.

"Hi, champ."

"Hi, baby. What's shakin'?"

"Hi, Muhammad. Who's the greatest?"

"Are you blind, man?"

"Hey, champ, how many rounds for Cooper?"

"If he tries to get rough—one's enough."

"You're the greatest, baby!"

He could no more escape that last line than he could his color.

"These people like me around when they've got trouble. Patterson, Joe Louis, Sammy Davis and other Negro bigwigs don't do that. Too busy cocktailin' with the whites. I don't need bodyguards. You don't need protection from people who *love* you."

I asked myself how he could believe that the sycophantic chatter we'd just heard was "love." Did he think that a good world was one filled with smiles and flattery—one where all things were bigger than life? I began to suspect so.

He trained hard. In the ring Muhammad let the sparring partners bull and spin him about as Cooper might do. He floated and ducked, causing them to miss badly. "Dance, baby, dance," his trainer, Angelo Dundee, purred from the corner.

"Hey, Angelo, could I have whipped Jack Johnson in his time?"

"Baby, you could have taken anybody in everybody's time."

"And that's the beautiful truth," Rahaman, his brother and sparring partner, cut in. Such questions, such answers, I realized, meant more to Ali than I had imagined in the beginning. He seemed to encourage it all. Often he had asked me, "Why would a big magazine like yours want to do a story on me? Am I really that big? Do people really want to know about me?" He expected affirmative answers and he nearly always got them. He clearly needed these assurances against the bad publicity he was getting.

Some days he would drive up to a school yard at recess. "Come here, all you beautiful black children!" And they came running as if he were about to hand out thousand-dollar bills. "Only difference in me and the Pied Piper is he didn't have no Cadillac," he would say. The adoring kids were more important to him than he was to them.

During those lazy afternoons he talked about that "crazy house" he wanted to build on a high hill—"where travelers could come by and say, 'That's where he lives, the heavyweight champion of the world.' " But just about any topic outside of Muslimism, boxing or himself made him tune out.

One day several boys came into the yard and two of them started sparring. "Hey, stop that!" he shouted at them. "You don't fight your brother—even in play. Now come on inside and I'll let you see some movies—of me beatin' up the 'Bear' and the 'Rabbit.' "

He continued the lecture as he threaded the projector: "They've been lynching your pappys and grandpappys and rapin' your mothers and sisters down here for years. There's plenty people to fight besides your brother. Catch you at it again, I'm gonna bop your heads together. Now, I'm gonna show the second Liston fight first, 'cause it lasts just long enough to warm up the machine."

He started the film and began announcing over the commentator's voice: "Here we go! Look, children! Looks like a turtle chasin' a jackrabbit! Now, watch close or you won't see it! *Rat-a-tat! Bop!* There it is! Now watch that clown fall flat on his face. There he goes! *Wham!*"

Muhammad ran up to the movie screen: "Git up, you bum. Get up and fight!"

When Patterson appeared on the screen Muhammad scoffed. "There's the Rabbit. Listen at 'em cheer. They love him. He's their black White Hope, children! Poor sucker! Now, here I come! Boooo! Boooo! Boooo! Boooo! Listen at 'em give it to me!"

I watched him closely. There was no joy in his heckling. Nobody could like being booed that much, especially not someone so concerned about "love."

I myself had wanted Floyd to beat him that night, and I told Ali so. He smiled! "I beat him so bad his breath smelled like saddle soap."

However, that fight bugged him. He was still trying to explain it in his bedroom late that night: "Patterson had no business in that ring with me—after saying he was going to bring the title 'back to

America.' But the crowd came for a show and I gave 'em one. 'Come on, sucker, git past that left,' I kept saying to him. The ref felt sorry for him, too. Maybe that's why I couldn't freeze him. But they didn't call that Patterson-Johannson fight sadistic. The Rabbit went down seven times."

His eyelids dropped for a few seconds. He had talked himself out. There was a little snore and he nodded himself awake. Then, looking out the window, he said, "I liked Floyd. He oughta quit. He's made lots of money. They'll never treat him as bad as they treat me." Then he dug his head into the pillow and went to sleep.

Some mornings, while he was winding up his training in Miami, I came upon him with his hands lifted, facing the East, mumbling prayers to Allah. Sometimes he seemed morose and disgruntled with everything around him. Then he would be in high spirits again—laughing, chattering, dancing, shadow-boxing in his yard, in the street, wherever there was room to throw a punch. It was never easy to know which of his different selves would be visible at a given moment.

I never witnessed the hate he was supposed to have for whites. But I did see him stand in the burning sun for an hour, signing autographs for Southern white children. And I did go with him on a visit to a young white hemophiliac one afternoon. On leaving the boy and his parents he remarked, "There are some good white folks around." I said it was nice of him to have made the visit. "Well," he answered, "he must have been a nice kid to want to see me."

Now and then his thoughts seemed far away. He would drop a conversation in midsentence without reason. Even when there was a great deal of noise around him, he would remain mute, meditative. One evening, in such a mood, he invited me for a walk. Just minutes before, he had been rearranging his scrapbook and I asked him why he didn't have a secretary.

"Oh, people don't ask me for much outside of autographs," he said. "No speeches and such things." He thought about that for a few paces.

"Do you know that Martin Luther King was the only Negro leader who sent me a telegram when I became champion of the world? The only one. I was just a dumb kid then, thinking all of them would be so proud of me—me being the champ and every-thing. I expected too much."

"You're so young yet. There's plenty of time to change—if you really want to."

"I want to. I'm sure I want to," he said, as though trying to convince himself. I repeated that he had plenty of time left and that the world had a lot to offer him.

After an intent pause, he said, "Nobody in this world ever of-fered me anything except Elijah Muhammad. Nobody."

Later that night, I went with him to the local mosque meeting. Muhammad Ali was dressed in the blue serge uniform of the Fruit of Islam. And, like everyone else who attended, he raised his arms and allowed himself to be frisked according to strict custom. Here, for the first time, I saw Muhammad listening eagerly to what someone else had to say.

Lucius Bey, the Muslim minister in Miami, started slowly, in a deliberately restrained voice. But soon the intensity increased: "The black man is indeed the greatest! His genes are stronger! No white man can produce a baby darker than himself! The most beautiful women in the world are black!"

"Teach, brother, teach!" Muhammad's voice led all the rest in the chorus.

"They say we hate the white man. We don't hate the white man! We just hate the way he treats us!"

"Tell 'em like it is, brother! Preach!" Now it was a duet between Lucius Bey and Muhammad.

"Why is the white man so anxious about Elijah Muhammad changing our slave names? Why? Africans are from Africa! Japa-nese are from Japan! Swedes are from Sweden! Where are Ne-groes from! Negroia?"

"Wake us up, brother! Wake us up!"

"Right now, the white man's being run out of all the black countries! And—now, listen to this—he wants us black people to go fight for him to stay there!"

Lucius Bey had hit home: *"Preach the truth! They want me to go right now!"*

"When the white man asks, 'What's your name?' and you say 'Muhammad Ali,' they say, 'That nigger's done woke up!' "

"Preach! Preach! Preach!"

Lucius Bey preached on—for an hour and a half.

Lucius Bey's "message" was still burning inside Muhammad the next day. Angelo got told off; sparring partners got their lumps; there was no horsing around in the camp that day, no movies, no children. And he kept spewing the kind of comment that had already made him a villain in the press. By evening the bungalow was dead quiet.

My original notion that there might be a different kind of story in Muhammad Ali had almost evaporated. I was going back to New York the next morning, and there now hardly seemed any need for me to go on to London.

Then, just before I left to go to my hotel, I took a chance and said to him, "It's not only white people, but a lot of Negroes don't like the way you act."

That cut him, deep. He erupted: "What do they want? I ain't promoting alcohol and sex, hugging on some white woman's head! So what if I am the first black athlete to stand up and say what I feel! Maybe I'm like the Japanese flier who sacrifices himself so others can live!

"Hate! Hate! Hate! Who's got time to go around hatin' whites all day! I don't hate lions either—but I know they'll bite! What does the white man care if I hate him, anyhow? He's got everything going for him—white Swan soap, Tarzan, Jesus, White Owl cigars, the white tornado, Snow White and her Seven Dwarfs! Angel food cake is white—devil's food cake is black, naturally!"

He ranted on and on. Lucius Bey's sermon had been tepid in comparison.

"One question before I go," I said after listening to him for most of an hour. "What about your draft situation?"

"What about it? How can I kill somebody when I pray five times a day for peace? Answer me! For two years the army told everybody I was a nut. I was ashamed! My mother and father was ashamed! Now, suddenly, they decide I'm very wise—without even testing me again! I ain't scared. Just show me a soldier who'd like to be in that ring in my place!

"I see signs saying 'LBJ, how many kids did you kill today?' Well, I ain't said nothing half that bad! I don't know nothing about Vietnam. Where is it anyway? Near China? Elijah Muhammad teaches us to fight only when we are attacked. My life is in his hands. That's the way it is. That's the way it's got to be."

He was wrapped up in himself—yes: still belligerent, still the mistreated kid against a hostile world. Yet, I reflected, he made some sense. The issue had never come up in my own home, but I knew I would have been ready to back up my own son if *he* had decided to resist going to Vietnam. Muhammad, however, was the heavyweight champion of the world. Did that give him a special responsibility to think and act differently? A lot of people clearly thought that it did. Yet I wasn't sure.

I didn't expect to see Muhammad again. But early the next morning there he was at my hotel door. "Hurry up, champ. You're about to miss your plane," he said. He spent the trip to the airport urging my driver through short cuts and around other cars. Carrying my bags, he ran all the way to the departure gate. Then his big hand held me back for an instant.

"I don't want to do anything that's going to hurt my people," he said. "I've been doing a lot of thinking since last night. I hope you'll be there in London."

I was sure he was making me a promise of some sort. "I'll be there," I said, and ran for the plane.

The London fog made Muhammad's plane four hours late. But the big crowd was still waiting. He stepped off smiling broadly, waving to all the cameras, reporters and the cheering crowd.

"Got any predictions, champ?"

"Nope."

"Any poetry, champ?"

"Nope. I'd have to keep my fingers together so you wouldn't say I was predicting."

"You've toned down considerably—a different fellow."

"It's just me, being myself."

Two days later the *Daily Telegraph* said: "Cassius Clay presented himself to an admiring British public yesterday as Muhammad Ali, a heavyweight champion of courtesy and charm."

He smiled when I showed him the newspaper: "Wait till the folks back home get a load of this."

"Do you really care about what they think back there?"

"I got a lot of boos," he said, "but—it's still home. I have to think about home."

The British found him to be a "decent chap." "Foxes" in mini-skirts, mods and rockers chased him. His telephones rang all day and all night. The adoration finally took its toll.

"You got a extra bed at your hotel?" he asked me in desperation. I said I had.

"Then you just took on a nonpaying guest, brother."

And each day after training he would come to my room, consume quarts of orange juice, check the sports pages and sleep. We talked of things we hadn't really talked about before—my family and his family. He woke up one afternoon and simply began talking about his childhood:

"I used to lay awake scared, thinking about somebody getting cut up or being lynched. Looked like they was always black people I liked. And I always wanted to do something to help these people. But I was too little. Maybe now I can help by living up to what I'm supposed to be. I'm proud of my title and I guess I want people to be proud of me."

I was astonished, and moved. It was the first time he had ever said anything like that. He went on:

"My mother always wanted me to be something like a doctor or a lawyer. Maybe I'd a made a good lawyer. I talk so much. I guess I got that from my father. I'm really kinda shy. Didn't get as much schooling as I wanted to. But common sense is just as good. My parents did what they could for me and my brother, scuffling down in Kentucky where things was hard. I bought 'em a new house and some furniture and two cars. I think they're proud of me now, no matter what people say. I'm glad I could get 'em out of a rut."

"Everybody will be proud of you if you will just give them a chance. Americans, Africans, everybody. Look how the British are treating you."

"Yeh, they sure are nice to me, all right. Wonder what makes 'em so nice? Have they ever been in any big wars?"

I thought back to the awful bombings in Britain during the Second World War. He had not been born yet. "Yes, several," I said.

Two mornings before the fight Angelo telephoned me: "The champ wants you at a press conference at ten this morning. He says he's going to say something you'll like to hear."

"I'll be there," I said. The conference would be at Isow's, a kosher restaurant where Muhammad took his meals. I went to Muhammad's room first.

"Here's what I'm going to say," he said. "Read it and tell me what you think."

It was a note scribbled in red ink, and it began by thanking everyone from the restaurant chef to the Prime Minister for his "kindness and understanding." Halfway through, Muhammad got to the point: "When I was campaigning for the championship, I said things and did things not becoming of a champion. But I'm champion now. And today I'm measuring my words. I'm measuring my deeds. I'm measuring my thoughts. By the help of the Honorable Elijah Muhammad, this is the new Muhammad Ali. And last, I want to mention something that is nearest to me—the country in which I was born. . . ."

("Wouldn't just 'my country' be better?" I asked. "No," he said, "Elijah Muhammad would like it better the way it is.")

". . . I thank the President of the United States and the officials of the government. And I thank my draft board for letting me come here to defend the title. Regardless of the right or wrong back there, that is where I was born. That is where I'm going to return."

"Beautiful, brother," I said.

Minutes later, dressed in a black silk lounge suit, Muhammad Ali sparkled with confidence and charm as he faced the battery of microphones and reporters. By now I was sure that what he would say came from an impulsive, well-intentioned heart. But I wasn't listening as he spoke. I stood in the back of the room, wondering whether his new high resolve could last.

It was possible, I decided. There would be times when he could, under the pressure of hostile questions, forget and say or do something hopelessly wrong. I decided to wait and see.

Three months is not the longest of trials, but it is a summer's worth at least and a time during which Muhammad Ali managed absolutely to keep his cool, despite some easy chances to lose it. The fight with Brian London had had problems. The press welcomed the champion back to England courteously, even warmly. But as the fight drew nearer and public interest in it kept dropping, reporters tried to stir things up by needling Muhammad. Muhammad merely guzzled down more orange juice and sparred even less. At a press conference, a reporter suggested to him that he looked fat and undertrained. Instead of answering, Muhammad turned casually to me.

"Where'd you get that foxy suit you got on, boss?"

"At my London tailor," I said.

"Well, call him up and tell him I want six just like it—all dark and conservative." Later, in Saville Row, he selected the materials in less than ten minutes. "And make me a vest for each one. I'm a gentleman now. I've got to look like one," he instructed the happy tailor.

As matters turned out, of course, the fight answered a number of criticisms about how well Muhammad Ali had trained and how hard he could hit. On his way into the ring, he had been serenaded with boos. The catcalls had continued as he prayed briefly to Allah before the bell. But when he jogged around the ring, as attendants helped poor London off the canvas, there were only cheers.

Back at the hotel he preened before the mirror in his new tailored suit. "Well, you changed their song real quick," I said.

"Yep, boss, I picked up a lot of new fans tonight. I won't be getting no more boos till I get back where I was born."

"Your face isn't even marked."

"Nope. Can't afford marks. The public likes pretty gentlemen fighters. So it looks like Muhammad has to stay pretty and be a gentleman forever and ever."

Someone laughed, but the champion seemed dead serious. And he just might do it, I decided. For, at last, he seemed fully aware of the kind of behavior that brings respect. Already a brilliant fighter, there was hope now that he might become a champion everyone could look up to. If only those back where he was born extended their patience, they would help buoy that hope. From where I had watched and listened, it all seemed so worthwhile.

On a peaceful April afternoon in 1968, terrible news flashed over my car radio as I drove through Los Angeles. "Martin Luther King has just been shot dead by an unknown gunman . . ." I braked the car to a stop, stunned.

The announcer's words kept spilling into the car with details—until finally they turned to a commercial expounding the merits of some dog food. The tone of his voice had lost all urgency, fallen back into a jargon of ordinariness. What was done would stay done seemed to be the essence of his manner. I sat by the curb, feeling suddenly isolated as traffic kept whizzing by. Why hadn't all the other drivers stopped as I had stopped? Didn't they hear? Didn't they contemplate the tragedy? Surely now the entire country would be caught up in the most hostile quaking of the black revolution. Despite all those other cars rushing past, there was for me a sound of silence; a crushing, respectful silence for the most revered of our civil rights leaders who had been gunned down. For a man who loved peace so much, no fate could have been worse. Throughout America a lot of black people would be praying; but some would probably be buying guns. Now, even those who had listened to him so hard might, through despair, decide to listen no more and take up arms as well. This I was thinking as I finally drove off.

I was suffering a bottomless hour when I reached my room at the Beverly Hills Hotel. I was about to pick up the phone when it rang. It was Philip Kunhardt calling from *Life*'s New York bureau. I knew Philip well, and understood his short interval of silence; it fell upon my own. How to say what he wanted to say was bothering him.

"Well—obviously you've heard the terrible news."

"Yes."

"This looks like one for you—if you want it."

"I want it."

"Okay. Get to Atlanta as soon as possible. Loudon Wainwright will meet you there, but we expect you to write the story." Martin Luther King was being readied for his final stop at little Ebenenzer Baptist Church. In less than an hour I was packed and on my way. Even before nightfall skies over dozens of American cities would be darkening to the smoke of arsonists—the black ghettos' answer to a white racist deed. The bloodthirsty spring had burst into flame, and the words that had been meant as warnings were much more than pretensions now.

Standing in the crush along the wall at Ebenezer my thoughts wandered back to those black funerals impaled upon my childhood. Mingling within the memories was the same odor of camphor, the sweet stench of carnations and the lamenting voice of the choir singing hymns so familiar to my childhood. But this time the coffin held a man who had made a lifework of being earthbound; who died while trying to help reshape the morals of a troubled nation; who, while in full cry against violence, came to his end

255

through violence. Now his voice, echoing off the ceiling and walls of Ebenezer, was letting us know that he had been to the mountaintop; that he had tried to love somebody, and that he didn't want a long funeral. The afternoon seemed to be overbalanced by his voice now concealed forever in his silence.

Then, like a river of blackness, thousands of us flowed behind two brown mules and the old flat-bed wagon that bore him to his grave. Oppression still flowed around us like a sea, but we would flow on, even against assassins, toward that extravagant dream that had persistently haunted him.

Truth looked at me hard as I flew toward New York to close out the assignment, and I had no intention of defiling it with polite talk from myself, or *Life* magazine. It was time to stay with reality. Racial uprisings across the nation had erupted like a volcano of blood and fire. People were dying. Buildings, stores and houses were burning, and history was taking notes on the carnage. I scrawled my anger on twenty sheets of yellow paper and handed them to the editors, and those pages banished whatever guiltlessness white men might lay claim to. The editors wrestled with their consciences for eight hours while I kept my eyes on their pencils. Finally, at four in the morning, the story went on the wire to Chicago where the magazine was printed:

". . . Dr. King spent the last dozen years of his life preaching love to men of all colors. And, for all this, a man, white like you, blasted a bullet through his neck. And this has just about eliminated the last symbol of peace between us. We must struggle to distinguish between his act and your conscience.

"It is not enough any more when you ask that all whites not be blamed for what one did. You must know how we really feel—before grass takes root over Dr. King's grave . . . his killer will remain a symbol of the white attitude toward blacks. We have grave doubts about your promises. We have grown to lack the patience to wait for God's deliverance. We want a new life. Our youth refuse to sit and wait to share in the affluence that you surround them with. They will cross your line—even if it means death. Dr. King's only armor was truth and love. Now that he lies dead from a lower law, we begin to wonder if love was enough. Racism still engulfs us. Blacks and whites are buying guns. Army troops stand ready, and our President is warned against going to

Atlanta. If the white man is truly stricken he must stay firm in his conscience—and the black man must see to it that he does. . . ."

Whatever else I had to say forsook any language of forgiveness. My words stared back at me when I saw them in cold print the following Monday, and I realized that my anguish had swept me dangerously close to hatred. It would be hard to get used to his silence.

TWENTY-ONE

More and more I was smitten with Genevieve Young. By now I had grown to admire her deeply; to love everything about her—the swarthy soft skin, the almond eyes, the long, dark floating hair; the way she smiled, talked, laughed and moved. Of every woman I had seen she was the one I hoped to go on forever seeing. The slightest touch of her made the moment golden. If waiting for her and she was overdue I became anxious and nervous. During such moments she was the heavenly present promised, but taking far too long to descend.

As she approached from the distance on Park Avenue one afternoon, my thoughts were saying hurry—hurry. Unable to wait I started toward her. Then we were rushing toward one another. Our closeness had grown into something neither of us could control, and there were moments ahead longing to be fulfilled. On that same summer evening we decided, after thoughtful consideration, to permanently bring our lives together. Passion and love stood aloof from fidelity—flowering flowering flowering until it seemed measureless. The price for it would be heavy but we were ready to pay it. Our love for one another had become so ardent and involving it was, at times, terrifying. From that day on we gave ourselves to it without restraint.

One morning, three months later, our world cracked apart. Elizabeth, with tears streaming down, said, "I'm pregnant." I felt suspended, wildly lost for any reasonable answer. My thoughts leaped to taking her in my arms; to expressing the kind of joy she obviously hoped for from me, but the fullness of another desire sent me stammering into a mesh of confusion. My answer shriveled into a sorrowful rebuff. "But, Elizabeth, we agreed to never having a child."

"I know, Gordon, but I want to have it and I intend to."

It was like being unexpectedly hit by a violent storm. "All right, Elizabeth. I'm sure everything will be all right." I accepted her decision, but out of despair. Then avoiding a painful look into her eyes, I smiled weakly, touched her cheek and turned away. The plans Gene and I had made were crumbling, and I put my thoughts to work, wondering now how I would say what I had to say to her. My thoughts came up with nothing helpful.

At lunch the next day I reached across the table, touched her hand and said, "Elizabeth is pregnant."

Without pause she pushed my hand aside and reacted exactly as I had expected: clenching her teeth, she burned a look of despair through me, got up and stalked off without another word. And I sat there for what seemed like an eternity, feeling alone. From then on working together would become impossible, and most editing would be done by telephone.

Elizabeth's beauty glowed as she swelled with our child, and I feigned happiness. It was a strange unlasting peace I made with myself, held together by the child that was coming. I would love it. There was no doubt about that. But neither was there any uncertainty about my continuing love for Gene. It was still the love that I awoke to every morning, and kept remembering. For me now, life was flowing so differently. Only a few weeks before I could never have dreamed that it would change so much. Gene, with her eyes and heart closed to me, seemed to have left me alone in my misery.

I never knew just how much Elizabeth knew about what was going on inside me. Perhaps she had no idea of what had really happened. I do remember that she went on planning for the birth of our child with a rather buoyant happiness. And since no one else knew, there was no one to confide in who might have helped bale me out of my woefulness. So for months I went about smiling with a lie on my face while sadness howled inside me.

Throughout 1967 I got many letters from David, who was now a tank gunner. They were filled with the horror of the ordeal, and with accounts of racism black soldiers were suffering at the hands of white officers: "We ambushed Charlie today and got several of them. Sgt. Young kicked a VC's body to be sure he was dead. He had to be; the bullet holes were showing from head to toe. Young asked for my knife, cut off the VC's finger and took his gold ring. I told him to keep the knife, and walked away. I'll be glad when this bloody mess is over. Every day you go out looking for someone to kill—and you're disappointed if you don't find them.

"Being an FO [Forward Observer] is hairy business. The odds are against you. Sgt. Paulson hand-picks Negroes and Puerto Ricans for this job. You would have to be lily-white to escape all the shit he gives us. I thought things would be different over here, but whitey, with a few exceptions, is the same throughout this whole damn organization. All the soul brothers are beginning to gripe."

I wrote him back: "I never thought this war would hang around until you became a part of it. Sometimes I wish you and Gordon had been born at another time. But there has rarely been a time when men were not killing each other. Hell is breaking out back here. Racial strife, especially in Alabama and Mississippi, is bad. But televised brutality of Southern lawmen is starting to fill the consciences of many whites. I mention this because it is something hopeful that might help you tolerate one evil while we, back here, fight another one.

"As for the prejudice you find there, understand that war does not always bring out the best in people. Surely you know by now that a bigot ambushed in a foxhole won't be concerned about the color of the soldier who saves him. Danger pulls people together. There are bits of venom in your letters. It doesn't fit you. Do what you have to do and get the hell out of there. Elizabeth is expecting, so you'll have either a brother or sister when you get back. Maybe both. When Elizabeth does something she does it big. I'm astonished at the quiet of this place with you gone. Harper follows me around growling for those bones you used to feed him. He's still a crazy dog. We miss you terribly. We love you and wish we could slice off a big slab of time from your absence, Dad."

On November 24, 1967, Elizabeth gave birth to Leslie Campbell Parks, a gorgeous, fat roly-poly dream of a baby with soft brown skin and big, inquisitive black eyes. And the latter was precisely what made me adore her all the more. When, through casual conversation, I mentioned Leslie's arrival to Gene, she said, "I'm sorry but I could never bear to see that child." She had completely absented herself from me after the publication of *A Choice of Weapons,* but I had called her for advice on an essay I was about to start on poverty in Harlem. It was unbearable not to have some contact with her. The letter she sent was terse and to the point: "You should take this ordinary black family and put their innermost thoughts into words. You will have to find the words, because they will not have them. Like the majority of human beings, they will not be accustomed to articulating their complex thoughts and emotions. You will have to find a way to convey all this to a white middle-class audience. The ghetto is truly a foreign country to them. You must bridge this gap; and you are uniquely equipped to do so by your color, background and sensibility.

"Your camera can show the facts, the present, the tangible. But only words can convey the web of thought and emotion, the influence of the past and the fears and hopes for the future. At the end of the text piece, having seen the photographs, your readers should feel what there is in the minds of the family, and what they have seen through your eyes.

"No one, black or white, can presume to speak for the Negro in a collective sense. All you can do is to show through a piling up of detail, incidents, and snatches of talk, what the existence of an impoverished Negro family is really like." She went on to say more, and in much the same manner. The letter was unsigned. When I called to thank her for it she replied coolly, "It isn't necessary. I am still your editor."

The letter we had been awaiting so long from David came on September 9, 1967: "I am at Bravo packing for home. It's hard to realize that I'll be seeing you soon. So many won't make it back. Now that I'm out, all the mud, blood and death seems unreal. It's hard also to realize I've taken other men's lives. I'm not proud of it, but out here it's either you or him. And you always hope it's him. It's strange, but I never got to hate Charlie, maybe because I never got to see him until he was dead. It was what he did to Greenberg, Gurney, Harris, Jones, Greenfield and the others I hated so much.

"All my buddies are on the woodline patroling, so I won't see them before I take off. I'm glad I'm not out there with them tonight.

"The camera is still in good shape, and I hope you'll like my pictures. The film's safely packed in my duffle bag. Well, I'm expecting a big turkey and plenty of sweet potatoes. I'll bring the wine. I can't wait to put my feet under a table again and enjoy Liz's good cooking. Seeya soon. Love, David."

Three days later David arrived for the turkey and the sweet potatoes. And we were thankful for his presence where for so long his absence had been; thankful too that he had cheated death. At last I could dismantle all the fears I had been carrying around. He was fully a man now, wearing the scars that earned him the Purple Heart.

But even today those awful months of war still curl inside him. Often, when recalling the cruelty, he sits shaking his head, reliving the wounds of the nightmare. Bladed like knives, they keep opening up, cutting into him. During such moments there seems to be nothing I can bring myself to say to help him forget the pain. Yet, I sometimes wonder if he should just shrug off the memory. Perhaps he, and the others who got back, are meant to constantly remind the future that it should avoid such disaster.

•   •   •

Finding a Harlem family who would allow me to poke about within the intimacy of their impoverishment wasn't easy. Those I approached were all overwhelmed by hunger and hopelessness, but it was their pride that prompted their refusal; working away within a shadowy existence, they still insisted upon clinging to their privacy. "We don't want our neighbors and friends to see how we live in this rat hole," one man said. I remember regarding him curiously. Only a few minutes before one of those neighbors had expressed his reluctance in much the same way. They were like compatriots hiding their misery behind the same dark tenement walls.

Bessie Fontenelle sat brooding with a kind of pride as I talked to her. The reason for her despair showed all around her—in the rickety furniture, the decaying walls and broken linoleum that covered the floor. "What good's to come of our showing people how we have to live?" she asked finally.

I explained that by doing so she, in a small way, might help others who shared her plight. She gave the idea a few moments of thought, then eventually agreed. After a week of pleading my pleas had been answered.

For the next seven days I showed up at the Fontenelles without a camera. Keeping my eyes and ears alert, I spent that first week melting into the confusion of the family, and getting to know them and the problems that confronted them every day. I had arrived late. The family's dreams, if ever they possessed any, had grown cold. Everything pointed downward.

The coming of winter was especially bad for them. Norman, the father, was without a job and there was no money or food left. None of the eight children had winter coats, and with the weather turning cold they couldn't go to school. Norman was a quiet, short, powerfully built man with defeat hanging off him. He had come to Harlem fifteen years before, with big plans, from St. Lucia in the British West Indies. "It's pretty there," he said wistfully. "I'd like to take my kids and wife there—away from this miserable place." The *place* was four flights up in an old brick building on Eighth Avenue. He had just turned thirty-eight; Bessie, his wife was thirty-nine. There were Phillip, fifteen; Roseanna, fourteen; Norman Jr., thirteen; Riel, twelve; Lette, nine; Kenneth, eight; Ellen, five; and Richard, three. Then there was a bad-tempered dog named Toe-Boy and a cat, who were really there to keep the roaches and rats in check. There were also goldfish, but one morning when I arrived little Richard was pointing at the bowl on the mantel. The heat had gone off the night before and the three fish were floating on the surface, dead from the cold. "Fishes dead, fishes dead," he kept mumbling.

Norman Fontenelle glanced at his son. "Three less mouths to feed. It's a wonder we ain't dead with them." He shook his head sorrowfully. "And to think we have to pay seventy dollars a month for this hole. Well, they won't get it this month. I'm down to my last penny."

I gave him the rent money and ordered some food from the corner grocery before I left. Thanks shone in his eyes but he remained silent. On the eighth day I brought along a small camera that fit into my pocket—using it sparingly and quietly, trying not to abuse their privacy. Then, in the quiet of my own home each night, I began entering the plight of the Fontenelles into a small diary.

NOVEMBER 6, 1967

Bessie Fontenelle appears to be a strong woman, especially in the early part of the day, when she looks younger than her age. As the day wears on she seems to age with it. By nightfall she has crumpled into herself. "All this needing and wanting is about to drive me crazy," she complained today. "Now I've got double trouble. Norman's a good man but when he's broke he takes it out on me and the kids. Gets a little bottle somewhere and starts nipping. Then he's mad at the whole world. Then the kids and I get it, especially little Norman. They don't get along at all now days. The boy keeps saying he'll kill him if he keeps beating on me. And I wouldn't be surprised if he didn't up and do it some day."

Bessie tries to give warmth to the place, but it remains a prison of filth. Her touch shows in the shapeless, soiled curtains; the dime-store paintings on the walls; the shredded scatter rugs covering the cracks in the linoleum; the wax flowers and outdated magazines. It's a losing battle for her.

I have yet to see the whole family sitting down and eating together. One of the kids will cry out his hunger and Bessie will scrounge up a sandwich of some kind. Norman Jr. seems to exist on seven-cent sweet potato pies from the grocery store. Little Richard was eating a raw potato today. Sometimes the kids will hungrily share one apple.

NOVEMBER 10, 1967

Lette came into the kitchen crying this afternoon. Norman Jr. had thumped her on the head. Bessie dropped her head into her hands. "Oh, God, if it ain't one thing it's another." Little Richard joined in the crying. His swollen lips were cracked and bleeding. "Oh, God, oh, God. That child's taking to chewing plaster off the wall." She put on some yellow ointment. Weary and distraught she lay down and began to moan. Kenneth sat down beside her. "You all right, Momma? You all right?" Little Richard is poisoning himself little by little eating the plaster. Norman Jr. was sticking a strip of masking tape over a hole next to his bed this evening.

"Is that to keep out the rats?" I asked.

"Naw. They would eat right through this stuff. It's to keep out the wind coming down the wall."

NOVEMBER 11, 1967

A surprise today. Bessie has a son by another marriage. Harry is in Brentwood Prison for drug addicts. He's been there for nearly two years. I went with her to visit him this morning. The prison library had several copies of *A Choice of Weapons*. "It's a good book," he told me. "Wished I'd read it before landing up here." I left them to talk out the hour together. She was in tears when we left. "Oh, God," she moaned. "I asked him if he was going off drugs for good when he gets out. He says, 'No, I can't promise you that. I wasn't on heroin, just cocaine—that's not so bad, Momma.'" She explained Harry further as we rode back to the city. "I did everything I could—even took him to the police myself. But once he was hung up there was nothing to do. I finally kicked him out to protect the other kids."

NOVEMBER 13, 1967

Going to the comfort of home each night is getting harder. I lie awake thinking about the futility and despair I've left behind—a world of gloom, hunger and a thousand little violences that attend each day of the Fontenelles' lives. Today

265

they were shut in by a heavy, wet snowfall, but it seemed as cold and desolate inside as it did out. The children lay on their sheetless bunks fully clothed and under blankets, suffering the cold and trying to do their homework. Roseanna read a comic book. Lette couldn't study; her glasses were chewed up by Toe-Boy. Dizzy spells take over if she tries to read without them. Welfare promised her a new pair two weeks ago but they haven't come yet. Bessie insists on homework. "They've got to get some kind of education. I'm hoping that just one of them will make it someday. Just one of them and I'll be thankful."

It is amazing to see how the kids keep their books stacked so neatly inside all the rubble. During rare, quiet moments they help one another with their reading. And for a little while the place seems to be filled with love.

NOVEMBER 17, 1967

Hunger, severe cold, rats and roaches sent Bessie with four of her kids to the welfare office today. I caught up with them there, pleading with the welfare man.

"How did it go?" I asked as she left.

"Promises. Promises. Promises. That's all I ever get."

NOVEMBER 20, 1967

Roseanna wouldn't talk to me today. She sat sulking with her head buried in her hands, barefoot with a black raincoat buttoned to her neck against the cold. "Momma whipped her for staying out all night," Kenneth whispered to me. Roseanna reached out to me for a little sympathy before I left. "I was at a girlfriend's house dancing, having a little fun. It got late and we were afraid to go home. So we just hung out till morning."

The girlfriend came by before I left. They sat in the shadows of Roseanna's room beside a bundle of rags, sharing a cigarette and hardly speaking. They seemed to share one another's misery.

A picture of Christ hangs on the cracked wall above Richard's bed. I asked Bessie if they were religious. "We used to be but we don't go to church anymore. Nothing to wear or put in the collection plate. You feel ashamed. It's hard

266

keeping faith with things going so bad. I teach the kids
prayers. That's about all I can do."

Ellen screamed. Toe-Boy had nipped her toe. Bessie sent
the dog scurrying with a well-aimed kick.

NOVEMBER 21, 1967

Norman Jr. is a strange mixture. I ran into him this
morning peering through the window of a fish and chips
joint. "Want some chips?" he asked hopefully. I told him I'd
love some. So we went in and filled ourselves with greasy
chips and fish. He talks defiantly of anybody who's white—the
police, the butcher, the grocery clerk. His eyes have the hard
glint of older men you see in Harlem. He seems dangerously
aggressive, and is powerfully built for a boy his age. Despite
the hostility he is overwhelmingly tender at times. He will
suddenly lift little Richard and smother him with kisses, or
stand fingering his mother's earring. "You're pretty, Momma,
real pretty," he'll say without a smile.

NOVEMBER 23, 1967

Snowflakes were swirling down through a broken skylight
and piling up in the hallway outside the door. I kicked the
snow aside, knocked and Bessie let me in with another
complaint on her lips. She had an armful of rags. "There's no
place to put anything. If we only had some drawers of some
kind to put things in." She began coughing violently, dropped
the rags and sat down. "The hospital says it's my nerves. They
want to open my throat and operate for some reason or
another. I'm not about to let them put a knife to my throat.
Never." She shook her head despondently. "Lord, I feel like
jumping out that window."

NOVEMBER 26, 1967

No heat at all in the place today. The oven was on when I
arrived and they were huddled together in the kitchen eating
warmed-over catfish for breakfast. They had all slept there on
a mattress the night before. Norman Sr. sat shivering in a far
corner.

"How's it going?" I asked him. The question was useless,
stupid, but it was conversation.

267

"Bad."

"Any hope for work?"

"I was out for shape-up at the railroad yard every day this week. Nothing—nothing doing." He motioned for me to follow him into the next room. "A lot of guys would have pulled out from their family by now and left them to welfare. I can't. All I want to be is a man—just a man, if they'd let me."

DECEMBER 1, 1967

I found Norman Jr. on a street corner warming himself over a garbage-can fire. Holes were in his tennis shoes and he shivered beneath a light windbreaker. I asked him why he was out in the cold.

"Poppa kicked me out."

"What for?"

"He's mad about having no work."

"Want to go home with me?"

"Naw, thanks. Momma will get me in some way. I'll be all right."

(I'll be all right. Suddenly I was remembering. They were words similar to those I had uttered to Crystal Graham the night my brother-in-law kicked me out into the cold many years before. Now, through young Norman I suddenly felt the futility of my own childhood rushing back, melding my youthful despair of that past frigid night to his—here in Harlem where he dwelled in yet another jungle of hunger and uncertainty. Through past heartbreak I sensed his heartbreak as he stood there shivering. And with night coming on there was no reason to think that his plight would disappear with it. Compassion, I realized, wasn't enough. He couldn't eat or drink it, nor would it stop his shivering or salve his misery. There wasn't even room in my thoughts to dream of better times for him and his family. The only thing to do about his hard, young life was to try and smooth it. Having bathed in the goodness of a father like mine, it was difficult to understand how any father—no matter what hardship hounded him—could throw him out into such cold.

I went upstairs. Bessie was stirring a large cauldron of boiling water on the stove. The other kids were already in bed. Norman Sr. was asleep on a bundle of rags and smelling of whiskey. "Things are rough around here tonight," she said softly. "One of his buddies gave him a bottle."

"What about little Norman? I can take him home with me."

"I'll slip him in after a while. Don't worry."

DECEMBER 2, 1967

Bessie was lying on the cot with little Richard beneath her arm when I got there this afternoon. Her face and neck were bruised and swollen. She managed a smile. "He gave me a good going over last night. My ribs feel like they're broken." She started crying. "I just can't take it anymore. It's too much for anybody to bear."

"Where is he?"

"In the hospital."

"Hospital?"

"Yes. I sent him there. When he got through kicking me around I dumped that scalding water on him—and it stuck because I put honey and sugar into it first."

Norman Jr. went with me to the hospital. He couldn't even recognize his father. What skin was left was still covered with honey and sugar. He was a hulk of running sores, horribly burned from head to foot. He sat on the bed's side daubing at his closed eyes.

"Hi, Poppa. This is Norman. I'm with Mr. Parks."

After a long silence he said, "I don't know why your mother did it, boy. I just don't know."

The outcome of the essay still troubles me, leaves me wondering about the serious problem of altering human lives. The Fontenelles lived in a rotting tenement across the world from Flavio da Silva's family, but they shared the same tragedy, and I became involved in their struggle to survive it.

After their story was published in March 1968, the Fontenelles, with money I asked for from *Life* magazine and what readers contributed, were able to buy a comfortable house in Long Island. There was new furniture; they had a front porch, grass, fresh air and schools for the children to attend. Norman Sr. was given a good job. An entirely new world had suddenly raced in upon the luckless Fontenelles and swept them from the filth and chaos of their Harlem tenement. The Fontenelles at last had good reason to be happy, and I was happy for them.

Then, at three o'clock one morning, Norman Sr. came in whiskied up and dropped a lit cigarette onto the sofa. In the roaring blaze that followed, the house was completely destroyed and he and Kenneth died, burned beyond recognition. In minutes, death and horror had replaced their happiness.

I had kept in touch with Mrs. Fontenelle. On one Christmas Eve several years later, I went to Harlem to pay her a visit, for she had returned there to stay. The family was now hopelessly scattered. The oldest brother and a younger one were back in prison paying for their drug habits; the three teenage girls were, according to their mother, "on the streets." She hadn't seen them for weeks. Only she and her youngest son, Richard, sat in the tiny cold apartment.

There wasn't much I could say to Bessie Fontenelle as I left that night. She stood, I remember, at the top of the stairs waving goodbye, saying finally what I could not bring myself to say, "Merry Christmas." Weakly I had called back, "Happy New Year."

I was thinking now that perhaps I had pushed them toward some improbable dream; played God by digging too deep into their lives. I had reported their plight with objectivity, but in the end my emotions, which by nature are subjective, took over. I had found them poverty-stricken and hungry, entangled in agonies, surrendering to whatever pride or respect they might have wanted for themselves. I had paused then to look back, and what I saw in the distance mirrored their situation—a kind of situation that should have grown weary with years and given up. But there it was, fresh as ever, gnawing away at the Fontenelles. I had simply yielded to a need to help them in some way. It had been impossible to lie contented in the arms of my own personal deliverance.

Disaster kept rushing through the Fontenelles, finishing them off one by one. Since the day I met them three had gone to their graves—two destroyed by a needless fire, one through drugs. Norman Jr. attended Roseanna's funeral accompanied by prison guards. To his mother, life by now felt like daggered teeth.

The afternoon flowed with sorrow when I attended Roseanna's funeral in Harlem during the summer of 1980. Ironically it was she who always expressed hope for a better life. On the coffin beside the bouquet I had sent was only a small gathering of pale yellow roses. I looked at Roseanna's dead young face, knowing that beneath the closed lids the eyes were still glazed with drugs. I glanced at Bessie Fontenelle. She was shrunken into her grief. The hope she had for her family was dwindling away.

As the small cortege rolled through Harlem en route to the gravesite, I saw other young black faces and knew that many of them were caught up in the evil of drugs, lost, wandering in their broken worlds, isolated from reality. More and more I had seen them, uptown and downtown, mere shadows of themselves moving into darker shadows, dull-eyed and staring through a maze of confusion.

On the first day of 1990 I called Bessie Fontenelle to wish her, and what was left of the family, a happy new year. She thanked me cheerfully, then began carrying me back through the years just passed. Little Richard was now married, and with a child of his own that he had named Gordon. "That boy is going to make it," she said proudly. "He doesn't even drink or smoke and he's a good musician. Can you believe it? He made twenty thousand dollars the past year. Well, maybe one of my kids will make it before I pull out from here." But then things began to collapse. Norman Jr. was back in prison for drug use. Riel, his younger sister, had died from an overdose two years before. Ellen, who had been on a *Life* cover, was in the hospital dying of AIDS. Her child of eleven months had already died of the same disease.

"Oh, Bessie, I'm so sorry. And how are you feeling?"

She sighed softly. "Me? I'm in bed with diabetes, and cancer is chewing me up. I guess I'm dying slowly. But all of us are doing that, so I'm not complaining. I'm used to hard times." A weariness crept into her voice. "Hard times moved in with me a long time ago. Now they're letting me into the project house, but it's almost too late."

Again, "I'm so sorry, Bessie." Suddenly it seemed that I had spent our entire relationship saying that. After I hung up everything turned backward. My hopes for the Fontenelles were also dying. Digging through the morass of their everydayness had demanded far too much of them.

It *was* too late. As if on schedule, death arrived for Bessie two months later. Huddled against a bitterly cold March wind on the day they buried her were only four of the ten children she bore—Diana (from an earlier marriage), Lette, Ellen and Richard. Norman Jr. grieved from prison. Harry was somewhere in Ohio. Richard explained, "He just couldn't make it here." Alongside their father, Norman Sr., four others lay in graves surrounding the one their mother was then lowered into. The final words of the obituary went with her:

> God saw the road was getting rough
> And the hill too hard to climb.
> So, gently he closed Bessie's loving eyes,
> And whispered, "Peace be thine."

Author and wife Elizabeth dancing on their wedding day. Grandson Alain Brouillaud at bottom of photograph. *Cecil Layne.*

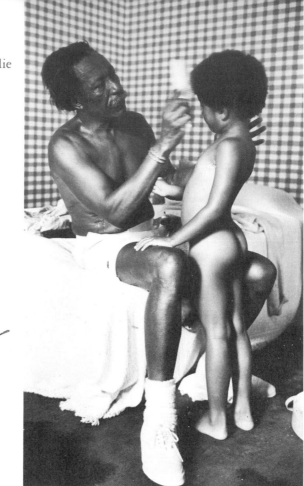

Author preparing daughter Leslie for wedding ceremony to Gene Young, August 26, 1973. *Jill Krementz*.

Author is wedded to Gene Young on August 26, 1973, at Pound Ridge, New York. *Jill Krementz*.

Author with Gene Young, leaving a party, 1975. *Courtesy of Gordon Parks.*

Author and wife Gene at work in bed, February 1974. *Alfred Eisenstaedt/Life Magazine* © *Time Warner.*

Author with sister Anna at mother's grave at Evergreen Cemetery in Fort Scott, Kansas. *J. K. Graham.*

Author with Rosa Parks at the banquet for the 1985 Springarn Medal, which the NAACP awarded Gordon Parks in 1972. *Juanita M. Cole.*

The author with Senator Nancy Kassebaum at a banquet in 1985 in Topeka, Kansas, at which he was named Kansan of the Year. *Richard Strickler.*

Author directing film *Leadbelly* from horseback near Austin, Texas, in 1976.
Paramount Pictures.

Author with cinematographer Hiro Narita, filming *The Odyssey of Solomon Northup* during May 1983, outside Savannah, Georgia. *American Playhouse.*

Author receiving one of twenty-four honorary degrees awarded him. Fairfield University, Fairfield, Connecticut. *John G. O'Connor.*

TWENTY-TWO

When summoning up the past I take into account the luck, which first touched me at my birth. Our family doctor, having pronounced me dead, was wrapping me for disposal when his young assistant asked to try something on his own.

"But the child's dead."

"Please—let me try."

Consent was granted by Dr. Cavanaugh and I was swished about in a tub of cold water like a slab of beef. Suddenly I started yelling, and they say I kept up the yelling for an hour.

Dr. Gordon was my savior's name, and that was the name I was given by my mother. Since then luck has visited me any number of times. When it came, and I was ready for it, I prospered. If I wasn't ready, it passed me by.

For years I, with everyone else, had justifiably believed that Hollywood would never accept a black director. So I was apprehensive as I sat opposite Kenneth Hyman, the man in charge at Warner Brothers Seven Arts Studio in Burbank, California. I was there at the urging of John Cassavetes, the actor, who felt, after reading *The Learning Tree,* that it should be made into a motion picture and that I should direct it. But I was there and it still puzzles me that he suggested my seeing Hyman; the two of them, according to Cassavetes, had argued violently and were barely speaking at the time. Hyman's very first question stunned me. "How long will it take you to get out here and start production?" Obviously my smile told him that I thought he was playing games. "I'm serious," he said hastily. "I love your book and I'm convinced that it will make a good film, and that you should direct it." He lit a cigar. "Who would you like to write the screenplay?"

It was happening fast—too fast. And I was still cautious. "I don't know any screenwriters out here."

"Why not write it yourself? You wrote the book."

"But I've never written a screenplay."

"You've never directed a picture either."

Carry him on, I was thinking. "Okay—I'll give it a try."

"Cassavetes tells me you're a composer as well."

"That's right."

The look I gave him now was loaded with all-out skepticism. "Okay—why not. I'll take that on as well."

"Fine. Now, you're going to be Hollywood's very first black director. There may be problems and you're going to need some clout. I suggest you act as executive producer."

Incredible. Smiling, I shook my head. "Well why not."

Provided Kenneth Hyman wasn't playing games, Hollywood's impregnable walls of bigotry were crumbling. When, a few days later, I signed the contract, the impossible no longer seemed impossible. But not until the news swept across the country did I relax. Singlehandedly, Kenneth Hyman had, in less than thirty minutes, broken Hollywood's unwritten law. He was in a good position to have done so—Elliot Hyman, his father, ran the studio.

But Kenneth had made the decision on his own and I, straddled with a pleasant burden, was determined not to let him down, nor those black people who would be counting on me to succeed. Several times before, in minuscule ways, there had been glimmers of hope—through Ingrid Bergman when she urged Roberto Rossellini to take me on as an assistant. He had refused. Later Peter Glenville, the British director, along with Hal Wallis of Paramount Pictures, offered me the opportunity to direct the opening titles of the motion picture *Summer and Smoke.* But after viewing Glenville's existing footage, I saw no way to improve upon it, and said so. Several years later, after Wallis had left the studio, John Cassavetes had wanted me as the director of a picture he was about to star in. The studio turned him down.

Now, after thirty-odd years, my photography, words and music were about to come together. And I had worked hard for this extraordinary moment. But the time for celebration had to be pushed aside. Quite well I knew that until *The Learning Tree* was actually in production I would not breathe easily. With only ninety days before the cameras would start rolling, there was so much to learn. This was, I realized, a chance for other blacks to work with me—and also behind the camera—for the first time in Hollywood. "I'm afraid none have been trained for that," Hyman replied when I made the request.

"But we should try," I insisted. Most agreeably Hyman tried and nine other blacks were added to the crew. One, Joe Wilcot, was taken on as a third cameraman.

It was necessary for me to have a highly experienced *line* producer, and Hyman introduced me to five men who he felt were capable of nursing me through the ordeal. For some reason I still find hard to explain, I chose the one who seemed to like me the least. Bill Conrad, I distinctly remember was the only one of the five who didn't shake my hand. Hyman, obviously surprised by my choice, approved it nevertheless. "Bill appears to be sort of an ornery cuss at first glance, but he knows the film business."

"He sure looks ornery, but I'm not looking to be coddled. We'll make out."

Conrad, I am sure, was a bit surprised himself. But sourly he began putting me through the hoops—grunting out camera angles in their proper and improper relationship to the actors who would

275

work before them. Matches represented the actors; a small match-box became the camera. Shoving a match to the right of the box, he would ask gruffly, "In what position is the actor?"

"Camera right."

He pushed the box a few inches to the right of the match. "Where's your actor now?"

"At camera left."

Around and around those matches and boxes went, with Bill grunting questions, and me grunting answers. "You learn pretty damn fast," he finally said.

"You're a pretty damn good teacher."

"Do you know anything about camera lenses and their focal lengths?"

I smiled inwardly. "A little."

"Hyman tells me you're to do the screenplay. Do you know anything about writing one?"

"I wrote the novel—if that means anything."

"That's a different kind of writing."

"I'm finding that out. I'm also finding that the screenplay is a lot easier."

He stroked his chin; a portly unshaven chin, then looked at me oddly. "How about actors? Have you ever worked with any?"

"A few—Laurence Olivier, Edward G. Robinson, Ingrid Bergman, Tallulah Bankhead, Helen Hayes, Henry Fonda, Tony Quinn and some others." He eyed me, awaiting an explanation. "I had to coax them into camera positions while covering Broadway plays for *Life* magazine."

"And how did you make out?"

"All right mostly. Olivier and Bankhead were a bit difficult."

"Now—I hear you're to also do the music. Have you scored a movie before?"

"No, I haven't."

He smiled as his brow lifted into a wrinkle. "Friend, that's going to be a toughie. Composing's not easy."

I thought of the piano concerto in Venice but didn't mention it. Instead I said, "It will be interesting."

Bill sat beside me, probably expecting the worst, when I faced department heads of the various groups who would work on the film—the electricians, grips, special effects, cameramen, makeup, wardrobe, trucking and props. The questions fell evenly and quickly. I was extremely nervous but this was not the time to show it. Right or wrong, my answers came back evenly and just as quickly.

"The cyclone—how many wind machines will be needed?"

I long-shotted a guess. "At least six—and very powerful ones."

"How many cameras will be operating during the sequence?"

An easy one. "Three if we need them. It depends upon how much power the wind machines can generate over the area."

"Is livestock needed for the cyclone?"

Another easy one. "Yes. Four horses and a herd of steers. We will also need wild birds, ducks and geese, as well as chickens. Three or four hound dogs wouldn't hurt. Four good horsemen should be on hand to control the herd."

"The script indicates the camera will be nearly a mile from the horsemen at one point. What about camera lenses and communication with the actors from that distance?"

"Bring a thousand-millimeter lens. I will direct by walkie-talkie. Be sure to have the most powerful units."

"What about cars, and what kind?"

"Nineteen-twenty models—Fords, Maxwells, Chevrolets, maybe an electric car or two."

It went on like that for two hours—everything from men's underwear to the kind of furniture that was to be brought along. At times I had become a little nettled, but again, that was no time to show it. Bill paid me a compliment as we walked toward his office. "Damned good job you did back there."

"Well, Bill, remember I lived through it. All I had to do was to think back. Some of it was outright guessing."

"Some pretty good guessing, I'd say."

"Thank you, *William.*"

Every day was knotted with problems to be untangled, but for me it was sweet labor. After three months of intricate planning and hard work, the crew was ready to depart for the location, my birthplace: Fort Scott, Kansas. The actors, crew and I went by plane as far as Kansas City. From there we would have to travel by car. My hometown's airfield could only accommodate the very smallest of aircraft. Even then stray cows had to be shooed off the runway for safe landings. As we motored over the prairieland nostalgia gripped me. I was coming back to where I was born; where, as a poor black youth, I had been the victim of white racism and intolerance. Now I was returning with nearly an all-white crew and millions of dollars at my command. We passed a few miles south of the Evergreen cemetery. There, in segregated graves, lay my mother, father, two sisters, a brother and several of my boyhood friends. Moments of anger crept in. Now I was in a good position to let the townspeople know how I felt about their intolerance before and after death. And I planned to do just that, now that the chance was about to arrive.

Though many Americans and Europeans had read *The Learning Tree* by now, possibly only five of the ten thousand residents of Fort Scott had done so. The local library had only one copy on its shelves. So even as the big trucks, loaded with every conceivable need for the filming, rumbled into the prairie town, trouble was brewing. The townspeople had been alerted. "Jack Parks's son is coming with a bunch of Hollywood people to make trouble for us." By the time the cast and crew arrived, a wall of suspicion had been built—and it didn't take long for us to feel its presence. Clouds of locusts would have received a warmer reception. A quiet hostility reigned. A farmer whose place we wanted to use yelled, "Git off my property or I'll git my gun! I don't want nothin' to do with that lying book about whites lynching Negroes!" We got off his property.

Things grew progressively worse until we called upon the mayor. Learning that we were about to move on to another town, and with a quarter of a million dollars to be spent with local merchants, he called the town's fathers together. In little time the residents, with chaste hearts, set aside their animosities—and within a couple of days Fort Scott was transformed into a rambling Hollywood back lot.

As the first day of shooting approached, Burney Guffey, my wizened cameraman, sensed my anxiety. "Listen," he advised. "When you go up on that big crane tomorrow morning, you're going to be nervous. Don't let your crew know that. Act like you've been up there a thousand times before. Bark out your very first order with authority." I laughed weakly, then went off to bed for a totally sleepless night.

Morning trundled in. When I reached the set the crew and

actors were waiting; the moment had arrived. I walked Kyle Johnson to the edge of what had once been my father's cornfield. He was to portray the part of Newt Winger, the role assigned to my own early life. Touching his shoulder I said, "Kyle, I lived and wrote it. Now I'm turning it all over to you."

"Don't worry. I'll give it my best."

I climbed into the crane seat and it lifted me high into the air. Beyond, as far as I could see, were the rolling green plains of Kansas where I had spent the first fifteen years of my childhood. The cornfield beneath me had been the only means my father had for keeping his big family from starvation. Now, with millions of dollars behind me, I had come back to re-create an experience long since passed. Several miles to the southwest was the segregated graveyard where my parents lay. I looked down at Kyle; he was ready. I nodded to the assistant director. "Cameras," he said softly.

"Cameras rolling." Burney Guffey's voice was reassuring.

"Action!" I shouted with *authority.*

Guffey was smiling. Squinting hard against the sun, Kyle Johnson started moving through prairie grass up to his chin. Soon the big wind machines were whirring, helping to whip up the oncoming tornado. *The Learning Tree* was on its way.

Making the film was a rewarding experience—and a traumatic one. It turned out to be one of the most difficult things I have ever attempted to do. The pressure had been excessive from the very beginning. A lot of people of all colors were anxious about the breakthrough, and I was anxious to make the most of it. The wait had been far too long. Just remembering that no black had been given a chance to direct a motion picture in Hollywood since it was established kept me going. No day was free of problems, but somewhere there were answers, and I lay awake late into the nights searching for them.

Being a part of the story's flesh and bone had its advantages. Out there, where the real drama unfolded, the past came around to be acquitted, to watch, to see that every move Kyle Johnson made faithfully emulated those I had made forty-odd years before —to nudge me constantly into the rightness of every scene and situation. If an actor's portrayal of some real-life character fell short of the mark, he was taken aside and rehearsed until he and I both felt he could improve his performance. This took time and, on location, time gets to be very costly. Big Hollywood crews, ceaselessly eating time and money, are subjects of a multitude of fearful tales. A luckless assistant to the costumer forgot to bring along red dye for a pair of long underwear, and three hours were lost while the town was combed for some. That estimated loss—ten thousand dollars. Booker Savage's longjohns wound up costing more than a Christian Dior ballgown. But the goal was perfection—for the actors and the crew. Everyone was aware of the historical significance of the undertaking, and everyone was giving the best of himself. It was heartening to know that certain crew members had refused other films in order to work on *The Learning Tree*. Never since have I seen a crew work with such rapport. Those were halcyon days.

Meanwhile, the townspeople had escaped their obscurity. Housewives, husbands and children, costumed for the 1920s, were playing out their roles as extras with dedication. The irate farmer who had ordered us off his property with a gun threat had even surrendered to the excitement. He was now the foreman of our trial jury, and loving every second of it. "I aim to give you one of those Academy Award performances," he assured me one morning. He had spoken with his customary sternness. An elderly juror who had difficulty hearing believed to the end that he was participating in an actual trial. "I know'd that Booker Savage was guilty right from the time I laid eyes on him."

And, like the old juror, the crew members got caught up in realism. They insisted that Estelle Evans, who portrayed my mother, be barred from the set during the filming immediately after her death. Understanding, Estelle kept to her room for two days. Even Kyle had become edgy. He came to my quarters at midnight, troubled by the scene he was to reinact the following morning: by sleeping next to his mother's coffin he would hope to lose the fear of death. "How did you actually feel at that moment?" he asked.

In the silence, I sat with him for several moments, remembering that frightful, lonely night. "Kyle, it was both terror-filled and strangely reassuring. I had gone alone in the dark toward what I feared most—death. But a few steps away lay the person I loved most—my mother. Somehow I felt she would understand why I was coming to her for the last time. Perhaps she would lift that terrible fear of death from my insides forever and take it with her. In the dimness I could only sense the shape of the coffin. Sweat popped out on me and I started to go back to my room. Instead I took courage and moved toward it. Then, I eased up the lid, shivered, and looked for a long moment at her in the crinkly white interior of the coffin, telling myself she was only asleep. 'I'm not afraid anymore, Mommy,' I heard myself saying. Then I eased down the lid, put my blanket on the floor, pulled it around me, and closed my eyes tightly. After a while the heartbeat slowed, the trembling eased and I began the struggle with sleep. Before long I was snoring softly." The hush over the set during Kyle's performance was no less than the hush that fell over my mother's death parlor on that bottomless night. Kyle had taken a moment that belonged to me and—for another enkindled moment—made it his own. The two intervals of silence had been separated by time. Over his came the soft whirring of the camera; over mine came the plaintive hooting of an owl. Kyle was emotionally exhausted, and the crew seemed spent; the quiet it kept was beyond belief. Normally I would have asked for another take, just for safety's sake, but my conscience peered at me, saying no.

I gave Burney Guffey a questioning glance. His thumb was pointed upward. His camera was contented with the performance. I asked Kyle if he was satisfied. Tears were still streaming down his cheeks. He nodded affirmatively, and I called for an early lunch.

Two days before we were scheduled to close out, Hollywood requested a reshooting of one underexposed scene in an apple orchard. By now the temperature had dropped below freezing, the grass had browned from winter, and the trees were leafless and bare of apples. I passed the problem on to the propman. He shrugged—no problem. The boys—Newt, Marcus, Beansy, Skunk and Jappy, would be practically naked and barefoot. For them—no problem. By morning the grass had been sprayed a summer's green and store-bought leaves and apples hung from the limbs. Heaters and blankets were brought in. July returned in December for an hour of shooting. The following day we "wrapped," forty-eight hours ahead of schedule.

281

Fort Scott seemed saddened when the trucks pulled out. For three months it had been engaged in a kind of excitement it would probably never experience again. Now it would fall back into the ordinariness of prairie life.

After three more months of musical scoring and editing, *The Learning Tree* was finished. Upon viewing it, Kenneth Hyman embraced me warmly and smiled. It was the kind of smile I wanted to see on the face of a man who had put his trust in me.

Later, on Broadway, my feelings mingled with nostalgia and quiet joy as I stood watching the throngs streaming into the theater for the premiere. Among them were my sisters Peggy and Lillian and my brother Clem, whom I had flown in for this night that I knew would be so special for them. The day before I had experienced several thorny hours at La Guardia Airport after realizing they were on the same plane, flying for the first time in their lives. Nervously I had paced up and down until their plane set down safely on the runway. My two sisters were still rigid with fear when I met them at the gate. Not so my brother. With a big smile plastered over his face he said, "Thanks for the skyride, Pedro. That's probably the closest I'll ever get to heaven." I remember so well that night how he stood on Broadway amid the bright lights, glancing up at the marquee emblazoned with *The Learning Tree*. "If only Momma and Poppa were here to see that," he said. Then arm in arm we had walked into the theater.

Nearly two years had passed since the filming of *The Learning Tree,* and *Life* had asked me back to cover the Black Panthers, who were being vengefully murdered by the police. Now, in 1970, the two enemy camps boiled with violent threats against one another.

The Panthers had first grabbed national attention when thirty of them—six women and twenty-four men—dressed in black leather jackets and black berets, marched on the California state capitol in Sacramento on May 2, 1967. Armed with .45's, .357 magnums, shotguns and rifles, and draped in bandoliers, they walked up the steps of the capitol building, and Bobby Seale read a statement by Huey Newton, their leader, protesting a bill then under debate making the carrying of firearms illegal. The bill was passed, but the Panthers were on their way. Against a background of summer riots and the growth of paramilitary groups all over the country, many whites suddenly found the Panther image a frightening and intimidating one. On the other hand, to a multitude of black boys in the ghettos the Panthers were "bad-ass mother-fuckers"—high praise indeed.

Night was falling when I entered the Panther headquarters on Shattuck Street in Berkeley, California. The young man who led me up the stairwell at the back of the building had fallen quiet. The Marxist theories he had bombarded me with on the ride from San Francisco had found me an unlikely convert. Now, as we climbed, the darkness grew fragrant with the odor of cooking. At the top of the steps he gave three short raps, waited a second, then gave four more. Each set of raps seemed to have a secret meaning. A door opened to a kitchen brimming with young people, men, women and children—all Panthers come to share a supper of rabbit stew. David Hilliard, the party's chief of staff, was at the stove stirring the contents of a big pot and, without changing rhythm, he observed me through dark glasses. "Welcome, brother. Be with you in a minute." He motioned toward two bearded Panthers who stood in a doorway. "Donald Cox, our field marshal, and my brother, June." They nodded. I glanced about the room; it was quiet despite all the people inside it. I sensed trouble in the quietness, nervousness in the faces. Everybody, even the children, seemed jittery. Something was wrong; the place was heavy with tension.

I went to read a large poster, framed and hung on a wall. It read:

WE WANT FREEDOM.

WE WANT FULL EMPLOYMENT FOR OUR PEOPLE.

WE WANT AN END TO THE ROBBERY BY THE WHITE MAN
    OF BLACKS.

WE WANT DECENT HOUSING FIT FOR HUMAN BEINGS.

WE WANT EDUCATION FOR OUR PEOPLE.

WE WANT BLACK MEN TO BE EXEMPT FROM MILITARY
    SERVICE.

WE WANT AN IMMEDIATE END TO POLICE MURDER OF BLACK
    PEOPLE.

WE WANT FREEDOM FOR ALL BLACK MEN IN THIS COUNTRY'S
    PRISONS.

WE WANT BLACK PEOPLE TRIED IN COURT BY THEIR PEER
  GROUP.
WE WANT BREAD, LAND, HOUSING, EDUCATION, CLOTHING,
  JUSTICE
AND PEACE.

The bowls were filled. Hilliard ushered me into a back room.
His brother and Cox joined us. I was offered some stew, but I
politely refused. Hilliard broke the silence. "What have you come
to do here, brother?"

"Oh, to get your side of the story—so that the rest of the world
can hear it." My words had been chosen carefully, but somehow
they sounded second-rate after I spoke them.

"That means hanging out with us, taking chances, brother. Our
lives are on the line. The pigs are out to wipe us out."

"I know. I'm part of all this, too. I have to take my chances."

"I'm curious. Do you think for a minute that that honky magazine you work for will print anything we've got to say?"

My mind's eye joined the cluster of editorial faces awaiting me
back in New York—all white, all skeptical. "I can only hope they
will—and somehow, I think they will. It's just another chance we'll
have to take." I wasn't sure. Hatred and fear for the Panthers was
feeding white America.

We were silent for several minutes. His memory, I knew, was
spitting up the terrible deaths that had come to several Panthers a
week before in Los Angeles. The faces of the three men, black and
glistening in the dim light, held anger and grief. Hilliard then
took a sheaf of paper from his pocket and laid it before me.
"Okay, brother, try this on them for size. See if they'll print what's
on that paper. It's all the Truth."

The universe became interminably still as I read, and the words
smacked against me like fierce waves. Now I began to understand
the agonizing quiet. Each sentence arrived with its cup of venom,
and what little respect I had left for law and order people slowly
crumpled:

Weapons to be employed: Rifles, shotguns, 33-MM gas guns, 37-MM
grenade launchers and Thompson machine guns. *The assault plans:*
Assign two-man squad to front with shotgun (solid slugs) and ar-
mor-piercing rifle to blast armor plate off upper windows. Upper
shields to be shot out, and use 00 buckshot to shoot out all lower

windows. Use rifle slugs to try and knock open main front door. Front and back guard lay down fire on the second floor. Assault squad (three men) armed with machine guns approach building from the south. Squad enter building through front broken windows and doors. Two men enter and move left and to right center of ground floor. Fire thirty rounds each up through the second story floor, and reload. The entire building should then be flooded with tear gas. The entire upper floor should be covered with intense fire. Assault squad will then proceed upstairs and bring down the wounded and dead. *The target:* The Black Panther Party headquarters on Shattuck Street in Berkeley. *The task force:* (in the event of a disturbance at the Panther Party office) the Berkeley police.

My thoughts returned to the kitchen; to a small girl who sucked her thumb and clung to her mother's skirt; to the freckled boy with large crossed eyes who sat on a bench with several other children. He had given me a look both quizzical and friendly, a look that I would find hard now to forget. They too would be blown apart in the crossfire, then dragged off dead—not knowing why they had died, because those who might have explained would be lying dead beside them.

The three Panthers awaiting my reaction had no doubts about the assault plans being carried out. A matter of time; a solitary disturbance of any kind would invite grenades and machine-gun fire. I expressed disbelief. "These plans are incredible."

"The pigs are incredible," Cox scoffed. He then handed me a news clipping in which Bruce Baker, the Berkeley police chief, admitted that the plans were *probably* the work of one of his sergeants. He was more concerned about how they had fallen into the hands of the Panthers. I put the story on the wire to New York later that night. The editors wired back: "Sorry—without proof document is unprintable." They fell a little short of accusing the Panthers of forgery. I wired back: "Check out statement with Chief Baker then wire back soonest." The answer sped back. "No outright denial from Baker. Proceed with caution. Good luck."

I rode with the Panthers for the next three weeks, and always within the shadowing of the police, following, watching our every move. At night their headlights glued to our rear windows. Every ride was a perilous mission, and invariably a brother or sister Panther was in some sort of trouble. I always returned to my hotel a little shaky, and happy to have arrived without mishap.

285

On one particular rainy night I rode in the back seat next to the young Marxist who had driven me to the headquarters. Lightning streaked through the darkness; the thunder was angry and volleying and the glare of a police car remained steady behind us. He turned and squinted into it. "Those filthy pigs. Man, how I'd love to blow the fuckers away. Bam! Bam! Bam! Blow them to hell and back."

"They're probably thinking the same way about us."

"No doubt about that." As we rolled on he was thinking hard, glancing occasionally at me. "A question for you, brother. Would you write your book *A Choice of Weapons* today the way you wrote it a few years ago?"

"Yes. I'd write it the same way. Why?"

"With our lives on the line, and those pigs with their guns trained on your ass? I can't believe it."

Cox was driving and I could see his eyes in the rearview mirrow. Both he and Hilliard were waiting for my answer. I eyed the young Marxist as I would a delinquent tomcat, feeling somewhat annoyed. "My good friend, I've got a 35-millimeter camera in my pocket. You've got a .45 automatic in yours. But I feel my weapon is probably more powerful than yours. Furthermore, my ass is out here with yours. If they start firing, I go the same way you go—for the same cause. So, don't give me that horseshit, because I'm not buying it." There was a heavy silence. I wondered if it was in my favor or disfavor. I could say that I didn't care one way or the other, but I did. I knew, of course, where the young man was coming from. Huey Newton hailed Karl Marx as a messiah, and he had sung his political theories to the party since its inception. His aims were, he said, "To give the members a chance to become objective in their appraisal of black people." But to hungry young blacks who were being slammed against the walls and frisked everyday, lectures about Marx's expositions on dialectical materialism were like having conversations without words. Such winged hypothesizing was too much for a hopeless dropout to grasp. Only the Harvard-trained Panther beside me seemed swayed by the complexities of the German socialist. I can't remember the young man's name. I do remember his being shot in a police ambush several weeks later and he died somewhere between his ideology and a reckless show of courage.

• • •

Now the Panthers were in deep trouble. Huey Newton was in prison at San Luis Obispo, doing fifteen years for killing John Frey, a policeman. Bobby Seale was in a San Francisco jail fighting extradition to New Haven, Connecticut. That state wanted to prosecute him for the murder of ex-Panther Alex Rackley. Twenty-one others were in New York jails for alleged bombings. What's more the police were stepping up their raids on Panther headquarters and homes.

The Panthers lived a semicommunal existence. Some cooked while others cleaned the rooms and offices. Telephones rang continuously, and Donald Cox usually answered. Teenage girls at typewriters and stencil machines gave a businesslike atmosphere to the dreary place. Huge posters of Panther martyrs and Third World heroes Mao Tse-tung, Che Guevara and Ho Chi Minh covered walls and street windows. Overlooking all of these from a commanding position was a huge poster of Huey Newton, sitting defiantly on a wicker throne—rifle in one hand and a spear in the other. Malcolm X posters were just arriving and a place on the ground floor was being found for them. On the outside of the building were pasted FREE HUEY posters, throwbacks to the angry days when he was fighting a first-degree-murder verdict and the gas chamber.

On one Saturday night the phone rang. Cox answered, listened, then summoned Hilliard. "The pigs are giving a brother some trouble." Hilliard stepped to the phone, listened, then said, "Sit tight. We'll be there." He, June, his brother, and Cox started down the stairs and I followed them to their car. Hilliard paused when he saw me. "Drop you at your hotel if you like. We're going past there." He added firmly, "We've got some very private business over in Frisco." I accepted.

I made my way through the plush lobby of the Mark Hopkins Hotel. It sharply defined the gap between the Black Panthers' world and the world they had set out to change. For a few uncomfortable moments I felt out of place, disloyal, even traitorous. The elevator door sprang open and whisked me up to a hive of thickly carpeted floors, soft beds and snow-white sheets. A prosperous-looking white family were leaving their suite. The blond teenage girl wanted to take in the waterfront the next morning. Her older brother was suggesting the golf course. "We have plenty of time," the mother said, "we'll enjoy it all." I wondered how the four of them would like to have rabbit stew over on Shattuck Street with some brothers and sisters of the Black Panther party. I smiled at the idea. The father smiled back, and I bade them good night. Before I fell asleep, I thought of the possible whereabouts of the three Panthers who had gone off to help a brother. And it suddenly came to me that I might not see them alive again. With the party's history that thought was easy to come by.

The Black Panther symbol first leaped into the civil rights movement in 1965 with Carmichael's formation of the Lowndes County Freedom Organization in Lowndes County, Alabama. The Black Panther was chosen because Stokely wanted to use a symbol diametrically opposed to the white rooster of the Alabama Democratic party. "The jungle Panther," he had said, "is respected for its savagery in defending its lair." Huey Newton and Bobby Seale hadn't formed their party as a direct adjunct to Stokely's organization, but it had blossomed after Huey had approached Stokely about expanding it to a nationwide political base. Having met on Oakland's Merritt Junior College campus, Huey and Bobby Seale, inspired by the symbol, and buttressed with a lawbook and an assortment of guns, set out to organize black young men in Oakland who shared their discontent, and there were quite a few around.

At a street gathering one hot night in June 1966, Huey put his finger in a cop's face and shouted, "We're not waiting for you to change! We are going to change you!" The Panthers grew. The police tightened their watch, harassed them and tried to flush them into the open for all-out warfare. Then, after two years, the Panthers made a bold move. They began tailing the patrol cars, watching for any brutality toward other blacks. They then advised them about taking legal action against the cops. Then came one skirmish after another, in which Panthers were killed.

Eldridge Cleaver, just out of prison, fell under Newton's spell and eventually became the Panther's minister of information. Harassed by state authorities, he fought back with vitriolic prose. Cleaver and seventeen-year-old Bobby Hutton were ambushed by the police one night. After the two surrendered, Cleaver, who had been shot in the leg, watched as Bobby was shot dead. Cleaver claimed the cops had told the boy to run to the patrol car, and was then mowed down. Berkeley became a frightened city.

Like the Muslims, the Panthers attracted young blacks with criminal records, and like them they rehabilitated former convicts. Thus the police labeled them, "A bunch of thugs." On October 27, 1967, Huey Newton and a friend, Gene McKinney, were driving along when they were pulled over by a policeman, John Frey. Then another squad car roared up with Officer Herbert Heanes. An argument started, and it was never clear what happened, but Huey got a bullet in the stomach, Heanes got several wounds, Frey was killed and Gene McKinney got away unscathed.

After a long and celebrated trial Newton was convicted, not for first-degree murder, as the Oakland police wanted, but for manslaughter, a verdict that snatched him from the gas chamber. It was obvious that the jury was never sure of who shot whom, or whether indeed Huey Newton was even guilty of manslaughter. When Officer Heanes testified, his account was riddled with contradictions. Huey, nevertheless, had been sent up for fifteen years. His jailing didn't halt the party's development. In fact the trial promoted an alliance with white leftist students who rallied to the Panther cry of "Free Huey!" The Panthers had hired Charles Garry, a white attorney, who did better by them than they had probably expected. It was his skillful defense that saved Huey Newton from the gas chamber.

After the gun control law was passed in California the Panthers shed their weapons and bandoliers. Street dress then replaced the black leather jacket uniforms being worn by young blacks all over the big-city ghettos. They were in effect, "cooling it." But the calm didn't last. It couldn't last. Unprovoked raids on Panther headquarters in San Diego, Berkeley and Sacramento were stepped up. The Panthers were shot at and the Panthers shot back. Some were wounded. Some were jailed and some were killed. The mayor of Sacramento rebuked the police for their "wanton destruction" of food the Panthers had assembled for their Children's Breakfast Program. Ed Cray of the American Civil Liberties Union said the cops not only destroyed the food but "pissed and crapped on the debris to be sure it could not be used again."

In Chicago before dawn came the most celebrated shoot-up of the ongoing warfare. In December of 1969, fourteen cops shot up a Black Panther's apartment. When the melee ended, the Chicago's party leader, Fred Hampton, and Mark Clark had been

289

gunned to death. Hampton, asleep when the attack came, never got out of his blood-drenched bed. Four other Panthers were wounded by gunfire. A Sergeant Growth, who had led the raid, claimed they had been fired upon first. After a week the *Chicago Tribune* printed a set of misleading and mislabeled pictures given to them by State's Attorney Edward Hanrahan, meant to confirm the police's story that they had faced a furious barrage of gunfire. Despite all *that* gunfire only one cop was nicked in the leg. These pictures drew a howl of protest from newsmen who toured the apartment. There was no proof of Hanrahan's claim. Bullet holes reported to be in the kitchen doorjamb were rusty nailheads. And there was no sign of any 12-gauge shotgun shells having been fired from Hampton's living room. Asked if he was responsible for the erroneous captions in the *Tribune,* Hanrahan replied, "No. We are not the editors." The paper had been left holding the bag.

CORONER: Sergeant Growth, did you consider the use of tear gas for the raid?

GROWTH: No, sir, I didn't see any need for it.

CORONER: Did you consider the raid dangerous enough to require extra weapons?

GROWTH: The fact that they were alleged to be Panther[s] . . . They were known to shoot a police officer, sir.

CORONER: Why didn't you take tear gas along to avoid the possibility of gun play?

GROWTH: (Haltingly) No tear gas was available.

In the Los Angeles' Watts area, the cops mounted a "frontal mission" on the Panther headquarters with high-velocity bullets, shotguns, tear gas grenades and satchel bombs. The Panthers gave back the fire. That the building still stood after the onslaught was a miracle. All the windows were blasted out and great chunks of bricks were ripped away. Only one sign was left unriddled. It read: FREE HUEY. FEED HUNGRY CHILDREN. The shootout lasted from five thirty-five in the morning until five minutes past ten. When the last clouds of tear gas cleared, thirteen Panthers, including two women, came stumbling out of the bullet-riddled building. The two women and six men were wounded. Three cops had also been wounded.

· · ·

And so the Black Panther history went. When I reached the Berkeley headquarters the next morning no one knew where Hilliard, his brother June or Cox were. If they knew, they weren't telling. Calvin, a heavily built Panther with a neatly cropped Afro, was acting as officer of the day. He sat behind a desk coolly issuing orders to party members who drifted in for various assignments. A white workman came in with a spraying apparatus. "Somebody called about some bugs you've got here," he explained. Calvin stepped over to him, raised his arms and searched him for weapons.

"He's clean," Calvin mumbled to another Panther. "Just keep an eye on his spraying." A tall white girl in hippie trappings sauntered down the stairs. Calvin turned on her. "Where'd you come from? Who let you in? Anyone frisk you upstairs?"

"Nope."

"Stand where you are," Calvin snapped. He summoned a sister from upstairs to do the frisking, meanwhile chewing her out for "gross negligence." "Don't let this happen again," he warned. "This chick could be a dope drop for the pigs."

When Hilliard and the others didn't show up, I called Charles Garry, the Panther's attorney and troubleshooter.

"Hilliard's on his way here. Come on over," he said.

I caught a ride to his office with Harold Holmes, a young Panther Calvin was sending on a party errand. Harold was boyishly thin and wrapped in an eloquent, chilly indifference. Like most Panthers, he was tight-lipped with strangers. Aside from a grunt or two, we rode in absolute silence. Only when I asked about the identity of the person in a picture on the inside of the windshield did he say something.

"That's Chairman Mao. He says you fight-fail-fight-fail until victory is ultimately won." Then he shut up until he let me off at Garry's office. "Power to the people," he answered when I thanked him for the ride.

Finally at three o'clock Hilliard and Cox walked in. Then Garry himself came in from lunch. He was a rather frail handsome man with a mane of straight white hair. To the party members he was "the white Panther." After greeting me he went into an inner office with Hilliard and Cox, and it was an hour before they finally emerged. Then Hilliard and Cox dashed for the elevator. "Right on, brother. More power to the people." Then they were gone.

Hell, it would be much easier to talk with Bobby Seale. He wouldn't be moving around so much. He was in jail. Garry, an affable man, eventually arranged for that. Indeed he took me to the jail himself.

"Concentration camps," he muttered once we were inside the main cell block. "Go in any penitentiary in California and you see nothing but black and brown faces—rarely a white one." I looked about at the faces peering at us from behind the bars. Their color bore out his statement. Only the guards were white. We entered a gray cubicle to await the arrival of the prisoner.

Shortly after, Seale, in blue faded prison denim and unlaced boots, came in. The two men shook hands and grasped thumbs—the gestures of a black greeting another black. Garry introduced me and for a few moments the three of us exchanged the kind of amenities people exchange in bars or living rooms. Our time with him would be short, and Garry had brought along a briefcase full of business papers. As he sorted them I told Seale I had seen his wife, Artie, and his son Malik the evening before. Perhaps the wrong thing to say to a man parted by prison bars from his family. But the hint of a smile came to his bearded face. "How are they?" he asked.

"Beautiful."

"How are you being treated, Bobby?"

A frown crept over his face. "Like an animal. Worse than big-prison treatment. They keep me in a one-man cell. There's no one to talk with, and you get cowboy books and funny papers. No decent literature's allowed. It's like they're hoping your brain will rot from apathy."

"What are the party's immediate goals?"

"Working at large voter registration in black communities—the only way to wrest control from the police; and we're working on breakfast programs to feed black kids in the black communities. We want about the same things Martin Luther King wanted. It's only our tactics that differ. The time for praying for deliverance and begging is over."

At a trial in Chicago a few months before, he had boiled over and the judge had ordered him bound and gagged. "How do you feel about that?" I asked.

"It's hard to describe. I was furious at the treatment I got there." He was silent for a moment. "My little boy was there that day. He came running down the aisle saying, 'I want my daddy.' I don't think the kid will ever forget that scene."

When Garry laid a sheaf of papers before him, I backed off to give them privacy. Looking from the small barred window, I could see row after row of other barred windows, knowing that inside them were many more black and brown faces—angry and isolated from society.

"Time's up." A guard stood waiting.

Garry drove along obviously in deep thought after we left the jail. Then, as if speaking to himself, he said, "The law as we know it today is irrelevant to the needs of our society. We need change —abrupt change." He smiled wryly. "You notice I'm not using the word revolution. You've got to be careful with that one you know."

It was dusk when we pulled up at the Panther headquarters. "What about the Panthers and their use of guns?" I asked before getting out.

"I tell them they have a right to kill in self-defense, or if they are subjected to brutality." A Panther spotted Garry from the entrance. "Right on!" he shouted. "Right on!" Garry shouted back as he drove off, his fist clenched in the Panther salute. "Right on!" I shouted back. My fist had also started up, and for a split second I started to let it drop. Then—what the hell? My arm stiffened firmly into the defiant gesture.

As I entered the building I was remembering the Berkeley police assault plan the Panthers had shown me—slugs bursting through the windows; the grenade launchers and submachine guns, the walls vomiting plaster under the intense fire. But inside the teenage girls were still at the typewriters, printing out words menacing to their own existence. I marveled at their calm. After a couple of days I realized they were doing what they felt they had to do. And I began to understand why the enemy was the police. Then, too, anyone who wanted the police to wipe them out also became their enemy—they served as targets for the police brutality.

A week later I left the Panther stronghold, wondering, but surely not knowing what would become of them. Hilliard's last words to me were, "For every Panther destroyed, eight will take his place." And I was thinking that there might well have been some substance to his boast. To more and more young blacks, the romantic appeal of their bold image was becoming irresistible. The Panthers had dared to use the word "revolution" because they wanted the system destroyed, not repaired. And they had lost faith in the ability of the system to repair itself—or in its will to do so.

New York was a severe contrast to the constant talk of police, assault squads and killing. Having put on my most formal self I was off to a theater opening. The evening was cold and warm hearth light flickered from some windows along Beekman Place. I hurried along looking to hail a taxi. Suddenly a squad car pulled up beside me and two cops jumped out, blocked my path and demanded identification.

"And why do I have to identify myself?"

"If you don't we're taking you in."

"Then I'd prefer that. Let's go."

They were looking me over carefully now. "Look, we can settle this right here. Just show us some identification." The cops were copping out.

"No—I'd rather that you take me in."

"Look, you're in a wealthy neighborhood where there's been several robberies lately."

"Do I look like a robber to you?"

"All robbers don't go around wearing little black masks."

"And all robbers don't go around wearing black faces." It was getting late, and I reached in my overcoat pocket for my wallet— to prove I wasn't a criminal. The cops' hands inched toward their guns.

"You two are pretty jumpy," I said, pulling out my *Life* card. I had always tuned out on the word "pig," but when those two fat faces reddened at the sight of that card, I, too, got the image— very clearly.

"Sorry, Mr. Parks." I kept walking. "Just doing our job. Just trying to protect you." I went on without answering, my thoughts on rifles, rooftops and pigs looking down from them. Malcolm X, Hilliard and Bobby Seale—all smiling at me from dark corners. ("Same old shit, brother. You can't escape it.")

I was not done with the Panthers. There was yet another from whom the party had inherited revengeful wrath, Eldridge Cleaver. But he was far away, exiled, and still roaring defiance against that

America he called Babylon. A couple of months later I flew off to Algiers to have a talk with him—a talk that his agent in Paris arranged for the price of ten thousand dollars. With a wife, a new child and no appreciable income, Cleaver was hurting. I found him with his wife, Kathleen, and their five-month old son, Maceo, outside of Algiers in one of those small, yellowish-white houses that line the Mediterranean coast. It was wet, windy and unusually cold for that part of the world, and the Eldridge Cleaver I envisioned seemed out of place there.

When I entered the house he was slumped in a chair, his legs stretched out, the infant slung across his shoulder. Gently he massaged the child's back. In the soft, rain filtered light from the sea, he looked like any other proud father trying to burp his son. But his thoughts were on a more violent thing, the killing of his fellow Panthers Fred Hampton and Mark Clark. "It was cold-blooded murder." He had spoken softly but with a tone rough as flint. I handed him clippings from the American press, most of which condemned the police action in the killings. As his eyes moved over the print his dark face was immobile. Maceo finally burped and Eldridge called Kathleen. "Come get this little Panther." As she took Maceo away, Eldridge frowned, "That little cat will give them hell one of these days." He lit a cigarette, took a healthy swallow of scotch and started reading again. I got up and looked about the house.

There were five rooms, including a tiled kitchen that also faced the sea. Emory Davis, the Panther's minister of culture, and his wife, Judy, occupied one room. Connie Matthews, an attractive girl who represented the Panthers in Scandinavia, had the other room. Off a dark hallway was the "workshop," littered with papers, typewriters, mimeograph machines, printing materials and party leaflets in several languages.

There was very little laughter in that house. Too many brothers were in coffins or prisons. The evenings were mostly spent talking about friends back in the States, revolution and death. Music consisted of Otis Redding blues, the soul-stirrings of Aretha Franklin, James Brown and protest songs by Elaine Brown. It was the cluttered, temporary shelter of a man in exile—where bags stayed packed and all precious things were portable.

Cleaver had finished reading the clippings when I returned. "Well, what do you think?"

"Crap. Unadulterated crap. So we have to be murdered and shot up in our homes before people become indignant. We have charged the police with ambush and murder over and over again. Now, after twenty-eight murders, people are taking a look. What are we supposed to do, pray for deliverance?" In a soft, dispassionate voice, he answered his own question. "Their deaths have to be avenged. The cops who murdered them must be punished in the same way they committed the crime."

"Right on, Papa Rage," Kathleen snapped. Her blue-green eyes were smoldering beneath a great copper-colored, bushy Afro. Her pale face, strong and intense, held a fearlessness equal to her husband's. "Right on," she repeated. Maceo began to cry. Eldridge took him. "He's angry. He was born angry—like a real Panther."

"Arthur Goldberg and Roy Wilkins are forming a committee to do some investigating on their own."

Cleaver scratched his beard and smiled for the first time. "They'll wind up saying the police were justified in shooting the brothers."

"They might find just the opposite."

"It doesn't make much difference what they find. It's too late for their concern. The brothers are dead. All that's left is the problem. The Panther is the solution."

"A lot of sympathy has sprung up, even among the moderates, since the killings."

"Sympathy won't stop bullets. It's the brother's job, and right, to defend his home. And there's only one way to do that. When cops bust through your door, put a gun in their faces and say, 'Split, mother!' There's alternatives. Call the UN, or the civil liberty boys, or the police station, and tell them you're being shot up. Then wait."

"What do the Panthers have to offer black moderates other than violence, or a fight to death?"

"Nothing. Not even condolences. They will bring about their own death through their apathy." He got up and moved across the room and stared out at the sea. He was big, well over six feet, broad-shouldered and powerfully built. "Violence? Our people are programmed into worse violence by Uncle Sam. Tell me, why should black boys have to go fight Koreans and Vietnamese boys, instead of the Maddoxes, Reagans and Wallaces at home? A white lunatic can attack a black man on the street. But when the cops come they first club the 'violent nigger.' Violence? We hate it. But is it violent to shoot a cop who breaks into your home bent on killing you? If so, the Panthers are violent.''

"So you don't see much of a future for the young black men in America.''

"Right now their future is in the hands of the Wallaces, Agnews, Nixons, Reagans, McClellans and their cops. The black youths in Babylon won't have a future unless they have the guts to fight for it.''

I thought of young Bobby Hutton, who had been shot to death in his presence. "It's amazing that your future didn't end that night Hutton was killed. You were right beside him.''

"I agree with you. It is amazing that they didn't rub me out too. Instead, they slammed me into Vacaville with a shot-up leg and revoked my parole without a hearing.''

"I'm surprised also that you were freed on a habeas corpus, especially with Reagan and his crowd all lined up against you.''

"That didn't stop them. They trumped up some more charges and ordered me back to prison. I knew if I went back I would be killed. So I split.''

"Are you ever going back?''

"Oh yes. I'm just on a vacation from Babylon. Two-seven-seven Pine is my address. Nobody is going to keep me away from it.''

"What about your writing here from Algiers? Your books sell well in the States.''

"You can't fight pigs with eloquence. I've got to physically commit myself.'' Now he asked me a question that pointed up a certain naïveté within him. "Do you think Reagan and his cops really want me back? Or do you think they would sleep better if I stayed lost?''

"Do you want them to sleep better?''

"I want them in a constant state of nightmare.'' He lit another cigarette, took a large swallow of scotch. Then looking through me he jolted me with another question. "Would you consider serving the Black Panther party as their minister of information?'' I spent several moments thinking that one over. His eyes told me he was dead serious.

"I'm honored, but—''

"We need you more than the establishment does."

"I'm honored," I repeated, "but as a journalist you certainly realize I would lose objectivity and credibility. I want to report to as big an audience as possible."

"I'm more concerned about young black strong cats following you into the party."

I went on to explain that my interests went beyond those of the Black Panthers, to other minorities and factions of the black movement who also wanted change. He eased off, suggesting that we leave it open.

Looking back to that moment I find myself displeased with my answer. I should have said: Both of us are caught up in the truth of the black man's ordeal. Both of us are possessed by that truth, which we define through separate experience. How we choose to act it out is the only difference. I recognize your scars and you acknowledge mine. You are thirty-five and I am fifty-seven. We meet over a deep chasm of time, the events of which forged different weapons for us. If I were twenty years old now I might well be a Black Panther. Then maybe not. I remember as a kid I was taught to take the first lick before I fought back. But a fist is not a bullet. I, too, would shoot a cop, or anyone else who forced his way into my house to kill me. You will be risking everything to go back to challenge a system we both dislike. I will continue to fight also, but on my own terms. I prefer to change things without violence—providing violence is not thrust upon me. If this is your position, too, then your weapons and mine are not as irreconcilable as you might think.

At dusk Kathleen brought in a bowl of lamb stew. Cleaver spooned a mouthful, talking all the while. "We won't be alone. A lot of whites relate to the same issues that we do. They're just as uptight, and the establishment will have to deal with them as well. Enough tear gas and head-whipping is bound to establish common ground."

"Do you welcome whites to the conflict?"

"Of course. There has to be some interconnection. We hope through some sort of coalition to bring change for everyone. I just don't believe that most whites will stand by and see a minority wiped out without trying to put a stop to it."

"And the Communists? Are they trying to infiltrate the party?"

"Black people don't need Communists to teach them about trouble. The jails in Babylon produce more rebels and revolutionaries than the Communists could ever dream of producing back there. An incredible number of those rebels are black, and their numbers are growing by the hour. We are out to tear down the system, not with fire, not with guns, but with solid political and scientific know-how. If it comes to guerrilla warfare, individuals will die. But individual tragedy can't block liberation for the masses."

"And what will you build in the rubble?"

"Social justice. If the blacks took power tomorrow and treated the whites like whites have treated blacks for three hundred or more years, I'd try to crush them too. We promise to replace racism with racial solidarity. There are no better weapons. We are disciplined revolutionaries who hate violence. That's why we aim to stop it at our front and back doors. Then we won't have to worry about our children dying in blood-drenched beds."

That night I left Cleaver on a wet, wind-swept street. His last words were about social justice, the kind that turns a blind eye to a man's color. I wondered if I would ever see him alive again; wondered about Malcolm X and Martin Luther King, both long since gunned down; wondered if Cleaver's promise, like their dreams, would go unfilled. Social justice would be much more difficult to come by than martyrdom.

Cleaver did come back, but in time his voice became increasingly calm. And the wall of defiance that seemed so shatterproof during the sixties slowly crumbled. Today his cohorts of that terrible time —Bobby Seale and Stokely Carmichael—refer to him as "Mr. Milktoast." Bobby Seale accuses him of betraying the party's principles and refuses to speak to him. Huey Newton, stabbed to death in 1989, avoided him on the street, and the once loyal Kathleen deserted him to get a law degree at Harvard. If you wish to see him now, you will have to search him out in places he would have brutally banished during the uprising.

Becoming associated with the Mormon Church is considered to be his most outlandish indiscretion, since its history holds it to be racist. Still there is an unyielding silence between Cleaver and those who won't break bread with him anymore.

Stokely shares no enthusiasm for Newton or Seale, nor they for him. The kinship has blown apart. The affinities that once forged them into a heroic brotherhood disintegrated with the unfolding of history. All of them have changed clothes and moved to quieter landscapes, vanished without hardly a sound. Seale, now lecturing in the African-American Studies Department at Temple University, and studying political science, recently published a book, *Barbeque'n with Bobby.* "Our only mistake during the black revolution," he says, "was not getting together with the NAACP, the Urban League and other fronts to hammer out common approaches. Otherwise I have no regrets. Those were gallant times. Today I'm telling kids to get an education, go to college, use your energy to help solve problems in our poor communities. I don't want any part of Eldridge Cleaver. First he tries being a born-again Christian, then hooked himself to the Reverend Moon. Incredible!"

During the fall of 1988 Cleaver, on his way to court in Oakland, telephoned me from a public booth. He sounded weary. "I'm tired of police harassment; they're trying to frame me again. I was moving furniture for homeless people and they accused me of burglary. A little while back they tried trumping up cocaine charges against me. They won't let me alone."

Stokely Carmichael now lives on Conakry, Guinea, where his loyalty to the late Guinean leader, the murderous Sékou Touré, put him under a cloud. In from Africa, he came to see me a while back. Coffee-colored, handsome and resplendent in a flowing pale-blue boubou, he looked like an Abyssinian prince. His voice was smooth, but his tongue was afire: "America is riper for revolution now than it was in the sixties. Black youth has more consciousness today. Get their dander up and they'll make me and the others look ultra-calm. There has been progress; but not enough. The only answer is to transform the spontaneous struggle into permanent organization. Shed blood."

Kwame Turé (for that is his name now) played down the courage I ascribed to him and the other young militants. "We had no more courage than Harriet Tubman or Marcus Garvey had in their time. We just had a more vulnerable enemy." I reflected upon what he said. The present surge of bigotry I see in this nation warns us that the enemy is regrouping. But then so are young black rebels. Racism seems ageless—like the passion of those who war against it.

I've heard the terrifying cry of "Burn, baby, burn!" in Watts and Detroit, seen block after block crumble into smoking, silent space. Later, walking the bloodstained streets, I remember being overwhelmed with despair. It was easy to conclude, even before the smoke cleared, that hatred was the loser.

TWENTY-THREE

Nobody likes good food and travel more than I. Consequently, the next assignment *Life* gave me was by no means a hardship. It was to photograph great food markets and restaurants around the world—beginning in Japan, going on to Hong Kong, Thailand, Germany, Africa, Italy, or any other place I chose to visit throughout Europe. After England I would finish in Paris.

Before departing, I called Gene to say good-bye.

"Good-bye. Have a nice trip." Her voice still had a sting in it.

"Can't we have one last lunch?"

There was a long silence. "If you insist."

We ate at a familiar place, but what few words were spoken were more fit for two strangers. Over dessert I showed her my itinerary. She studied it silently while sipping a demitasse, and I allowed my eyes to dwell upon her, knowing it would be months before such a pleasure would come again. She scribbled something on a note pad. "Interesting trip," she said as we got up to go. Outside the restaurant she shook my hand stiffly and handed me the folded note. "Please—read it later." And with that she strode off without even a backward glance. I stood for a few minutes watching her disappear into the confusion of the traffic.

Well, a block away was *later,* and hurriedly I unfolded the note, read it and felt like an oak tree falling. Very simply it said: "It would be nice to meet you in Paris." Sweet songbirds were singing—even above the noise of the afternoon traffic.

The next two months were held together with letters, cablegrams and overseas telephone calls. Then we both hurried to Paris. The sublime week at the Hotel Crillon brought us to the logical conclusion, and from there she flew to The Hague in the Netherlands. Wellington Koo, her stepfather, was serving there as a world court judge, but the journey was to apprise her mother of our decision.

"Mummy—Gordon Parks and I have decided to divorce our respective spouses and get married."

"But, Gene—isn't he a black man?"

"He is for sure."

"Well—you must have given it proper consideration."

"We have indeed."

"Then, I guess that is that."

And that was that.

Saying good-bye to Elizabeth was, after eleven years, deeply disturbing. Even more disturbing was the realization that there would be long separations between my daughter Leslie and me. The parting called for spirits, so Elizabeth and I sat down to a bottle of good French wine and drank to one another's happiness. She was painfully sensible to the very last drop, promising that she would see to it that Leslie and I spent as much time together as possible. And I knew she would live up to that promise. When I attempted to soften the moment with regrets, she waved me off. "There's no more wine. I distrust my emotions without it. Let's quit while we're still ahead. Don't worry too much about Leslie. I'll explain things the best I can."

After a respectable wait, Gene and I were married at her sister Frankie's country house up in Pound Ridge, New York, on August 26, 1973. My "best" men were David and my grandson, Alain. Leslie, who was almost six, arrived in a lovely pink sundress—which I preferred she wear. However, beneath her arm she carried a long, ruffled dark dress—which she preferred to wear. Tempers quietly flared. The guests were arriving so I demanded that she obey me. Being an obedient child, she did. But as she left the room she turned and said, "Heh, Dad, I know this is your wedding day, and I want you to be happy—but I won't be happy in this outfit." I then demanded that she wear what she wanted to wear.

Remembering Gene's proclamation (I never want to see that child) had me a bit worried about their meeting. They met in the hallway a few minutes later. "Momma Gene!" Leslie cried out with a big smile.

Breaking into an equally big smile, Gene melted and came to her with open arms. "Leslie, darling, I'm so happy that you came!" From that day on Leslie would have two mothers.

We said our vows on a sloping green lawn banked with flowers. Relatives and close friends from the publishing world attended along with a sizable part of the Chinese community, some from as far away as the Orient. As is their custom, Chinese children address older family friends as "Auntie" and "Uncle." I was now *Uncle Kao Teng Pai,* which means high achiever. At the reception I felt right at home. A gathering of Chinese makes almost as much noise as a gathering of blacks. The food had been prepared by a chef from the Chinese mainland, and the music was exhilarating. To the strains of it, Leslie took me to a high bank of the lawn and insisted that I dance *alone* with her. And as we danced my world was afire with happiness.

The wedding was over. The years ahead were set aside for love and work—in our sunny apartment high above the East River. Orange morning sun splayed through the spacious windows. Evenings sparkled with sailboats plying the river. Christmases were spent with Leslie, skiing the mountains at Vail, Colorado, and vacationing in the Caribbean. After eleven years of waiting, things were as we had longed for them to be. The only things to overcome now were the trials of marriage.

The Learning Tree had placed Hollywood solidly into my future—deeper into a prosperous but sketchy world of dreams and illusions. To direct a motion picture was demanding, difficult and wearing, but it was a joy broken off from all the others. *Life* magazine had allowed me to know a good existence, yet I sensed that it was just a stepping-stone, not a pinnacle. Feeling now that I had expended all I could to it, I left the staff to work under a contract that would give me more freedom. The tie was not permanently cut, but directing was foremost in my mind. Fortunately Gene found excitement in my filmmaking as well.

Jim Aubrey, the tough, inflexible boss at MGM Studio, handed me my second Hollywood film. Titled *Shaft,* it was the story of a virile, suave, black Harlem detective. Frankly, I didn't hold great expectations for its success, but it offered me a chance to expand my knowledge of directing. What's more, it was a film that could give black youth their first cinematic hero comparable to James Cagney or Humphrey Bogart, but not least of the persuasions was the salary I was to recieve.

After an exhaustive search I had chosen Richard Roundtree for the role of Shaft, not because of his film experience, because he had none, not even a screen test. It was my son David who had prodded me into taking a look at him. When I agreed to give Roundtree a test he looked dumbfounded. Having glanced at a row of experienced film actors waiting on the sidelines, he shook his head in despair. "I just knew I didn't have a chance," he told me later, "so I really didn't give it a real try." But I had slapped a fake mustache on him and slung a holstered gun over his shoulder, and someone read him the lines. After seeing his rushes the following morning I called Jim Aubrey. "I think I've found him. I'm sending you several takes. Let me know what you think."

Aubrey called back immediately after seeing them. "You've got him. Sign him up."

Jim (known throughout the industry as the "smiling cobra") threw in some suspenseful hours when, three months later, we were about to commence shooting in New York. The crew was intact, the actors set and dozens of locations selected when he telephoned Joel Freeman, the producer—just twenty-four hours before the cameras were to roll. His order was terse, formidable and impossible to believe. "Tell Gordon to cancel out New York. We've decided to make the picture out here." He had hung up without giving Freeman a chance to answer, and his face was a yard long when he gave me the news.

"Well—screw him!" It was time to test the cobra's bite. Instead of following orders, I hopped a plane for the West Coast. Hollywood wasn't Harlem with its hard, gritty atmosphere. Shooting beneath palm trees wasn't shooting beneath the tired tenements around 116th Street. It just wasn't what the script called for. If Aubrey couldn't be turned around, then he could damned well call in another director.

My mind was glued to that decision when I sat down next to him at his big conference table. All around it sat his staff, and having already felt them out individually I knew I had their support. I also knew that they were not about to express that support openly.

Ice was in Aubrey's voice when he spoke. "You don't take orders very well, Mr. Director."

"Not disastrous ones, Jim. It's impossible to shoot that picture out here. It would wind up just another TV skit. I just can't understand your wanting to shoot it here. It has to have the smell of New York."

"The studio can't tolerate a picture going overbudget right now. Winter's coming on out there, and you're bound to run into a million problems. That's mainly why I want it shot out here— lenses and cameras freezing up. All such crap."

Quickly I summoned up an answer; one that I didn't have complete faith in. "That's the least of my worries, Jim. The equipment I've got has built-in heaters. I can make subzero days look like they're sweltering with heat."

The staff smiled. I smiled. The cobra frowned. "Sounds like so much bullshit to me."

Bullshit? It was elephantshit, but I kept slinging it out until it sounded like fleashit. "I'll come in *under*-budget, Jim. Just have faith."

He glanced at me with his cold blue eyes. "I want to talk this over with production. I'll call you in ten minutes." I'd laid every kind of shit on him there was. I went to an office and waited. Ten minutes to the very second he telephoned. "Okay. You've got it, but if you screw up, your ass is mine."

"You're in good hands with Allstate, Jim. Keep the faith." Three hours later I was on a plane back to New York.

Roundtree himself gave me a jolt the following morning just before he was to go before the camera. He was walking across the room with a towel and razor.

"Don't foul up the mustache," I said. "It's just the right length."

He looked startled. "But Freeman told me to shave it off."

"Shave it off and you're out of a job."

"Hell—I didn't know. I was just taking orders."

"Well, you've got the latest orders. Follow them."

Freeman was entering the room. "Why did you tell him to get rid of the mustache, Joel?"

He looked puzzled. He really didn't know, but I did. Richard Roundtree was about to become the first black leading man who would wear a mustache on the silver screen. It was another one of those unwritten laws lurking within the minds of Hollywood's film barons. A mustache on a black leading man was just *too* macho. Freeman had fallen prey to the absurdity without realizing it.

For reasons I failed to understand, Aubrey sent me to London to preview *Shaft* to the British press. It was a most disheartening experience. "I say, I'm most confused. What does shaft really mean?" a critic asked.

I thrust my middle finger into the air, twirled it around, then upward. He colored deeply. "Oh, really! And he goes about calling those tough blokes 'mother.' Now, what's that all about?"

There were several women in the audience. Scratching my head, I replied, "I'm afraid you're going to have to figure that one out for yourself, old boy."

"*Shaft's* not going to make it in the British Isles," I warned Jim Aubrey when I got back to Hollywood.

My telephone jarred me awake at three o'clock in the morning when the film opened in New York. It was my son David. "Dad, you've got to get up and get over to Broadway! Right away, Dad!"

"David, do you realize what time it is?"

307

"Please—get up, Dad. You've got to see this to believe it!"

I understood his urgency when I got there. The line was completely around the block, and growing. *Shaft* was a hit, throughout the world—even in England. Black youth had their first big romantic hero. Now Hollywood had the green light for black suspense films—and they exploited them to a mercilessly quick demise with a rash of bad screenplays. But Jim Aubrey had kept the faith, and I went on to make two more films for him—*The Super Cops* and *Shaft's Big Score.*

I attribute *Shaft's* success to several things: a fine screenplay by John D. F. Black; Richard Roundtree's outstanding performance, and Isaac Hayes's great theme music, which later won an Academy Award for best song—the very first for a black composer. But extremely important to me was the number of blacks used in the crew. The number had doubled since the filming of *The Learning Tree.* Slowly it seemed that the doors to blacks working behind the camera were opening up. Perhaps Hollywood was taking notice. I watched as it took two steps forward, then three steps back, hoping that the next move would be an unrestrained leap—the kind that blacks could feed on forever.

TWENTY-FOUR

Over the years I had received a good number of letters from Flavio da Silva, and always a Christmas card. In one letter that came in October 1967, the English was fair, the scribbled handwriting a bit shaky: "How are you my good friend Gordon Parks and how is your family? If I could see you I would be very happy. Do you remember the watch you gave me? It is broke and I don't no where to fix here in Brazil. When you go here I want to talk about many of things we know to talk about. Dear Gordon do you help me go back to America? In São Paulo I break the typewriter you give to me. Could you get me another one when you come back? I always remember you and hope you always do remember me. Your good friend Flavio José Luiz da Silva." Then we lost touch.

Years passed. I was in a Buenos Aires shop trying on a pair of shoes when a clerk walked over and spoke. "I remember you. You're the one who befriended the little Brazilian boy up in the favela."

"Yes. That was a number of years ago."

"Is he still alive?"

"Yes, I'm sure he is," suddenly not knowing for sure.

"What year was that?"

"Nineteen sixty-one." Suddenly it struck. Flavio was a short plane trip away. In less than three hours I was on a plane to Rio. By now, if he was still alive, Flavio would be twenty-seven—a full-grown man.

Upon reaching Rio I called José Gallo and he hurried to the airport to meet me. We embraced and stepped back to observe one another. His hair was streaked with gray now, and the lines in his face had deepened. "It's good to see you back in Rio. It's been a long time."

"And how does it go with you, José?"

His face crinkled into a smile. "I'm walking slower, talking less and breathing harder."

"And Flavio, have you seen him?"

"Not for a year or so. I do know he has a house of his own, and a wife and a child. Two I think."

"It all seems like a dream now."

"More like a nightmare sometimes. But God must have been with him."

"And how's your family?"

"Oh—the wife's ailing a bit. But everything else is the same." This meant that there had been no upswing in his son's mental disability. But then he had never really expected much of a change. He had confronted that sad passage in his life years before, knowing the sorrow of it would be lodged in his chest forever.

We drove on for about an hour, reaching back through the memories of those last days the Da Silva family had spent in the favela. The neighborhood where we finally stopped was a little over a mile and a half from Flavio's mother and father's place.

310

There was a neat row of houses painted in pastel pinks, greens and blues, all about the same shape—square bungalows surrounded with low concrete walls of the same pastel shades. Tall palm trees towering above the houses lent a tropical grace to the area. José Gallo's eyes narrowed to a squint as he searched for the right number. "Ah, this is it," he said dryly. "This is where he lives." And he braked his old Volkswagen to a stop.

A tremor of guilt swept through me. There had been no way of notifying Flavio that we were coming since he had no telephone. The tiny yard aproned the green house, and the yard was as clean as a church pew. A small locked gate hinged to the concrete wall barred our way. Gallo cupped his hands around his mouth. "Flav," he shouted. A few seconds elapsed before Gallo called out again. The door opened and Flavio appeared. He looked hard at us, seeming puzzled. Then a smile broke over his face. He came to us silently and reached over the wall to embrace me. "I cannot believe this. Gordon Parks, my friend. José, where did you find him?"

"He found me," Gallo said, smiling.

"Come in. Come in, Gordon Parks. My family has waited so long to see you." We crossed the yard and entered the house. Inside were Flavio's wife and two small children. He introduced them proudly. "This is my wife, Cleuza, and our sons, Flavio Jr. and Felipe Luiz." Cleuza smiled shyly. Her hair was jet black and her eyes were a soft brown.

"So, you are Flavio's lovely wife, Cleuza. I'm glad to meet you."

Confused, she rubbed at her forehead. "You lovely wife to meet Cleuza?" she asked.

Flavio smiled and touched her cheek. "No, Cleuza, you are my lovely wife and he is glad to meet you." He smiled. "Her English is not so good."

"My wife you lovely wife!" She threw up her hands, laughing. *"Fala Portuguese,* Flavio! *Fala Portuguese!"*

"She gives up too easy. But she will learn. She is very smart. That is one reason I married her." A beautiful girl appeared in the kitchen doorway. "Gordon, do you remember this bad one?" Flavio asked.

My mind raced back over the years, over the dirty, hungry

311

young faces of the Da Silva household. There was no resemblance to anyone I could remember. "I give up. Who is she?"

Flavio spoke to her in Portuguese. "Say your name, silly girl. Say your name to Gordon."

She broke into a shy grin. "Isabel," she said in a near whisper.

Isabel! The scowling, clawing, ill-tempered Isabel, who once sank her teeth into me and stuck me with a pin. I used to call her Bitter Flower. I asked Flavio if she remembered me.

"No, she will not. I have asked many times before. She was only three then. She lives with me now and she will someday amount to something I am sure. That's why I have her live with me." Then, pridefully, he took us through his house. It was small but spotlessly clean. There were plenty of sparkling pots and pans. Each child had his own bed. The bathroom with a bidet was a far cry from the wooden toilet that served over twenty-five thousand back in Catacumba.

When Flavio asked us to stay for supper we refused, but when Cleuza told us she had made a fine *feijoada* we changed our minds. Flavio was now working as an armed guard for a wealthy family who were afraid that their children might be kidnapped. He roamed the property at night and got off work about six o'clock in the morning. He received a fairly decent salary, but he disliked carrying the big gun on his bony hip. "I don't like what a gun stands for. I would never want to take a life—no matter what."

The following morning Flavio arrived at my hotel and we went to the poolside for breakfast. There were things from the past he wanted to get off his chest. "I was happy to be going on that plane with you that night, but I was scared inside. I kept saying to myself, 'Where are these people taking me to way up here in the sky?' Then, at the hospital, those doctors kept saying things I couldn't understand." He laughed. "I thought they were going to chop me up and feed me to the pigs. They were like policemen in white uniforms."

"You wouldn't take off your clothes until I took mine off."

"I thought somebody would steal my pants and shoes. If they stole yours, then we would be naked together. I wasn't so dumb, huh? Oh, I was so happy with those shoes. When they cut them up I felt like dying. Those were the prettiest shoes in the world. I still think so." He smiled. "You know, I did lose my pants and I never did find them." He paused and shook his head. "Things were so strange, the language and everything. I didn't know if I would ever see my sisters and brothers again. They kept putting me in rooms with strange-looking machines with all kinds of lights blinking. It was scary. The doctor from Argentina thought we could talk together, but he couldn't understand me and I couldn't understand him. He thought I was an idiot, and I thought he spoke awful Portuguese. It was crazy—just crazy."

"The doctors were trying to save your life."

"I thought they were trying to kill me! They stuck needles in me and poked their fingers in my mouth and ears. 'Say, ah!' 'Jump up and down!' 'Hold your breath!' 'Lie down!' 'Stand up!' They hit my knees and made them jump. They even tickled the bottom of my feet. These crazy policemen, I kept thinking. They're nuts! One stuck a stick down my throat and got my breakfast all over him. Boy, was he mad. The next time he did that he stayed a long way from me. It was a long time before I felt everything was going to be okay. After a few months I knew everybody was trying to help me get well. When Gallo sent me pictures of my family I felt a lot better."

He was quiet for a while, gazing out to sea. Then, as if he had been dreaming, he returned to reality, spoke in Portuguese, caught himself and switched to English. "I want you to know something very important. When I got back here from Denver I was sent to São Paulo to school. Well, I got kicked out so I came back home. And it was like the favela all over again. My mother was always sick with new babies and I had to do all the washing and cooking." He shook his head sadly. "Gordon, I don't want you to see that place now. It is like a pig pen. It would shame me for you to see it. My father lost his truck and he was always fussing about me going out and getting a job. I didn't know much, but I did get a laborer's job, but it was too big for me. I just couldn't carry those heavy pipes and machinery, so I got fired." He gazed into space. "But I wanted to make something of myself so I wouldn't disappoint you and all those nice people who helped me. I wanted to invent things and work on planes or study animals and insects." There was another long pause. "Do you believe what I have told you?"

"Yes, I do, Flav."

"Then, Gordon, I would like to go back to America. Please help me do this. In America I can live better and do something good for my family. I feel like an animal in a trap here." He was quiet, finished, having at last said what he had really come to say.

I hardly dared to consider such a futile plea.

"I have friends in America, Gordon, who still want me. I can stay with them while I study and learn. Then when I have a good job I can send for Cleuza and the children. That is how it would work, Gordon."

I knew of some of the friends he referred to, but he seemed to have forgotten that some of them were dead and that others were not able to assume such a responsibility. Most of the staff at the Asthma Institute were no longer there, and many of his fellow patients had not been as fortunate as he. They, too, had died. I carefully explained all this, saying finally that even *Life* was gone— no longer being published.

"But I still have friends someplace in America. I know they won't forget me." It seemed impossible for him to understand that there were those who would always care *about* him, without being able responsibly to care *for* him. "If only my father had let me stay there, I would be somebody by now. Don't you believe so?"

"Yes, I'm sure, Flav."

His yearning was honest, poignant. He would go on believing that only in America would he have another chance. He got up to leave, drained, yet hopeful that he had got his message across, that in some way I could perhaps help. We walked slowly through the lobby, then out to the bus stop. The overloaded vehicle screeched to a stop, its doors opened like jaws and swallowed him up. As it roared off I could still see him moving toward the rear, waving as he went.

Both Flavio and Gallo had a surprise in store for me. The day before I was to leave they drove me along the Copacabana beach, then on past the lagoon that separated the radiant white homes of the rich from Catacumba. So, the surprise was to be a revisit. I hardly looked forward to it. A heavy gray fog blanketed the area as we approached it, giving it a dull luster that matched the day. Finally Gallo pulled to the side of the road and stopped. We got out and looked skyward. Cristo Redentor loomed up through the grayness. My eyes searched the fog beneath it, but in vain. Catacumba was no more. "It was bulldozed away shortly after your story appeared," Gallo said. It was staggering. Where once there

314

had been thousands of shacks clinging to the mountainside, there were now only acres of unkempt grass. "Where did they all go?" I asked.

"They are scattered all over, in other favelas—Penha, Cordovil, Jacarepagua and Quitungo-Guapore. They moved from hell to purgatory."

The final day of my visit was a gloomy one. It had rained for twelve hours. At noon Flavio and I sat in my room eating and observing the hunchback mountain looming up above the beach. It seemed to be melting under the heavy downpour, "It's a bad day for you to leave, Gordon." He lit his tenth cigarette.

"You smoke too much, Flav."

"I know. I will stop soon." He opened the old *Life* to the picture of himself stuffing food into Zacarias's mouth, then to one of himself lying ill in bed after an attack. "I was sure going to die if you had not come."

"Possibly not."

"Oh yes. I knew. I didn't know what death was, but I knew something very bad was happening to me. I was so sick sometimes I didn't care what happened. I just worried about how my brothers and sisters could live, with me dead." He glanced at a picture of the shack perched on the mountainside. "It's a shame. My father's house now is just like the favela was. All those kids living with my mother, and not a one lifts a finger to help her at the hard work. Luzia's got two children and only she knows who the fathers are. Maria went off to work with some family in another city. We never hear from her because she can't write. Don't know if she's dead or alive. Maybe we'll never see her again. I still try to help Momma, but one single *andorinha* [swallow] can't make a summer." He got to his feet, spent from his quiet anger. "I must go now, Gordon, to sleep so I can be at the airport tonight." He seemed to be talked out. He was leaving, then remembered something. From a shopping bag he pulled out a small package and handed it to me. "This is from Cleuza and me. Open it on the plane, okay?"

"Okay."

"Tonight, Gordon."

"Tonight, Flav."

Flavio and Cleuza were already at the airport when Gallo and I arrived. The parting was awkward. "Isabel, you be a good girl now."

"Sí."

"I'll never forget that wonderful *feijoada,* Cleuza."

"Sí."

"I will miss you, Flav, my good friend."

"You won't forget to write, Gordon."

"I won't, and you be sure to answer."

My flight was called. "Well, that's it," Gallo said.

Flavio pulled me aside. "Please, Gordon, try to get me back to America."

I wanted to say finally, "Stop dreaming, Flav. It's impossible." Actually, I said, "I will try. I promise I will try." Then I hurried on, leaving him once again hoping for a miracle. As the plane became airborne depression swept over me. How could I truthfully respond to his desire to return to something that existed only in his memory. Perhaps I had already shuffled his dreams too much. Just knowing him had amounted to an incredible experience. But what had that experience really meant? Catacumba was no more, but there were other favelas. The Da Silvas were better off, but crumbling into the danger zone again. Flavio, despite the doctor's prediction, was still alive, striving and full of love. Now that his life had been spared, I hoped he wouldn't waste it chasing a futile dream.

Five minutes out over the sea I opened the package Flavio had given me earlier that afternoon. It was a handsome black billfold with a note: "Happy Father's Day, Gordon. We love you." Inside were small pictures of Felipe, Flavio Jr., and Flavio Sr. with Cleuza. I opened the *Life* magazine and placed the two Flavios next to one another. The resemblance was startling; their faces seemed to merge as one. Perhaps then, this was the point of Flavio da Silva's story—showing his son, his alert brown eyes and healthy body, a body not hampered by malnutrition and poverty. Such a father as Flavio would never allow that.

We were banking northward now and climbing. In the darkness below, on the road to Guadalupe were Flavio and his family—he with his hopes tied once more to mine. For a few minutes I allowed myself to think that perhaps another miracle for Flavio wasn't so farfetched. That ennobling spirit that rallied hundreds of thousands to his side was still there, and so was the courage that made millions of others acutely aware of the dreadful scourge of poverty. Even today, with his forty-second year of life closing in, that spirit, that courage, still compels him. Now and then I get a letter from him, and invariably it is still filled with hopes of coming back to America. And I write back, knowing that as time passes nothing is changeless.

TWENTY-FIVE

Hollywood, rich as it is with opportunity, is forever threatening—even to the men who reign over the studios. For them, too long a lunch can prove precarious. Some have returned to find their castles locked up, and when they knocked, nobody opened the door. Some with extraordinary talent arrive, bringing with them a glimmer of hope. Then you awaken to hear that they are gone.

Frank Yablans, who used to run Paramount Pictures, might have done himself in by taking an extended lunch, but I'm inclined to think he erred by trying to instill integrity into his studio's moldy concepts of entertainment. In any case, the door was locked when he returned one afternoon, and nobody answered his knock. Another "Hollywood shuffle" was taking place inside.

Yablans had assigned me to direct *Leadbelly,* a film based on the life of legendary folksinger Huddie Ledbetter. It was ready to be screened just as Yablans was locked out. The new studio head, Barry Diller, viewed it with me instead, complimented it generously and promised me his "zealous support." Then, according to one of his young underlings, he went back to his office and gave the verdict—"Kill it."

"I couldn't believe it," the young man said later.

Such an abrupt death was forestalled by Charles Champlin, the prestigious critic for the *Los Angeles Times.* I had screened the film for him the morning before, and that following weekend he had predicted that it would surely be one of the year's best. He then recommended it to the Dallas Film Festival. It won first place there. Now, I thought, the studio would really put its weight behind it. Instead *Leadbelly* was sent on an abbreviated tour of dilapidated theaters around the country, including a San Francisco porno palace, then allowed to expire. I fought; the press fought with me, but to no avail. Puzzled by the feeble promotional campaign, another *Times* critic had written, "You can't kill art. It is indeed a fine film, and it will live on."

Leadbelly was not the only Yablans film killed; several met a more absolute death. And this was not necessarily an unusual occurrence for Hollywood; it seems to have a passion for slaughtering worthy things. I look back at the experience grimly nevertheless, having admired the subject and his music. A demanding contract had kept Gene and me apart for nearly a year and a half. As the picture died, her patience was slowly dying with it. *Leadbelly* was proving to be costly.

After directing five motion pictures in Hollywood, I was still fascinated with its seductiveness and its challenges. Yet, sometimes I couldn't help but think of it as the grand illusion; the place of deals—made in restaurants, cocktail lounges, bistros, swimming pools, limousines, planes and bedrooms, deals that often didn't bear fruit. Multi-contracts could be as impermanent as the paper they were written on; yet, filmmakers and actors ceaselessly arrived to pawn their souls for dubious futures. Some had dreams that did unfold and allow them some heroic years, but there was always the ugliness and debauchery to wade through.

Hollywood's most badgering problem is that of producing meaningful motion pictures without subjecting its studios to bankruptcy, and its public can be as unpredictable as the wind. Studio executives, repeatedly out of touch with the box office, indulge in head scratching—trying to feel the pulse of that giant octopus they must cater to. Failures bunch up, take the form of a monster and start chewing up contracts.

Homes in Beverly Hills are imperial. Swimming pools are so numerous one could swim across the city. Lawns are well groomed and the streets are clean as angel's ears. Sidewalks are handsomely paved, but rarely do you see anyone walking. Walking there seems at times to be unlawful. Nothing revs up a Beverly Hills cop's suspiciousness more than someone out for a leisurely stroll, and a black stroller invites instant trouble upon himself. If he is driving he shouldn't drive too slowly—especially if he drives a Mercedes-Benz, or perhaps a Rolls-Royce. Having had the experience of staring into the gun barrels of two white Beverly Hills lawmen one night, I can attest to that.

"What was I stopped for?" I asked.

"We stop any black man driving too slow in this neighborhood. You're driving a Rolls. How do we know you didn't steal it."

After enduring the ritual of providing proof of ownership for the car, and my residence, which I'd acquired in 1972, I watched them holster their guns as they further explained, "Don't forget, we're here to protect you, your Rolls and your home."

I was so grateful, once more, for police protection.

Despite its vigilant lawmen, Beverly Hills was an easy place in which to dream—providing you have had a successful run of films. Mine had lifted me into this honeyed paradise where, among well-known strangers, I could concoct dreams, hit tennis balls and swim. It was not an inglorious interlude. And regardless of what one hears to the contrary, there was intellectual stimulation to feed on. All the fine writers, poets and thinkers hadn't deserted those hills. Furthermore, I was thankful to be far from New York's sirens, honking cabs, trucks and buses for a while. It was a lofty but legitimate place for dreaming.

But you won't find many black actors, actresses or filmmakers in Beverly Hills. Their work is a hard sell across America. And progress for them is still shadowy and slow moving in Hollywood. Certain actors and actresses prefer idleness to the kinds of roles available to them. After years of cultivating their diction, they are pushed into gutter language by casting people who twist their minds into psychological knots. One black actor, in to read for a part, and having greeted me with Oxfordian English, suddenly reverted to gutter talk when he began reading.

"Why," I asked, "did you change your manner of speech? The script doesn't suggest your doing so."

He thought for a moment, laughed pensively and replied, "You are perfectly right, you know. But invariably I am asked to put 'black juice' into my voice. That's what I was attempting to do a moment ago."

Black producers and directors, if they are to survive, must begin channeling their efforts into pictures that are universally acceptable. America is not the only country on earth. I'm not suggesting they go elsewhere, or that they give up on black films. I am suggesting that they broaden their horizons, and prepare themselves for any worthy project that means survival. No one has the right to tell you how *not* to dream, or to fix marks where one's dreaming should stop. The truth is, Hollywood still harbors a racist industry, and it will keep shutting doors to blacks as long as possible. But doors, after sufficient pounding, have a way of opening. The trick is to be ready when one does. Another Kenneth Hyman may be sitting inside.

But actors, actresses and filmmakers of all colors are caught up in the rubbish of Hollywood's industry. Its vendors of that rubbish leave things up to the public. If the public keeps demanding, and paying, for the rubbish, it will be fed more rubbish. That is the problem that creates the aura of big-studio thinking, and I can't swallow that thinking. If Hollywood comes looking for me, it must bring along something worthwhile; otherwise I will be gone, walking in another direction—and in a different pair of shoes.

Problems had left Gene and me in a hallowed peace for over five years, then they had entered our door and were refusing to depart. Gene was spending her life editing my writing, as well as that of several other authors. In one year she worked on three best sellers —Nancy Mitford's *Zelda,* Stephen Birmingham's *The Grandees,* and Eric Segal's *Love Story.* Along with this she was attempting to pull my ragged life of photography, music and films together. The paying of bills, balancing checkbooks and attending to our social calendar was left to her. It seemed now that we were always trying to shake free of work in order to enjoy one another. My love and admiration for her never paled, and I was awed by her quiet energy, although she probably never thought so. Like my father, I have lips that tend to flatten against one another when they shouldn't. She seldom talked about her work, and to me it dwelled in a world beyond my comprehension.

Yet, it hadn't been all work during those first years. There had been pleasant weekends of swimming and tennis at Frankie and Oscar's up in Pound Ridge, skiing at Vail, trips to England, the Continent and vacations in the Caribbean. At times it had been a dreamy existence, laced with exotic Chinese dinners at her mother's house.

But now, in the sixth year, we were becoming like fading portraits of ourselves, and my long absences on the West Coast reduced our lives to mundane telephone conversations—rug cleaning, piano tuning and other domestic things we would rather have not talked about. Time then went slowly.

While unpacking my bags at the Beverly Hills Hotel I found a note between my shirts, and afterward I kept it close to my heart:

> Ah, love, let us be true
> To one another! for the world, which seems
> To lie before us like a land of dreams,
> So various, so beautiful, so new,
> Hath really neither joy, nor love, nor light,
> Nor certitude, nor peace, nor help for pain;
> And we are here as on a darkling plain
> Swept with confused alarms of struggle and flight,
> Where ignorant armies clash by night.
> > Matthew Arnold, "Dover Beach"
> Dear Gordon, I love you and miss you, G.

Over and over I read that poem. Later, I lay in bed thinking, remembering those early years. She was lovely then—even lovelier now. I adored her eyes. When moonlight touched her face it took on the color of everything that was beautiful.

The following day I penned this verse and sent it on to her:

Before I took my mother's blood and breath
        I loved you.
When you broke the silence of your first hour
        crying
Through ovaled eyes under some foreign sky,
I had already begun to guard your days.
        Each moonfall after,
I tossed a lotus petal into my river of hopes
Until an endless bouquet covered the oceans
        that parted us.
Through winter-locked and hungered days,
        in
The trials of many doubtful years, and over
Hourless and mistaken roads I searched for you.
If, as you say, during pillow talk, you do not know me,
        It is because I am you.
I have been you for a thousand years.
Our love is older than the air.

Despite our love, the bad cards kept falling. When she moved to J. B. Lippincott as vice president, I was extremely proud of her— so proud I set out to do something I had done many years before, when Sally and I were having difficulties. I entered an expensive Park Avenue store, picked out a lovely gown and telephoned her to meet me there. I had never asked about the price. It made no difference. She was now a vice president, and deserving of the best.

She arrived, tried on the dress and indeed it looked as though it had been inspired by her. Then suddenly sweat popped out on her nose.

"Heavens! Gordon, have you seen this price?"

I scanned the figures. "Well—well, I thought those were just stock numbers. But it makes no difference. I want it for you."

"Never. It would be vulgar."

We settled for a coat costing a few thousand less. It pains me now that neither Gene's coat, nor Sally's, solved the problems of the man who bought them.

Gene's responsibilities were doubled by now, and even small problems became gigantic ones. Unsigned, terse orders replaced the hasty love notes that used to garland my mirror. No longer was I at the door to greet her when she arrived evenings; unfailingly, some difficult passage harnessed me to the typewriter about that time. Something was snipping at us, severing us painfully, slowly, like a dull knife. Every conversation left us bruised. We tried applying Band-Aids, but they were no good for wounds spreading into angry sores.

An interview she gave to a magazine about our life together shoved us deep into quicksand. It was witty dialogue, but loaded with hostility, and hostility fired our language when we discussed it. The moment turned on us. She rose to her feet, burst into tears, hurried into the bedroom and slammed the door shut. Night passed with me in the darkness of our living room. And I was still there when dawn edged over the horizon—knowing the day ahead would dissolve into another darkness. Lying on the sofa, I stared at the ceiling; it swirled with good memories. She dressed for work in silence; and in that silence we both knew that it was over. Our marriage was broken, crumbling into hurtful remembrances. From that morning on we never found much to say to one another; our time together was vanishing quietly like a shadow. But I realized then that never twice would I know such a love. It was too late. When after a month she was gone, loneliness poured over me. The memories kept streaming in, and though I tried shaking them off, I couldn't. There were far too many. I loved her still.

The azaleas I had given her on Valentine's Day are, after ten years, still blooming. Her wedding bouquet, which I kept in my study for several years, finally grew brittle, then crumbled. Reluctantly, I placed it in the wastepaper basket—the last vestige of our vows.

Before the Black Revolution it had been all but impossible for whites to understand that black Americans looked at color as a political reality; that it was this reality that powered the uprising. Out of desperation the black man had finally pushed patience aside. Frankly he was saying, "I no longer bow to racism."

Black youth emerged from those blazing summers with positive images of themselves: "Black is beautiful," became their cry. This assessment of themselves was a respectable distance from my own youthful concept of blackness—when racism in America had made it a dirty word. Our schoolbooks never presented black heroes for us to emulate; only white achievers stared at us from the pages. Hollywood bombarded us with shuffling, grinning, slow-talking actors like Stepin Fetchit and others that sent us homeward with shame. Then even to be called black could justify a fight.

But by the end of the turbulent sixties, black youth, ennobled by the color of their skin, shouted pride from every corner of the nation. Through struggle they had come to uncompromising terms with their heritage, and embarked upon a journey that altered their ambitions. Their self-discovery was a splendid thing, but beyond it lay a danger. In their passion to express the virtues of this realization it was easy to become so occupied with blackness that they overlooked certain opportunities that might push them even further ahead. There are a lot of doors waiting to be unlocked, and with so many possibilities, it isn't enough just to talk, read, write and sing blackness to a smattering of black people.

Slowly, very slowly, America is granting recognition to black achievement that, only a few years before, it would have ignored. And, at times, the white press appears to be somewhat curious about a black person's acceptance of it. In Washington, a white reporter questioned me after President Reagan presented me with the National Medal of Arts at the White House in 1988. "How do you feel about receiving the award?"

"I hope that it will encourage minority youths."

"Your people must be proud of you."

"My people?"

"Yes—black people all over the country."

"I hope they are."

"Have you received congratulatory letters or telegrams from any of the nation's leaders?"

"A few."

"From whom for instance?"

"Well—Kassebaum, Dole and Carlin, the former governor of Kansas."

"And the black leaders?"

"Well—none so far."

His eyes widened. "Does that bother you?"

"No, because I'm certain they are happy about my being here. They helped me to get here. I got the Spingarn Medal from the NAACP and the Frederick Douglass Award from the Urban

325

League. Both are the highest recognition one can get from these two organizations—and they are just as important to me as the one I just received." The interview ended.

A French television crew was awaiting me at my New York apartment when I arrived. When the camera rolled the young lady who was to question me made her first inquiry: "How do you feel about living in this elegant apartment—especially in this part of town?"

I shook my head and laughed. "Are you serious?"

"Very serious. Do you have any reservations about living here?"

"Oh yes—to be sure I do. I so much regret that my apartment is not twice as elegant, and twice its size."

She winced and went on to other questions that were just as insidious. Then checking her notes she said. "You are listed in the World's Who's Who as having twenty honorary doctorates. It would interest our French viewers to know if any of those happened to come from a white college or university."

"All—but one."

"Now, I must ask if you are serious?"

"I am."

"That's strange. Isn't it rather disappointing for you?"

"Not really. They're taking their time—watching, waiting and being sure that I first prove myself worthy." When, after two hours, the young lady departed she seemed to be puzzled by some things she couldn't understand.

I remember well a question thrown at me by a white Algerian reporter during a radio broadcast from Paris. The question was meant to undo me. *"Paris Presse* quotes you as saying that you advise black youth to ignore their blackness when applying for jobs at white enterprises. Are you not asking them to forget their past?"

"No. I'm simply advising them not to go in weighted down with blackness to the extent that it sets them apart. Nor do I advise them to call a white firm first to announce that they are black. Otherwise they might be asked to come around in February—Black History month. No I don't ascribe to that kind of thinking. I want them to work the year round. You, for instance, didn't state your color when you telephoned me for this interview. Why should I?"

. . .

I have never gloried at being the first black photographer to enter those closed doors at *Life* magazine, *Vogue* or any of the other places. I like to feel they were opened for my race as well as me. I did realize that I was making fresh tracks, but I never carried the responsibility around on my back like a sack of stones. I simply did my best without asking favors because I was black. Time and again those tracks have been filled, and this is reason to rejoice. Only through hard work did I gain a sense of security and independence.

I have learned a few things along the way. The lesson I value most is to take human beings as they are, to take the measure of them; to accept or reject them, regardless of their wealth, impoverishment or color. I've learned not to expect any more, or less, from a black stranger than I would a white one. It all depends upon the stranger. Experience has kept this attitude flowing. Consider the admixture of kinships that influence my thinking. Of three mothers-in-laws I have acquired at different times, one has been Swedish, one black and another Chinese. In turn, I have been father-in-law to a Frenchman, a Jew, a Britisher and a Yugoslavian—and you might add my father's Cherokee heritage to this very grand mix.

Like my family, my friends represent such a pastiche of hues, I no longer assign to them colors. They are friends, and that is more than enough. The closest of them could hardly be called homogeneous—a black, a Chinese, a Frenchman, a German, a Jew, an Irishman, and a white Southerner from Louisiana. Altogether they are like one big sheltering tree with different colored leaves. That's the way things are and I don't welcome any changes.

I have painful memories of having endured those poison markets that hamper subjugated racial groups in this country. Recalling my own experience is like looking back on a sequence of burned squares wherein people wrapped hatred around me like tangleweed and attempted to impede my growth—unyielding, insensitive people obsessed with the belief that blacks, Indians and Mexicans were meant to live as second-class citizens. Hapless victims, millions of those died keeping their silence. Perhaps I was born with a stubbornness that my tormentors failed to take into account. Now, I glance back at them and manage a smile, knowing they remain puzzled for letting me slip through their nets. Perhaps I owe them for the injustices they heaped upon me; for it was such injustice that engendered my craving to escape their intolerance.

It now appears that as I have grown, so has my home state of Kansas grown. With quiet dignity it has acknowledged its shortcomings, placed me on the list of its favorite sons by selecting me as Kansan of the Year, declaring Gordon Parks Day. And Fort Scott, my birthplace, devoted an entire week to my endeavors a few years ago. Perhaps the nation, in honoring me with the National Medal of Arts, was also bestowing honor upon Kansas. In a circuitous way Kansas had driven me to it. My resentment has withered, and I emerged free of any scars of an imperiled childhood. But there was a huge price to pay for our greeting one another in peace.

I have lived through change. Undoubtedly certain segments of the black population have experienced progress. There are more home owners, college students and graduates, and an increase in the proportion of black people with decent incomes. These make up the middle class. But there is, however, the overwhelming large underclass that, because of increasing unemployment, sinks deeper into poverty, and white America now confronts the realization that what it thought was a black problem is actually a white problem as well. Stubbornly, those to the far right refuse to look at that problem in terms of those who have plenty, and those who have nothing. And they would have us believe that legality achieved through the civil rights struggle has little or no meaning. They are, at best, cripplers of a worthy purpose.

Long before I went back to film *The Learning Tree,* I had become a stranger to Fort Scott, Kansas. Except for my sister Anna, and the few friends left behind, there was so little to return to. The rest of my family had scattered to different parts of the country. An occasional visit to Anna was precious but loaded with foreboding. Invariably she insisted upon my paying a visit to the Gordon family, for whom she worked. My mother had also been a maid in the household, and their son Clifford and I got along well together— in a rich-boy poor-boy way. The problem was Mr. Gordon. He could never quite understand how one of Sarah Parks's boys could have been employed by a big magazine like *Life.* Scratching his head, he would inquire of Anna, "Was he one of Sarah's light-skinned ones? Do they take him for white maybe?"

"No, sir, Gordon's too dark to be taken for white." Her answer only brought on more head shaking.

I made my visit in 1949 to the Gordons my *very* last. A light rain was falling when Anna telephoned to tell me the family was gathered and waiting. Calming her worst fears, I assured her that I would be coming shortly.

"Oh, brother, they'll be so happy. Mr. Gordon especially wants to see you. And, brother—it's raining and there's no shelter over the front door. Now I don't want you to get wet, so it would be better if you came in the back way."

"I'll be there shortly, sis."

I loved Anna dearly, but I betrayed her and got wet coming through the front door.

The family was gathered and waiting—especially Mr. Gordon. Clifford and I embraced warmly. I shook Mrs. Gordon's hand and smiled at the big question mark covering Mr. Gordon's face as he greeted me. Then I sat down in his big leather chair. Anna brought in hot cocoa. "Oh, brother dear, you're in Mr. Gordon's chair!"

"It's all right, Anna. It's all right." Mr. Gordon took off his bifocals and looked closer. "So you're the one who used to scaddle about with Clifford."

"It's me for sure."

"Now tell me something. Just last week I saw all those pretty fashion models in *Life* magazine and your name was attached to them as photographer. Did you actually take those pictures?"

"Dad—"

"Quiet, Clifford. I'm asking questions."

"Yes I did, and many more. They were taken in Paris."

"Paris. Now—now—do you yourself tell them how to stand—and fix their clothes the way you want?"

"I do. Sometimes I have an assistant who attends to adjusting the skirts and dresses if I'm busy at something else."

"Then you're not the only colored as Anna says working at the magazine?"

"I am."

"But your assistant—he's white?"

"She's white."

While Mr. Gordon reached for a bottle of peach brandy, neither Clifford nor his mother could suppress their smiles. After an hour of such questioning Mr. Gordon fell quiet. I got up, bade them good-bye, kissed Anna and exited through the front door. Glancing back through the window I saw Mr. Gordon—still scratching his head. Another session like that would surely have left him bald. That was home—the place I attack in dreams some nights. Echoes from the past, painful things to be remembered and remembered—the chilling terror of being locked inside that evil-smelling embalming room with the battered corpse of Captain Tuck when I was nine; the racial insults and brutalities whites heaped upon me back in Kansas; the segregated grade school and the discriminating acts of Fort Scott's high school; the fright of nearly drowning in its Marmaton River; the senseless shooting of two friends by Kirby, the white, lawless lawman; my banishment on that subzero night by my brother-in-law; the homeless nights of loneliness and hunger; the frigid Minnesota nights when I rode streetcars until dawn for shelter; the demeaning days working at that Chicago flophouse; the bigotry that kept up its harassment in Washington and New York—even when I was being thought of as successful. These and so many other incidents had littered my mind until it screamed retreat. Yet, I also remember dwelling in my father's temperate house where lamplight fell on me, while outside bluebirds and bob-o-links twirped in their flights—when the whole family went to the porch to eat ripe melons beneath a waxing moon. These were the good things not to forget.

Time has allowed Fort Scott and me seventy-odd years to reconcile our differences. Though the bad memories have often gnawed me to the quick, I eventually went back there to find more decent things to tack on to those bitter remembrances. The years had piled up like grains of sand, then cemented themselves into a firmness I could at last deal with. Something bigger was lifting me above the earlier bigotry and abuse, granting amnesty to those who once found pleasure in their indiscretion. In 1985, the Native Sons and Daughters of Kansas selected me as Kansan of the Year, and that announcement sent a message smashing against the wall of misunderstanding that had stood for so long between us. The bronze plaque Governor John Carlin was to present to me on the night of my acceptance in Topeka would help proclaim our truce.

There, with a thousand others, was Senator Nancy Kassebaum. Senator Robert Dole had come to congratulate me earlier, then left for Washington. Now I could only hope that for other black people throughout the state Kansas's intentions would forever remain sincere. Both the state and I had seemed to emerge from the terrible past.

Recognition from Kansas had long since begun its trail—with the governor's medal, honorary doctorates and achievement awards. And I was indeed grateful to have received them. But I remember that on this very special night, during the second quarter of the first hour, there came a hint of the state's collapsing back into its old ways. With honest compassion Clarence Rupp, the master of ceremonies, read what he felt was my finest verse, "Kansas Land." I had written it many years before, and with conscientious conviction. Now, with Governor Carlin at my side, I was about to hear it from a white, native Kansan's own lips.

So gentle was Mr. Rupp's voice when he began, it seemed to weave the words together with silk:

> I would miss this Kansas land that I was leaving.
> Wide Prairie filled with green and cornstalk;
>> the flowering apple,
> Tall elms and oaks beside the glinting streams,
> rivers rolling quiet in long summers of sleepy days
> for fishing, for swimming, for catching crawdad
>> beneath the rock.
> Cloud tufts billowing across the round blue sky.
> Butterflies to chase through grass as high as the
>> chin.
> June bugs, swallowtails, red robin and bobolink,
> nights filled with soft laughter, fireflies
>> and restless stars,
> the winding sound of crickets rubbing dampness from
>> wings.
> Silver September rain, orange-red-brown Octobers and
>> white Decembers with hungry
> smells of hams and pork butts curing in the
>> smokehouse.

331

He stopped, finished. I, along with others who knew the poem, gasped. Clarence had omitted the last two lines. My heart quailed, and filled with governable fury. I arose to accept the honor from the governor, who had come to stand beside me. Turning to Mr. Rupp, I thanked him for the reading, smiled at him, then recited the two lines he had deleted:

> Yes, all this I would miss—along with the fear,
> hatred and violence
> we blacks had suffered upon this beautiful land.

In all my life I have never heard such a huge silence. Mr. Rupp paled. The governor graciously made the presentation. Katie Strickler, a close friend of many years who knew the poem well, sat staring with anger at Mr. Rupp. Then suddenly the audience rose to give me a standing ovation. I put a conciliatory hand on Mr. Rupp's shoulder before going to sit down.

He never mentioned "Kansas Land" when he drove me to the airport the following morning. In the quiet of the misty countryside there was even more quiet. Flying eastward, I again thought back to my family lying in those segregated graves—there in the misty distance beneath the seal of bigotry. Would it be disrespectful if one day I chose not to join them there where racism had set them apart? The thought grew into a problem. Perhaps I wouldn't allow myself to be lowered into a grave garlanded with weeds and a dead tree—a few feet across the dirt road from where whites lay in a beautiful, wooded greenland. I had warred against segregation for so long.

Back in 1968 I let Fort Scott's mayor know my thoughts about segregated burial. Two days later his office sent a gentleman to tell me that a decision of great importance had been made. Sarah Parks's remains were to be disentombed and moved to the *white* side of Evergreen.

The pleasure so firmly set in the man's eyes faded with my answer. "Your offer is remarkable, but my mother, I am sure, would prefer to lie among those she loved so much. Thank you nevertheless."

"But the mayor thought that this would please you."

"Wrong is still wrong until it is completely done away with. Cut

332

the weeds, mow the weeds, plant new trees, pave the road on that side—and stop segregating the dead from now on."

For a long moment he stood helpless, then broke the silence. "I'll tell His Honor what you had to say, but I know he'll be very disappointed."

"I'm sorry about that."

He coughed a couple of times then disappeared.

Remembering my childhood in Fort Scott, going back there is like returning to a battlefield where a truce has been signed. The gifts it has handed me lately are not the whole truth of the place. Yet, the dark clouds that hung over it during my youth there have thinned out, and other black youths can see a little light in the skies, despite the Southernish attitude that still exists there. And it will always be the identity of my brutal past. There are still rich whites and poor blacks. All others exist somewhere in between those who govern and those who still scrub the rich man's floors.

During Christmas I received a card from a white friend there whom I have come to respect highly. It held a message that wished me the gift of faith, the blessing of hope and the love of peace. The postscript read: "Every Memorial Day I drive by Evergreen and look at your family stones to be sure they are well kept."

Sara Marble Emery had not forgotten. Time had not dimmed her memory, nor was she pretending that my birthplace was at last utterly charming. She *was* saying that I was to keep faith; that I was not free to cancel my hope for Fort Scott, Kansas. She is not to worry. My hopes, and hers, are worth far too much. Still, I wonder if when I go west Sara will find my stone there, and also see that it is well kept. It is autumn; time perhaps for me to make up my mind. But I find it disturbing to choose my final place in the earth. Most likely it recalls my childhood fear of the prairie's darkness.

TWENTY-SIX

As my children watched me grow, I too watched them grow. Leslie, an excellent skier, has emerged a sensible young lady with a talent for writing, and the kind of beauty that equals her mother's; David, working in films and instructing at a tennis clinic, remains a nonconfirmed bachelor, still a bit boisterous but inwardly compassionate; Toni deserted music for the camera, and has just successfully completed her first assignment. Long divorced from Jean Luc Brouillaud, she is now married to Derek Parsons, a British film editor. Her son Alain is grown now, a businessman and also a tennis instructor. Gordon Jr. finally realized his dream of working with horses and acquired a ranch with thirty of them. He went on to become a successful film director—making such motion pictures as *Super Fly, Three the Hard Way* and *Aaron Loves Angela*. But fate left him where he fell—where he had gone to Kenya to direct a film in 1979.

On April 3, at half-past three in the morning, the telephone snapped me awake. "Nairobi, Africa, calling Mr. Parks."

"Yes, this is he."

"Your party is on the line, Nairobi, Go ahead."

It was Jimmy Richardson, Gordon's assistant director "Pops?"

"Jimmy?" There was a long silence. "Jimmy?"

"Yeh, Pops—I'm calling with terrible news."

The world started spinning and slowing at the same time. A lot of horrible thoughts flashed through my mind but I knew and I spoke the most painful words I have ever spoken. "Gordon's dead — I feel it, Jimmy. I feel it."

"Yes, Pops—and I'm terribly sorry."

A heart attack? A mauling by an animal? A shot from a gun? With such possibilities racing through my head I drummed up the courage to ask, "My God, Jimmy, how did it happen?"

"His plane spun in during takeoff. Three others went down with him. It was pretty terrible."

The moment every parent dreads had arrived, and lying very still I was trying desperately to take hold of it bravely; trying as well to choke off the reality. "Oh, God, it's so hard to believe. But it's happened. It's happened. I'll get there right away. I want to be near him all the way home."

"Pops, please listen to me, and try to understand. There is no use in your coming now. I hate telling you this, but there was an intense fire. Only ashes are left. I'll fly back with them day after tomorrow. You may want to come later for some reason, but not now."

Closing my eyes against his words, I saw Gordon's body lying there, taking shape—but with no flesh, no pulse, just smoldering hot ashes. "Jimmy."

"Yeh, Pops."

"Save a part of him to spread on Kilimanjaro. Gordon loved that mountain."

"That will be done before I leave, Pops."

"Well, Jimmy—there's not much left to say. Call if you need anything, and let me know when you arrive."

In a trance I dressed with deliberate slowness. I saw no sense in hurrying to carry such news, and I pulled on each piece of clothing with painful preciseness. To the doorman I mumbled, "My son's dead. Please get me a taxi."

"Your son's dead?"

"Yes, my son's dead—burned to ashes."

"I'm sorry, sir."

"Yes—my son's dead." As I waited I looked east toward the river. Both it and the pale dawn light glinting off the water seemed to be in mourning. Why him? Why so early into his life? I drove to where his wife, also named Leslie, was asleep, and I rang the doorbell.

"Who is it?"

"Pops, Leslie. Open the door."

Such despair was on my face that she gasped. She stood with her hands folded over her stomach—swollen with my dead son's child. How, I was wondering, could I bring myself to tell her that he was only ashes now; that she was a widow carrying an unborn child. Mercifully I was spared that. The truth suddenly struck. "Oh Lord! Something's happened to Gordon! Something's happened! I know it!"

"He's gone from us, Leslie. Jimmy just called from Nairobi." With a mournful shriek, she collapsed into my arms, crying until there were no more tears to give. It had grown suddenly cold. I put a blanket about her shoulders and asked her to lie down. She refused. Instead she stood there moaning. "This poor child inside me will never see his father. This poor child will never see his father." She was still standing there when I left two hours later— to telephone Gordon's mother, brother and sisters. I couldn't bring myself to mention the ashes. That would have to come later.

All day long television stations showed pictures of me, erroneously reporting *my* death in a plane crash in Africa, and I wished they had been right. Gordon, so young, the director of three notable films, was headed for a distinguished career. But death had caught him on the way up. When someone called the stations to have the mistake corrected, he was confronted with one of those lamentable drawbacks of technological progress: "We are terribly sorry, but that particular news slot is locked into today's computer program, and there's absolutely nothing we can do about it until tomorrow morning."

Several times during the remainder of that day when I answered the phone, a gasp, then silence came from the other end of the line.

Years later, Gordon III, the grandson Gordon left to me, landed on my chest as I awakened one morning. Lifting my mustache he said, "Grandpa, I have never seen your lips before." Then, in a brief puzzling way, he added, "But then I've never seen my father either." Any meaningful reply failed me. Perhaps he had said it all, but still I wondered what brought his young mind to place the two discoveries side by side. Perhaps I was seeing a future with the kind of poetry I probably wouldn't live to know.

Just recently I came to know a lovely young lady who had been subliminally present in my life for twenty-four years—without my being aware of her. She came floating in through a letter so gently that it left me somewhat speechless. Her name was Sara, and she had written me from a small town up in Maine, sending photographs of herself, her husband and their two-year-old daughter, Dannah. She explained that she had been adopted by a couple who gave her love and a good family life. Yet, during most of that life she had been in constant search of her real father. She was now twenty-four. Her birth mother, whom she had come to know and love just three years before, had decided to help end that traumatic search. Touching a photograph of me that appeared in a magazine, she had said, "This, Sara, is your grandfather."

Sara's letter had been tender, mildly desperate and pleading. ". . . I now find that your son, David, is my father. I do want so much to know him, and to know you. For years I have wanted this. Would you please send my letter on to David. I would so much appreciate it."

I read and reread the letter, looked at the photographs over and over again. There was no doubt: my son's features were deeply etched into hers. The only thing to come to now was the truth. David was not only a father; he was a grandfather as well—and I a great-grandfather.

I sent the letter and pictures on to him, knowing they would carry waves of shock to wherever it reached him in Texas. Then, without awaiting his answer, I telephoned Sara on the following Sunday morning.

"Sara, this is your grandfather calling."

"Gordon?"

"Yes, Sara—this is Gordon."

During the few moments of silence that followed, I sensed the flowing of tears. Finally she spoke, and a bit apologetically. "I'm sorry. I'm just a bit overwhelmed. Oh, I knew you would call. I just knew it. Oh, Gordon, I'm so happy—so happy."

My eyes dimmed a bit now. "And I'm happy too, Sara. We must see one another as soon as possible. I sent your letter on to David."

There was another silence.

"Sara, are you there?"

"Yes—yes I'm here. Do you think he will call?"

"I'm sure he will. But you must give him time. Remember this will all be new to him as well."

"I know—I know."

We talked on until there wasn't much to say between a granddaughter and a grandfather who had never met or, for that matter, never knew each other existed. Twenty-four years of empty space lay between us.

Eventually David called Sara, and shortly after he telephoned me. He was still stunned, but exuberant with praise. "She sounds wonderful, Dad—just wonderful."

My ballet, *Martin,* was about to be premiered in Washington, D.C. Sara wanted to be there, and I wanted her there—along with David, my daughters Toni and Leslie, and my grandsons, Alain and Gordon III. David came to New York for two days, and together we worked at calming the tension funneling through him.

Still unstrung, he was in the hotel lobby to meet Sara when she arrived in Washington. I longed to witness their first moments together, but those moments were for them—and not to be intruded upon. So I paced about the room, waiting, eager to see this new grandchild of mine. Eventually they came through the door with arms interlocked. Smiling wistfully, and free of any doubt about our love and kinship, Sara fell into my arms, her long search over. It was a good, warming moment for the three of us. Sara was as beautiful and lovely a grandchild as I could have wished for, and for the next two days she was all but crushed with family love —which she returned with confiding warmth. I was grateful for her presence; it assured me that no longer was I a missing great-grandparent; that life is a strange circle where sometimes things move inexplicably behind—yet ahead of one another.

As for the three wives in my life, I invariably unveil memories of them when they were at their finest. Each one gave me many good hours, and the beauty of those hours grows plump with time. No doubt my inability to reach the summit of their expectations had a lot to do with the storms and disasters. Sometimes I am inclined to think that ambition carved my image out of stone; that the persistence of it crushed Sally, Elizabeth and Genevieve under its weight. Fortunately those hostilities that assailed us failed to hold us in bondage. I am still here if they should need me; and if I should be in need, they are there for me.

Looking back I would have nothing new to ask of them. That part of me they found so incomprehensible still wears its misgivings, and I'm afraid that I will be forever entangled in its flux. My past is bent around circumstances I can't seem to escape; circumstances laced and interfused in such a way that they keep me moving toward boundaries that seem at times unreachable.

EPILOGUE

I've known both misery and happiness, lived in so many different skins it is impossible for one skin to claim me. And I have felt like a wayfarer on an alien planet at times—walking, running, wondering about what brought me to this particular place, and why. But once I was here the dreams started moving in, and I went about devouring them as they devoured me.

Since I was exiled here, it was impossible to remain by just standing still. I became an actor and gave myself the name of "I" and it was I who had to search out the cycles that helped me play the roles of my exile. Not only did I play myself; it was also necessary to take on the roles of others who were shrewder than I, and masters of their own plots. Yet, hidden in the sorcery of those plots were things to help me unmask them. I had only to listen to their lines, then concoct lines of my own—to question me, then lead me toward the daily answers.

I still have a passion for living, so this is no farewell, but rather the gathering in of observations I hope will make someone else's trials easier to bear. Our daily lives are knotted with sufficient worries, and the climate of the universe, with all its makings of death, keeps us wrapped in fear. Since Hiroshima the entire world goes to bed with murder on its mind; morning finds it thankful to be in one piece. What I give here is meant to show how I try to drum up courage to keep going.

I still don't know what compels me off into different directions. Perhaps the early years on the prairie have something to do with it —my putting a wetted finger up to catch the drifting of the wind, or the feel of oncoming rain or snow. Maybe my small black finger expanded into a greater consciousness that helps presage the right or wrong of things headed my way. Even then as a child there were things I knew—like the coyote's howl or a hawk's cry. Yet, there were so many things to learn. Sometimes now, I go back to the prairie riverbanks to gaze into the water I envied for flowing off to places I would never see, but places I have been to since and learned from.

The prairie is still in me, in my talk and manners. Out there I still sniff the air for weather, know the loneliness of night and distrust the sky when things grow too quiet. And I find it hard to forget the hatred and violence I knew there. Our old clapboard house, standing against the storms and tornadoes, still leans into the oak tree shade where I used to sit and dream in the huge silence.

The years to follow convinced me that nothing is more noble than a good try. Throughout the coming and going there was so little space for idleness. Time was too small. I have yet to figure out what life is really all about, and I doubt that I will ever come up with the answer. I do find a certain fascination with the unpredictable. The transitory years we wade through are what they are —what we make of them. I'm still happy to be here, and I'm clever enough to know that my date of departure remains time's secret. I trust time. It has been my friend for a long while, and we have been through a lot together. Now I ask only that it lend me enough of itself to say a proper good-bye; to thank it for giving me faith when others chose to doubt me; for refusing to let me hate those who chose to hate me. It taught me that triumph or failure can be hypocritical, and that both should be looked at with beseeching eyes.

Life has frightened me now and then, and if I've ever shown uncommon bravery, I've failed to notice it. I still dream big at times, but when my dreams pull apart, as they sometimes do, I don't press the panic button. Only a chosen few are selected to rise above their true height.

I'm not positive about tomorrow. The geography of it may be snarled with roads I've never walked. It may come plunging in with contradictions, speaking a language I've never heard before. If so, listening won't be enough. I will listen closely, shutting out all disguised voices. Too often those voices, dressed in Sunday clothes, have made their way into my ears, changed outfits and begun tearing my tomorrows to shreds. They are like scavengers with iron teeth who dine on insecure souls. I no longer want any part of them.

I've been given several names—Mr. Dreamer, Mr. Striver, and occasionally Mr. Success. I've tried on all three for size. The first two fit rather well; the third still has a slight feel of discomfort. Success is filled with the agony of how and why—in the flesh, nerves and conscience. It takes you down a lonely road and you feel, at times, that you are traveling it alone. You can only keep walking. During the loneliness you get to know who you are. Then you face the choice—of holding on to everybody's friendship, or losing the one you have made with yourself. Success can be wracking and reproachful, to you and those close to you. It can entangle you with legends that are consuming and all but impossible to live up to. Then what the mirror reflects might well be weary of all the confusion. Looking deep into it one sees the washed-out days; the hidden intentions that broke apart and disappeared in the tide of all the circling and swirling. Then you are left wondering if you are all you set out to be; if what was to be done is finally done. There's only one past to talk with, to say what you did best, or allowed to go wasted. By then you are locked into your fate, and you are whatever you are, waiting for the final door to slam shut.

INDEX

GORDON PARKS has written twelve books of poetry, fiction, and nonfiction, including *The Learning Tree, A Choice of Weapons,* and *To Smile in Autumn.* Although he never graduated from high school, Parks has received over fifty honorary doctorates and awards, including the National Medal of Arts, presented to him by the President of the United States in 1988. His photographs and paintings have been exhibited throughout the world, and his recent ballet, *Martin*, for which he wrote the music and libretto, premiered in February 1990 in Washington, D.C. Parks lives in New York City.